Historic Cities
nd Sacred Sites

Cultural Roots
for Urban Futures

Ismail Serageldin ■ Ephim Shluger ■ Joan Martin-Brown *Editors*

THE
WORLD
BANK

The
Government
of Denmark

MINISTRY
OF CULTURE
BRAZILIAN
GOVERNMENT

Banco Safra

UNESCO

Contents

Part VII   Preserving the Sacred Sites and Cultural Roots   333

Part VIII   Partnerships in Action   383

Sacred tree and a shrine, Beith Hanania Galilee, Israel.

Acknowledgments

The Editors are grateful to the support received from the World Bank, the Government of Denmark, the Ministry of Culture of Brazil, and Banco Safra in Brazil to produce this volume. We are also grateful to the authors for sharing their knowledge, wisdom, and inspiration, and for their sustained scholarly interest in completing this book.

We would like to thank the co-sponsors, who provided resources to the Symposium on the Preservation of Historic Cities and Sacred Places, organized at the World Bank in May 1999, during which some chapters in this volume were presented and discussed. These co-sponsors were: Aga Khan Trust for Culture, American Institute of Architects, CEC International Partners, Center for Jewish Art of the Hebrew University of Jerusalem, Council of Europe, Eisenhower Foundation, Government of Brazil, Inter-American Development Bank (IADB), International Centre for the Study of the Preservation and Restoration of Cultural Property (ICCROM), International Council on Monuments and Sites (ICOMOS), J. Paul Getty Trust, Norwegian Agency for Development Cooperation (NORAD), Organization of World Heritage Cities, United Nations Educational, Scientific, and Cultural Organisation (UNESCO), United States National Park Service, World Bank, and World Monuments Fund.

We appreciate the expert contributions to the symposium of Roberto Chavez, Kreszentia Duer, Alexandre Marc, Bezalel Narkiss, Brooke Shearer, and Achva Stein. Our warmest thanks go to Debra Cooper and Marc Halcrow for their tireless support in putting together the symposium and to the following colleagues for their behind-the-scenes support: Fatiha Amar, Katrinka Ebbe, Yoko Eguchi, Inas Ellaham, Edie Fattu, Arlene Fleming, Marina Galvani, Tomoko Hirata, Sarwat Hussain, Tsige Makonnen, Christine Stover, and Feroza Vatcha.

Several individuals advised us on this publication, including Michael Cernea and Bezalel Narkiss. We deeply appreciate the work of Alicia Hetzner, principal editorial consultant, and the contributions of editorial consultants Christine M. Smyrski-Shluger, Sheldon I. Lippman, Alison Raphael, and Jacqueline Edlund-Braun. Paola Scalabrin and Randi Park coordinated the print production. Finally, our gratitude goes to the team at ULTRAdesigns for their invaluable work in designing this book.

Ismail Serageldin
Ephim Shluger
Joan Martin-Brown

Ouro Preto, Minas Gerais, a national monument and a World Heritage Site.

Introduction

The urban population of the developing world will triple over the next two generations. For the first time the majority of humanity will be classified as urban rather than rural. The economic and social consequences of this huge demographic shift are the context for this volume. Public authorities are challenged to be effective in guiding change, under the severe strain of scarce public funds. One of these challenges is to protect urban heritage.

A great proportion of the 100 historic cities and nearly 200 sacred sites on the World Heritage List are located in the developing world. How do historic cities fare against the population pressures, crumbling infrastructure, and eroding economic base of the developing world? And what about historic sacred sites, which resonate so strongly with individuals and with nations? Sacred sites are as much at risk as the urban tissue of historic cities.

This book investigates the tolls that overpopulation and poverty often take on historic cites and sacred sites. More importantly, it demonstrates that taking care of humanity's cultural heritage can regenerate the self-esteem and self-identities of disempowered peoples and revive moribund economies. Cultural heritage preservation and poverty reduction are closely intertwined.

The fight against poverty and exclusion requires promoting solidarity and a better understanding of the obstacles to participation and empowerment of the disenfranchised. Solidarity and empowerment cannot occur unless the sense of common purpose, shared values, and affinity with others is anchored in a notion of a common culture. The self-esteem of the poor and the sense of community of local action groups are built on trust, common language, and a shared heritage. Historic and sacred sites are part of that shared heritage.

Recent studies on social capital, or social cohesion, and on the effectiveness of the poor's responses to challenges have emphasized that a sense of shared culture is crucial to a people's success in overcoming poverty. However, the building blocks that create this sense of a common culture are only partially recognized in the prevailing economic development paradigm.

The Comprehensive Development Framework (CDF), advanced by World Bank President James D. Wolfensohn, pioneered the specific inclusion of culture and identity as essential elements of a more holistic development approach.

This concept of culture in development does not view culture as an elite activity for the few but as the essence of being for all. Eduard Sekler states in this book:

> There are many ways in which a cultural identity is formed and maintained. Much of...the process has to do with the intangible cultural heritage of a body of traditions and usage, rites, poetry, song, and dance. A great deal of all of this is passed on orally through generations. Consequently, its survival is always threatened....
>
> Tangible cultural heritage has the great advantage over its intangible counterpart that with proper care it will remain authentic over centuries. As long as historic monuments remain without falsification and misleading imitations, they will, even in a neglected state, **create a sense of continuity that is an essential part of cultural identity.**[1]

This volume makes an important contribution to the understanding of culture's function in nurturing economic development by addressing one element in the development of identity: *the sense of place*. The sense of place and the feeling of roots are major components in building social cohesion, or social capital. The concept of roots introduces the physical dimensions of the location, the buildings, and the spaces that have special significance to people and that help define identity and sense of belonging. Kevin Lynch has argued in *What Time Is This Place?* that individuals' sense of well-being and resulting effective action depend on stable references from the past that provide a sense of continuity.[2] Historic cities and sacred sites are the very references that connect past, present, and future. Lynch stresses that governments should protect built heritage so that cities can be "collages of time": spaces that express continuity of time as layered by natural elements, human habitats, and monuments.

The preservation of historic cities and sacred sites requires sensitive treatment and an understanding of the essential as compared to the less important. It also requires skillful institutional and financial engineering of the viable economic reuse of the historic quarters as much as the techniques of restoration. Many of the most important lessons of how to successfully manage change in the urban fabric of cities and the preservation of their historic significance and character have come from the industrialized world. Therefore, the case experiences depicted in this book come not only from the South and the East, but also from the North and the West.

The purpose of this volume is to expand the dialogue on state-of-the-art preservation approaches based on actual cases set in a range of economic and social contexts. In this evolving field practice informs theory as much as the other way around.[3] The range of human activities involved in cultural heritage preservation is immense. The present collection provides the reader with a rich treatment of the issues, approaches, and experiences for preserving the cultural roots of urban futures.

Cultural Roots

Cultural matrices contain elements of the human collective memory—language, beliefs and rituals, myths, and values. These are represented through a variety of art forms and are transmitted from generation to generation. Cultural references and signs are essential to the formation of national, group, and individual identities. The preservation of cultural heritage is central to protecting a sense of who we are—a meaningful reference in our culturally diverse world. However, Nobel laureate Wole Soyinka has warned:

> ...culture is a matrix of infinite possibilities and choice. From within the same cultural matrix, we can extract arguments and strategies for degradation or ennoblement of our species, for its enslavement or liberation, for the suppression of its productive potential or its enhancement.[4]

Decisions that affect culture and the responsibility for such choices must be predicated on a clear and transparent process, which, to be genuine and representative, should be open and participatory, hence inclusive and empowering of local communities.

From an operational point of view, preserving tangible cultural assets in their multiple forms may influence development project performance. It may also determine whether local communities take "ownership" of the results of project activities, which determines whether the benefits are sustained over time. Evidence from recent social fund programs suggests that positive synergy can be created by linking cultural concerns with poverty reduction programs. To be effective, development processes aimed at mitigating poverty must understand culture, or take culture into account, for two reasons. First, culture influences what is valued in a society. In particular, it shapes development outcomes that the poor will value. Second, culture influences how individuals, communities, and informal and formal institutions respond to developmental changes. In these ways the knowledge of culture facilitates effective poverty reduction.

In the 1990s cultural preservation movements energized public opinion around the world concerning the importance of protecting cultural assets. They elicited technical support to halt the progressive degradation of built heritage and to rescue heritage at risk. From Brazil to Italy, and from India to the Netherlands and Norway, civic groups have successfully advocated for improved heritage preservation approaches. Typical issues dealt with the need to improve legal mechanisms, to adopt national strategies to protect local and national listed heritage, to improve preservation management approaches, and to link built heritage and sacred places with protected areas. In many countries public policies have responded to such appeals by improving pertinent legislation and by adopting new mechanisms to finance the reconstruction and conservation of historic cities and neighborhoods.

In 1995 UNESCO's World Commission on Culture and Development published *Our Cultural Diversity*. This report advanced new perspectives on the role of traditional and contemporary cultures and their importance in socially and economically sustainable development.[5] The report argues convincingly that the prevalent model of development based solely on the narrow yardstick of economic growth is outmoded. That model ignores both the environmental consequences and cultural dimension of development. The report concludes that, above all, cultural diversity is here to stay. It is a manifestation of the limitless creativity of the human spirit. Its aesthetic value can unfold in multiple ways and stimulate the production and marketing of new and unique products. Finally, cultural diversity is a reservoir of knowledge and experience of social and environmental interactions that can inform improved sustainable approaches to using natural resources and protecting built heritage.

Historic Cities

Efforts to preserve historic architecture and revitalize historic cities and sacred sites have gained new momentum throughout the world. The focus on historic centers such as Fez, Morocco; Ouro Preto and Olinda, Brazil; Quito, Ecuador; Bilbao and Barcelona, Spain; St. Petersburg and Moscow, Russia; Bergen, Norway; Mostar, Bosnia; and Lijiang, China--is reshaping and reviving the economy of old cities through built heritage preservation and new cultural projects. Changing attitudes and approaches toward conserving and re-adapting architectural heritage, historic cities, and sacred places are proving to be good public policy and sound economics.

Protecting built heritage for any historic city is a political as well as a historical and a cultural process. Decisions about what to remember and what to preserve require complex iterative processes involving many actors, including political leaders, and representatives of civil society, the public and private sectors, and funding institutions. The public policy challenges include adopting new laws to protect cultural property, nurturing the array of local cultural and artistic manifestations, and regulating new development to mitigate its possible negative impacts. Public policies and regulations are also essential instruments to promote the formation of partnerships for the reconstruction, preservation, and management of historic cities, cultural landscapes, and sacred sites.

Increasingly, culture and economics are interlinked. Cities and their cultures can take leading roles in economic transformation, mainly through the service sector. In many cities it is the fastest growing sector, steadily replacing industry and manufacturing. This trend is generating new employment opportunities, contributing to the increased production and consumption of cultural goods and services, and stimulating local art markets.

Urbanization

Urbanization is a historical trend. Historic records indicate that cities existed 8,000 years ago. Important urban centers flourished at the turn of the thirteenth century with the rise of the urban mercantile societies in Italy and in the other countries of Western Europe and Asia. The longest commercial route, the Silk Road, stretched halfway around the world, from Italy through Central Asia and Mongolia, to China and Japan. It left behind a precious strand of heritage cities, including Samarkand, Bukhara, and Kaifeng.

During the Industrial Revolution in England and later, in the United States, cities experienced exponential population growth, enabling the concentration of great material wealth through economic growth cycles that led to new standards and forms of urban living. Mass media visionary Marshall McLuhan anticipated the nature of the contemporary cities in a globalized world:

> Cities were always a means of achieving some degree of simultaneity of association and awareness among men. What the family and the tribe had done in this respect for a few, the city did for many. Our technology now removes all city walls and pretexts.
>
> The oral and acoustic space of the tribal cultures had never met visual reconstruction of the past. All experience and all past lives were now. Preliterate man knew only simultaneity. The walls between men, and between arts and sciences, were built on the written or visually arrested word.

With the return to simultaneity we enter the tribal and acoustic world once more. Globally.[7]

The urban industrial centers built between the nineteenth and early twentieth centuries were products of great technological innovations in transport, trade, and communications and a new social division of labor. The legacy of that era can still be experienced in the preserved districts of central cities, which feature period buildings, that is, markers of architectural styles, along with urban parks and cultural institutions. Developing country cities experienced a later but intense process of industrialization and urbanization. There, population growth rates have surpassed the abilities of their societies to equip cities with adequate infrastructure and provide the population with basic social services. In the centrally located old neighborhoods of cities in many countries, irreplaceable baroque and neoclassical architecture coexists with later industrial structures—warehouses, sheds, train stations, and terminals—juxtaposed with the skyscrapers and office buildings of the modern city.

Urbanization has taken place on two opposite fronts: as formal and legal, and as informal and irregular, development.[8] This manifestation of cultural, social, and economic disparity has profound implications for the form and function of contemporary cities. The duality can be clearly seen in large developing country metropolises with important historic centers, such as Rio de Janeiro, São Paulo, Cairo, Bangkok, Bombay, and Mexico City, and is, in fact, the defining feature of their built environments. Within the boundaries of these cities the modern city built by private developers and defined within the framework of detailed urban legislation co-exists with the three- or four-times larger urban fabric erected by the poor in the gray area between legal and illegal, formal and informal. The "precarious peripheries" of chaotic land use and dwelling patterns found in the sprawling settlements of the poor have led to the total disconnection of these poorly serviced areas from the city center, where jobs and cultural and economic opportunities are concentrated.[9]

Policies to protect environmental and cultural endowments in a rapidly urbanizing world are inadequate. Population growth, the influx of rural migrants to cities, and an evolving economic base challenge the ability of cities to provide livelihoods. Deteriorating infrastructure, overburdened social services, rampant real estate speculation, and government incapacity put enormous pressure on city cores, which are often places of invaluable architectural and urban design heritage. The degradation of the urban environment limits the abilities of a growing, shifting population to establish communities with adequate and decent housing. Inner-city neighborhoods of large centers worldwide are besieged, with the middle class and economic activities either fleeing the historic core or destroying its fabric by the demolition and reconstruction of older buildings.[10]

Preserving Urban Heritage

In many cities the obsolescence of built heritage has led to the crumbling of urban infrastructure and public services. Both conditions contribute to the decline of inner-city property values. The loss of original communities and their replacement with newcomers transform the old neighborhoods and can bring a host of social problems arising from poverty. Typically, under these conditions the old city centers undergo significant functional changes as well. The business functions remain in the central districts surrounded by obsolete and decaying private and public property.

The challenge of rescuing at-risk heritage is the inevitability that development means change and that not all that is old must, or can, be preserved. Nevertheless, many parts of the old can be adaptively reused.

A positive response to the challenges of historic cities and sacred places is feasible, even under seemingly intractable conditions. Such a response must protect the urban context and the sense of place, revitalize the economic base of the old neighborhoods, and meet the legitimate expectations of residents. A comprehensive action strategy is needed to keep historic centers alive and protect their valuable urban history, social fabric, and cultural patterns of building. It must also reinforce their links to the surrounding modern districts. The strategy must include a framework for concerted action that includes government agencies working with the private sector and an array of experts and conservation groups. Partnerships can be stimulated when there are in place a tax structure that creates incentives and legislation that reduces the risks of investments. This "enabling environment" encourages individuals or corporate investors to bid for the rights to own and maintain historic properties.

However, more often than not, local administrations are inadequately staffed or not organized to process requests for the approval of conservation projects or to grant licenses. Exhaustive planning reviews, cumbersome procedures, and rigid or unclear regulations have deterred new investments in many cities, which often are desperately seeking to attract and secure new investments to bolster their stagnant economies. An investor un-friendly environment is often found in cities undergoing economic transition.

On the other hand, in cities cited in this book, such as Ahmedabad, Bergen, Bilbao, Ouro Preto, Olinda, Recife, and Rio de Janeiro, bold strategies for sustainable urban development have been combined with streamlined administrative procedures and financing instruments to produce remarkable results. The strategic objective is predicated on mobilizing private resources for urban redevelopment with a strong emphasis on preservation of the built heritage. In addition, by recasting public investment programs to improve urban infrastructure and service delivery, many cities are able to leverage resources from individuals and corporations to restore and conserve historic dwellings, palaces, religious buildings, cultural centers, theaters, libraries, and public spaces.

Financing Urban Heritage Preservation

In response to practical issues the World Bank and the Inter-American Development Bank, among many other institutions, have adopted an operational approach to appraise the economic value of cultural heritage and have developed methods to estimate the benefits and costs of heritage projects. Without financing there can be no projects. The chapters on Brazil's *Monumenta* Program and the proposed project in Split, Croatia, provide insights on financial analysis and proposed instruments to determine the value of built heritage in specific projects. In both cases the complex project designs and interventions in historic cities aim to establish links whereby general revenue may be used and public and private funding blended. Cross-subsidies are almost invariably part of such arrangements. The chapters in Part VIII examine key institutional arrangements in project development, touching on ways in which successful collaboration and partnerships are set up among the array of actors involved in financing built heritage.

The Issues

The 51 chapters of this volume are organized in 8 Parts on specific themes. Each Part is accompanied by an Editors' Note—an executive summary highlighting the key points contained in each chapter.

Part I seeks the philosophical and spiritual origins of historic cities and sacred sites. The aim is to establish a holistic understanding of the legacy of religious, symbolic, and cosmological references that have engendered historic cities and sacred places. Spiritual archetypes determined the structure of earthly holy cities such as Jerusalem, Mecca, Assisi and the Isle of Ise. The treatment of sacredness of place in the Eastern and Western spiritual traditions is compared. Seyyed Nasr offers a historic and philosophical perspective on the meaning of space in sacred places and historic cities. Stefano Bianca examines the future of sacred places in the contemporary world and makes the point that historic cities are an underestimated cultural asset. Bezalel Narkiss compares the architecture of synagogues, churches, and mosques to demonstrate their cross-cultural influences on one another over centuries. From a contemporary architectural perspective Norman Koonce reminds us that the stewardship of built heritage and its preservation are essential intergenerational commitments to cultural continuity.

Part II discusses the governance, planning, and management of cultural patrimony based on fresh policy and operational material from new empirical research and original conceptualizations. Case studies focus on cities in Brazil, the Middle East, the Netherlands, North Africa, North America, and Norway. Michael Sorkin raises the issue of authenticity in the contemporary architecture of large metropolises, such as New York. Findings from places as diverse as Brazil, Jordan, Lebanon, the Netherlands, Norway, and Tunisia indicate that cultural policy instruments such as an earmarked line of financing as well as incentives are essential to elicit private sector participation in cultural production and heritage preservation. Brazil's Minister of Culture Francisco Weffort quotes Robert Reich to say that in a globalized economy, "only labor is national." Weffort speaks of labor as including education and culture—to be understood not only as knowledge and erudition but also as the exercise of creativity—the source that transforms imagination into practice. Therefore, from his point of view, to develop, Brazil should have a policy of investing in culture and cultural industry.

Part III is devoted to one of the most important yet rarely discussed issues of built heritage at risk: the range of rescue strategies, which include reconstruction, transformation, and the adaptation of historic structures to new uses. The first two chapters describe successful reconstruction efforts in Assisi, Italy, and Lijiang, China, in the aftermath of intense seismic episodes. Other chapters cover the transformation, adaptive reuse, and rededication of historic buildings in Venice, Italy; Tampico and Tlacoltapan, Mexico; and Recife, Brazil.

Part IV addresses the issue of urban and cultural heritage preservation during periods of economic transition. This theme is clearly connected to the issues presented in Parts I and II: public policy, governance and cultural heritage preservation in a changing world. Both operational research and project experiences prove that citizen participation in decisionmaking and planning is the *sine qua non* for achieving optimal levels of continuity in heritage preservation management.

Part V analyzes processes and instruments to appraise heritage investment projects, the role of incentives in the transfer of funds from central governments to local authorities, and strategies to attract private businesses to revitalize the economies of historic cities. One such instrument is to establish a public-private corporation with the mandate to manage redevelopment and preservation of historic centers. Also covered is the program to revitalize "Main Street," the historic town centers in the United States abandoned for suburban sprawl and shopping malls. Ahmedabad, India, reversed economic decline by strengthening municipal management and gaining the confidence of investors, resulting in the issuing of municipal bonds, which led to the financing of urban and heritage preservation projects. The U. S. National Park Service Historic Landscape Initiative established new working principles and standards to protect the integrity and physical conditions of cultural landscapes. With the funding of private investors by the International Finance Corporation and other agencies, the Old Stone Town of Zanzibar was able to restore its neglected built heritage and turn the town into a tourist destination.

Part VI covers the technical applications: surveying, valuing, and documenting heritage. These are the essential activities that pertain to both decisionmaking regarding preservation and managing change in built heritage. Heritage designation is a dynamic process. Documentation and listing are instruments used to manage change to historic buildings. Landscapes can be viewed as manifestations of cultural belief systems. Documenting such systems is a complex undertaking that requires proper definition and procedures. A special section containing articles organized by the Center for Jewish Art depicts the ongoing research, survey program, and virtual reconstruction using computer-aided design (CAD) of Jewish architectural heritage, which the Center has conducted in 37 countries. Also examined are the most pronounced types of synagogues and the symbolic and liturgical origins of the placement of their elements. Research on the sequence of design steps of two major monuments offers new insights into the generative and constitutive processes of architectural design in the early eighteenth century. Also documented are the *shtetls* in Poland, the urban fabric of *melah* in Morocco, the Jewish presence in the Cape Verde Islands, sacred spaces in conflict areas, fortress-synagogues, and the wooden sacred buildings in Eastern Europe.

Part VII is devoted to sacred places and cultural roots. Chapters on North American indigenous cultures and the traditional ritual of *Kuarup* among Brazilian indigenous people reflect a common perspective: that nature and landscape are part of the cosmology and spiritual endowment of these peoples. In this conception the whole Earth is a sacred place. It contains powerful forces that need to be cared for to maintain a balance between the community and the nature. Other subjects are the religious and political centrality of the sacred site of Axum in Ethiopia, the eight centuries of close cultural interaction among Muslims, Jews, and Christians in medieval Spain (*Convivencia*); and the importance of non-built sacred places. UNESCO's Laurent Levi-Strauss concludes, "At a time when social diversity is everywhere leading to fragmentation, it is only...cultural memory that will maintain the indispensable bonds that enable a mosaic of people with different origins and different cultures, and of different generations, to live together."

Part VIII collects a wealth of international experience from private nonprofit institutions, foundations, and regional development banks working with national and local governments and communities on heritage preservation projects. Lawrence Hannah describes a partnership to rebuild Mostar as part of post-conflict reconciliation in Bosnia-Herzegovina. Eduardo Rojas draws lessons from private sector participation in recent revitalization efforts in select Latin American historic cities. Harold Williams stresses the need to incorporate a cultural dimension in sustainable development. Marilyn Perry examines the growing corporate commitment to cultural heritage preservation and conservation. Luis Monreal documents the remarkable growth of corporate contributions to culture in Spain. ■

Notes

1   E. Sekler, "Sacred Spaces and the Search for Authenticity in the Kathmandu Valley," this volume, 354.

2   K. Lynch, *What Time Is This Place?* (Cambridge, Ma.: MIT Press, 1972), 235.

3   Some chapters of this volume initially were presented in preliminary form at the Symposium on Preserving he Architecture of Historic Cities and Sacred Places, organized at the World Bank in May 1999. A draft symposium proceedings of the same name was prepared for Conference on Culture Counts: The Financing, Resources, and Economics of Culture in Sustainable Development, held in Florence in October of the same year. The present volume takes off from that point to present a much expanded, scholarly treatment of the multiple facets of current thinking and practice on the preservation of historic cities and sacred places and the challenges of development. Additional experts have contributed new conceptual and operational material, and the text is vividly enhanced by nearly 300 images.

4   Cited in James D. Wolfensohn, Opening Keynote Address, J. D. Wolfensohn, L. Dini and others, eds., "Culture Counts: Financing, Resources, and the Economics of Culture in Sustainable Development. Proceedings of the Conference, Florence, Italy, October 4-7, 1999" (Government of Italy, World Bank, and UNESCO, Washington, D.C., 2000), 11.

5   World Commission on Culture and Development, *Our Cultural Diversity* (Paris: UNESCO, 1995) as cited in "Culture Counts."

6   D. Hayden, *The Power of Place: Urban Landscapes as Public History* (Cambridge, Ma.: The MIT Press, 1995).

7   M. McLuhan, "The Media Fit the Battle of Jericho," Explorations Six, July 1956.

8   This section draws on E. Shluger, "Culture and Development in Brazil—Promoting Public-Private Partnerships in Heritage Preservation," Policy research report prepared at the Latin American Public Scholars Program, Woodrow Wilson Center, Washington, D.C., 1999.

9   R. Rolnick, "Territorial Exclusion and Violence: The Case of São Paulo, Brazil," Working Paper Series (Urban Program, Woodrow Wilson Center, Washington, D.C., 1999).

10   This section draws on I. Serageldin, "Very Special Places: The Architecture and Economics of Intervening in Historic Cities," Culture in Sustainable Development series (World Bank, Washington, D.C., 1999).

Dome of the Rock mosque, Jerusalem: interior.

Part I

Preserving Historic Cities and Sacred Sites: The Problematique

Editors' Note

The authors in Part I examine the complex origins and rich legacy of the religious symbolisms attached to the structures of historic centers, houses of prayer, and sacred sites. The first three chapters examine the design principles and make comparative analyses of the designs of early temples, synagogues, churches, and mosques.

Seyyed Nasr examines early philosophies on the formation of cities, their physical forms, and their spiritual importance. According to certain major religious traditions, the city was likened to the body and modeled after it. As such the city was a confluence of the physical, the psychological, the emotive, the intellectual, and the spiritual. For example, Mecca is the supreme spiritual city of Islam in which the Ka'bah at the heart of the city corresponds to the human heart. Although much of the historic city of Mecca has been destroyed through successive urban renewal projects, the center survives, establishing a direct relationship to the spiritual heart, the heart of the city, the heart of the Islamic universe, and the human heart.

In the West early Christian philosophers advanced the notion of the city as a reflection of a divine kingdom. Similar ideals were also found in Far Eastern traditions. In the first half of the eighteenth century Immanuel Swedenborg wrote about the archetypes of cities, which transcended their physical reality. In the same way that a tree grows out of the "principles" (blueprint) contained in a seed, Swedenborg saw the underlying principle of the city—its "seed"—as being in the world above. Many traditions believe that the sacred cities are a crystallization in space and time of a reality that belongs to the spiritual world.

However, since the seventeenth century, in the West the dominant view has been that space is a purely quantitative reality. This view leaves little room for qualitative and symbolic space. Swedenborg argues, however, that a sacred historic event, an exceptional life with spiritual significance, or a mythic "event" can invest art, architecture, and places with those qualities. Great cities that remain spiritual centers, such as Jerusalem, Mecca, Assisi, or the Isle of Ise, are based on archetypal realities that determined their earthly urban reality, notwithstanding the onslaught of transformations, destruction, and time.

Bezalel Narkiss clarifies the cross-cultural influences and interrelationships among the structures of the houses of worship of the three major monotheistic religions. He draws evidence from the comparative study of the first known synagogues, churches, and mosques. The structures built with windows placed above the columns, known during the Roman Empire as basilicas, are found not only in the fourth-century church of San Giovanni and the Basilica of St. Peter of 333 A. D., but also in the sixth-century synagogue in Sardis. The Al-Aqsa Mosque built in Jerusalem between the eighth and tenth centuries has a basilical shape similar to the churches and synagogues of that time. These circulating influences continued as late as the twentieth century, when synagogues were built reflecting the large, theater-like churches of the time that incorporated fashionable Neo-Moorish, Neo-Gothic, or Neo-Romanesque styles. Although the interrelationships among synagogues, churches, and mosques throughout history are very complex, Narkiss clarifies some of the basic influences on the architectural design solutions.

Reflecting on the function and the future of holy places in the contemporary world, Stefano Bianca points out that traditional cultures understood how various layers of reality—material and spiritual and essential—coincide. They mirror one another through the chain of references and analogies implied in the relationships between the macrocosm and microcosm. Implicit with accepting this integrated vision of reality means that sacred places cannot and should not be dissociated from their mundane environments. One of the basic concerns of traditional civilizations was to establish permanent connections between the visible and invisible, the quantifiable and the qualitative, the ephemeral and the timeless. The author argues that historic cities are an underestimated cultural asset. In societies in which religious traditions are strong, historic cities can be seen as the surviving engines of cultural identity and creative diversity, which in recent years have begun to be integrated in the international development agenda.

Reminding us that heritage preservation is an essential intergenerational commitment, Norman Koonce quotes Jonas Salk that it is incumbent on us "to strive to be good ancestors for future generations." The last two chapters focus on varying ways that cultures transmit traditions and knowledge from one generation to next to ensure that heritage is properly cared for by concerned communities and that cultural continuity is preserved despite the encroachments of modern development.

The Grand Shrine of Ise is one of the foremost sacred places in Japan. Isao Tokoro describes the celebration of faith through the holistic process by which the shrine is renewed by rebuilding the structure and every object within it every 20 years. The shrine is constructed completely of wood, which necessitates this different kind of "preservation." The tradition of this periodic renewal, and the requisite skills, have been transmitted through generations for 1,300 years. There is much to be learned from the Grand Shrine of Ise, as it possesses elements of both old and new, and transmits the wisdom of its legacy to each new generation.

The Spirit of the Cities 1

W hen we speak about historic and sacred sites, it is of utmost importance to understand why they are signif-icant. Even if we are not philosophers or architects, while walking through the narrow streets of Carcasone in France, Fez in Morocco, Isfahan in Persia, or Benares in India, we feel that we are in an ambience that touches us very deeply. It is another space, another place. But our present-day worldview pre-vents us from taking such an experience seriously. It is a worldview that reduces the human being to molecules banging against each other and the cosmos to dust that has evolved over billions of years into its pres-ent structures. It is a worldview, therefore, that makes the word "spirit" ultimately meaningless, simply a poetic metaphor with no correspon-dence to objective reality as far as the accepted, legitimized structure of knowledge in our world is concerned.

Fortunately, the total domination of this stifling worldview is now coming more or less to an end. Many people speak earnestly of the Spirit, although still too few are aware that it corresponds to an objective reality. The rea-son historic cities are also sacred cities is that before modern times, it was taken for granted that all cities and all human life were touched by the Spirit. That is why there was no need for historic preservation before our time. That is why the very act of preservation is an anomaly that is made necessary to preserve something that in the past was always normal and part of human life. In the same way a thousand years ago we had no museums because there was no need for museums, because before mod-ern times human beings lived in the matrix of the sacred. If we take histo-ry back a few centuries, what is historic is also in a sense sacred.

Assisi, where St. Francis lived and died, is 700 years old. It is a sacred city precisely because it was the locus of a religious culture that could give rise to a being such as St. Francis. The same is true of other historic sites if one goes deeply into their history. As for ourselves, we actually live in an exceptional period of human history, the only one we know that denies the reality of the spirit in its general cosmology. It therefore builds cities and buildings based on a view of the human being that is two dimensional and earth bound, a view characterized by the stifling reign of quantity over quality, of the profane over the sacred.

Seyyed Hossein Nasr

Seyyed Hossein Nasr is University Professor of Islamic Studies at the George Washington University, Washington, D. C.

City as Reflection of the Human Body

In many traditional sources—Islam, Hinduism, the Chinese tradition and Christianity, and many other religions—the human body itself is often-times compared to a city or kingdom, with all its political and social functions. There is a famous book by Ibn 'Arabi, the celebrated Andalusian mystic, whose very title, *al-Tadbirat al-ilahiyyah fi islah al-mamlakat al-insaniyyah* ("Divine Governance of the Human Kingdom"), indicates its content. The content concerns how to govern the city or kingdom of the human state whose various functions are compared to that of a polis, which is comparable to the body. The famous *Rasa'il* ("Treatises"), written a thousand years ago in the cities of Basra and Baghdad by "The Brethren of Purity," contains a whole section on how the body is like a city.

The body as envisaged in such sources is not the same body whose anatomy is studied in modern medical schools. It is the body as understood traditionally, which means the locus of the confluence of the physical, the psychological, the emotive, the intellectual, and the spiritual, which is not to be confused in any way with the psychological. The city was not only compared to the body and the body to the city, but the city was the body expanded macrocosmically, providing the loci for all these elements. The heart corresponded to the center, and the various parts of the body corresponded to various functions in the city, as we shall see in a moment.

It is amazing how universal this concept is. One can think immediately of the examples of sacred cities of Islam, especially the City of Mecca, the supreme spiritual center of Islam. According to numerous treatises written on the subject, the *Ka'bah* at the very heart of the city corresponds to the human heart. Much of the beautiful City of Mecca has now been destroyed through modern urban design. Nevertheless, the center survives, which demonstrates the direct relationship between the inner heart, the heart of the city, the heart of the universe, or at least the Islamic universe, and the human heart.

There is the example of the Ming Tang in classical China, in which a three-dimensional magic square dominated the numerical symbolism of the 12 chambers of the Ming Tang, which always added vertically to the number 11. This number symbolized the wedding between Heaven and Earth. It was here that the emperor resided, he being the bridge between Heaven and Earth and representing precisely the function of man in his universal aspect.

The space of the cathedral symbolizes the form of the Body of Christ, as represented by the cross. It was in consideration of this space that the old European cities, which retain their beauty for people today, were planned always having a cathedral in the middle.

To come back to the question of the body and the city, all of our limbs are organically tied to the function of the heart. We are an overly cerebral civilization and always identify thinking with the head. We must recall that there is also "heart knowledge." The heart as the seat of the intellect and organ of intuitive knowing is mentioned in the Bible, the Upanishads, Chinese classical texts, the Quran, and so many other sacred writings of the world. The heart is the seat of intelligence, not the discursive and divisive intelligence that is associated with the brain and the mind, but unitive, integrated intelligence that knows by immediacy and in a synthetic manner.

This heart-center is, therefore, at once the center of life and the center of intelligence that emanates from the center to all the parts of the body. In the traditional and sacred city the heart always corresponds to the place of worship. It is from that center that all of the other parts of the city grow and to which they are organically related.

What are the powers and functions that we have within ourselves? We possess an intellective and religious power and function. We have an active aspect associated with our will. We make and produce things, and we live a life that must be lived according to certain laws.

All of these powers and functions of the human being associated with parts of the body and the mind are reflected in the traditional city. It always had spaces and sites for the following functions:

1. The intellective and religious function. Why do I put these together? Because through most of human history, among those very people who created the cities that we call historic cities, the religious and intellectual functions were united—whether in the Egyptian and Babylonian priesthood, the Brahmins, the Mandarin class, the Islamic '*ulama*', or the medieval Christian priesthood. In traditional societies the functions of the theologian, priest, and scientist were united in a single organ that was conceived as the heart of society, while from another point of view it corresponds to the head, as one can see mentioned in certain classic Hindu texts.

2. The active element. It includes on the one hand the political and military functions of the city, and on the other the mercantile functions.

3. The production element. It includes farming and arts and crafts.

All of these are functions for which the living city had to provide architectural space as organically unified as are the heart, the head, the arms, and the feet of the human body. Furthermore, in the traditional ambience these spaces were always related to the heart-center, as are parts of the human body to the human heart.

Wonderful examples of this principle exist in the classical cities of the world. Since I know a little bit more about the Islamic world than other places, my examples come from that world. In what remains of the traditional cities of the Islamic world, such as Fez or Isfahan, one always sees this organic interrelationship between the mosque or religious center and the various spaces associated with functions that are always related to the center. In this pattern there is an unbelievable unity that comes from the integration of the various functions of the city with the heart-center.

Without the heart-center, which is always related to the Sacred, as in the case of the microcosm, in which the heart of human beings is the seat of Divine Presence, there can be no veritably human city. We have forgotten the heart-center of ourselves as well as of the world around us. This is the reason that we feel in such inhuman ambiences in modern cities that we build based on planning that does not have a heart. This is why the historic cities always give us a sense of intimacy, of belonging, of being at the center. In these sacred and historic cities there is always a center, which reflects our own center. This point is what really distinguishes the traditional city from much that has been built in the last two or three centuries, especially the last century. The distinction is between the possession of a center or lack thereof. We have lost our own center, so we build cities without centers.

City as Archetypal Reality

Another important philosophical point has been discussed in many different traditions, yet appears strange to us because it lies outside of our worldview and does not make any sense within the paradigm that dominates our minds. It is that traditional cities have a kind of archetypal reality. They are not just physical conglomerates that were built as an ensemble. They reflect a reality from the spiritual world in the same way that, according to all traditions, what is below is a reflection of what is above. In the Western tradition, this concept is identified with Plato and the Platonic ideas and is well known in the West, even if not accepted in the prevailing Western *Weltanschauung*. There are other examples of this concept such as *menok* and *getik* in the Zoroastrian religion, and *nama* and *rupa* in Hinduism. The city itself was conceived to be a kind of reflection on Earth of a celestial, archetypal reality.

Many architects have expressed that idea for individual buildings. They have asserted that they have had a direct inspiration and vision of the whole edifice before its design and construction, in a sense like a poet who suddenly writes down a poem after having received it in its entirety through inspiration. Such architects have created buildings on the basis of an archetypal reality that has "descended" on them.

But this idea is also true of sacred cities as a whole. There is a whole literature, for example, in the Islamic world about the mythical cities of

Jabulqa and Jabulsa, cities belonging in a sense to the subtle world, which in traditional cosmology precedes the physical world in which we live. One is the city through which we enter into this world situated in the seven climes, and the other is a city through which we go out from this world to that higher abode that Islam's visionary geography calls the eighth clime.

In the West the Swedish visionary, Immanuel Swedenborg, wrote extensively of his vision of the archetypes of cities and not just their physical reality. In the same way that a tree grows out of the principles that are contained in its seed, such visionaries saw the principle of the city as the embodiment of its "seed" in the world above. The seed of a pear tree will never grow into an apple tree; it always gives pears. The whole pattern of the growth of the parts of each tree—the leaves, the colors, the form of the branches—is contained in the original principle, with modifications due to the external ambience.

The same reality holds true for traditional architecture and urban design. Many traditional sources believe that sacred cities are in a sense like the crystallization in the world of space and time of a reality that belongs to the world of the spirit. They believe that these cities develop according to principles and laws contained in the "idea" of the city in question in the archetypal world, much like the growth of the plant from its seed.

This idea is closely related to that idea of a holy place, of a sacred site, and what we could call sacred geography. Thanks to Descartes, we today have quantified dimensionality. Space for us is a purely quantitative reality. Some people are trying to change that view now, but for the last 400 years, that has been the dominant point of view in the West. This quantified view of space leaves no room for qualitative and symbolic space. In contrast we know that all sacred art, all sacred architecture, and all holy places are created precisely on the acceptance that a reality, a sacred historical event, an exceptional life with spiritual significance, or a mythic "event" has qualified a particular place or space. For those living in the religious reality of that world, that space is not the same as just another space. Assisi is not like the rest of Tuscany. Mecca is not just another city in Arabia like Taif.

The idea of qualitative space, of sacred geography, of certain sites that attract the sacred, are universal among traditional people. China has developed the extensive science of as *feng shui* concerning this qualitative and sacred geography. Other civilizations have not elaborated it so systematically but have nevertheless spoken about it in different ways.

Some historians have written that as soon as Christianity and Islam appeared, they simply took over the cemeteries of religions that existed before and converted them to Christian and Muslim cemeteries because this was the easiest thing to do. Or it is said that Christians and Muslims simply took over the various temples of the Greeks or the Zoroastrians and built churches or mosques in their place.

There was no shortage of space at that time, as in today's modern cities. Why is it then that so many Byzantine churches are built on top of Greek temples? Why is it that the most extensive and beautiful mosque in Persia, in my view, the Jamiy' Mosque of Isfahan, began to be built at the site of an old Zoroastrian fire temple and only later expanded in the area next to it? In India this occurred over and over again. In Europe one can see many Bogomil funerary sites in Yugoslavia. When those poor Muslims of the Balkans who are being massacred every other day became Muslims, they built their cemeteries there. All of these examples point to the idea that there are certain sacred sites and places on earth.

The fact that many have lost the sense of the sacred does not change the character of that reality. Even those of us who have lost the sense of the sacred, however, feel something of the presence of the sacred when we go to those places. That is why they are so precious and that is why preserving them is so important.

A center becomes sacred for many different reasons. One is sacred geography, the nature of the topography, the subtle forces involved, and all that goes with those types of traditional sciences, especially sacred geometry. Another has to do with certain events, either mythical or historical, but pertaining to sacred history. Babylon, Athens, Rome all had mythical or religious beginnings. The same is true for Benares; Madura, the birthplace of Krishna; Kyoto; the Isle of Ise in Japan; many places in China; many sites in the New World—the Hopi reservation. In the reservation in which the Navajos settled after being nomadic people, their pattern of settlement began with a vision that identified the sacred centers. These then determined where the settlements in New Mexico and Arizona were located.

Examples of these principles are legion. I will just draw one example, which also touches us very deeply politically and historically today. That is the City of Mecca, the center of the Islamic world. It is called in Arabic *Umm al-qura*, that is, "Mother of all cities." Of course, in days of old, for each civilization its world was *the* world, because it was a sacred world.

Today the sacred quality is lost, but, strangely enough, the idea in its secularized form has manifested itself in another way. Eurocentrism also sees its view of the world as the only worldview. In the old days people were at least more honest about it. Therefore, *Umm al-qura* does not mean "Mother of all cities" on earth, but "Mother of all cities" in the Islamic world, that is, the source or principle of all legitimate cities. There are many mystical treatises in Islamic languages about the interrelationships among various cities, such as Mashhad in my own home country of Iran, in the province of Khorasan, and their inward relation to Mecca.

Figure 1. Among the great contributions that Islam has made to architecture is the use of two- and three-dimensional geometry. Geometric forms not only organize space but are used at all scales of the building. The three-dimensional *muqarnas*, or "stalactite form," is unique to Islam. Usually used as a transitional element between two surfaces, for example, at a corner, it dematerializes space. Calligraphy, part of the tradition in which the word of God is expressed in written form, is another significant contribution. Such texts on buildings are called epigraphy and are a very important sign of Islam.

According to Islamic eschatological sources, when the *Mahdi* comes at the end of the world, he will put his back to the wall of the *Ka'bah*, call out to those destined to aid him, and those in Khorasan and elsewhere destined for the call will hear his appeal. This, many will claim, is merely folklore. But it is not important how modern people judge such assertions. The important thing is the significance of this way of looking at things for the understanding of the creation of sacred space and sacred cities (figure 1).

Another interesting case is one in which the archetypal city of three different religions meets in one, single reality on earth, Jerusalem. This is the reason that the problem of Jerusalem is so intractable politically. It is not simply one city among others. For 2,000 years the Jews said "Next year in Jerusalem," and finally, after 2,000 years, they have come back to that holy city. The Muslims have been there for 1,400 years, and nothing in the world is going to change the sacred character and significance of Jerusalem for them. The Christians have been there for 2,000 years. The Church of the Holy Sepulchre, and all the events of the end of the life of Christ, are related to the city.

Therefore, in a sense, the city is a meeting of archetypal realities that determined its earthly urban reality, some of which has been destroyed by the creation of profane architecture in recent years. However, no matter how much Jerusalem has been vilified by high-rises at the very place where Christ is supposed to descend at the end of the world, it does not change the ultimate nature of the sacred city. It will retain its sacred character as long as those religions that hold this city as sacred remain alive and their sacred sites remain protected in that holy ambience.

I want to mention one more important point. I have mentioned that the traditional city, the historic city, is always built on the basis of the primacy of the spirit, beginning from the heart and expanding outward—not first building a business district and then making a church in the suburbs for people to go to on Sundays. It is always growing from the inward to the outward, like us, like the fetus in the womb of the mother. In addition the city is the place from which come the great moral calamities of human history. Basing himself on a verse of the Koran that asserts that there is no city that will not suffer punishment from God before the end of the world, the great Tunisian philosopher of history, Ibn Khaldoun, alludes to the significance that cities have not only as centers of knowledge, art, and luxury, but also of decadence, disruption, and corruption.

Of course, at this stage of history we are now witness to the reenactment of the famous myth of Cain and Abel—that is, it is the cities that are destroying the nomadic people and the world of nature, which the nomads always guarded and protected. We have either killed off the nomads, the other half of humanity, or settled them forcing them to become sedentary. We have forced them into settlements or obliterated them physically. And now the cities grow like a cancer, precisely because we have decided to forget our brother, who is also our other half.

But ultimately, as long as we live as human beings on earth, the truth is always present. Sacred cultures will not disappear completely. At this moment we are destroying both our historical heritage and our natural heritage with a rapidity never seen in human history. Not even Genghis Khan could do things like what we are doing through "development." At this time I believe there is nothing more important than to realize that what remains of our historic cities, of our sacred sites and sacred places, is significant not only for national identity or archaeological records but also for our own identity as human beings. It is through these sites that we remember who we really are, where we come from, and where we shall go at the end of our earthly journey. Thus, the significance of such cities and sites is far greater than any immediate economic, political, or even cultural factors that we might consider. Such places are necessary for our spiritual health. They are necessary for our continuation as human beings. The preservation of our sacred sites and historic cities is not only an investment in culture. It is also an investment in the continuity of our existence here on earth and in the meaning of our lives as human beings. ■

Synagogue-Church-Mosque: A Comparison of Typologies

2

T here is a relationship of dependence among the structures of the houses of worship of the three monotheistic religions. These relationships have been distinguishable since the early centuries of our era, when the first known synagogues and churches were established. One of the earliest types of synagogues is represented by the first-century Gamla Synagogue in the Golan (figure 1). The single hall is divided by rows of columns surrounding the inner walls of the edifice. It contrasts with the Greco-Roman Temple of the Roman Empire, in which the row of columns surrounded the outer walls of the building.

On a panel painted on the western wall of the Dura Europos Synagogue of 244 A. D., the high priest Aaron is standing near the tent of meeting in the desert, depicted as a Roman temple (figure 2). This strange rendering is related to the common pictorial language of the late Roman Empire, which represented any sanctuary in the shape of a Greco-Roman temple.

Dura Europos Synagogue itself is a small, wide hall with no row of columns inside or outside. Its western wall with a central Torah niche faces Jerusalem in accordance with the practice of the Prophet Daniel, who faced Jerusalem while praying.[1] The niche holding the Torah and its direction are this synagogue's most important elements.

The entrance of the fourth-century Synagogue of Capernaum, typically elongated with an interior rows of columns, faces Jerusalem, and the synagogue has no Torah niche (figure 3) similar to that of Gamla. The location of the Torah in this type of synagogue is not

Bezalel Narkiss

Bezalel Narkiss, recipient of the 1999 Israel Prize and founder of the Jerusalem Index of Jewish Art, is Nicolas Landau Professor Emeritus of Art History at Hebrew University of Jerusalem.

Figure 1. Gamla Synagogue, first century: reconstruction of ground plan.

Figure 2. Dura Europos Synagogue, Dura Europos, 244 A. D.: west wall panel with Aaron the high priest in front of the Tent of Meeting in the desert.

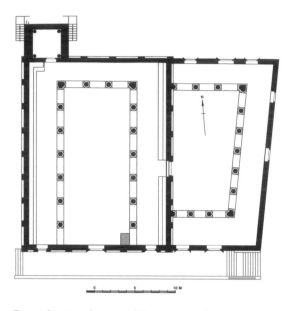

Figure 3. Capernaum Synagogue, fifth century: ground plan.

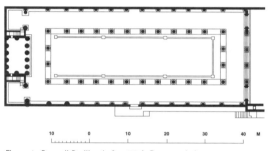

Figure 4. Pompeii Basilica, before 78 A. D.: ground plan.

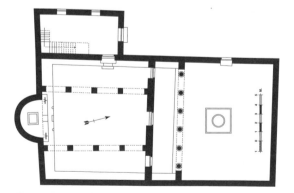

Figure 5. Beit Alpha Synagogue, sixth century: reconstructed ground plan.

known and creates a problem for historians. It may have been placed in a movable ark.

In the Roman Empire the shape of such a building with rows of columns within the walls is known as a basilica, such as the one that existed in Pompeii before the destruction of the city in 78 A. D. (figure 4). The most important element in a basilica is the upper windows above the columns that bring light to the main hall. The Jews probably chose the basilica as a model to build their sanctuary because the former was a civic building and had no connection to a religious edifice.

The synagogue in Sardis, on the western shores of Turkey, was constructed in an existing first-century basilica of a gymnasium, which had been relocated from the city. Originally, it may have had a movable Torah Ark. However, in the sixth century, the Jewish community fitted two *ediculi* for the Torah scrolls in the southwestern entrance of the hall, opposite the wide apse. It was during this period that the location of the Torah Ark was fixed on the wall facing Jerusalem.

The smaller basilical first-century Synagogue of Ostia, the Port of Rome, was built specifically as a synagogue, with the entrance facing Jerusalem. However, in the sixth century, an *edicula* as a Torah Ark was added to the right of the exit.

The Beit Alpha Synagogue in the Lower Galilee was constructed in the sixth century with an apse that incorporated the Torah facing Jerusalem to the south (figure 5). This new feature may have been influenced by the construction of Christian churches in the fourth century.

One of the earliest fourth-century churches was San Giovanni in Laterano, built as a double-column basilica in 324 by Pope Sylvester. It was constructed with an apse facing the Holy Sepulchre in Jerusalem and fitted with an *edicula* in its center (figure 6). Other fourth-century churches in Rome, such as the Basilica of Saint Peter of 333, are constructed in similar shapes, which continued throughout the Middle Ages. The mid-sixth-century basilical Church of Saint Catherine in Sinai (548-565) is constructed similarly, with the apse facing north toward Jerusalem.

For the builders of the early mosques it must have been an easy way to construct the main hall, as in the Great Mosque of Damascus of 709-715. Instead of the deep apse, a small apsidal *mihrab* was an indication of the direction of prayer. Facing south toward Mecca, the basilical structure with rows of columns was constructed as a wide hall to accommodate more participants' facing Mecca. However, the interior toward the central entrance, Bab El-Barid, is not different from any church or synagogue entrance at the time. The facade is, of course, wider than any church or synagogue.

The rapid spread of Islam during the seventh and eighth centuries disseminated the structure of the mosque throughout the Islamic Empires. The Mosque in Cordoba, started by Abdul-Rahman the First in 784, remained one of the most sumptuous buildings for two centuries. The double-arched columns are part of the earliest stage of the mosque (figure 7). However, the basic wide construction, with a pronounced *mihrab* in the southeast toward Mecca, is visible even from the rooftops.

The earlier Al-Aqsa Mosque, which was started in 705, exposes a similar structure, although broadened in 1035 (figure 8). The basilical shape seen from the main entrance is not different from any sumptuous church or synagogue (figure 9).

The place of Al-Aqsa Mosque on the Temple Mount in Jerusalem was determined by the night flight of Mohammed on his *Burraq* (winged steed), but the earlier Dome of the Rock is placed in a more prominent situation on the mount. Built by Abdul-Malik from 688 to 692, the Al-Haram-ash-Sharif was meant to divert the Muslim believers from Mecca to Jerusalem (figure 10). As a round building the Dome of the Rock was not meant to be a mosque, but a memorial structure commemorating the sacrifice of Ishmael on the Temple Mount. Similarly, the neighboring Christian

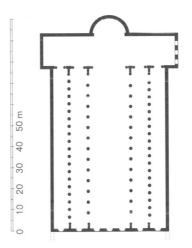

Figure 6. San Giovanni in Laterano Church, Rome, 312-24 A. D.

Figure 7. Great Mosque, Cordoba, double arched sea of columns, 784-86.

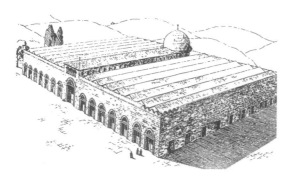

Figure 8. Al-Aqsa Mosque, Jerusalem, 705–1035: reconstruction.

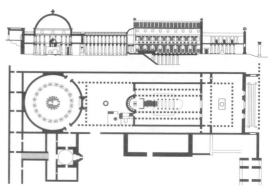

Figure 11. Holy Sepulchre and church, Jerusalem, 326–34: reconstructed ground plan and section.

Figure 9. Al-Aqsa Mosque, Jerusalem, 1035: interior of central aisle.

Figure 12. Memoria of Sta. Constanza, Rome, 337–54: interior.

Figure 10. Dome of the Rock, Jerusalem, 688–92: exterior.

Figure 13. Hagia Sophia, Istanbul, 537: interior.

Figure 14. Hagia Sophia, Istanbul, 537: exterior.

structure, the Holy Sepulchre, commemorates the burial of Christ. Indeed, the Dome of the Rock has the same measurements as those of the round *memoria* over the empty tomb constructed by the architect Zenobius in 326–334 for Helena, the mother of Constantine the Great (figure 11).

The Constantinian round memorial structures of the Ascension of Christ have the same proportions. The round *memoria* over tombs was common in Rome since the days of the Republic, like that of Cecilia Metella, the wife of Sula. It continued in similar structures, with the Tomb of Augustus and that of Hadrian, the Castel-Sant-Angelo.

The most prominent Christian *memoria* in Rome is the Mausoleum of Santa Constanza, the sister of Constantine, built and decorated between 337 and 354. Like the Holy Sepulchre and the later Dome of the Rock, the round Santa Constanza was built as a basilical type with windows above the columns, giving light into the Main Hall (figure 12). These could have been the origins of the more sumptuous, round, centralized churches.

Justinian the First, who built the Hagia Sophia in Constantinople in 537, claimed that he outdid Solomon in constructing a sanctuary. He probably did much more regarding the shape, spaciousness, lavishness, and daring (figure 13). The main achievement was the enormous dome resting on four pillars. This, and maybe other domes, inspired a Christian Syriac poet to compare the church dome to that of the Dome of Heaven, carrying the Almighty and its host of angels, related to a hierarchy of the Church on Earth.

There is no doubt that the magnificence of the Church of Hagia Sophia influenced the centralized structure of many edifices in the East as well as in the West (figure 14). Interestingly, after the Turkish conquest of Constantinople and the use of Hagia Sophia as a mosque, this structure

Figure 15. Selimiye Mosque, Edirne, 1569-75: exterior.

Figure 16. Selimiye Mosque, Edirne, 1569-75: interior with *mihrab, minbar,* and *dikka.*

was used as a model for other mosques. The Selimiye Mosque of Edirne was built by the famous architect Sinan for the Sultan Selim in 1569-75 on the model of Hagia Sophia (figure 15). However, the interior of the Edirne Mosque is somewhat lighter than that of the Hagia Sophia and exposes the *minbar,* the *mihrab,* and the *dikka* (figure 16).

The seventeenth-century Blue Mosque in Istanbul is similar to those from the outside, but has a blue-tile luminosity inside.

The influences of what was considered the fashionable Moorish style in architecture of the nineteenth-century modern synagogues are noticeable all over Europe, as in the Hungarian Synagogue of Szeged. Its dome is no less impressive than the monumental Torah Ark.

In the late nineteenth and early twentieth centuries under the influence of large, theater-like modern churches, synagogues were built after the same manner and shape. This form changed the idea of a two-pole structure of the traditional ancient and medieval synagogues into a single center, toward Jerusalem, by combining the Torah Ark and the *bimah* in one place. During the same period the Neo-Gothic, Neo-Romanesque, or Neo-Moorish styles were common to the new sumptuous churches and synagogues. Even the more contemporary structures that started to develop between the two World Wars did not change the concept of the theater-like interior of churches, mosques, and synagogues.

The interrelationships among synagogues, churches, and mosques throughout their histories are much more complex than these brief comparisons, but I hope to have clarified some of the basic influences and origins of new creations within the basilical and centralized structures. ■

Glossary

Apse   Semi-circular or polygonal recess, arched or dome-roofed, especially in churches, and later in synagogues

Bimah   Literally, "platform." In the Ashkenazi synagogue a raised platform on which a desk is placed. The Torah scrolls are placed on the desk while they are being read.

Dikka   In a mosque a raised platform supported on columns on which prominent Muslims are seated while studying or praying.

Mihrab   In a mosque an arch-shaped niche indicating the direction to Mecca.

Minbar   In a mosque a high pulpit for the imam, accessed by a single flight of steep stairs.

Torah   Literally, "Pentateuch," the five books of Moses in the Bible. For the synagogue the Torah is written by hand on a continuous parchment scroll, wrapped around staves, and placed in the Torah Ark, or chest. Each week a different portion of the Torah is read.

Note

1 For specialized terms see Glossary at the end this chapter.

3 Resources for Sustaining Cultural Identity

Stefano Bianca

Stefano Bianca is director of the Historic Cities Support Programme of the Aga Khan Trust for Culture in Geneva and a practicing architect, urban designer, and author.

It is indeed an auspicious opportunity to link the debate on urban conservation with considerations on the function and the future of holy places in our contemporary world. Discussing the role of the sacred today does not seem the most obvious thing to do. It may even cause embarrassment, because in a modern context the sacred is often felt to be either unreachably high, above "normal" life, or totally detached from it. To address the topic properly therefore will require readiness to reconsider (and even to question) the assumptions of our conventional modern perspective by looking from a different point of view at the issues. This will not only apply to the topic of sacred sites and historic cities, but also to the corollary theme of the genesis of cultural identities, as raised at the end of this essay.

Traditional cultures knew that the various layers of reality, from the material to the spiritual plane, coincide. Thus they can mirror one another through the chain of references and analogies implied in the relationships between macrocosm and microcosm. Accepting this integrated vision implicitly means that sacred sites cannot and should not be dissociated from their more mundane environments. They are in fact the places in which the world manifests itself in its most real and most concentrated form. Other, perhaps more tangible, expressions are secondary reflections and outgrowths of the inner sap of the tree of life, so to speak. Establishing permanent connections between the visible and the invisible, the quantifiable and the qualitative, the ephemeral and the timeless, was one of the basic concerns of traditional civilizations.

Thinking through the holistic traditional perspective can be an eye-opener for anyone interested in the more essential aspects of culture. Doing so will reveal that the prevailing modern notion of the sacred as being separate from the "real" world is a mental distortion. It is based on a deliberate reduction and fragmentation of reality to accommodate more simplistic quantitative and mechanistic manners of perception. This approach is in clear contradiction to the spirit in which most sacred places were established and experienced in the past. Introducing and cementing an artificial dichotomy among different layers of reality not only risks marginalizing sites. It also means reducing their significance to highly abstract, if not sterile, connotations, depriving the sacred of its potential as a creative impulse in the construction of a truly human and lively environment.

Reconsidering our perception of sacred sites may also enable us to throw new light on historic cities, which tend to be underestimated cultural assets. In societies in which traditions are still alive, historic cities can be seen as the surviving engines of cultural identity. They are not defunct relics of the past overcome by a present that will in turn be superseded by the future. They convey the inner dimension, the soul, of an unfolding human development process. This process is based on the crystallization of the acts and beliefs of human beings in time and space, resulting from the investment of creative imagination, social interaction, and responses to environmental conditions.

Once we admit the idea of a continuous presence of creative forces, the past remains alive while the seeds of the future germinate. On the contrary curtailing the sense of an overarching presence means opening an artificial gap in cultural continuity. The resulting chasm between past and future not only empties the present of much of its substance and significance but also affects the qualities of the past and the future. History then runs the risk of being mummified and relegated to the department of the sciences, while coherent and creative innovation is in danger of being aborted or replaced by the stillborn phantoms of a unilateral "progress." In either case the sense of a living cultural identity is at stake. It can flourish only through a sustained identification of people with a continuous and interactive process of creation, as reflected in a meaningful built environment (figure 1).

In most of the Western World such identification processes have been disrupted by the "Modern Movement," which deliberately, and for good reasons, refused the depleted architectural symbols of the nineteenth century. Nevertheless, in doing so, that movement also rejected the need for spiritual and emotional content as implicit or explicit motives of architectural expression. This rejection meant that the common cultural ground that existed between earlier periods gave way to a serious divide that has never been overcome. Thus, the natural fluidity between past and the future was blocked, stifling the creative communication between human beings and their cultural matrix and fragmenting their vision of the world. This in turn allowed rigid and fatal dichotomies to emerge, with which we struggle today: "Modern" versus "Traditional," "Rational" versus "Emotional," "Cultural" versus "Technical," to name a few.

Figure 1. Interior of Old Dispensary, first building restored by the Aga Khan Trust for Culture in the Old Stone Town Project in Zanzibar.

Figure 2. The balcony overlooking the interior courtyard of the
Old Dispensary before restoration.

Figure 3. The balcony overlooking the interior courtyard of the
Old Dispensary after restoration.

Historic cities offer, at least potentially, the opportunity to overcome the
effects, if not the causes, of that relatively recent mental and physical disintegration. This holds true especially for societies less affected by the modern industrial civilization and closer to the roots of their social and spiritual resources. There, beyond constituting mere cultural memories, historic
cities should be able to act as productive nurseries of cultural continuity
(figures 2, 3). Clearly, this can not be achieved by reproducing frozen architectural forms. It must be sought by sustaining and encouraging the internal patterns of life that have generated the existing built environment and
that may be capable of internal renewal under changed external conditions.

By investigating the growth patterns of historic cities, we find that the formation of cultural identity can work in two ways, because cultural identity may be understood as both the origin and the result of the identification of human beings with their physical shelter. We will also see that the
genesis of cultural identities is no gratuitous process. It depends on human
beings' existential experience of human values and on their possibility of
practicing a dialogue with an all-encompassing reality. In the course of
this dialogue individuals discover and develop their own deeper beings.
While this dialogue eventually may refer to shared universal values, it is
equally concerned with producing tangible embodiments in terms of

meaningful forms, shapes, and places. By necessity, the results of this crystallization will be differentiated according to the "medium" and the circumstances imposed on respective human expressions. These variables engender parallel but different cultural identities, typical for specific societies, communities, and individuals. Deep-rooted cultural identities and creative diversity do not contradict but, in fact, condition each other.

Patterns of cultural identity take time to develop. They are woven through numerous cycles of interplay between deep and largely spontaneous human impulses; and "productive" resistances set up by a given environment, a given social order, and a given set of shared ethical codes. It is this creative interaction that, through experience, integrates the human mind and roots it in meaningful cultural patterns. This interaction turns information into knowledge and eventually produces shared emotions, shared values, and shared physical expressions. To survive, therefore, cultural identities depend on continuity and tradition, while they also have the faculty of adapting, evolving, and innovating—so long as they remain connected to their sources and are supported by collective endeavor.

Over the past decade cultural identity and creative diversity have become recognized issues in the international development agenda—a positive fact in itself. Yet the implementation of such qualitative concepts has to be pursued at levels, in domains, and under conditions that elude theoretic constructs and the prevailing means of information and communication. Relying on the easy shortcuts of "virtual" experiences offered by modern technology would mean depleting or flattening existing cultural differentials and settling for abstract identities, which are no longer underpinned by lived and practiced values and sustained collective experiences.

Nurturing cultural identities, I would submit, can succeed only through re-anchoring the lives of individuals and communities in the deeper layers of a primordial reality. This reality is all-encompassing in that it links past, present, and future. It is also limited in that it can be grasped and materialized only through individual realizations at "grassroots" levels in a given time and place.

The fact that spiritual values are essentially *beyond* forms, yet have to be experienced *through* specific forms, is a condition of human existence. Without the interplay between a transcendent vision and a tangible human embodiment, "culture" will remain either meaningless or unproductive, and so will the creation of the built environment ■

4 The Grand Shrine of Ise: Preservation by Removal and Renewal

Isao Tokoro

Isao Tokoro is a professor in the Institute for Japanese Culture at Kyoto Sangyo University, chair of the Compilation Committee of the Geirin-Kai, head of the study group on Missing Ancient National Documents, and a member of the Society of Historia Juris and the Legal History Association.

The Grand Shrine of Ise may be called the foremost sacred place of Japan. Its history goes back more than 1,000 years. The shrine buildings are built completely of wood, so compared to sturdy stone architecture, its preservation has been more difficult. Another rare example is the Hôryûji Temple in Nara, built in 607 A. D. However, in spite of this handicap, the architecture and religious ceremonies of antiquity at Ise have been transmitted almost unchanged to the present day.

How was this possible? The major reason is the institution of a system called the *Shikinen sengû* (the removal of the Shrine every 20 years), in which the architecture is freshly reconstructed, and the religious treasures are reproduced exactly like the originals. Thus the Shrine is totally renewed every 20 years.

This system was instituted around the end of the seventh century and has been observed faithfully for the past 1,300 years. Recently, in 1993, the sixty-first regular removal and renewal of the Grand Shrine of Ise was held on a magnificent scale. In this sense the Grand Shrine of Ise is not an archeological site excavated more than 1,000 years ago. Rather, it is a new, invigorated sacred sanctuary. It is permeated with the force of everlasting youth *(Tokowaka)* of human life, as it forms a symbiotic relationship with nature.

Granary-style Shrine Preserved Since the Yayoi Period

The image evoked by the name "Grand Shrine of Ise" is perhaps the unique buildings. Divine Brightness Style *(Shinmei zukuri)* is the basic architectural style of Shinto shrines, seen everywhere in Japan. These are designated as Divine Brightness *(Shinmei)* shrines, and consist of a central post *(Hottate bashira)*, raised floor *(Taka-yuka)*, openings at the longitudinal ends *(Hirairi)*, triangular-shaped roof with protruded rafters *(Kirizuma)*, and thatched roof *(Kayabuki)*. The supreme model of this Divine Brightness

Figure 1. Making fire. Land and sea products offered to gods are cooked by sacred fire, made by a lighter of ancient design.

Style *(Shinmei zukuri)* is the main shrine building of the Grand Shrine of Ise. The main shrine building, therefore, is pointedly called the "Singular Divine Brightness Style" *(Yuiitsu shinmei zukuri)*.

The noteworthy point in Divine Brightness Style architecture is the posts that support the edges of the roof *(Munamochi bashira)*, because the wood pieces extend horizontally to either side of the building. These roof-sustaining posts appear in the drawing of the ancient copper bell-shaped artifacts *(Dôtaku)* which were cast during the middle Yayoi period about 2,000 years ago. Similar posts seem to have been used in raised-floor buildings of the Yayoi period. The existence of such posts can be deduced from excavation of post holes, and it appears that such buildings were used as granaries in tribal hamlets of the period.

From the above, it can be surmised that the archetype of Divine Brightness Style might have originated from raised-floor granaries. Such a granary might have been built by every few houses to store communal grain.

Figure 2. Inner Shrine: aerial view. The sixty-first *Shikinen Sengû* ceremony, marking the completion of a new shrine building, was held in 1993. The sixty-second ceremony will be held in 2013.

Figure 3. The *Kinensai* Ceremony is held to pray to Amaterasu Omikami for the happiness of the Emperor's family, the prosperity of Japan, the welfare of Japanese people, and a bountiful harvest.

Figure 4. Daily *Omikesai* Ceremony. At the *Mikeden* building in the Outer Shrine, offerings made in Ise Shrine's fields are served to gods every day in the morning and evening. Since the days of Emperor Yuryaku about 1,500 years ago, these ceremonies have been held without a single day's intermission.

Figure 5. Misomahajime-sai Ceremony to soothe the mountain god, prior to felling trees. Since Japanese cypresses on the mountain have not yet grown fully, for several centuries cypresses from Mt. Kiso have been used for rebuilding.

Chronologically, the granaries go back to the Yayoi period, when rice agriculture became disseminated in Japan. Moreover, the buildings may not have been mere granaries. People might have believed that if unhulled rice seeds were stored on a shelf during winter, new life, which is the soul of rice (*Ina dama*), would be generated and embodied in rice seeds.

With this life, the belief might have gone, one seed that was planted in the forthcoming spring would multiply 10,000-fold. Hence, to the ancient people, the granary-storehouse was sacred and mysterious. In this way, the raised-floor architecture became established, specifically as a sacred place that enshrines the soul of rice. The original simple style became more sophisticated as time passed from the Yayoi period to the Tumulus period (fourth to sixth centuries). The architectural development must have been completed prior to the mid-sixth century, when Chinese-style Buddhist temple architecture was transmitted to Japan, along with Buddhism. Buddhist architecture was different from Shinto style; the style of the former was grand and luxurious, with stone foundations, painted walls, and tiled roofs.

The town of Ise is located east of Yamato, present-day Nara. It is a sacred place because the sun rises from this direction. Amaterasu Omikami, the supreme deity of the Inner Shrine of the Grand Shrine of Ise, was worshipped as the Ancestral Goddess of the Imperial Family, as well as in her own capacity as the Sun Goddess. It is thought that this goddess was enshrined in Ise during the reign of Emperor Suinin, probably at the end of the third century. Furthermore, it is said that Toyouke Omikami, the great deity of the Outer Shrine of the Grand Shrine of Ise, revered as Divine of food and industry, was enshrined during the reign of Emperor Yûryaku in the latter half of the fifth century. At the Inner Shrine, the supreme Shinto shrine architectural style called Singular Divine Brightness Style *(Yuiitsu shinmei zukuri)* mentioned above, gradually developed into perfection. Subsequently, the Outer Shrine was constructed by imitating the Inner Shrine, which may be the reason that the two shrine buildings are almost identical.

Removal and Renewal Every 20 Years

The original, constructed more than 1,000 years ago, was a wooden building whose posts were erected by digging shallow holes in the ground, with a thatched roof. The longevity of such a building, located in Ise, in a wooded area with high humidity, is said to have been about 30 years maximum. Moreover, it was and is extremely vulnerable to strong winds and fire.

Yet it is not entirely impossible to preserve the original style semi-permanently, even though it consists of wood and bamboo. An example unprecedented in history is the Grand Shrine of Ise. At the early stages

Figure 6. *Shokujusai* Ceremony. In Ise Shrine the building believed to be the residence of the god is rebuilt every 20 years. Divine treasures (clothing and furniture) attached to the building also are remade. A ceremony called *Shikinen Sengû* is held to mark the movement of the god from the old residence to the new one. The building is made using about 13,000 Japanese cypresses of different sizes.

the buildings were repaired as needed, and a complete renewal took place whenever the deterioration became irreparable.

The Jinshin War took place in 672. During the battles Prince Oama worshipped the Ancestral Goddess Amaterasu Omikami enshrined in Ise from a great distance. After he won the war, he ascended as Emperor Tenmu, and dispatched Princess Oku to Ise to serve as the Imperial Sacred Priestess. Emperor Tenmu made an effort to set up an administrative office at the Grand Shrine of Ise. Subsequently, Empress Jitô succeeded Emperor Tenmu, and observed the late Emperor's intentions in governance. In particular, she instituted the system of regular removal of the Grand Shrine of Ise every 20 years. In the fourth year of her reign (690) the rite of reconstructing the great shrine building of the Inner Shrine was performed, and in the sixth year of her reign the rite of reconstructing the great shrine building of the God Toyouke Omikami of the Outer Shrine was carried out, both by her decree. These were the first in the series of twentieth-year reconstructions. After the Edo period, the interval became a full 20 years, which means that the reconstruction is carried out in the twenty-first calendar year.

This special year is called the Year of Regular Ceremony *(Shikinen)*. In this year renewal of all the sanctuaries takes place, and when it is finished, the rite of removing the Divines *(Sengû)* is performed. These ceremonies have been carried out to the present day.

The system does not merely involve reconstruction of the shrines. The decorations and furniture of the shrines, and more than 1,000 items (divided into more than 100 groups) of sacred treasures and garments are newly produced and installed. These are handiworks of great finesse, equivalent to national treasures.

Figure 7. Making offerings to the god at the *Kannamesai* Ceremony. Five times each year (at the *Kinensai*, *Kannamesai* and *Niinamesai* Ceremonies, and *Tsukinaminomatsuri* Ceremonies in June and December), the Emperor makes offerings to the god at Ise Shrine.

Thus, over the past 1,300 years, some lapses occurred. Total reconstruction and refurbishment was delayed by more than 120 years during the civil war period in the latter half of Muromachi period (mid-fifteenth to mid-sixteenth century). At this time the revival of the system was brought about by lesser-known people, such as a nun *(Nun Keikôin Seijun)*. Nevertheless, complete renewals of the Grand Shrine of Ise including treasures and garments have been repeated, most recently in 1993 as the sixty-first such enterprise, since antiquity.

Endeavor to Transmit Wisdom—Thinking Ahead a Few Hundred Years

How were such past achievements possible? Great amounts of money and human resources were and are required for the renewal, but it does not mean that sufficient money and manpower were enough for the enterprise to be carried out.

In the deep mountains of Mt. Hiei, at the Central Hall *(Konpon Chûdô)* of Enryakuji Temple, Monk Saichô (later Great Master Dengyô) opened the Heavenly Platform (Tendai) Sect of Buddhism, reciting a poem *(Waka)*:

Akirakeku nochi no Hotoke no	Brightly
Miyo mademo	*may this fire of the Law*
Hikari tsutaeyo	*pass on and light up the later generations*
Nori no Tomoshibi	*of the believers of the Buddha*

The religious light that he lit still burns brightly as a guiding lantern today, after 1,200 years. This is because the monks have been replenishing the fuel for the lantern, observing and preserving the precious teachings of their founder, the Great Master Dengyô.

Shrine administration is carried out at the Grand Shrine of Ise. For example, to reconstruct the Shrine building, over 10,000 pieces of Japanese cypress *(Hinoki)*—roughly 10,000 cubic meters—are necessary. In the first few hundred years the cypress trees were cut from Mt. Kamiji or Mt. Takukura behind the sanctuary. Eventually, good cypress trees were located in the mountains upstream of the Miya River, or at Osugidai Plain in Wakayama Prefecture.

After the Middle Edo period, Mt. Kiso in the Owari domain, which is located in the inner part of Mino Province (Gifu Prefecture) came to be designated as Mt. Misoma. After the Meiji Restoration of 1868, an 8,000-hectare-wide forest managed by the Imperial Household Agency in Kiso area became the "Forest for Preparation of Shrine Construction."

Yet the high-quality cypress wood of Mt. Kiso will not last forever. Therefore, it was decided in 1923 that about 3,000 hectares of Jingû Forests (Mt. Kamiji, Mt. Shimaji, Mt. Mae, and others) under the management of the Grand Shrine of Ise were to be procured as the growing field to supply the wood for Shrine construction. In other words they became the secondary Shrine Forest. This grand plan looks several hundred years into the future. Here, the cypress trees take up 50 percent of the area, and the other 50 percent is taken up by coniferous and broad-leaved forests. By cultivating them successively for 200 years, more than 3,600,000 koku, or 1,008,000 cubic meters, of cypress wood will be obtained. This is approximately 30 times more wood than is necessary for a single renewal, which requires only 120,000 koku (33,600 cubic meters) of cypress wood pieces.

The wood used for the reconstruction is mostly 60 centimeters in diameter at 1 meter above ground. Such a tree is about 200 years old. However, the wood pieces called *mihishirogi*, which make the casket that enshrines the most important deity, or the main roof-edge-supporting posts erected at both sides of the main building of the Inner and Outer Shrines, must be superb. For this purpose, more than 30 wood pieces with diameter of over one meter are used. Such trees must be grown for more than 400 years. In this way the authorities (Shrine Department of Forestry) continue the work day and night, thinking ahead about 10 renewals (200 years hence) or 20 renewals (400 years hence).

Preparation for the renewal starts eight years in advance. The first of the series of ceremonies are the Yamaguchi Festival and Konomoto Festival, which are held within the Shrine premises. Subsequently, the *Miso-Ohajime* Festival is held within the mountain forests in Kiso, to offer gratitude to the deities of the mountain for producing and fostering the required wood pieces. When a cypress tree is cut down, without fail a new cypress seedling is planted to replace it. After the removal ceremony the old wood used to erect the shrine for the 20 previous years is dismantled, and distributed to other Japanese shrines to be reused, as it is still quite satisfactory.

Figure 8. Each April trees are planted on a nearby mountain by shrine staff for future use as timber for rebuilding. The Shokujusai ceremony is held to mark this occasion. About 200 years from now, the shrine building will be rebuilt using solely Japanese cypresses from the mountain.

Retrieving Purity and Power through the Religious Right

The reason the Grand Shrine of Ise was preserved in its original state of more than 1,000 years ago is precisely that it was not built with durable stones or bricks, but with wood, which is prone to rotting. To preserve a purity suitable for the Divines in wooden architecture, it was necessary to constantly renew everything.

The timbers used in a wooden building could last longer than 20 years, but in turn, 20 years may have been considered the maximum to preserve the purity of the building. Moreover, if it were renewed every 20 years, the Shrine carpenters and artisans who build and produce the sacred treasures and garments could pass on their skills and technology to their disciples, and the disciples can experience the teachings by participating in the process. If the renewal were not carried out every 20 years, the Shrine buildings would not be pure and clean. Moreover, in the interim the superior skills and craftsmanship of the artisans and carpenters might become extinct. Thus, since the institution of the system, a tremendous amount of work has accumulated as the involved people observed the system strictly. The culmination of such effort is the Grand Shrine of Ise, which can be considered a crystallization of Japanese wisdom and discipline. It stands tall today, embodying the technology of its constant renewal.

The significance of the removal is found in the following religious ceremonial processes. First, beautiful sacred treasures and garments are placed to decorate the newly built shrine. Then the Divines remove to the shrine. Finally, sacred food and liquor *(Shinsen)* are offered to the Divines.

At the Grand Shrine of Ise, which the Japanese people have nicknamed "Dear Old Ise" *(O-Ise-san)*, food such as grain, vegetable, fish, and shellfish *(Jukusen)* are cooked and offered to all the Divines at the Dining Building of the Divines *(Mikeden)* of the Outer Shrine in the morning and in the evening. In the middle of the ninth month of the lunar calendar (present October), the Thanksgiving Festival for the Divines *(Kanname-sai)* is held at midnight. A meal that consists of rice from the year's new crop and sake are offered. The highlight of the annual festivals is the Grand Thanksgiving Festival for the Divines *(Dai-Kanname-sai)*, which is held every 20 years, in a renewed set-up within the newly constructed building. This is the grand festival of the renewal of the Grand Shrine of Ise. Through this religious rite it is believed that purity of mind is retrieved; one seeks rebirth of life force, which prevails with new power. As a result, the sacred force of everlasting youth *(Tokowaka)* is maintained.

The Treaty on the Protection of World Heritage Sites divides world heritage in two groups. One group covers heritages in natural environment, and the other, cultural environments. The treaty also recognizes combinations of natural and cultural heritage. Many of the Japanese sacred places, Shinto shrines, including the Grand Shrine of Ise, originated from *Yorishiro*, which means a symbol for the Divines. These Divines were believed to be the deities of nature, or ancestral deities. Shrines as their dwelling places served as the central spots from which festivals, rites, performances, and other cultural events originated and were performed every year. In this context, nature and culture are indivisible, forming one entity. In other words human beings are able to live on thanks to the benevolent blessings of nature and ancestors. Human beings, in turn, respect nature and ancestors as Divines, simply and unpretentiously. Such faith is kept alive in the Japanese shinto shrine, a sacred place still active in the modern age. There is much to learn from the Grand Shrine of Ise. It is alive with everlasting youth, as it possesses elements of both old and new, and thus inherits and transmits everlasting wisdom. ■

5 Stewardship: An Architect's Perspective

Norman L. Koonce

Norman L. Koonce is executive vice president and chief executive officer of the American Institute of Architects; he serves on the boards of the Boyer Foundation for Advanced Studies and St. Paul's Cathedral Trust in America.

Historic cities *are* sacred places. While he was researching a vaccine for polio, Dr. Jonas Salk told me that he had been experiencing a dead-end at every turn and wanted to distance himself from the work. He then went to a thirteenth-century monastery in Assisi for a retreat, and the spirituality of its architecture was of such great inspiration that he was able to do intuitive thinking far beyond any he had ever done before. Under that influence, he said, "I designed the research that I thought would result in a vaccine, went home to my laboratory in Pittsburgh to validate it, and it was indeed correct." The influence of architecture has a great effect on our lives.

This is a spiritual currency—the richness that our historic cities share with and through mosques, synagogues, temples, cathedrals, and all those other precincts that we call sacred places. They are where we lay up our highest spiritual treasures, where we go to be spiritually refreshed.

No one culture or no one country owns a monopoly on such places. They have been created by the peoples of the world and belong to the peoples of the world. They are our common heritage. They are evidence of and a reaffirmation of our humanity.

Unless we honor the achievement of those who have created these sacred places—the patrons, the craftsmen, the architects, the people—unless we celebrate their continuing value, their power to elevate and enrich the human experience, unless we become advocates for resources as precious and irreplaceable in their way as the rainforest and fertile soils, it is not likely that we will develop the critical mass to protect, preserve, and perpetuate the historic cities and sacred places necessary to our spiritual well-being.

This idea is as old as the Greek writer Simonides, who wrote circa 500 B.C. that "The city is the teacher of man." History is not a gravestone; it is not a vault nor a mausoleum. It is living, adding layers, staying vital and green. To be loved, our historic cities and sacred places must have friends. They must be used; they must be a part of the fabric of our lives.

In one sense the task of preserving the architecture of our historic cities and sacred places is easier than it was even a few decades ago. Increasingly, governments are coming to appreciate the value of historic cities and sacred places. There is a dawning realization of the environmental issues that are part of what I might call the ethic of historic preservation. They are tourist destinations. They are engines for economic development.

At the same time, the task is more difficult than ever. Populations are growing. Developing nations must feed their people and offer the promise of a better life. Too often, governments regard preservation and development as opposite poles. In too many cases progress is ushered in to the sound of the wrecking ball. It is an attitude that I as an American can say has done great damage to our historic cities and sacred places.

But even here, in our market-driven economy, there has emerged an appreciation for the sense of place, for the roots of pride that come when we do not silence our historic cities and sacred places, but allow them to continue to speak to us, to our children, and to our children's children.

Three things are required to keep this nourishing conversation alive. First, the political will, the sense of urgency, patrons, role models. These all come under the heading, *leadership*. Second is *access to financial resources and provision of financial incentives*. Third is the *availability of the professional and technological resources* to the developing nations of this world, who stand the greatest risk of losing extraordinary heritage. Such a loss would not simply be theirs; we all would be poorer. It would be an irrevocable diminishing of life.

Since the National Historic Preservation Act in 1996 was passed, thousands of towns, cities, localities, and all sizes of sites in the United States have felt the positive impact of commitment to the ethic of stewardship. We have developed a wide arsenal of preservation technologies. Indeed, our oldest subgroup within our organization is its Historic Resources Committee, founded in 1890.

About eight years ago the American Architectural Foundation embarked on a national campaign to restore its headquarters, the historic Octagon, in Washington, D.C. (figure 1). The decision was made to pursue and indeed define a state-of-the-art restoration that would recover the Octagon's past and at the same time give it a viable future. In the relatively short life span of this nation the Octagon qualifies as an historic place. It was designed by the first architect of the United States Capitol, Dr. William Thornton. It became the anchor of the residential development of this city shortly after L'Enfant's Plan for Washington, D.C. was laid out. It became a refuge for President and Dolly Madison when the White House was burned, and it was the site in which the Treaty of

Figure 1. The Octagon, Washington, D.C., 1801. Now the Museum of the American Architectural Foundation.

Ghent was signed, ending the War of 1812 and remaining the accord for peace between the U.S. and Great Britain. In 1897 the Octagon became the national headquarters of the American Institute of Architects. It was here that the Macmillan Plan was drafted, which restored the integrity of L'Enfant's grand design for this city. It was here, too, that our National Trust for Historic Preservation put down its very strong roots.

In restoring the Octagon we learned a great deal about research, technologies, public education, and how to gain support. Out of such efforts there comes not only an architectural legacy but also a renewed sense of community. This is the magic that awaits us in our historic cities and sacred places. Jonas Salk often shared this phrase: "We must always strive to be good ancestors for future generations." Let us become that. ■

Part II

Governance: Planning and Management of Heritage Preservation

Editors' Note

Good governance is an essential condition for a sustainable conservation and management of historic heritage. Part II focuses on the range of public policies and strategies adopted in Brazil, the Netherlands, Norway, the United States, and the Middle East and North Africa. Common to all are the efforts to strengthen the legal and regulatory framework for heritage preservation; to decentralize responsibilities for rebuilding and maintenance from central to local agencies; and to provide incentives for private sector participation in preservation programs.

Francisco Weffort's chapter on Brazil examines challenges posed by a multi-ethnic and multicultural society. It raises the question of the relevance of cultural policies in a globalized economy. Weffort quotes Robert Reich to say that in a globalized world economy "'only labor is national.'" Weffort says that when we speak of labor, we are speaking about education and culture understood as knowledge and erudition, but also as the exercise of creativity. Creativity is the source that nourishes the imagination and the instrument that transforms imagination into practice.

Pedro Taddei discusses the Monumenta Program, which aims to strengthen capacity of Brazilian municipalities to maintain and preserve national listed monuments. The government established a municipal revolving fund to ensure that rents from renovated buildings are collected and earmarked for new investment projects in heritage restoration. The Monumenta *program is expected to raise public awareness concerning the sustainable preservation of national monuments and to celebrate Brazil's cultural diversity.*

In the Netherlands, where 76,000 historic buildings and sites are registered, the responsibility for their protection is distributed among the state, municipal and provincial levels of administration. Alle Elbers discusses a new mechanism—the National Restoration Fund—created to encourage private preservation efforts. A private foundation manages the revolving fund to disburse low-interest loans to owners of historic buildings. A survey conducted by the Dutch Ministry of Finance indicates that the revolving fund has already generated steady profits and is projected to continue to do so over the next five years as it creates new jobs and contributes to economic development.

Siri Myrvoll takes us to Bergen, the second largest city of Norway and one of the oldest historic cities of Europe, which is listed on the World Heritage List. The historic center, which includes the wooden medieval harbor of Bryggen, is being preserved while it continues as a living part of the city and not as a museum. The primary goal of urban management in Bergen is to protect the cultural landscape and the historic identity of the historic center, which is threatened by heavy traffic and new construction.

How to define the value of urban preservation? In his chapter on the protection of architectural heritage in expanding metropolises, Michael Sorkin reflects on public perception of authenticity, which is often confused by simulacra in contemporary architecture. People often accept the virtual recreation of historic buildings in movie-making or the contemporary reproduction of great architecture. The risk is that many cannot tell the difference. Sorkin argues that the best line of defense for authentic historic architecture is authentic contemporary architecture. "However, if all space-making is caught in a matrix of simulation, then neither old or new can enjoy the freedom of its own space," he says. He concludes that the ultimate peril of accepting imitation is that we become actors rather than citizens, pretending to be part of an environment that fools us into thinking it is real. The "new urbanism," an ascendant movement in the United States, strongly suggests its neo-conservative inclination: a nostalgic return to an idealized lifestyle of a distant past.

In discussing the protection of cultural patrimony through development projects, Michael Cernea points to the complexities involved in translating policy and conceptual support for historic city preservation into operational programs, and the difficulties in funding such projects. Cernea explores how World Bank-assisted programs address myriad technical, socioeconomic, and political issues related to the identification, design, preparation, and implementation of cultural heritage activities and projects. Studying a range of sectors and projects, Cernea asserts that when urban infrastructure works undertaken to address sector problems are designed with cultural sensitivity and heritage awareness, their contribution can be long-lasting even if they do not explicitly invest in historic building restoration. The implication for development agencies is that their projects' portfolios do play a role, directly or indirectly, in the comprehensive endeavor of sustainable preservation of heritage sites.

Brazil: Challenges of a Multiethnic and Multicultural Society

6

Brazil is a nation of multiple ethnic and cultural roots, but it is not a multiethnic and multicultural nation as understood in many places, for example, in North America. Although this may appear to be a chronological contradiction, a Brazilian is first and foremost a Brazilian and then *oriundo* (of other origin). As a Brazilian, one can, for example, recognize his or her Italian origins and value them, as I do, but probably will not call himself an Italian-Brazilian.

The concept of roots in Brazil is difficult to define chronologically, because these roots can re-emerge from the uppermost branches of the family tree. Characteristic of the vitality of the Brazilian culture is that we have formed a nation not only from indigenous and Portuguese Catholic roots, but the nation renews its roots and to a certain degree creates new ones. The Africans, who were brought by force, intermarried with the indigenous peoples and the Portuguese, and became an essential part of our cultural roots. But at the end of the millennium even the triad of indigenous, Portuguese, and African did not fully reflect our ethnic and cultural diversity. A great variety of Europeans, Arabs, Japanese, and, more recently, Koreans and Hispanic Americans, reaffirms and recreates our roots.

Colonization

From the outset, the cultural formation of Brazil is the convergence of a great number of different ethnic groups. As in other Latin American countries, the Iberians, protagonists of the great feats of circumnavigation of the fifteenth and sixteenth centuries, inaugurated the maritime roots by which the diverse other peoples arrived. Our nation was the setting upon which numerous invasions and colonizing campaigns were staged, primarily by the French and the Dutch as well as the Portuguese (figure 1).

Francisco C. Weffort

Francisco C. Weffort is the Minister of Culture of Brazil, a professor of political science, and an author.

Figure 1. Igreja da Sé in Olinda, Pernambuco was one of the early settlements established in northeast Brazil by the Portuguese colonizers.

The Catholic Influence

As is well known, the Catholic Church was one of the pillars supporting the great maritime discoveries. The presence of its missionary orders, particularly the Jesuits, was remarkable in our country during the entire colonial period until the rise of Enlightenment in Portugal in the eighteenth century. The missions have left an indelible mark on the formation of Brazil. Today, their numerous artifacts constitute the most important historic and artistic heritage under federal protection. Of the approximately 1,000 listed monuments, 332 are churches and chapels, the oldest of which dates from the first half of the sixteenth century. Countless colonial chapels are located in remote areas, hundreds of kilometers from what is known as civilization, where indigenous villages had formerly existed and been converted or where colonizers had explored mines (figure 2).

The Jesuit campaigns of conversion were culturally intense, lengthy, and extended over a wide territory without regard to the frontiers between the Portuguese and Spanish possessions. The artifacts of the *Sete Povos das Missões* (Seven Nations of the Missions) are noteworthy, and they still connect Brazil, Argentina, Paraguay, and Bolivia. During their campaigns, the missionaries developed the basic principles of the language considered predominant among the indigenous peoples. The language, which was called *Tupi Guaraní* or *lingua geral* (common language), disseminated from the North to the South as a vehicle of conversion.

The *lingua geral* was of great importance in the cultural formation of Brazil. Its influence can be seen by the large quantity of indigenous words that have been incorporated in our language, rendering it difficult

for the Portuguese to understand. Nonetheless, only in this century have we recognized the great diversity among the different indigenous peoples. When the Portuguese first arrived in Brazil, there were about 1,200 different indigenous groups. Today, there are only around 200, each with its own diverse culture. Only in recent decades have we been able to identify and recognize this diversity, this cultural richness. Perhaps it is no coincidence that this recent trend of recognition has occurred at a time when the indigenous populations are starting to grow again. I do not want to affirm that we have addressed all of the problems afflicting them, but rather that this recognition corresponds in some way with an improved self-esteem among indigenous groups.

Figure 2. Bird's eye view of Ouro Preto, with the Church of São Francisco De Assis, a national monument and a World Heritage Site.

The Indigenous Influence

We could prolong indefinitely a discussion of the contributions made by the indigenous peoples to Brazilian culture, from our most typical dietary customs, the frequency with which we bathe, our relationships with water and probably with nature and our bodies, the habit of using herbal medicines, our music, the way we treat infants, to our coats and tails, the ethnic features of our *caboclos* (mestizos), and the types of housing in the interior of the country. A large number of influences and features demonstrate not only the diversity and breadth of these contributions but also their permanence. These contributions have made Brazilians feel "Brazilian" since the first Europeans established themselves in Brazil.

The African Contribution

Besides the contribution of the indigenous peoples, the contribution brought by the Africans to Brazilian culture is fundamental. Brought as slaves to substitute for indigenous labor, the Africans rapidly intermarried with the indigenous and Portuguese people, recreating their own customs, forms of expression, and religions. Today, their influence over all Brazilian culture is profound, all-encompassing, and inextricable. As with the indigenous peoples, the African contribution extends to our dietary customs, our music, our way of dress, our ethnic features, but overall is most pronounced in the syncretism that developed throughout the centuries between the African religions and the Catholic religion (figure 3). Prohibited from practicing their own religions, in many places the slaves developed new religious manifestations in which their divinities are represented by saints from the Catholic liturgy.

Figure 3. Marketplace in Salvador, Bahia selling beads, seeds, and sea shells used in Afro-Brazilian religions.

Over a long period Catholic parishes absorbed some of the African rituals. The most eloquent example is that of the *Irmandade de Mulheres Negras*, or Sisterhood of African Women, devotees of Our Lady of Good Death. These lay sisterhoods were composed of elderly women who, during the time of slavery, performed funeral ceremonies for the souls of the deceased slaves who had been prohibited by the Church from receiving the last rites. Some of these sisterhoods exist to the present day in an unstable relationship with the hierarchy of the Catholic Church. Besides being Catholic, many of the Sisterhood members are *Mães-de-Santo* (*Candomblé* priestesses) and maintain their own sacred places, where they practice *Candomblé*, the Afro-Brazilian religion. *Candomblé* is probably the most important religion in our country. It mobilizes a large proportion of the Brazilian population from all ethnic groups on the day of its most popular saint, Iemanja, Goddess of the Seas (figure 4).

The Jewish Contribution

Since the first maritime expedition to our continent in 1500, *Cristãos novos* (Christianized Jews) and Jews held diverse civil and military positions. In the early seventeenth century, when the Dutch Prince Mauricio de Nassau established the headquarters of the West Indies Company in Recife in the Brazilian northeast, the first rabbi arrived in Brazil. Of Portuguese origin this rabbi had lived with his community in the Netherlands, taking refuge from the Inquisition in Portugal. In the Americas he was the founder of the first Jewish Synagogue on the new continent, the Kahal Zur Israel Synagogue. For over 25 years the religion of northeast Brazil developed into prosperous colonies that were tolerant of different religious and ethnic groups. When the Portuguese reconquered Recife, the Jews took refuge in the Antilles Islands and later in New Amsterdam, today's New York, where they were also pioneers.

These seeds sown in Brazilian soil remained inert for more than two centuries. They began to flourish at the end of the nineteenth century and the dawn of the twentieth century with the arrival of a new contingent of European immigrants subsequent to the abolition of slavery in Brazil.

Figure 4. Salvador, Bahia, is one of the first Portuguese settlements in Brazil and a renowned center of Afro-Brazilian culture.

Presently, we are engaged in recovering the traces left from the colonial period by the Jewish community, to celebrate their invaluable contribution to the formation of our culture.

The theme of pluralism in our cultural, ethnic, and religious origins has gained pre-eminence in recent years because the country was celebrating the five hundredth anniversary of the arrival of the first Europeans, which coincided with the passage of the millennium. We are also coming to the end of the historic period that started in the 1920s and 1930s, during which Brazil developed from an agrarian, underdeveloped country into an urban industrial nation and, with the sixth largest economy, a world economic power. Due to its demographic, economic, and social characteristics, Brazil is one of the most important nations in the world today. The City of São Paulo has reportedly the largest concentration of German capital outside of Germany. It is the largest Swedish industrial city outside of Stockholm. It is also the third largest city in the world.

Since the 1930s Brazil has had a remarkably successful economic development. However, that does not mask, but rather accentuates, the extreme social inequalities and great regional disparities that still exist in Brazil. Upon the completion of the five-hundredth anniversary of the arrival of the Europeans, we are entering a new era. One of its characteristics is that, besides our own internal economic crisis of 1999, we participate in the crises of the world. We are proving that we are capable of surviving crises, imported as well as internal.

Developing a Cultural Policy

What is the relevance of a national cultural policy in Brazil in a global-ized world at the turn of the millennium? Professor Robert Reich, Secretary of Labor in the first Clinton administration, affirms that in a globalized world in which capital seeks fast yields, *only labor is national.* When we speak of labor, we are speaking about education and culture. Culture is understood to be knowledge and erudition but also the *exercise of creativity*, in other words, the source that nourishes the imagination and the instrument that transforms imagination into practice.

In this context culture must be within the domain of state policy if we want to project into the future an image of the place that is our coun-try in this globalized world. Paradoxically, the globalization of the world economy is bringing culture and development together. Frequently, glob-alization brings about not the weakening of a national and local culture but their strengthening. In Brazil we can observe the strengthening of national and local cultures.

The technical means of production have also evolved to the point that there is no economic reason for uniformity, which previously had been imposed by assembly-line industrial production typical of the machine age. This fact, allied with the communications revolution, seems to be causing consistent demand for specificity, for diversity, for the most dif-ferent forms that local and national production can supply.

If we wish to build a country capable of exacting from globalization its greatest rewards, we must democratize the image of our cultural heritage, making it open and pluralistic, closer to the reality of our structure and roots as a nation and to the development profile of our economy. ■

Policies of Historic and Cultural Heritage Preservation in Brazil

7

Pedro Taddei Neto

Pedro Taddei Neto, an architect and urban planner from São Paulo, is director of the Monumenta *Program of the Ministry of Culture in Brazil.*

I n many countries that experienced economic cycles based on agricultural or mining activities, entire regions were occupied, developed, and then suddenly abandoned because of soil erosion or mine depletion. So it was in Brazil with the cycles of sugar, gold, and coffee. From 1500 to 1800 with the abrupt decline of the principal economic activities, large segments of the population migrated in search of better opportunities, abandoning all the built infrastructure, such as cities, roads, ports, and processing plants. They took with them their financial resources and entrepreneurial skills. Ironically, it is exactly because of this sudden decline that innumerable treasures of imperial and colonial art and architecture have survived intact (figure 1).

At the end of each economic cycle since the arrival of the Portuguese conquerors, the built assets remained in the ownership of the rural oligarchy, the Catholic Church and its charitable institutions, and the government. From the beginning of the twentieth century, with the advent of industrialization and urbanization, numerous historical ensembles succumbed to the pressure of real estate speculation; underwent programs of urban renewal, as in the center of São Paulo or Rio de Janeiro; or were reoccupied by low-income groups. Such is the case of Pelourinho in Salvador, Bahia. Once the splendid center of the first capital of Brazil, it was transformed into one of the country's largest enclaves of poverty (figure 2).

In other cases entire cities, which in more prosperous times had been provincial capitals or important business and cultural centers, were surpassed by new towns during industrialization. These regional development poles were better located for new economic frontiers and new communication networks.

Figure 1. Town center of Ouro Preto, Minas Gerais, a national monument and a World Heritage Site.

This took place in Ouro Preto, the rich capital city of the gold cycle, which was powerful until the end of the eighteenth century. During the nineteenth century Ouro Preto declined economically and at the dawn of twentieth century was superseded by Belo Horizonte, a city planned for the development of Brazil's largest mineral province, with the highest production of iron ore (figure 3).

In 1936 in response to this challenge President Getulio Vargas signed a decree that regulated the protection of historic patrimony. Although Vargas had ascended to power by force, he was an ardent nationalist and assembled a group of vanguard intellectuals connected with the "Modernist movement." They simultaneously looked to the past as well as to the future and used history to legitimize the "Nation-Building" project. The movement focused on the cultural and ethnic characteristics of the Brazilian national identity, which the adherents referred to as "the Roots." The search for cultural roots led to the unintended development of an ethnocentric aesthetic: an expression of the triad "White, Portuguese, and Catholic." This official aesthetic was anchored in the "Brazilian Baroque" period, that is, in the dominant style of colonial art and architecture.

Figure 2. Decaying buildings in the old center of Salvador, Bahia.

Today, as a result of that ethnocentric position, most federally protected buildings in Brazil pertain to the colonial period. Of the 50 historic centers and approximately 1000 individual buildings and sites listed in federal historic registers, 40 percent are Catholic churches or institutions. This represents only a modest proportion of Brazil's historic and cultural heritage. The other 60 percent, which are monuments from different periods, are protected by state and municipal legislation. A significant number of monuments are not listed and protected (figure 4).

Figure 3. Bird's-eye view
of Ouro Preto, Minas Gerais.

In these last two categories are monuments of diverse styles representing
different periods, above all an important collection of cultural assets representative of the Imperial period and the first decades of the Republic, characterized by European Eclecticism. These artifacts, left by the groups outside
of the "White, Portuguese, Catholic" triad over the course of our long history, have deteriorated or were lost to the cycles of new construction.

There are numerous examples, such as the archeological sites that
remain from the more than 1,200 indigenous groups who lived in Brazil
before the arrival of the Portuguese. In addition there are the living cultures of the more than 200 indigenous groups or the hundreds of
Terreiros de Candomblé—sacred sites of the Afro-Brazilian cult,
Candomblé, which has been extremely important in the formation of our
national culture (figure 5). More than 400 *Quilombos* also exist today,
frontier communities established by runaway slaves. The first Jewish
temple in the Americas was built in Brazil. The Kahal Zur Israel
Synagogue, established in Recife, Pernambuco, is a witness to the important presence of the Jewish community from the earliest days of the
Colonial period. Only now are we trying to restore and protect it.

After the abolition of slavery in Brazil new waves of immigration brought
Italians, Germans, Poles, Japanese, and Arabs, among others. These new
immigrants brought their cultures and participated in the growth of the
nation, but an insignificant number of monuments representative of
their cultures have been listed or protected.

Until recently, the official policy with its ethnocentric focus contributed
to distancing the patrimony from the people, who could only tenuously

Figure 4. Richly ornate baroque interior of the Church of São Francisco, Salvador, Bahia.

identify with the symbols of the rural oligarchy: the culture of White-Portuguese-Catholic.

On the other hand, cultural heritage legislation generated during the Vargas period was characterized by centrism and paternalism. It entrusted the federal government with the final responsibility for the conservation of historical assets.

In general owners of historic buildings had limited means, and they relinquished the properties to the mercy of the public sector. The municipalities that collected meager taxes from these property owners shirked the responsibility for conservation of these buildings.

Progressive neglect on the part of these public agencies led the federal government to a vicious cycle. With an increased burden on the budget, routine maintenance was reduced. Without maintenance the neglected properties deteriorated, requiring costly capital reconstruction works. When these restored properties were not regularly maintained, they sooner or later required the same repairs again.

Figure 5. Preparing for a *Candomblé* ceremony, Salvador, Bahia.

In this manner local communities as well as tourists became more and more distanced from cultural heritage. Even worse, with increased budget constraints since the 1970s, the federal government limited the scope of its listings and reduced the number of monuments added to the historic register.

With the adoption of new cultural policies in the 1990s, the face of Brazilian cultural heritage is changing. Under the leadership of the Ministry of Culture the first measures have been taken to protect the assets that, until now, have been neglected. The turning point occurred when private-sector partners became involved in this domain—attracted by a federal law that awards tax-based incentives program.

The first stage of the federal program of sustainable restoration of urban historic patrimony is being executed in partnership with four municipalities (figure 6). The *Monumenta* Program is based on the following mechanism in each project city: the rents accrued from the buildings, restored with the program funds, are collected in a municipal revolving fund, earmarked for restoration work. These funds will be reapplied in new areas scheduled for restoration.

The new funding mechanism will lighten pressure on the federal government. It will enable the government to deploy its budget resources more flexibly, both in extending its regulatory and legal protection of cultural property as well as in maintaining the federally listed monuments, which fall under its responsibility. ∎

Figure 6. Adaptive reuse of the old buildings on Rua do Bom Jesus, Recife, Pernambuco.

8 Preservation Policies and Financing in the Netherlands

Alle Elbers

Alle Elbers is director, Bouwcentrum International, the Netherlands, which is affiliated with the Union of International Buildings; and is a member of NIROV, the Dutch Institute of Physical Planning and Housing.

In the Netherlands a distinction is made between historic buildings registered by the state and those registered by local authorities. This distinction is especially important in respect to the difference in legal protection and the possibilities for subsidization.

Historic Building Stock

In total 76,000 historic buildings and objects are registered (table 1). The majority of the registered historic objects were built before 1850 (figure 1). Some years ago an inventory was made of valuable objects created from 1850 to 1940. Only a small portion of these (approximately 12,000) will be added to the list of protected state monuments by the year 2000. Meanwhile, a new survey is being prepared to inventory the interesting buildings, objects, and ensembles created after 1940.

Table 1. Historic building stock, the Netherlands

Category	Number
State monuments	45,000
Municipal monuments	30,000
Provincial monuments	1,000
Total	76,000

Source: Bouwcentrum International 1999.

Figure 1. Koudenhorn 66-70, Haarlem, the Netherlands.

About 80 percent of the historic stock consists of houses (figures 2, 3). The other 20 percent consists of churches, castles, civil works, windmills, and smaller objects. A substantial part of the historic building stock is located in small towns and villages.

Role of Main Actors

The main actors in the field of preservation are the state, municipalities, and the private sector.

The State

The main responsibilities of the state are to (1) develop policy and legislation, (2) provide subsidies, and (3) develop and disseminate knowledge and experience. In the last decades several policy plans were developed that show a gradual shift from object-oriented policy to policy to preserve historic structures. Today preservation of historic structures, ensembles, and archaeological sites is a very important issue in physical planning. Other developments that can be observed are shifts from restoration to maintenance, from lump-sum subsidies to financing, and from the state to municipalities; and strengthening the role of the private sector.

The Historic Buildings and Ancient Monuments Act rules preservation in the Netherlands.

This Act settles:

1. Designation and registration of cultural heritage
2. Designation and protection of historic urban and village areas
3. Procedures for obtaining a permit to restore a protected monument
4. Means of coercion (in case upkeep of monuments is threatened or illegal construction activities are taking place)
5. Subsidies and allocation of subsidies.

Figure 2. Kasteel de Haere,
Olst, the Netherlands.

Figure 3. Bociwual, Culemborg,
the Netherlands.

The system of subsidies is quite differentiated. In the case of restoration the amount of subsidy depends on the type and function of the monument and sometimes also on the category of owner.

Some examples are:

1. Restoration activities for churches and windmills are subsidized to a maximum of 70 percent of the (approved) restoration costs.
2. A private organization (foundation) whose main objective is to contribute to the preservation of historic buildings also can obtain a subsidy of 70 percent for all types of monuments.
3. A 60 percent subsidy can be obtained to restore monuments owned by municipalities.
4. For all other monuments a subsidy can be obtained to a maximum of 50 percent.
5. More than 10 years ago a special subsidy was introduced for the maintenance of churches. Today this type of subsidy also is available for other categories, mainly objects that no longer have an economic function.
6. A special subsidy has been introduced for the upkeep of country houses, including the park belonging to the country house.
7. Last but not least there is a tax incentive for owners of historic buildings. They are allowed to deduct maintenance costs from their incomes.

Municipalities

In the Netherlands subsidies are allocated via the municipalities. They have to deal with preservation in a very planned way. Every four years they have to make a complete inventory of the need for restoration of listed monuments (table 2). Based on this inventory, the available budget is allocated to the municipalities. After deciding on the subsidy budget, local authorities draw up a multiyear plan, which is the base for allocation of subsidies to investors.

Municipalities fix the amount of subsidy an initiator will receive, issue the permit for restoration, and conduct the restoration process.

Table 2. Distribution of historic building stock by size of municipality

Population	Percent
Fewer than 100,000 inhabitants	35
30,000–100,000 inhabitants	25
Fewer than 30,000 inhabitants	40

Source: Bouwcentrum International 1999.

Private Sector

The third main actor in the field of preservation is the private sector. First are the investors in preservation and upkeep. These could be private owners or private firms, but also a specific private entity, such as the Limited for Urban Renewal. In most large cities in the Netherlands municipalities and (primarily) local firms together establish such limited partnership companies. The main objective of such a Ltd. is to safeguard historic buildings. In case an owner is not able or willing to restore his or her property, the company can purchase it, restore the building, and sell or let it. Profit will be used to realize the main objective: the upkeep of historic buildings. Limited companies are exempt from paying taxes.

The private sector is very well organized. Almost 350 organizations on the national, regional, and local levels represent the interest of owners of monuments. They all are members of the National Contact Monuments Foundation, which represents these private initiatives to the authorities at all levels and can be a catalyst in the exchange of knowledge and information among the private organizations.

National Restoration Fund

The National Restoration Fund is one of the private institutions (foundation) that plays an important role in the upkeep of historic buildings. In 1986 a new method was introduced to subsidize historic buildings. If the owner of the building is a tax-paying entity, part of the lump-sum subsidy is transferred to a low-interest loan. The interest is 5 percent below that of a commercial loan. For the investor the effect of this transfer is largely compensated by a higher tax deduction.

The National Restoration Fund was established to provide low-interest loans. To do so, the Fund receives an annual budget from the state, currently 15 million Dutch florins (Hfl 15 mln). Redemption and interest return to the Fund to be reused to finance restoration. Thus, a revolving fund has been created.

The "revolved" money now is used to realize additional restoration in the sector. In time it is expected that the Fund will be able to finance all activities without budgetary support from the state.

Within 15 years of its founding, the Fund's additional restoration activities already exceed restoration works from the regular budget (table 3).

Preservation Is Profitable

In the beginning of the 1990s the Government of the Netherlands concluded that, despite all past efforts, the restoration backlog was considerable. Investments in the sector should increase to catch up this backlog

Table 3. Development of revolving fund
(in Hfl*1000)

Year	Revolving fund	Loans	Extra available
1986	295	0	0
1990	15,725	11,400	2,350
1995	72,750	12,000	7,500
2000	140,000	15,000	23,000
2005	195,000	15,000	30,000
2007	235,000	15,000	36,000

Source: Bouwcentrum International 1999.

within a reasonable period of time. Before deciding to provide extra budget, the minister of finance first wanted to have an insight in the effects of such an extra impulse. The results of a survey showed that private investors would triple the state's total investment (subsidy). Because of this multiplier effect, 75 percent of the subsidy would come back to the treasury within one year. In the long term the return would exceed 100 percent, which means that investments in the preservation of historic buildings contribute to the economic development.

Based on the above conclusion, the minister of finance could be convinced to provide additional budget for the sector. ■

9 Strategies for Preserving the Historic Identity of Bergen

Siri Myrvoll

Siri Myrvoll is director of Heritage Management for the City of Bergen, Norway; a member of the Norwegian national committee of ICOMOS; and its representative on CIVVIH, ICOMOS' international committee on historic towns and villages.

Bergen, the second largest city in Norway, is one of Europe's historic cities. Never a planned city, it grew centered around its natural harbor as a self-structuring settlement, which kept its main features despite many devastating town fires (figure 1). The particularly destructive fire in 1702 A.D. was largely responsible for the town's present version. Founded by King Olav Kyrre in 1070 A.D., the city center, as is every true historic town, is a compound of periods, both as to settlement structure and town plan. Its history may be traced both in the living town and in its underground—the up to 8-meter-thick archaeological deposits on which the present town is built.

History and its remains have provided Bergen with its "identity"—the particular "personality" that is a vital part of its charm. The historic center may be divided roughly in five parts, each with its separate identity: the medieval town, the post-medieval settlements on Nordnes and in Marken, the "new" harbor in Skuteviken, and the replanned "1916 district."

The medieval town is situated on the northeast side of the Vågen harbor. It consists of the wooden medieval harbor quarter, Bryggen—one-time headquarters of the Hansa merchants in Bergen—and the town proper, Vågsbunnen, whose town plan, settlement structure, streets, and alleys date to the Middle Ages. Most of the district's buildings date back to the seventeenth and eighteenth centuries but with medieval foundations. Some even have intact vaulted cellars.

North of the medieval center, in Sandviken, the seventeenth- and eighteenth-century city extensions are remnants of a harbor with large wooden warehouses erected to cater to the extensive worldwide trade of the wealthy and cosmopolitan Bergen merchants of the time (figure 2). Until the mid-nineteenth century Bergen was the largest shipping port in Scandinavia.

The 1880s saw an economic surge. Tall apartment buildings of the period take up large areas outside the historic center. But even within the old

Figure 1. The City of Bergen seen from Mount Fløien. The medieval shoreline is on the right.

town they can be found towering side by side with the small wooden dwellings—a historic record of the unrestricted building boom between 1880 and 1899. The last catastrophic fire in 1916 also left its mark in an entirely new, beautiful and monumental, planned shopping area. In other words history has shaped the various parts of the town and has provided Bergen with its special character.

In addition Bergen is the proud host of a World Heritage Site. The Hanseatic wooden harbor quarter, Bryggen, holds a special place in the cultural heritage of Bergen because of its importance for local, but also for national and world, heritage (figure 3). This district was inscribed on the UNESCO World Heritage List in 1979.

While being a historic city, Bergen is also very much alive. Its history may be seen as a document of the activity and developments through the centuries. Throughout its past the city has continuously met and dealt with new challenges and demands. It is *not*, and *must never* be treated as an outdoor museum!

With its historic monuments and city fabric Bergen itself is a heritage site, and the management of its urban development constitutes a major challenge. Its management is also a great responsibility to

- Preserve and pass on the historical heritage, which is of local, national, and international value
- Maintain Bergen's particular identity
- Accomplish the above without strangling the living modern city, the economic center of the Norwegian west coast.

Figure 2. "Maaseskjaeret," monuments of the eighteenth-century international stockfish trade: one of the many wooden warehouses in Skuteviken/Sandviken.

Through the years the challenge of heritage management in Bergen was handled in two ways:

1. Through setting the focus on the preservation of the "objects" by listing monuments of outstanding value for protection, primarily architectural monuments such as the banquet hall of king Håkon Håkonsson built in 1260 (figure 4), or the old town hall of 1556. Archaeological monuments and ruins also were automatically protected by Norway's Cultural Heritage Act.
2. Through inventorying and listing "valuable" buildings and building categories on special inventory maps, with designated value classifications. Categorization by age also has been used to classify value.

These surveys were intended to aid town planners in their work. Unfortunately, they came to be regarded as "the whole truth," the quick and final solution to heritage protection. What was not on the list could be removed. No account was taken of the ever-growing list of "new" heritage monuments, such as industrial heritage sites, which were prominent in Bergen. They had importance in understanding industrial history but also could be of high architectural merit.

As an example, industrial monuments, built in the eighteenth century in connection with the international harbor activities, were a particular feature of the Sandviken identity but were not on the protection lists. Complete and well-preserved environments of cultural heritage value were also left out—environments that today are receiving more and more attention. New research and development of cultural heritage studies result in awareness of more types of sites needing protection. The tendency today is to shift from the protection of the *objects* to the management of *contexts*, what might be designated "the historical cultural landscape." In the towns this shift presents a challenge: how to incorporate this development in urban planning?

Figure 3. World Heritage Site Bryggen, Bergen's old harbor quarter.

The living historic city is the object of pressures large and small. A major problem is traffic management. The Bergen city center is built on harbor infill. In some areas the infill is more than 8 meters thick. Not only are these deposits of great archaeological interest, but also they are badly suited as foundations for the heavy traffic of the modern city. The World Heritage Site of Bryggen is particularly endangered, and the major four-lane through-road in front of the site is exacerbating the situation. The narrow streets of the medieval city are unsuitable for modern vehicles. Air pollution from the traffic is also a cause for concern regarding the protection of the ornaments of the medieval stone churches. Parking on its own is a problem—neither a World Heritage Site nor historic church-yards are respected.

New development of sites in the city center also can threaten the monuments when no respect is shown for the historical cultural landscape, or knowledge of its features is insufficient. As an example, new apartment buildings in the well-known "harbor warehouse style" are being built in the old town residential areas far from the harbor. Signs and posters, too, can damage the overall impression of the city, as can the many window replacements, roof terraces, and balconies added to the eighteenth-century wooden houses. These all are minor details, but, if left to develop on their own, they may cause larger areas to lose their identity and historical quality.

To handle these pressures, the basis for planning and development must originate in knowledge of the historic city structure and the elements vital to the city's identity. Documentation of historic structures and incorporating their main features on an overall scale in planning should ensure development within the framework set by the city itself, and put a stop to the continuous conflicts between protection and large-scale urban development. In addition, planning should pay greater attention to

Figure 4. The Bergenhus castle and banquet hall built by King Håkon Håkonsson.

the heritage context and less to the single object. The main goal should be protection of the historical cultural landscape, as this landscape constitutes the city's identity.

How to ensure this? In addition to protection by the Cultural Heritage Act, larger areas in Norway may be protected through the Planning and Building Act, with special handling restrictions. The local development plans of the two medieval districts of Bryggen and Vågsbunnen are particularly detailed in their protective clauses, but large areas of the city centers have similar statutes. However, the restrictions focus mainly on the protection of buildings and objects.

The Heritage Management Office in Bergen has developed a better tool for urban planning along the lines suggested for Bergen, that is, based on context and identity rather than on single monuments. This new method presents the historic foundations for the urban development of a district through a Geographic Information System (GIS) map series for urban planners (figure 5). These maps comprise:

1. Early topography
2. Settlement structure
3. Communication lines
4. Special features and listed objects.

These four elements are considered the important features of a district's character. Such maps are being developed for all master plans and will be components of the basic planning tools used in the Department of Urban Development for new development schemes (figure 6). The maps are available on the department's computer network with recommendations from the Heritage Management Office on handling the various topics. Plans are then discussed, and heritage management plays an active

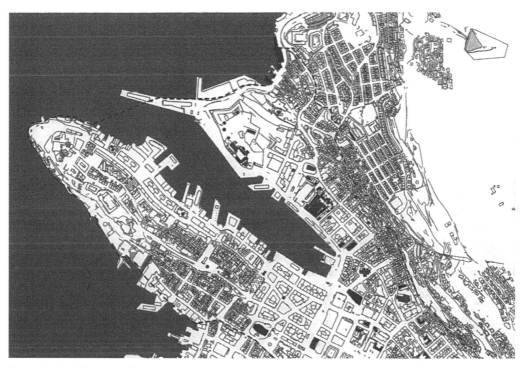

Figure 5. Heritage Management GIS map showing features and buildings protected by the Cultural Heritage Act (darker areas = automatically protected, that is, older than 1356; gray = younger features listed for protection).

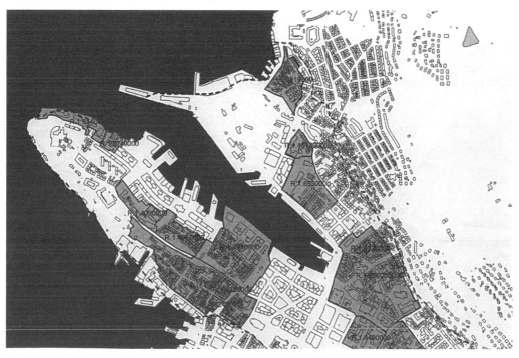

Figure 6. Heritage Management GIS map showing local development plans with protection clauses.

> *Box 1. Heritage management and the sequencing of the planing process, Bergen*
>
> - Establish planning program.
> - Consult Heritage Management Office.
> - Incorporate cost of heritage planning in total planing budget.
> - Heritage Management Office engages consultant; documents and writes up the planning area.
> - Transfer results to GIS (ARCVIEW).
> - Produce report with Heritage Management Office recommendations.
> - Transfer heritage charts on files to the local server as "look-up charts" available to the Planning Office.
> - Develop final plan. Consult Heritage Management Office on details.
> - Present final plan for political approval.

part in the planning process from start to finish. In this manner we hope to achieve modern urban development with integrated heritage management (box 1).

The main heritage challenges in a historic urban center are to protect its historic identity and maintain the quality of the centuries-long traditions, while promoting and strengthening the living city. The goal for Bergen is to present the town to the visitor and to its citizens as Bergen, not as just "any other town"! ■

Protecting Architectural Heritage in Expanding Metropolises

10

W hat is preservation? To begin with, it is a natural part of city life, a consequence of the general process of urban respiration. The built environment comes and goes: some parts stay, others vanish. We are all continuously modifying our environments under a wide variety of influences, from the tremendous sway of technology and culture to the intimate particulars of our own fortunes and families.

The modes of construction that characterize our environments impart to each work of architecture a kind of half-life. Whether we are homeowners or tenants, builders, or official guardians of the civic weal, we are constantly confronted with occasions and opportunities both to respond to and to regulate the life cycles of the buildings we inhabit. This quotidian stewardship is more than mere maintenance—quite different conceptually, although not necessarily technically. What distinguishes preservation from maintenance is a special supplement of value, something beyond the everyday necessity of ensuring the safety and integrity of a structure.

That value is cultural. Preservation is always an investigation into a system of beliefs and desires. As an artifact of democratic culture (or of some form of structured decisionmaking), preservation imparts construction with the value of consent. The self-identities of societies that preserve are bound up not simply with the appearances of the structures they produce but with the process by which they agree on what is to be saved, what modified, and what destroyed.

Authenticity

Where do these values originate? Preservation always engages the idea of authenticity. While this is a highly vexed concept, and often used as a

Michael Sorkin

Michael Sorkin is an architect and author working in New York, sorkin@thing.net, http://www.thing.net/-sorkin

cudgel, it has special resonance and accessibility in environments that have been continuously inhabited. Such *architectural* authenticity is deeply coded in its parent societies in a raft of practices and procedures that constitute the legibilities of indigenous strategies of building.

Just as important as architectural authenticity, however, is *social* authenticity, the pattern of life as lived, the ecology of living. A society defines its own values via the reverence and respect it accords to different styles and formats for living. *Historical* authenticity flows from this fit between form and life and from the exigent protection that culture accords it. Any other definition is too dry, too artificial, too alienated from the arts of living. Historical authenticity always entails a vector of witness. This is the notion that the walls do, in effect, have ears and eyes and have overlooked and heard the events great and small that characterize the particularities of their parent cultures.

Finally, the more purely *phenomenal* strain of authenticity is much harder to codify. We know our cities and places by their moods, by an ineffable set of phenomena that cannot easily be characterized but that we lose at our great peril. These are characteristics that escape quantification, that are simply unreproducible by deliberate means, that can be retained only if larger cultural continuities survive.

Thus, a mood that we would preserve in its originating setting demands that the compass of preservation be far broader than the limited context of structure or district. Preservation begs the question of ecology, the skein of global interdependencies that knit systems together. A sustainable idea of preservation demands that we take a nuanced view of the larger settings in which the objects of our immediate attention sit.

Preservation and Its Simulacrum

There is a little parking lot not far from my studio in Tribeca in lower Manhattan (figure 1). Several years ago it was swarming with workers who were busy constructing two "historic" buildings. The two buildings looked very nice indeed and fit very well into the surrounding context. They were of a scale and level of detail that is rarely built in New York anymore, the kinds of buildings that the neighborhood would seem to need. But on closer inspection they turn out to be no more than facades, stage-sets (figure 2).

Who but Hollywood could have been responsible? For weeks the neighborhood had been papered with posters apologizing for the inconvenience the filmmaking might entail. The flyers also explained the reason for the construction of the two preternaturally authentic looking "buildings." The set was to house the key scene in a film: the meeting between waitress Bridget Fonda and policeman Nicholas Cage. The brochures

Figure 1. A parking lot in Tribeca in lower Manhattan in New York City before construction of two "historic" structures.

claimed that location scouts had scoured the entire city looking for a suitable luncheonette in which to shoot the scene but were unable to come up with a single site that satisfied their requirements for "authenticity." Hence the decision to build the simulacrum, more "authentic" than any of the available realities.

The point I am making is not exactly fresh but it is no less problematic for its familiarity. As culture is increasingly globalized and the architectural forms of authenticity become ever more easy to manipulate and reproduce, we risk a condition of general architectural mendacity. The onslaught of Disneyfication—building Ludwig's Castle or the Alhambra in Tokyo or Orlando—is the condition of world architecture today because doing so is possible and popular. If nothing else, this trend sets the terms of the debate.

While there is nothing wrong per se with the creation of spaces of fantasy and entertainment, the phenomenon does pose real risks to the idea of preservation. The risks center on two issues. First, the corruption of the aura of genuine authenticity puts a great strain on its retention. If we cannot tell the difference, if the environment lies to us, the task of preserving it becomes both impossible and trivial.

Ironically, a second question concerns innovation. The best defense of an authentic historic architecture is the complement of an authentic contemporary architecture. However, if all space-making is caught in a matrix of simulation, then neither old nor new can enjoy the freedom of

Figure 2. The "buildings" constructed for a movie background.

its own space. Ultimately, the peril of the Disney effect is that we become actors rather than citizens, pretending to be part of an environment that simply fools us into thinking it is real.

Of course, much superb historic architecture has long since left the circumstances of meaning responsible for its original invention. Obviously, it is ludicrous to try to "preserve" traditional societies to preserve traditional architectures. However, we must engage in a continuous process of judgment, of selecting what is best in our social lives and in the settings we create for them. Given the constant pressure of change, preservation always entails a choice. It marks our values.

From the viewpoint of urban and architectural preservation, a useful concept—a type of value—is that of *climax*. This sense of climax describes a state of ecological perfection, for example, a forest that, like the great western stands of redwoods, has reached a final stage of growth and entered a condition of homeostasis. Such grand sustainability—that of a self-regulating, essentially closed system carrying on forever—is a powerful model for judging the achievements of architectural and urban form.

This model is particularly important to cities because of their fundamentally dynamic character. Recognition of climax forms becomes a crucial means of regulating and stabilizing the engine of growth, of asserting the character of the genius loci, and of organizing structures of social consent in the environment. The idea of climax is also a very direct way of engaging the issue of authenticity.

If one were to speak of climax forms in New York City, some of the architectural expressions that come to mind are the rows of nineteenth-century brownstone houses or the set-back skyscrapers of Wall Street. One also thinks about the characteristic ways in which buildings interact with parks and other open spaces. The long walls of buildings that ring Central Park or the more sinewy line along Riverside Park are typical architectural responses to a valued landscape and to the possibilities for the long view. Every great city produces its special forms, from the Georgian squares of central London to the labyrinthine Medina of Fez. All of these represent social compacts made into form.

In the United States the idea of preservation has emerged as perhaps the strongest value in city planning in general. This trend is a recognition of the sorry record of modernist urbanism's respect for the past and its pathologizing of the city as well as, conversely, its own failures to produce an environment of delight comparable to the best of our historic urbanisms.

Because of these oppositional origins, the rise of American preservationism continues to be structured as an essentially adversarial process in which government or private developer initiatives are fought by citizens with the power to say no, whether to the highways, "urban renewal", or the demolition of beloved old buildings that have so often deeply threatened private happiness. The demolition of Penn Station is widely regarded as a local turning point. While this adversarial process has resulted in many important victories, the system has left the city badly bereft of new ideas.

As a result, we New Yorkers live in a city that is extremely timid about any physical planning that does not fit some historic model or that seems to have too much reach. Because we cannot agree on any contemporary forms, preservationism has become not simply an address to the past but the main mode of inventing the future. This tactic itself threatens the authenticity of the past by submerging it in a sea of forms that are simply copied soullessly from old models, deforming their context to strip them of their last vestiges of aura. As sprawl and hypergrowth relegate historic cities to statistical and literal margins, a more creative approach is demanded.

A project that we did a few years ago concerned, among other things, centers, which I believe are critical to the legibility, functionality, and conviviality of cities. The project is in East New York, way out in Brooklyn and far from the center of town. The neighborhood both sits on one the city's margins and offers a home to the marginalized. East New York is a very poor neighborhood and a museum of virtually every failed modernist social housing typology.

But East New York has two tremendous resources. The first is an engaged and activated community with a network of self-help and political organizations. The second is a great abundance of vacant land owned by the municipality. These two assets, it struck us, might be used to leverage a dramatic transformation in the neighborhood. But what sort of transformation might this be, given the essentially unsatisfactory character of both the existing neighborhood—gapped, decrepit, and without legible central places—and of the variety of solutions proposed down the years?

The most common solution in the United States today is the preservationist-inspired "new urbanism." These architects—very much in the ascendancy at the moment—would suggest an appeal to precedented form, to some version of a theory of original intent, a neo-conservative holy writ. For them the keys would be to rebuild "original" densities and forms, a recreation of the putatively superior physical relationships of past years (with the hoary presumption that happy social relations would follow).

But what actually were the original intentions of the builders of East New York? To locate the poor far from the city center? To provide a vast reserve of substandard, over-crowded housing? To offer the absolute minimal levels of amenities and public space? These are clearly historical intentions that deserve no reverence, never mind reproduction. While there are crucial social ecologies to nurture and preserve, the importation of pre-packaged nostalgia for a halcyon past that never was is a formula for myopia and disaster. A more critical approach seems to be in order.

But how to begin? Architecture comes from either memory or invention. These are by no means mutually exclusive. I am an advocate of starting from scratch conceptually, rather than radically hemming in possibilities from the start. It is always easier to draw back than to take a great leap, and one wants the benefits of both freedom and constraint when operating in the urban context. We begin, then, by sweeping the imaginative decks clean while at the same time preserving what is already built and established.

In a very conceptual sketch of the project one can see a new kind of formal energy as it begins to swim about the neighborhood. Although abstract, certain patterns should be legible: first, the preservation of existing buildings without exception, and second, a dramatic increase in green space and blue space. The second point is inspired both by a broader vision of what the good city ought to be like in terms of its balance of built and green spaces (and by a dramatic dearth of such spaces in East New York) and by existing community enthusiasm for urban agriculture. This is a community in which there is already some farming on behalf of the homeless.

Figure 3. Step One:
"Plant a Tree in the Street."

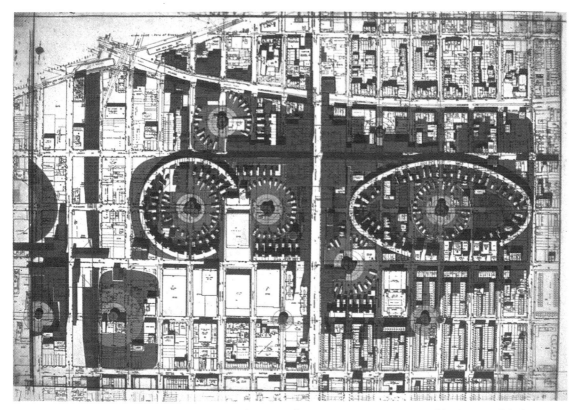

Figure 4. A plan for East New York showing acupuncture points (tree plantings), low-density green villages, and consolidated and densified urban centers.

Given this mood of change, we wondered what might be the minimal intervention required to begin to leverage this transformation. We concluded that planting a single tree in the midst of an intersection might be a good beginning (figure 3). We anticipated several consequences. First, traffic would surely be calmed and pedestrian-oriented collateral means of circulation through the blocks might develop. Second, we imagined that in the lee of certain acupuncture points, a lower density, very green, texture of houses and gardens might grow up in a series of pockets (figure 4).

Third, however, we thought, paradoxically perhaps, that the new low-density areas would force a consolidation of high-density, street-related activities in several compact new centers. One of the problems of East New York is its surfeit of street-space and its inability to form cogent and congenial central places. Although the scheme is in many ways a radical one, its ultimate effect is to reaffirm and to preserve the most fundamental forms and values of urban life.

The point is that strategies for preserving historic architecture and cities are locked in a dynamic with strategies of innovation. For either to succeed, they must enjoy a productive symbiosis. If we treat preservation as the antidote to, or antithesis of, innovation, we will not simply deny ourselves the boon of new thinking about sustainability, technology, social life, and community. We also will run the risk that by losing its relevance to the living city, preservation itself will also lose its capacity to inspire and its power to contain our most precious memories. ■

At the Cutting Edge: Cultural Patrimony Protection through Development Projects

11

dvocating is easy; acting is difficult. This adage applies to advocacy for historic city preservation. Moreover, when "acting" entails heavy financial investments, many soul-searching—or "how-to"—dilemmas surface rapidly.

This chapter addresses some of these "how-to" questions that center on one theme: how to translate policy and conceptual support for historic city preservation into operational development programs.[1] This question may appear deceptively simple, but it raises complex issues of substance. Development projects pursue *poverty reduction and employment creation objectives.* Integrating these objectives into patrimony preservation is not yet a beaten path.

More specifically, this chapter explores how World Bank-assisted programs address such substantive problems. Over the last several years Bank explicit statements of support for cultural heritage (CH) preservation have become widely known. Less known, however, is what occurs on the ground, and how such assistance is provided.

This chapter discusses some far-reaching strategy issues concerning development support to patrimony preservation, by examining several cases and project stories—real stories about real projects. The chapter attempts to distill some answers and nuggets of experience from crafting actual development projects that support patrimony preservation and management, while at the same time attempting to reduce poverty in historic cities, increase employment, and encourage small-business incubation. The specific projects analyzed are located in historic cities of countries in the Middle East and North Africa. Most of the cities are on the World Heritage List (WHL).

Michael M. Cernea

Michael M. Cernea, anthropologist and sociologist, has worked for many years as the World Bank's senior adviser for social policy, and is the recipient of international awards for applied anthropology and public policy and a prolific author.

Difficult technical, economic, and institutional questions have confronted the World Bank and the country governments in preparing and designing these projects. Specific questions include how to *incorporate investments* for preserving the cultural monuments of the past in projects focused on triggering change and building for the future.

The cultural component of each project discussed in depth represents an innovation, because each project design is virtually unprecedented in Bank assistance to the given country. Learning how these innovations emerged and how these path-opening projects were prepared and designed may offer new options and ideas for those involved in preparing future assistance programs.

Cultural Components or Stand-alone Culture Projects?

Designing an investment in cultural heritage raises many new questions for country officials and World Bank specialists alike, because until recently this domain was little explored. One initial, but basic, strategy choice faced in project design is between two possible routes:

1. To design fully dedicated, *self-standing culture support special projects,* or
2. To exploit opportunities available *within* many *regular* projects financed in other sectors to *incorporate major patrimony support project components in cross-sectoral development programs.*

Future projects will face this choice, and such strategic questions will recur.

Linking patrimony preservation with regular programs in multiple other sectors of the economy differs significantly from interventions, usually small scale, that focus exclusively on restoring one or a few built structures. The latter are very important too, but typically are limited to conservation and/or repair works, have relatively limited financing, and cannot undertake broader institutional capacity building. Rarely have massive interventions for cultural heritage preservation and management been integrated in large-scale development programs within various other sectors of national economies. Therefore, integrating substantial heritage components as parts of larger *cross-sectoral* development programs, and using opportunities available in these programs—otherwise forgone—is an approach at the cutting edge of work in CH preservation. The stakes in its success are high, because it adds value, mobilizes additional financing for CH, multiplies impacts, and reduces costs of broad institutional support to CH. If this approach proves successful and is embraced on an increasingly large scale, the benefits to patrimony preservation primarily, and to development generally, will be considerable.

The several interventions designed from 1996 to 2000 for Bank projects in the Middle East and North Africa (MENA) are themselves important storehouses of accumulated knowledge about what can or cannot be done. They form a "menu of possibilities" that will enable future operations to build on approaches that have undergone the exacting test of implementation. The requirement will be not to copy them mechanically but to select from the available options the one that fits best and retailor to the given country and sector. The following sections take stock of these "best practices." Undoubtedly, further work will bring additional design innovations responsive to country needs and circumstances.

Two Routes

Within the region both strategic project routes are being used.[2] A large project in Tunisia has taken the *fully dedicated* project route. Projects in Jordan, Lebanon, and Morocco have taken the *component* route. The West Bank and Gaza Bethlehem 2000 project combines the two approaches. The range of sectors and project design options is:

- Urban improvement option in the Morocco Fez *Medina* project
- Tourism option in the Jordan Petra–Wadi Rum project
- Post-conflict option in the Lebanon reconstruction project
- Capacity creation and restoration option in the West Bank Bethlehem project
- National program option in the Tunisia cultural heritage project under preparation.

The component approach is able to capture the synergy among sectors resulting from cross-sectoriality, such as between urban development and cultural heritage, or between tourism development and heritage conservation. Cross-sectoral approaches are a powerful development tool. Moreover, when institutional capacity in the country's cultural sector is weak, starting with a CH project component may prudently build capacity and models for subsequent larger, stand-alone operations.

Also worthy of notice is what is being avoided: *enclave-type projects*, which would focus on only one or several isolated monuments taken individually from their context and outside intersectoral linkages and opportunities. When governments outside the Middle East and North Africa region have requested them, the Bank's Board of Directors has expressed reservations regarding enclave projects.

A stronger institutional framework in the country's cultural sector justifies consideration of a full-fledged project. That is the case in Tunisia, where a large-scale preparatory study of the nation's built heritage, together with a strategy preparation effort, are underway, with support through Italian and Japanese donor grants and experts. This type of project requires more complex preparation, as will be shown later.

Which specific project-design options have been chosen in the Bank's Middle East and North Africa Region so far? We have found an array of such options, which are described and analyzed individually below.

Urban Development Option: Morocco

Because the region's heritage assets are located primarily in urban settlements, links with urban infrastructure projects are indispensable. To date the Fez *Medina* Rehabilitation project is the centerpiece of efforts to explore the "space for linkage" between the two sectors. Valuable elements also will be highlighted in the forthcoming Lebanon Cultural Heritage and Tourism Development project.

Interestingly, at the pre-identification stage the Fez urban project started conventionally, with little intention to support heritage preservation and no consideration of how the Fez population itself regards the city's heritage.[3] Many technocratically inclined project planners perceived Fez *Medina* not as a resource, but rather as a bottleneck to modern urbanism. It lacked access roads for emergencies (ambulances, fire trucks, police) and adequate roads for services (garbage disposal, deliveries). Almost one-quarter of Fez el Bali was inaccessible by motorized vehicles, while other areas suffered badly from lack of parking. Heavily polluting industries nestled in the vicinity of dense residential areas caused health hazards, increased waste production, and deteriorated the housing stock.[4]

The engineering consulting company invited by the government and the World Bank to produce a project feasibility study submitted a technical design that proposed cutting large transportation crossroads through historic districts, thus demolishing valuable cultural assets. The proposed plan was generally insensitive to the cultural value of the *Medina*. In fact, some agencies in Morocco itself were so concerned with facility of access as to underestimate the importance of preserving historic buildings. UNESCO, which in 1976 had placed Fez on the World Heritage List, communicated to the Bank its strong objections to the proposed technical solutions (figure 1). The Bank examined and embraced UNESCO's objections and proposals.

After considerable discussion among the Bank and relevant country agencies, the Bank and the Government of Morocco set aside the consultants' technical proposals, and began project preparation virtually anew based on different principles. The new principles put the *cultural value* of the *Medina* and the goal of *reducing poverty among its inhabitants* at the center of the project's new concept and design. The new approach, more refined both socially and technically, confronted head-on the problem of combining preservation with response to modern needs. In the process, it found trade-offs and original solutions. The result is the project design under implementation, to which UNESCO contributed and fully supports.[5]

Figure 1. Fez *Medina*, Morocco.

Reducing Urban Poverty

The new design is characterized by a three-fold combination: it harmoniously integrates (a) basic *urban improvements* (in roads, type of transportation, vehicles, and services) with (b) *preservation and enhancement of historic assets* and *Medina's* distinctive characteristics, both within (c) an urban program geared to *reduce poverty and increase employment* in the *Medina*, improve the quality of life, and make Fez more accessible to worldwide visitors.

The *poverty-reduction orientation* of the Fez approach to cultural conservation deserves special highlighting, even though only its key features can be outlined here. Fez *Medina* is not only a World Heritage celebrated site. Foreign tourists are less aware—because they are not led to see it—that Fez is also a pocket of concentrated, abject mass poverty. The pre-project survey found that 52,700 people (36 percent of Fez *Medina's* population of 150,000 inhabitants) live below the poverty threshold.[6] This is a far higher proportion than Morocco's national poverty average for urban (10.4 percent) and rural (28.7 percent) inhabitants. Housing occupancy density in Fez Medina far exceeds acceptable levels, and half of the Medina housing stock is decayed.

Targeting primarily the population living below poverty levels, the project will help create some 10,000 jobs over 15 years, channel benefits to artisan groups working in the *Medina*, and improve living standards through better communal services.

Another poverty-reduction initiative under the Fez project is the organization of emergency assistance to historic dwellings at high risk of collapsing, which are usually inhabited by the poorest people. A monitoring system relying on the inhabitants will promptly signal to project management the buildings that start showing signs of imminent collapse.

This system enables project managers to intervene rapidly, taking action to reinforce the valuable building and thus protecting inhabitants' lives, the buildings themselves, and ultimately reducing reconstruction costs.

Breaking New Ground in Project Processing

Fez is the first large urban-cum-cultural-heritage project assisted by the World Bank in Morocco. In the process of making culturally informed technical choices, it has generated a host of non-routine solutions for its institutional, financing, and implementation arrangements (on financing and risks). The Fez project is similar to another Bank-assisted operation in an Asian historic city—the Lahore Urban Development Project in Pakistan[7]—and has benefited from the region's experience with an earlier project in the Hafsia area of the Tunis *Medina* carried out in the 1980s (box 1).[8] Yet it has much enriched the analytical methodologies and solutions employed in these earlier operations.

Compared to average World Bank project processing standards, the Fez project was one of the most complicated and exacting to prepare. It involved breaking new ground in preparation work, and it had to incorporate distinct, heritage-related, risk-reduction measures. Its institutional and financial arrangements took a long time to negotiate with both the central government and the Fez municipalities, but produced ground-breaking local and central financing approaches, with high replication likelihood. Bank managers and staff had to devote more than the usual effort to bring this project to implementation. They had to overcome conceptual and bureaucratic rigidities as well as the inexperience of national agencies with such innovative projects.

For these reasons some Bank insiders consider it legitimate to ask: should the World Bank engage in such complex and time-intensive projects at all? Surely, pioneer projects take more time than average to prepare and process. Time pressures work against such projects. Yet if the Bank declined such projects, it not only would forgo new learning and fall back on misguided carbon-copy approaches to complex problems but also would fail to respond to country demands and needs.

The decay of Fez had long represented a problem growing from bad to worse, despite Fez's placement on the WHL in 1976 and the international safeguarding campaign launched by UNESCO in 1980. The campaign raised intellectual awareness about Fez but failed to generate the financial support required for significant rehabilitation works. It is for this reason, and counting on the Bank's comparative advantage, that the Government of Morocco asked the Bank to help "break the long-standing deadlock which has deterred any comprehensive rehabilitation project in Fez"[9] and requested a loan to finance the Fez project. During the next five years the Bank's intervention will help mobilize considerably more financial resources than have accrued to Fez over the almost 20

Box 1. Successful rehabilitation of Hafsia

Tunis offers an early and successful example of how to incorporate a historic city rehabilitation program as a component into a "regular" urban development project. The Tunisia Urban III Development Project approved in 1982 (total cost US$60 million) included a rehabilitation component for the Hafsia Quarter II in the town center of the Tunis Old Medina. The project rehabilitated valuable buildings and recreated the old covered *souk*, which organically re-connects the two parts of the old city.

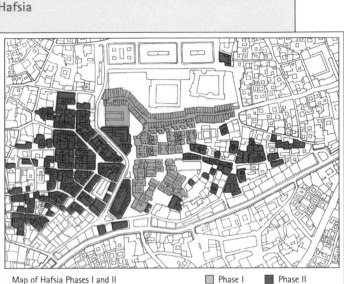

Map of Hafsia Phases I and II   ☐ Phase I   ■ Phase II

The key questions raised at the time, in the 1980s, were whether a second phase of this project would be able to do more than just promote a physical implant of a few new houses. The response over the past 10 years has been spectacular....The second phase has not only confounded the skeptics with its success; it also won the unique distinction of a second Aga Khan Award for Architecture in 1995 (figure 2).

...the Municipality of Tunis, the Association pour la Sauvegarde de la Medina (ASM) and the Agence de Réhabilitation et Rénovation Urbaine (ARRU) have succeeded in reducing the high population densities in the old *wekalas*.... Rehabilitation of the structures through credit schemes has worked extremely well in all but the rent-controlled, non-owner occupied structures. The success of the project in 1995 in nudging the government to finally remove the rent control law effectively lifted the remaining obstacle to commercially financed rehabilitation of these non-owner occupied rental units.

The second phase of the project, Hafsia II, is a financial, economic and institutional success. Cross-subsidies have made the project as a whole financially viable. Rates of return on public investment have been high. The multiplier effect of private to public funds has been of the order of three to one.[1] All of this has been accompanied by a sensitive treatment of the urban texture, and an integration of the old city with its surrounding metropolis.[2]

> Ismail Serageldin, "Very Special Places: The Architecture and Economics of Intervening in Historic Cities," Culture Unit, Social Development Department, World Bank, Washington, D. C., 1999, 39-42.

The results of the *ex-post* financial analysis of revitalization efforts at Hafsia are very encouraging. The overall project was financially profitable, thanks largely to the revenue generated from land sales, housing, and shop sales by the project implementing agency (ARRU), despite relatively high resettlement costs. A study carried out by a Harvard University team found the internal rate of return (ex post) to be about 11 percent.

1 Harvard University Graduate School of Design 1994.
2 Harvard University GSD 1994.

Figure 2. Hafsia Quarter II, Tunis: new housing design respects the scale, materials, and uses of the public space of the existing urban historic fabric.

years since it was placed on the WHL. The Government of Morocco also relies on the Bank's comparative advantage in promoting interagency donor coordination and mobilizing supplementary grant aid over and above the borrowed financing.

What lessons, if any, can be derived from the strenuous efforts to prepare and process this project?

Before Fez the World Bank had not thought through solutions to technical and cultural problems in typical *Medina* contexts. Therefore, it had to pay a price in time to learn how to avoid known and unknown pitfalls. Nevertheless, it succeeded in breaking the "long-standing deadlock" in Fez. The *process* that led to the project's final content yielded wider policy and strategy lessons about how to *deliberately link* cultural heritage preservation to mainstream urban development programs.

The valuable messages of the Fez project experience, so far, are:

- Cultural heritage conservation and rehabilitation *within* large urban infrastructure renewal projects are a valid project design opportunity. Conservation and infrastructure renewal are both feasible *within the same* development project.
- Modernization of urban standards and upgrading of infrastructure in old cities, however important, is *not* a license for insensitive and wholesale "clearing" and sacrificing of historic areas.
- Infrastructure that is technically *appropriate* to cultural and topographical requirements can be creatively designed to make modern

amenities *compatible* with the retention and preservation of the original social fabric. Urban mechanical equipment if being custom-manufactured for Fez.

- Projects such as Fez that combine the objectives of the urban and cultural sectors can offer *additional routes to reach basic economic development goals: poverty reduction and additional employment generation.* They significantly enhance the effectiveness of development investments.

- Addressing the urban built heritage as a coherent continuum within its social context can prevent the pitfalls of "monumentalism" at the expense of the surrounding socio-cultural fabric.

- Not every urban development project in an old town must contain major cultural heritage preservation components. But when opportunities exist, failing to exploit intersectoral synergy between infrastructure and culture foregoes important benefits.

- Projects that link the urban and culture sectors tend to require more preparation time than conventional urban projects. They demand coordination among sets of institutions. Accumulated lessons may optimize the "critical path" for future preparation of comparable projects.

Lessons from Fez are being transferred to other Bank-assisted projects. In Lebanon, for instance, the historic towns of Saida, Tripoli, and Tyre (a recently declared World Heritage site), will be assisted under an urban/tourism development project, in which culturally sensitive urban infrastructural improvements will receive project support (see below). In Yemen studies initiated to conserve vernacular architecture in historic cities follow the same principles as in the Fez project. In Morocco itself, given the country's large number of historic *Medinas*, the Fez *Medina* project may become the forerunner of a line of urban/cultural interventions with great benefits for the country's poor and the general population, and with rewards for the global community. In fact the Government of Morocco has requested the World Bank to provide technical and financial assistance for a new urban-cum-cultural heritage project in the historic city of Pleknes.

Urban sector projects have considerable potential to enhance the preservation of built heritage *even when they do not manifestly include cultural heritage* components. This can be called the "indirect support" potential inherent in urban projects (see last section of this chapter).

Tourism Options: Jordan

Because of the inherent link between major heritage assets and economically thriving tourism, projects in the tourism sector provide another set of options for incorporating cultural components.

The World Bank's 1978 decision to cease lending for tourism[10]—a decision that some questioned even at the time—has been fully reversed in recent years. Nonetheless, the 1978 decision resulted in a long hiatus in the Bank's financial support for the budding tourist sector in North Africa and the Middle East. The Bank's support for culture and cultural tourism during almost two decades also was negatively affected and limited.

In Jordan the 1997 Second Tourism Project reversed the 20-year hiatus that followed the first Bank-assisted tourism project in Jordan (1976). During those 2 decades the Bank financed 4 urban development projects in Jordan, providing loans totaling more than $105 million. However, none contained substantial and explicit heritage-oriented provisions. With hindsight it can be said that important patrimony support opportunities were missed in these four projects due to inattention to cultural heritage.

The new project started from three basic premises: (1) tourism is Jordan's second largest source of foreign exchange revenues; (2) the main motivation for tourism to Jordan is the country's heritage and ecological sites, not its limited beaches; and (3) the peace process opened up vast additional tourism potential and cultural opportunities. Capturing these opportunities would require Jordan to develop the tourism sector in a sustainable and multifaceted manner across the country, which implied *simultaneously improving* the maintenance and management of the cultural patrimony.

Integrating Tourism with Support to Heritage

How does the Jordan project employ its options to incorporate support for heritage conservation in the design of a tourist operation? Tourists come to Jordan (1.1 million in 1996) primarily to visit Petra, a World Heritage Site (figure 3); Jerash; and Karak. Increasing tourist flows, however, entails hazards as well as benefits.

Predicating tourism growth on intensified visitation of heritage sites demanded safeguards against risks to patrimony assets. The criteria applied by the project team were:

- Enhancing the sustainability of heritage sites through the formulation of a coherent tourism *and* cultural strategy
- Selectivity (identifying the most promising sites among multiple choices)
- Integrating heritage in contextual community development by building in incentives for the local population to protect the heritage
- Balanced management of tourist flows over valuable heritage spaces to prevent excesses over carrying capacity
- Maximizing local and overall benefits from limited investments.

The project team was struck by the discrepancy between how much Jordan had to offer for tourism and the absence of a coherent tourism

strategy.[11] Foremost on the minds of the project team was *combining development with heritage safeguarding*; that is, ensuring long-term sustainability that responds to cultural, environmental, and physical criteria. The 1997 Bank-assisted tourism project, specifically its Petra component, set as its goal to address the problems highlighted by UNESCO's 1994-95 study concerning overcrowding at the Petra Sanctuary and the need for access-management plans. Other problems identified by UNESCO in the archeological sanctuary, such as uncontrolled urbanization and asset management deficiencies, are also explicitly addressed in the Jordan Second Tourism Project.

Figure 3 The famous temple carved into rock, a great tourist attraction, Petra, Jordan. Petra means "rock."

In particular the project report emphasized the need to preempt the increased risks to heritage from expected growth in tourist flows. Without specific consideration of "carrying capacity" issues at cultural heritage sites, excessively increased tourists flows could harm heritage preservation.

The tourism project also finances infrastructure works convergent with the project's objectives. Among these are a 60-kilometer road rehabilitation effort in the Petra region and on urban spine roads, Wadi Musa town center improvements, flood control measures, urban regeneration provisions, land-use planning, and solid-waste management. Each of these components is capable not only of providing additional (direct or indirect) protection to the monuments and improving the experience of tourists, but also of creating *new employment* and improving the quality of life of the local population.

Tourism Diversification: Rehabilitating New Sites

Characteristic of this project's approach, and relevant to its replication value is the sense of balance and discerning selectivity with which it made investment choices among the many sites in need of assistance. To maximize investments for the sake of both tourism and culture, the project seeks to bring into the circuit previously neglected heritage sites.

Jordan's towns and villages with potential for heritage tourism have been unevenly treated in the past; choosing among them was not simple. The project's files reflect that many sites were considered for investments, including Azrak, Qasr Amra, Qasr El-Hallabat, Pella, Hemmeh, villages at the Dead Sea, Wadi Rum, Jerash, Mount Nebo, Karak, Madabe, Aqaba, Um Qais, and Petra.

After carefully pondering alternatives, the project team made some unconventional decisions and selected two sites—Petra and Wadi Rum—for immediate project investments. Giving priority to Wadi Rum over other, far better known tourist destinations was an unusual, but well-reasoned, decision. Two additional sites (Jerash and Karak) were selected for a pilot program and for carrying out feasibility studies toward future project preparation. Thus, the foundations for subsequent longer-term projects were laid during the initial phase.

By selecting the relatively small Wadi Rum site, along with well-known historic Petra, the project enables Jordanian authorities to experiment simultaneously on two models for the cultural heritage sector. On the one hand it can concentrate investments on a major site of world fame to realize its full potential and enhance its sustainability. On the other hand it can bring into the universal circuit several other of Jordan's less known, small- and medium-level sites, of which Wadi Rum is typical.

This second model carves out room for grassroots entrepreneurial initiatives, channeling economic and social benefits to the inhabitants of areas surrounding the lesser known sites. Wadi Rum's selection is also justified by its location close to Aqaba, Jordan's main site for non-heritage tourism. The project will make Wadi Rum more attractive to international tourists and in time will add a cultural dimension to what now is primarily beach tourism in the area.

Post-Conflict Reconstruction Option: Lebanon

The validity of the Jordan tourism-cum-heritage option is being tested during its implementation. Already a new urban project under advanced preparation in the Middle East, the Lebanon Cultural Heritage and Tourism Development project, finds considerable inspiration in the Jordan project.

Post-conflict reconstruction creates opportunities for either (a) incorporating CH components in various investments required by reconstruction in all domains, or (b) consolidating CH activities in a unified project, addressing only the built heritage.

Conventional wisdom has held that post-war immediate needs are so many and pressing, and resources so stretched, that hardly any attention can be paid to culture and heritage. Lebanon proves this conventional wisdom wrong. Decisionmakers with vision—as opposed to those with blinkers—tend to take a long-term, macroeconomic view to reconstruction, and program it to endure for future generations.[12]

Reconstruction of urban or transportation infrastructure after the calamities of war and civil war requires distributive and technical decisions concerning areas that may host enormously important heritage. Ignoring heritage is a sure recipe for making the wrong reconstruction decisions, soon to be regretted and challenged for what they overlooked or the damage they inflicted. Therefore, post-war reconstruction, indispensable in any case, also must be seen as an *opportunity* to address intrinsic heritage preservation needs in the respective areas.

Modernization and Respect for History

This rationale is embodied in the request of the Government of Lebanon to the Bank to provide assistance for a major reconstruction effort that would *explicitly include, not avoid, heritage preservation investments.* This rationale could be seen as valid for other countries in comparable situations.

Certainly, the reconstruction of Lebanon is advancing on a much larger scale than can be covered by the upcoming Bank-financed project. The project will concentrate on several urban segments that heavily involve precious heritage rehabilitation. This orientation also is expected to increase financial resources, as the Bank's involvement is likely to catalyze financing from other donors for cultural heritage rehabilitation.

Lebanon's government aims to turn the pressing need to repair conflict-caused destruction to towns into an opportunity to modernize Lebanon's urban centers, their major routes, equipment, and services. But this modernization is guided by a strong respect for history and heritage. The approach is to reconstruct in such a way as to create better architectonic contexts for the historic buildings. The challenge of the project is to underscore the cultural value of the urban patrimony, while enhancing its economic potential.

Specifically, the Lebanon Cultural Heritage and Tourism Development project will provide direct support for the rehabilitation of such major archeological sites and cultural assets as: the Imperial City of Tyre (on the WHL), the Sea Castle in Saida, the Citadel St. Gilles, the Old Town and the Tawba mosque in Tripoli, and the Temples and the Umayyad Mosque in Baalbeck. Work will also take place in the city of Baalbeck, which is on the WHL.

A Development-Oriented Perspective

The development perspective taken during project planning assumes that the rehabilitated sites will help revive Lebanon's status as a major tourist destination, lost during long years of conflict. The heritage sites are not treated as enclaves but are integrated in the surrounding urban socioeconomic fabric, with consideration of population flow patterns, traffic, hotels, and mix of commercial and social activities. The anticipated benefits from tourism, which, given the locations' dismal states, otherwise would be largely forgone, would go a long way toward recovering the project's investments. The salvaged and enhanced spiritual and educational value of the heritage thus would be virtually "free of charge." Overall, the project includes a balanced combination of historic building rehabilitation, regeneration of old town centers (Saida and Tripoli), conservation of archaeological sites, construction of visitors' centers (in four locations), and improvements in urban services infrastructure.

In addition, and with a view to future CH needs, the project will budget technical assistance for further planning and the formulation of a national heritage preservation strategy. This strategy will lead to the next stages of heritage protection, and possibly to a master plan or national program for cultural heritage preservation and management in Lebanon.

Certainly, as development perspectives improve for other post-conflict countries—such as Algeria, Iran, and Yemen—the Lebanon experience will offer a valuable body of knowledge that can be adjusted to the circumstances of these countries (figure 4).

Restoration and Capacity Building Option: West Bank

The West Bank and Gaza Bethlehem 2000 project embodies a distinct experience with heritage management. The project convincingly shows how the World Bank can help *build institutional and management capacity in the cultural sector from the ground up.* To one or another degree, as emphasized in prior sections, institutional strengthening is a feature of every Bank-assisted project. Yet the West Bank Bethlehem case is emblematic.

The project came about in response to an urgent local and international call: a request to the World Bank from the Palestinian Authority (PA) of West Bank and Gaza and the international community at large to take a leading role in preparing Bethlehem and its surroundings for the Millennium celebrations. The project was prepared and appraised in

record time, and embodies an extraordinary model of Bank partnership and cooperation with the Palestinian Authority, UNESCO, the Vatican, the Government of Italy and other governments, and various universities and scholars directly interested in this unique task.

Figure 4. Sana'a, Yemen: the multi-story, highly decorated houses are well-known architectural heritage and the subject of numerous studies and preservation efforts.

Institutional Challenges

From the start institutional capacity building emerged as the project's make or break challenge—more difficult by far than the civil works required in the project.

The incipient municipal structures were far too fragile to undertake the task and required time to mature. The "Bethlehem 2000 Steering Committee," initially established by the PA to prepare for the celebration, was encountering major problems of its own and soon had to be replaced. Furthermore, no other bilateral or international donor was prepared to confront the institution-building challenges. UNESCO was ready to provide technical and artistic advice for rehabilitation works, but could not offer the institution building and vast financial support needed. Some donors declared willingness to provide grants for individual infrastructure and cultural components, yet none was in a position to integrate the immediate work with the West Bank's long-term program. In short, the institutional bottleneck was such that the entire effort could be stillborn, or limited to bricks and mortar.

The key question was how to turn the preparations for this one-time event into an opportunity to address long-term development needs? The World Bank emerged as the agency best placed to help the PA to capitalize on this short-duration project for the long term; to establish the institutional, financial, and programmatic framework needed immediately for the celebration.

All participants clearly recognized that the celebration, while religious in content, had strategic development potential for the West Bank's cultural and tourism sectors. At stake in this project were major cultural preservation issues with which the Bank was relatively inexperienced, and risksæpolitical, economic, and technical. These risks were increased by the request to complete the project very quickly.

Five alternatives were considered. They ranged from a "minimalist" scenario, with a narrow focus on infrastructure rehabilitation only, to the "maximalist" case, incorporating long-term tourism and private-sector development. Given the significance of the occasion, the former was clearly insufficient. The maximalist option was clearly beyond local capacity and the Bank's own capacity to prepare a maximum-scenario project, given budget and staff constraints. An alternative between the two extremes, based on needs and realistic feasibility, was called for.

The final Bethlehem 2000 project, at a total cost of some US$100 million, allocated *unusually high funding (40 percent) to institutional and capacity building support,* plus technical assistance. The allocation included direct assistance to area municipalities (mainly for reforming their managerial, financial, and accounting systems and undertaking studies), the Ministry of Tourism and Antiquities, and the Ministry of Culture (for developing a cultural heritage preservation policy and a corresponding legal framework).

The intensive infrastructure and heritage rehabilitation component received the remaining 60 percent of the Bank funding. This consists of essential infrastructure and adaptive reuse of historical cores of Bethlehem, Beit Jala, and Beit Sahor. The project will also improve services: drains, water, sewerage, and parking.

Estimates of potential visitors to the Holy Land for the Millennium celebrations in the year 2000 ranged as high as 4 million people. These visitors also will temporarily benefit from the improved capacities. Therefore, in the most direct sense, the Bethlehem 2000 project is a cultural service to the world, not only to the borrower.

Closer to home, the target for poverty-reduction goals is the 100,000 persons in the larger Bethlehem area. The local population will benefit directly from investments in civil works, artisanal production, and businesses servicing tourists.

The ongoing Bethlehem project puts the Bank's pivotal role in capacity creation to an exacting test. The implementation experience of the tight three-year execution period is being closely monitored. While the PA will emerge from the project with a higher institutional capacity platform on which to build, the Bank is positioned to gain unique experiences in emergency response to major heritage preservation demands.

National Program Option: Tunisia

Including cultural components in projects in traditional economic sectors is not the only way to support CH preservation. The other option is *full-scale* projects dedicated primarily to culture-sector activities.

Distinct from the approaches taken so far in Morocco, Jordan, Lebanon, and the West Bank the national cultural heritage project under preparation in Tunisia pursues an option not yet selected in any other Bank-assisted project. It consists of developing a *comprehensive countrywide strategy* for cultural heritage preservation and building capacity for a long-term master plan, with step-by-step activities consistent with one another. In this sector master plans will have to be revised and adapted to emerging needs, new demands from related sectors (international tourism), and resource inflows. Therefore, one objective is to cultivate Tunisian in-house competence to monitor and understand international markets and respond adequately. The Tunisia Cultural Heritage Management and Development Project now under preparation is the vehicle for generating such a master plan. This special stand-alone project is obviously a more ambitious option than those taken in other projects. However Tunisia has better institutional capacity in this sector than many other countries.

The primary reason for adopting this challenging option was the government's preference. Tunisia, the Bank was told, has a long and mixed experience with piecemeal donor support for one or another of its historic monuments. The Government of Tunisia felt it to be in the best interest of the country to take stock and get a comprehensive view of the heritage domain. It wanted to ascertain its strength and potentials; identify its weaknesses and short- and long-term needs; develop a national inventory of its assets; and—based on all this—formulate a coherent, long-term strategy for heritage preservation. The Bank agreed, and Japan and Italy offered grants to cover the costs of preparing the national project.

Tunisia has a high density of heritage sites countrywide, and faces two common, yet major, problems: (1) accelerated degradation and (2) inadequate capture of the patrimony's vast economic potential. Degradation is due to well-known natural, economic, and social causes: weathering, economic and technological change, pressure for land, under-financing, population growth, theft, limited community involvement, and little private-sector support. Tourism has only partially helped to harvest the patrimony's economic value. Because tourism in Tunisia is oriented mainly toward coastal destinations, opportunities for cultural tourism remain severely underused. Moreover, per capita tourism revenues have been relatively stagnant or even decreasing. The government indicated to the Bank that it wished to reorient its strategy and encourage higher-value *cultural* tourism.

Need to Prioritize and Sequence

The tasks of a countrywide, heritage-focused project are daunting. It must cover a multitude of sites, respond to a wide range of needs, and balance a broad spectrum of complex issues. Therefore, the preparation team was asked to follow a two-fold orientation: (1) to place first on the agenda sector-wide issues that would impact most individual activities, and (2) to pursue a set of immediate "results on the ground" that would demonstrate effectiveness, create momentum, and evolve into models replicable through the longer-term strategy.[13]

The strategy, now at an advanced stage of preparation, defines three primary goals: institutional capacity building, private-sector mobilization, and improved conservation technologies and management approaches.

To achieve convincing "results on the ground" early in the project, the preparation team identified eight priority sites for immediate conservation and management activities. These are expected to pilot and confirm the strategy. Work on the selected sites should provide the operational opportunities to strengthen institutional capacity.[14] Criteria for selecting, prioritizing, and *sequencing* work on the eight cultural sites were devised. Each selected site would enable the project to confront another critical issue and test the response to it.

Worth highlighting also is that the approach taken offers great *flexibility* to the government and the Bank as to the final content of the investment project (or projects) that will result from the preparation. The feasibility studies have yielded a comprehensive, although preliminary, countrywide report covering multiple possible actions.[15] Yet the countrywide coverage of the *preparation* study does not compel a countrywide coverage through the immediately resulting *investment project.* Resources and capacities for tackling everything at once do not exist.

Comprehensive preparation allows ranking of priorities and less urgent tasks. It facilitates sequencing investments in time and space. The final definition of the project will therefore be able to plan for several phases over a longer period. The challenge will be to select those activities that address CH priorities and contribute most effectively to poverty reduction and employment generation. Financing will also be easier. The availability of a coherent national master plan will enable the government and the Bank to mobilize soft financial support from other donors. Donor agencies are much more likely to respond to the appeal and needs of a master plan than to piecemeal requests.

A comparable comprehensive approach was taken in Yemen for the preparation of a national cultural heritage project encompassing Yemen's three historic cities on the World Monuments List (figure 5). Yet in this case the route taken did not prove to be the most promising. It soon became obvious that, given the very weak existing institutions—whose capacity could not be improved quickly enough—a countrywide project would be overextended. The project preparation process was thus redirected in midstream toward first preparing a country strategy paper, an in-depth institutional diagnosis, and a heritage inventory. (The inventory is financed by an Italian grant, while the Bank provides implementation management and non-lending assistance.) This experience reinforced the lesson that implementing countrywide programs through stand-alone projects can be undertaken realistically only when existing conditions are favorable (figure 6).

Indirect Support to Patrimony Safeguarding

All of the options examined in the sections above involved CH-support activities that required World Bank financing. Yet some types of Bank-assisted projects in MENA, particularly urban sector infrastructure projects, have considerable potential to help in the preservation and sustainability of the built heritage *even when they do not explicitly include cultural heritage components*. The study that I conducted of cultural heritage programs in the Plena region concludes that this potential must be used by the Bank more systematically.

Obviously, the way in which general infrastructure upgrading in old towns is carried out affects—directly and indirectly, positively or adversely—the built heritage. The spectacular mud-brick buildings of Sana'a and Shibam, for instance, were constructed on dry soils, for very limited and controlled in-house water husbandry. In recent decades the advent of piped water exposes such historic buildings to new and severe risks, such as inadequate equipment for public water supply, anarchic behavior by inhabitants prone to making haphazard connections through uninsulated walls, and uninformed and careless in-house water management. These all result in water leaks, seepage, cracked walls, destabilized foundations, and ultimately collapsed historic buildings. Normal municipal services projects can do a great deal to arrest such damaging factors of CH destruction.

Figure 5. Yemen: richly decorated facades rise up to nine floors. The tall buildings of Old Sana'a are built exclusively from hewn natural stones and baked clay bricks.

Traditional urban settlements across the Middle East and North African countries suffer from typical infrastructure and service deficiencies that sap the durability of many historic buildings. The most frequent dysfunctionalities are:

- Water supply: defective systems, insufficient capacity, leaking pipes
- Drainage systems: absent or dysfunctional
- Sewerage: systems open to the surface
- Streets: unpaved, become mudholes and disease-breeding pools in rainy months
- Garbage disposal system: absent or insufficient, resulting in garbage accumulation
- Housing stocks: deteriorating
- Land tenure: complexities and uncertainties over ownership of land and structures hamper infrastructure improvement and maintenance.

When urban infrastructure works undertaken to address these problems (under domestic or international aid programs) are designed with cultural sensitivity and heritage awareness, their contribution to CH preservation can be long-lasting *even if they do not invest explicitly in historic building restoration.* The contribution is often modest, but it is real. This spillover effect often is a matter of how the project area is determined. Frequently, it is possible to select some locations in which defective or absent infrastructure systems, such as a routine water supply or drainage project, also put heritage buildings at risk of collapsing. The beneficial impacts of the same investment for one project can thus be multiplied.

Such preferential selection presupposes *awareness* of existing heritage at risk, and may involve minor trade-offs. However, if such awareness is lacking when conventional urban infrastructure projects are designed, important potential benefits from infrastructure upgrading may be forgone.[16]

The implication for development agencies is that their entire urban infrastructure portfolio—not only one or another flagship urban cultural heritage

Figure 6. Fish market in historic Sana'a. Although it faces pressures from urban growth and new construction, Sana'a's original urban core is intact, economically active, and vibrant.

project—does play a role, directly or indirectly, in the comprehensive endeavor of sustainably conserving heritage sites. For this reason careful consideration of socio-cultural variables and impacts of all "regular" projects is required, even when direct investments in cultural public goods are not envisaged. ■

Notes

1   This chapter draws on research for a large cultural strategy study about patrimony preservation and management in North African and Middle Eastern countries, to be published in 2001: M. M. Cernea, *Development and Cultural Heritage Preservation* (Washington, D.C.: World Bank, forthcoming).

2   The criteria for deciding which route to take have been (1) the nature of the country's request to the Bank, (2) available objective opportunities, and (3) institutional strength in the cultural sector.

3   F. Navez, "Projet de Sauvegarde de la Medina de Fez, Evaluation Sociale," April 1995 (processed).

4   An earlier (1991-92) United Nations Development Programme study, "The First Conservation Project for the Fez Medina," identified these as critical problems that need to be addressed with priority.

5   See L. Lévi-Strauss, "Sacred Places in Historic Cities," in this volume.

6   Navez, "Projet de Sauvegarde de la Medina de Fez." See also N. L. Tagemouati, "La Medina de Fez a-t-elle une valeur d'échange?" (processed).

7   D. Hankey, "Case Study: Lahore, Pakistan: Conservation of the Walled City," Environmentally and Socially Sustainable Development Network, World Bank, Washington, D.C., 1999.

8   Harvard University and Association Sauvegarde de la Medina de Tunis, "The Rehabilitation of the Hafsia Quarter of the Medina of Tunis," Project Assessment (mimeo), World Bank, Washington, D.C., 1994.

9   "Morocco: Fez Medina Rehabilitation Project," Staff Appraisal Document, World Bank, October 7, 1998.

10   Minutes of the Meeting of the World Bank Executive Directors, Staff Notes, November 1978.

11   The following excerpt from a presentation made by the project preparation team leader, Tufan Kolan, vividly describes the country situation and the team's reasoning: "When we first got into this project, we realized that Jordan did not have a coherent tourism strategy.... The Department of Archeology was working with some 19 donors, supporting excavations here and there, with great dispersion among numerous sites. The value added by the Bank resulted primarily from placing the focus on a coherent strategy for developmental tourism. I am referring to a three-pronged strategy which combines tourism development, cultural heritage enhancement, and urban regeneration. We suggested that a longer time frame would be necessary, thinking about the Bank's involvement over a ten-year period rather than preparing just a sporadic operation, and that we would favor phased investments starting with the highest priority and moving onward. Within

such a coherent strategy, we must have policies that support the private sector in tourism and we must have the right institutions. On the investment side, the ten-year sector strategy should be accompanied by an investment program which makes investments in phases. And the third step was to link policy, institutions and investments in determining the priority sites."

12 D. Gressani and J. Page, "Reconstruction in Lebanon: Challenges for Macroeconomic Management," Middle East and North Africa Social and Economic Development Group (MNSED) Working Papers Series 16 (April), World Bank, Washington, D.C., 1999.

13 See C. Delvoie, "Tunisia: Cultural Heritage Management and Valuation Project," Regional Operations Committee (ROC) Meeting for Project Completion Document Review memorandum, World Bank, Washington, D.C., September 21, 1998. See also F. Amiot, "Tunisia Cultural Heritage Project." ROC Review of the Project Completion Document Decision Memorandum, World Bank, Washington, D.C., October 7, 1998.

14 M. Gautier, F. Amiot, and J. Taboroff, Back-to-Office Report, memorandum to Sonia Hammam, World Bank, May 4, 1999.

15 "Rapport Préliminaire: Projet de gestion et de valorisation du Patrimoine Culturel" (mimeo). (Diraset-Empreinte et Communication–Groupe Huit, Tunis, February 1999.

16 This aspect is distinct from the situations addressed in the World Bank's Operations Policy (OP 4.11) concerning safeguarding of heritage, which warns against "damage by commission" rather than by omission. These policy guidelines explicitly require that infrastructure projects take safeguarding precautions prior to and throughout all civil works.

Part III

Rescuing Heritage at Risk: Reconstruction, Transformation, and Adaptation

Editors' Note

The chapters in Part III examine the built heritage at risk and the range of rescue plans developed for its conservation, transformation, occasional reconstruction, and adaptive reuse. Although the destruction of a monument or an ensemble of monuments may be caused by natural disaster, most experts agree that vulnerability to decay is often aggravated by inadequate safeguards, inadequate inspection procedures, and deferred maintenance—in other words, neglect. The first two chapters depict successful reconstruction efforts in Assisi, Italy, and in Lijiang, China, in the aftermath of intense seismic episodes. The second group of chapters covers transformation, adaptive reuse, and re-dedication of historic structures in Venice, Italy; Tampico and Tlacoltapan, Mexico; and Recife, Brazil.

Giorgio Croci describes decisions made in sequencing the reconstruction of the Basilica of St. Francis of Assisi. These start with the examination of the structural damages and the engineering solutions proposed, especially the urgent measures taken right after the earthquake to prevent a complete collapse of the vaults and tympanum. With the deformation of the structure it was feared that further destruction of the roof of the chapel would occur, damaging the frescoes and works of art dating from fourteenth and fifteenth centuries. The second stage of the work involved the consolidation and restoration of the Basilica's interiors using state-of-the-art technologies.

Geoffrey Read and Katrinka Ebbe document and analyze the post-earthquake reconstruction and conservation of the Old City of Lijiang, a project assisted by the World Bank. Lijiang's 800-year-old urban design of meandering canals and roads is home to 10 national minority groups. Lijiang is a designated World Heritage Site. In response to widespread destruction from earthquakes the Chinese government issued guidelines on how structures should be strengthened to make them safer and more resistant to quakes. Regulations were also issued to upgrade the housing stock, and provisions were made to protect the historic character the Mu Fu Complex. The goal was to mobilize resources quickly and re-establish normal life in the city, while protecting its unique cultural heritage. Coordination among agencies, empowerment of the local community to participate in upgrading, assistance in heritage management tourism planning, and institutional capacity building are all priorities in this type of an intervention.

Deterioration of the natural environment of the Venetian Lagoon is threatening the ensemble of monuments in Venice. Protracted deterioration of the city's marine environment, rising water levels (acqua alta), and high tides, as well as a massive loss of industrial jobs and of the resident population over 30 years, have damaged the city's economic capacity and hence its capacity to protect its unique heritage. Maurizio Sabini examines the rehabilitation of the Arsenale and the re-use of the historic warehouses of the old navy yard for a high-technology industry and information technology research center. These new commercial uses are expected to generate jobs and pave the way for the economic recovery of Venice.

Alfonso Govela provides a detailed account of the work of his team of architects in Tampico and Tlacoltapan, Mexico. In Tampico they rebuilt and adapted the old Customs House, or Aduana, and the Edificio de la Luz, both structures refitted for new uses. Their experience shows how abandoned and neglected structures can be recovered by the private sector for useful and attractive use. The transformed buildings have proved economically viable and are important political symbols of recovery in the downtown area. In contrast, the reconstruction experience of the historic center of Tlacotalpan, because it was designated a World Heritage Site, attracted greater scrutiny and involvement by experts and officials. The firm's experience in Tlacotalpan demonstrated that preservation actions regulated by complex approval procedures by state, federal, and international agencies are often slow in being implemented.

Carlos Alberto Vieira relates the identification through bibliographic and archeological research of an early seventeenth-century building in Recife, Brazil, which housed the first synagogue built in the New World. The Kahal Kadosh Zur Israel Synagogue was built by the community of Portuguese Jews brought by Prince Mauricio de Nassau in 1630 to Northeast Brazil. These Portuguese Jews had immigrated to the Netherlands to escape the Inquisition courts. After the expulsion of the Dutch from Brazil, this community of Jews escaped by going back to Holland or by drifting into the Caribbean and eventually to New York, then known as New Amsterdam. Their legacy had been all but forgotten. Through the Fundação Safra, a private foundation in Brazil, reconstruction works are under way. The refitted building will house a seventeenth-century interior of a synagogue and a research and documentation center, with documents to be brought from Portugal and the Netherlands to celebrate the legacy left by the Jews in colonial Brazil.

Reconstructing the Basilica of Assisi

12

The Basilica of St. Francis of Assisi, the imposing pilgrimage church built in Italy from 1228 to 1253, is famous not only as a holy site but also for the wonderful frescoes by Cimabue and Giotto that cover its walls and vaults. These frescoes, which represent scenes of St. Francis' life and episodes in the history of the Catholic Church, are considered milestones in the history of painting in the Western world (figure 1).[1]

History, Damage, and Collapse

The Basilica of St. Francis has endured many earthquakes; yet none produced damage as great as that of September 26, 1997. The quake destroyed the vaults near the facade, the vaults near the transept, and a portion of the left transept (figure 2). It also caused large cracks and permanent deformation all over the vaults, leaving them in a very precarious and dangerous situation.

Besides the accumulated impacts that past earthquakes of different characteristics may have produced on the Basilica, other factors in the past have increased their vulnerability. The tympanum consists of a cavity wall with two faces and an inner fill. Its partial collapse was caused by the decay of the mortar that joined the bricks of the external face with the inner fill. The first damage was produced on September 26, but it was the quake of October 7 that created a large hole in the wall.

The collapse of the vaults was produced by a large volume of fill, mainly broken tiles and other loose materials that had accumulated in the springer zones over centuries of roof repairs. Under seismic actions this fill, lacking any cohesion, slides from side to side, alternatively stressing the opposite side. Moreover, the loose fill follows the movement of the vaults, opposing their recovery, thereby causing additional permanent deformations. When the September 26 quake hit the Basilica, it is very likely that permanent deformations that reduced the curvature, and therefore the bearing capacity of the vaults, had accumulated as a consequence of previous earthquakes.

Giorgio Croci

Giorgio Croci holds the Chair of Structural Restoration of Monuments and Historic Buildings and is professor of Structural Engineering in the Faculty of Engineering at the University of Rome La Sapienza; is a consultant to UNESCO, ICCROM, the Council of Europe, and the Italian Ministry of Foreign Affairs; and is president of the ICOMOS International Committee of Analysis and Restoration of Structures in Architectural Heritage, mail@giorgiocroci.com

Figure 1. Frescoes on the walls and vaults of the Basilica of St. Francis of Assisi.

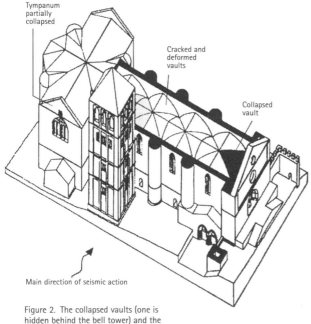

Tympanum partially collapsed

Cracked and deformed vaults

Collapsed vault

Main direction of seismic action

Figure 2. The collapsed vaults (one is hidden behind the bell tower) and the damaged tympanum in the Basilica.

After the September 26 quake a general model and a global stress analysis of the Basilica was carried out. A non-linear model of the vaults confirmed the decisive role of the fill (figure 3). When the horizontal acceleration reaches about 0.2 g (gravity acceleration), relevant tensile stresses are produced. The deformation shown by the mathematical model is perfectly in agreement with the failure mechanism of the vaults filmed by Umbria Television. The failure resulted from the progressive loss of curvature of the ribs. Then a "hinge" was produced in the middle, and finally the rib collapsed, drawing the vault down with it.

The collapses were concentrated on these specific zones as a result of the direction of the seismic action. It was mainly perpendicular to the nave axis; thus it behaved globally like a "beam," for which a kind of restraint at the ends was provided by the stiffness of the façade and the transept. The result was that high normal and shear stresses were produced there, in addition to the "local stresses" resulting from the weight of the fill (figure 4).

Urgent Measures

Urgent measures were required immediately after the earthquake to prevent the global collapse of the tympanum and vaults. The surviving vaults all were affected by large cracks distributed both on the intrados and the extrados (figure 5). As already mentioned, curvature was lost in several zones.

The danger that the standing vaults might collapse, and the consequent risk to human life, precluded the possibility of supporting the vaults from the ground level. Instead, a platform was suspended from the roof above the vaults with the double function of inspection and providing a base for working over the vaults (figure 6).

The urgent measures taken in the first month after the main earthquake can be summarized as follows:

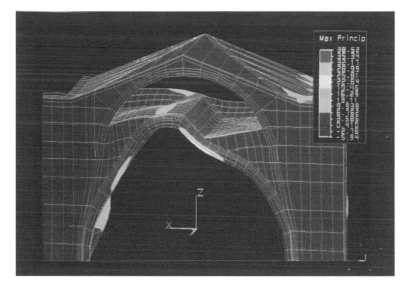

Figure 3. Stresses and deformation of the vault.

Figure 4. One of the modal deformations of the vaults caused by seismic actions.

Figure 5. Cracks and deformations in the vaults.

Figure 6. The small flying bridge suspended from the roof to inspect and strengthen the vaults.

Figure 7. A crane lifts up a second crane to be placed in the inner courtyard of the Convent.

- Removal of the huge load represented by the fill in the springer zones of the vaults
- Filling the cracks with a salt-free mortar to limit possible damage to the frescoes
- Applying bands of synthetic fibers over the cracks of the extrados.
- Suspending the vaults from the roof with a system of tie bars, having first inserted two springs to maintain the force at the design value, independent of thermal effects and minor vibrations.

As regards the tympanum, the risk was that if it had collapsed, it would have destroyed the roof of the chapel below, destroying frescoes and works of art of inestimable value. After long reflection it was decided to use a huge crane 50 meters tall to reach the tympanum and remove the bricks and loose fill.

But such a crane could not pass through the narrow gate into the inner yard. This problem was resolved by using two cranes. The first, outside the Basilica complex, lifted the second one over the roof of the building and deposited it in the inner courtyard (figure 7).

Organizing this operation involved anchoring two cantilevered steel trusses on the two walls of the transept. The trusses were designed to support a 4.5-ton steel frame structure in the shape of the tympanum, a triangle 8 meters high and 17 meters at the base. Then the empty spaces in the tympanum and big holes were filled with polyurethane foam to provisionally stabilize the masonry.

Consolidation and Restoration Project

The problem of the definitive restoration and consolidation of the Basilica, especially as regards the vaults, without risking damage to the frescoes and without compromising the historical value of the original vault structure, was very delicate. The choice has been to realize on the extrados a series of small ribs, following a pattern typical of Gothic structures (figure 8), leaving the original structure clearly visible.

These ribs are made of a light and very strong composite material made of a central timber nucleus and aramidic fibers embedded in epoxy resins. The ribs are built *in situ*, so that it is possible to follow the deformed shape of the vaults.

As regards the cracks that have compromised the continuity of the vaults, it was decided to complete the first injections in the emergency situation using a mortar that satisfied very specific and severe conditions. This mortar is salt-free and compatible with the frescoes. It is sufficiently fluid to penetrate and diffuse in all the cracks and micro-cracks and to be injected in dry masonry (no use of water is allowed). Finally, it has good strength and bond capacity so that it can establish structural continuity through the cracks.

Figure 8. Ribs made of a central timber nucleus and external aramidic fibers.

The reconstruction of the collapsed vault has been another major problem. Fortunately, painstaking research identified several frescoed bricks that could be reused to rebuild the vaults. It has been necessary however to produce new bricks with the same constituents and similar characteristics as the original ones.

The Basilica was reopened to the public in November 1999, two years and three months after the earthquake. That is a record for swift action. It was possible because we were charged with all the responsibilities, and we had the powers to take any decision without waiting for any approval.

Conclusions

The operations carried out, first to save and then to consolidate and restore, the Basilica of St. Francis of Assisi all have followed the same philosophy. That is to place the most up-to-date techniques and technologies at the service of the culture in order to respect the historic value of the ancient building and to obtain adequate safety levels, changing the original conception as little as possible.

Some of these technologies, never before applied in the restoration field, have been studied expressly for this occasion. They offer interesting new possibilities to safeguard architectural heritage and open new perspectives in the cultures of conservation and restoration.

Envoi

Most literature on preservation of built heritage refers to the meaning of the building to the people. However, few attempt to study the many natural phenomena that put our architectural heritage at risk.

An earthquake caused the collapse of the Basilica of St. Francis of Assisi.

Figure 9 (above). Bukhara Mosque prior to reconstruction, Uzbekistan.

Figure 10 (above right). Reconstructed plan of the seventeenth-century city center of Bukhara.

The effect of rising dampness associated with soil settlements caused the collapse of one of the four minarets of a mosque in Bukhara, Uzbekistan (figures 9, 10). During a UNESCO mission to Uzbekistan, we advised of the risk of this situation, but, unfortunately, a few months later, we were called again to look at the situation after one minaret had collapsed.

Soil is also settling under the Tower of Pisa (figure 11). Through a restoration project using under-excavation, 10 percent of the tilt will be recovered. In this technique we remove bits of soil on the positive side of the inclination to produce an artificial tilt on the positive side. In a way this is going back to the future because, when we recover 10 percent of the tilt, the tower will be in the same position that it was three-and-a-half centuries ago. We have verified that this is a totally safe procedure.

Decay and natural process are severely accelerated in the tropics. For example huge trees have grown over the structure of the temple in Angkor, strangling it (figure 12). In that case UNESCO suggested that the trees be protected as part of the cultural heritage so that the trees have to be maintained as well as the temples.

The worst of all threats, however, are produced by human beings. Wars often deliberately aim to destroy not only the building as a material and physical entity but primarily as representatives of their culture. During the war in Croatia the United Nations flag could not prevent wide disasters. The old town of Dubrovnik, so quiet and peaceful, without any military

interest, was partially destroyed by bombs. It is quite pathetic that desperate attempts to protect a historic building can do little against a shell.

The destruction of the Sarajevo Library and the destruction of the Mostar Bridge took place far more for their symbolic meaning as links between different ethnic groups than for their intrinsic architectural value.

Too little is done to protect architectural heritage. Too often actions are taken to repair, consolidate, or restore only after the damage, the decay, the collapse, and the spoiling of our architectural heritage have occurred. Rather, repair and applying global preventive measures and strategies should be ongoing.

However, even if prevention and conservation must remain our primary tasks, decay and destruction are not the only problems that we face. Habits and customs of people are changing. Traditional uses of buildings cannot be maintained in a modern society. Towns are growing rapidly. The environment is more and more aggressive towards cultural heritage. To preserve cultural heritage, education of the public and governments—local, national, and international—is essential. ■

Figure 11 (above left). The campanile of Pisa Cathedral built in 1174, has eight stories of ascending, encircling arcades. Due to soil subsidence at its foundation the tower leans dangerously to one side. Through under-excavation, about 10 percent of the tilt will be reversed.

Figure 12 (above). Archeological remains of the temple in Angkor, Cambodia, are the object of conservation work to expand knowledge of the ancient Khmer Empire. Specialists have recommended preservation of both the stone work and the overgrowing trees.

Note

1 A visitor to the West Wing of the National Gallery of Art in Washington, D. C. will find in the rooms dedicated to the beginnings of Western art outstanding works by Cimabue and Giotto.

13 Adaptive Reuse of the Arsenale Complex, Venice

Maurizio Sabini

Maurizio Sabini is an architect in private practice in Trieste, Italy.

The Arsenale, an old military shipyard and dock area, has existed since the twelfth century and had been completely abandoned and in decay. The redevelopment of one small portion of the complex has been one of the most economically successful and culturally meaningful interventions in the upgrading of Venice (figure 1).

Venice is a world-famous urban wonder, an architectural jewel miraculously set in the middle of a most delicate, complex natural environment, the Venetian Lagoon. The lagoon environment has fallen into severe jeopardy due to several factors. These factors are the industrial district constructed at Porto Marghera; deep canals dug throughout the Lagoon for large cargo and oil tanker traffic; pressure exerted by the construction of human settlements around its borders; and ecological problems caused by increasingly polluted

Figure 1. Arsenale, Venice: aerial view.

river effluents. Moreover, in recent decades climatic changes resulting in a rise in sea level, combined with soil subsidence, have caused the City of Venice to suffer the now oft-recurring phenomenon of *acqua alta*, or exceptionally high tides. In 1966 a record high tide, measuring 1.94 meters, brought the attention of the international community to Venice.

The city also has suffered from an alarming deterioration of its social fabric and demographic structure, with an exodus of younger inhabitants from the historic city to other coastal cities. The outflow is due primarily to the unaffordable costs of rehabilitating old buildings to modern living standards, the mounting pressure of tourism on the property market and public services, and the limited job market increasingly dominated by public institutions and tourism (figure 2).

In a drastic demographic shift over the last 50 years the resident population has dropped nearly 55 percent, from 150,000 in the late 1940s to 68,000 in 1998. By Italian standards Venice has a relatively low density of 90 inhabitants per hectare, compared with 200 to 300 inhabitants per hectare in other Italian historic centers. The average age of the population is increasing rapidly, from 35 in 1971 to 45 in 1997.

To address the loss of the industrial and mercantile economic base and more than one-half of the population, as well as the environmental problems, the local administration took several actions in recent years. These were to (a) develop systems to control the high tides, (b) construct a new sewerage system and dredge the canals, (c) implement urban renewal projects, (d) diversify the urban economy, and (e) create more affordable housing to attract new residents to Venice.

It is within this strategy that the redevelopment and reconversion of the Arsenale was conceived. Located at the edge of the historic nucleus of Venice, the Arsenale was established in the twelfth century for the construction of the first Venetian fleets, then venturing on the Crusades and conquering

Figure 2. Mass tourism, as here in Venice, benefits historic cities economically but also puts pressure on the property markets and public services and can limit job markets.

strongholds in the southeastern Mediterranean. At the end of the sixteenth century the Arsenale occupied 26 hectares, boasting one of the first examples of industrial production based on the assembly line. At the time the 3,000 workers employed at the Arsenale could produce 7 warships every month.

After World War I, with the limitations imposed by its historic structures and by the environmental conditions of the Lagoon, primarily the shallow canals, the Arsenale ceased to be a major military shipyard. From then on, although it is still owned by the military, its dry-docks were used by private ship-repairing firms.

In the early 1980s discussions about the redevelopment of the area were advanced. A more comprehensive planning concept began to emerge based on a broader system of urban relations across the Lagoon in which the Arsenale compound would be endowed with a mix of different uses. Several architectural visions were examined as to the feasible uses of the various Arsenale sectors and to phase in the implementation.

In 1991 a consortium of private and public companies was formed called Consortium THETIS, with the twofold objective of developing technical projects and building the THETIS center itself (figure 3). The center consists of 4,500 square meters of covered area and 6,500 square meters of open space, thus accounting for only 3 percent of the Arsenale's overall area. The project introduced a host of modern technological facilities into the historic warehouse structures, one of which was built in the sixteenth century, while preserving the physical integrity of the old buildings (figure 4).

Furthermore, the design followed a reversibility concept so that the old warehouses may be reconverted into new uses once the current project

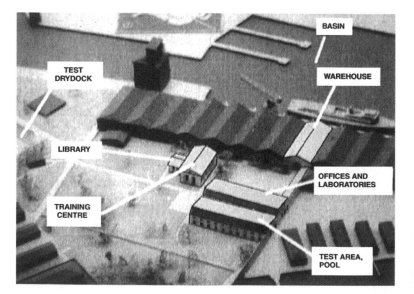

Figure 3. THETIS Center, Venice.

ends. The THETIS center is built to house a new engineering company that develops innovative products and technological applications in marine and environmental technologies, telerobotics, and laboratory test facili ties, transportation safety, monitoring systems, environmental safety systems for coastal cities, and maintenance and state-of-the-art information systems. These services are planned for the local, national, and international markets (figure 5).

Figure 4 (above left). THETIS premises, Venice: exterior, showing historic warehouses.

Figure 5 (above). THETIS premises, Venice: interior.

The rehabilitation of the Arsenale has represented a great opportunity to upgrade the City of Venice and its lagoon environment, and THETIS is a particularly successful example of adaptive reuse. The success of THETIS is attributed to the following variables:

1. Careful planning of the operational, financial, and management aspects of the projects, with the cooperation of public and private agents, before starting the actual physical design.
2. Creation of an operating structure, the Consortium THETIS, prior to the construction of the center, thus enabling the consortium to benefit from a pre-existing portfolio of clients and contracts, and technological know-how.
3. The market-oriented technological assets of the consortium and culturally sensitive overall development concept merited external financial support from the European Union.
4. Synergies created with local research centers.
5. Adoption of structure-friendly approach of architectural design based on a reversibility concept.

In sum the exemplary value of the THETIS project lies in a revitalization of the historic areas approach that is not simply tourist-oriented but, rather, eco-sensitive and focused on generating new productive activities and richer and more diverse cultural growth. ∎

14 Post-Earthquake Reconstruction and Urban Heritage Conservation in Lijiang

Geoffrey Read and
Katrinka Ebbe

Geoffrey Read, principal municipal engineer, Urban Development Sector Unit, East Asia and Pacific Region, World Bank, was task manager for the World Bank's reconstruction project in Lijiang. Katrinka Ebbe, a cultural heritage consultant at the World Bank, prepared the case study on the Lijiang project.

n February 1996 an earthquake measuring 7.0 on the Richter Scale struck northern Yunnan, China. It resulted in the loss of life and widespread destruction of dwellings; businesses; schools; hospitals; and the water, power, and transportation systems. This chapter presents the results of a World Bank-assisted earthquake reconstruction program and community heritage conservation work in the Old City of Lijiang in Yunnan.

The World Bank provided a credit of US$30 million to reestablish daily life and economic activity as quickly as possible by helping to reconstruct the Old City's basic service infrastructure, dwellings, and community facilities (figure 1). To comply with local historic conservation guidelines, the community decided that the city's buildings must be reconstructed in their traditional architectural forms. Moreover, US$7 million of the credit was set aside to rehabilitate cultural heritage assets that had sustained severe damage. The rationale for these investments was the local importance attached to preserving cultural heritage and the need to help the Old City reconstruct an efficient, supportive environment for daily living and enterprise.

Cultural Heritage in the Old City

Due to the harmonious fusion of different cultural traditions and its uniformly traditional cityscape, in 1997 the Old City of Lijiang was designated a UNESCO World Heritage Site. The urban fabric of this 800-year-old city is uninterrupted by twentieth-century construction or other incompatible development. Old Lijiang is also unique because it did not

102

Figure 1. The cost for earthquake reconstruction in Lijiang, China, was estimated at US$482 million.

evolve according to the same rectilinear pattern as many older Chinese cities on the Central Plains. Instead, its mountainous setting has shaped streets and lanes that hug the hills in natural topographical patterns. The Old City's remarkable water-supply system has also shaped its development. The Yu River brings water to the edge of Lijiang, where the river branches into multiple streams and channels providing fresh water to every part of the Old City (figure 2). The size and shape of housing parcels have been adapted to take advantage of this natural water source.

Lijiang also developed a unique style of housing in response to local conditions and traditions. Since the city has always been prone to earthquakes, the buildings' wooden frames are built to be flexible, and the upright timbers are canted slightly inward to increase stability. Special attention is paid to the architectural detail of homes, especially to gateway arches, doors, windows, balconies, and roof beams. Most wooden elements (beams, pillars, railings, and eaves) are elaborately carved with representations of lions, musical instruments, flowers, birds, fish, and

Figure 2. Many of the Old City's 354 bridges are local gathering places, Lijiang, China.

vignettes from folktales. Courtyards are paved with colored stones depicting the same images in mosaic patterns.

Lijiang County is known for its vibrant, living culture. The area is home to 10 national minority groups. The Naxi are the most numerous, accounting for just over half of the county's population. The Naxi have kept their traditional way of life, and ethnic dress is widely worn in the area. Most Naxi subscribe to an eclectic mixture of Buddhist, Taoist, and indigenous animist beliefs known as Dongba. Dongba rituals and beliefs are recorded in an ancient pictographic language that is still read and translated by Dongba priests. Naxi music dates back to the Han Dynasty (207 B. C.-220 A. D.). Even though this music is forgotten in the rest of China, it is still played in Lijiang. Using ancient instruments, local music societies play for their own enjoyment as well as for tourists.

Earthquake Damage and Response

The 1996 earthquake caused significant damage to the Old City's historic buildings, bridges, paving, and infrastructure. However, most catastrophic was the destruction of numerous homes. Residents' low income levels and dislocation made rebuilding a daunting task. To aid in the rehousing, the World Bank worked with the Lijiang County Construction Bureau to support grants for home repair and provide guidelines on reconstruction techniques.

In many cases the traditional construction technique of loosely attaching walls to timber frames allowed the frames to shake without collapsing. However, even though the frames stood, the mud brick walls often collapsed, resulting in some injuries and deaths. Consequently, the reconstruction program emphasized more earthquake-resilient materials and techniques.

Within a few weeks of the earthquake the County Construction Bureau issued the "Design and Construction Technical Requirements for Houses in Lijiang Prefecture." This set of guidelines explained the reinforcing techniques and materials that should be used to make housing safer during future earthquakes. The recommendations included using vertical and horizontal reinforcement poles and netting in walls, and fired, hollow-cement brick instead of sun-dried mud brick. In support of the existing regulations on historic preservation residents were also warned against using nontraditional materials or visibly contemporary building techniques.

To initiate the housing repair grant program a village committee appraised the damage on each house and placed homeowners in one of three grant categories. Depending on the degree of damage, homeowners received grants of US$95, US$120, or US$300 to purchase of materials. In addition to the grant program residents relied on mutual self-help groups. Families organized themselves to focus on completing the repair of one house and then moved on to focus on another. Construction

Box 1. Housing repair grants and earthquake-resistant construction

Ms. Li received US$300 from the housing repair grant program, Lijiang, China.

Ms. Li reported that she was visiting friends in another village when the earthquake struck, and that she immediately prayed to the gods that no one in her house was injured. When she returned home, she was grateful to find her family unharmed, but her 100-year-old house was badly damaged. All the interior walls needed to be rebuilt, the roof was leaking, and the timber columns were out of alignment.

Pooling her $300 repair grant with those of the three other families living in her courtyard house complex, she bought the materials for repairs. Because of the high demand for construction materials, supplies were scarce and prices had gone up 30 to 50 percent. Even so, she and her neighbors were able to rebuild and comply with reconstruction recommendations by using fired, hollow-cement brick for the walls.

Bureau staff report that often the amount of private money put into housing reconstruction was 5 to 10 times the amount of the grants.

Upgrading in the Context of Historic Cities

It is important to note that the World Bank's earthquake reconstruction programs are designed to restore facilities only to the level existing prior to the earthquake. In the case of historic cities it is often difficult to strike a sensible balance between replacement and improvement, particularly when existing facilities are outdated or inadequate. Whatever the degree of upgrading, however, two overriding principles in this work are that (1) urban development should not result in the loss of significant historic assets; and (2) infrastructure work should be designed to be compatible with the local architectural scale, form, and materials and the existing social fabric.

Homes and infrastructure in the Old City are severely substandard in comparison with what is found in the adjacent, newer parts of Lijiang (figure 3). Since China is projecting increasing incomes and a rising standard of living over the next 20 to 30 years, it is especially important that the Old City be upgraded to keep pace with residents rising expectations. The Earthquake Reconstruction Program identified a clear need to develop activities and guidelines to improve housing and upgrade infrastructure while preserving the World Heritage quality of the city's historic buildings.

There are several possible scenarios for an historic urban area with substandard conditions when its population has the opportunity for a higher standard of living. First, as incomes rise, ad hoc improvements made without clear conservation guidelines could destroy Lijiang's chief cultural asset, its uniformly historic cityscape. Second, wealthy residents could move to more modern areas of the town, leaving the Old City with a population financially incapable of maintaining the historic properties. Third, if tourism increases (as planned by Chinese authorities), a substantial amount of housing could be converted into businesses, stripping the area of its residential and social character.

These are classic patterns of decay in historic urban environments all over the world. Clearly, the ideal in Old Lijiang will be to facilitate the current population's ability to remain in place while encouraging upgrading that maintains the historic urban environment. A design study to develop appropriate and cost-effective means of upgrading housing while maintaining the historic quality of the interior and exterior design would address:

- Safe and aesthetic installation of basic services such as electricity and sanitation
- Construction and material improvements to provide thermal insulation and increase wind- and waterproofing
- Adjustments to the traditional layout of rooms to incorporate modern lifestyles.

Improvements to Lijiang's urban infrastructure also are needed to ensure the sustainability of the Old City as a safe and healthy place to live. To maintain the city's historic quality and atmosphere, unobtrusive routing and coordination of these services is critical. Carefully considered design guidelines are, therefore, extremely important for this work. They should include:

- Design solutions for the installation of street lighting, telephone lines, and water and drainage services compatible with historic streetscapes
- High-quality materials and installation techniques to minimize the need for maintenance disruptions.

Box 2. Increasing average age of the historic city's residents

Yang Jing Hua and his wife, Lijiang, China.

Yang Jing Hua's family has lived in the same house in Lijiang for 200 years. Most of the younger generation has moved to modern apartments in the new part of the city, but they like the old ways and the atmosphere in the Old City. They use wood and charcoal for cooking and heating.

Many older couples like the Yangs care for their grandchildren in the Old City while their married children live and work in new Lijiang. Young couples say they need the time to focus on work and like the idea that their children are being raised in a traditional environment.

Even though many families in Lijiang still value the traditional lifestyle of the Old City, urban planners know that the present trend of outward migration of the young is a dangerous sign that predicts a downward slide in income levels and ability to maintain housing.

An additional challenge, common to many historic cities, is Lijiang's extremely dense city plan and narrow streets, which lack adequate access for fire fighting and other service vehicles. Specialized small-scale, non-polluting service vehicles for emergencies and services such as solid waste collection need to be located or developed to address this problem.

Tourism Development

In addition to its population's rising expectations for an improved standard of living, the Old City faces another challenge: the Chinese government's plans to focus on tourism in the Lijiang area. In 1998 1.53 million

Figure 3. Much of the housing in the
Old City lacks sanitation facilities and
electricity, Lijiang, China.

tourists visited Lijiang Prefecture and generated US$11.36 million in
tourism-related income. As is true world-wide, these numbers are
increasing every year. Tourism holds great promise for positive outcomes
in Lijiang. It can diversify and generate economic development, create
jobs, supply the funds necessary to maintain historic sites and promote
cultural understanding.

However, tourism also brings the possibility of negative economic and physical impacts on heritage assets and the host community. Possible negative
impacts include destruction of inadequately managed historic or natural
environments, congestion, pollution, and over-use of community facilities.

Lijiang's most unique and valuable asset is its traditional ethnic community.
The latter is also the most vulnerable to the negative impacts of tourism. As
has happened elsewhere, residents of Lijiang could become hostile toward
tourism if they are continuously confronted with visitors who have dissimilar lifestyles and higher incomes, or if their culture is not respected by visitors. The continuous presence of such outside influences may cause long-
held social values to erode and age-old cultural practices to be discarded.

The choice that must be made between economic development through
tourism and maintaining a community's way of life is sometimes extremely
difficult. One answer lies in the fact that the size and diversity of the tourism

market means that there are many different options in the type and scale of tourism development communities can pursue. Communities may choose to develop mass market tourism that is served by large hotels and provides many service sector jobs. In contrast, communities can choose "study group" tourism, which brings limited numbers of visitors who stay in locally owned and operated bed-and-breakfasts. A third alternative is the development of eco-tourism or adventure tourism, in which visitors "rough it," sleeping in tents and requiring little in the way of infrastructure or services.

To enable Lijiang residents to plan for tourism development and effectively manage the changes it brings, several basic principles should be considered.

Community Control

Community residents must be involved in creating comprehensive tourism development plans. Ideally, communities will be in control of identifying the heritage assets, setting objectives, designing development strategies, implementing strategies, and evaluating success.

Informed Choice

Communities should have full information on the likely consequences of their tourism development choices. For instance, planners should help communities think through the differences between large hotels owned by outsiders versus small, locally owned bed-and-breakfast development.

Impact and Feasibility Studies

The potential for positive benefits, as well as negative consequences on the local population, heritage, and environment must be carefully considered through impact assessments. Rather than basing expectations for revenues on assumptions, feasibility studies that use tourism industry expertise should be done to evaluate the real potential of the tourism market.

Community Benefits

Development must be planned so that all residents have equal access to the benefits of tourism. Training and loans for local residents are one way to ensure that tourist hotels, restaurants, and shops are developed and controlled at the local level. Using tourism profits for community services such as health centers or literacy classes is another way to distribute the benefits of tourism.

Authentic and Sustainable Development

Heritage resources must be developed according to internationally acceptable criteria and standards of authenticity. The tourist experience should be authentic, reflecting the area's true culture rather than false or artificial images. The development must be sustainable, that is, have adequate planning and funds for quality operation and maintenance over time.

Respectful and Educational Programming

Engaging educational programs and interpretation should be presented to assist visitors in understanding the heritage, culture, history, religion, and way of life in the local area. Visitors also should be given guidance on local taboos and cultural attitudes.

Regional and National Planning

Tourism development must be grounded in the realities of regional and national policies, priorities, and resources. For instance, even isolated sites are subject to the impact of national decisions on infrastructure development. New roads and services can encourage increased numbers of visits to historic sites but also create the opportunity for other development that results in pollution and overuse.

The residents of Lijiang deserve respectful tourism that brings benefits to their community. The most effective way to ensure this is to facilitate their informed participation in the process of planning and developing the tourism. Because much of the value of the tourism experience in Lijiang lies in the culture and lifestyles of local residents, successful tourism development will depend on avoiding negative impacts on their way of life (figure 4).

Historic Site Conservation: Mu Fu Complex

One of the major tourism sites in Lijiang's Old City is the Mu Fu Complex. In 1382 a local ruling family by the name of Mu began building its administrative compound in the Lijiang area. For the next 340 years each successive Mu leader enlarged and embellished the 22,000-square-meter administrative center. The rectilinear site included administrative, ceremonial, religious, business, entertainment, and domestic structures that progressed up the side of Shizi Mountain, culminating in an elaborate temple at the top.

In 1723, the local family was replaced by an imperial appointee, and the compound began a gradual deterioration. Many buildings were destroyed or damaged by earthquakes and fire. After the formation of the People's Republic of China in 1949 some contemporary buildings were added to the site, and some existing buildings were converted to government offices. The 1996 earthquake caused additional damage, prompting local officials to use some of the earthquake reconstruction loan to restore the complex and develop it as a tourist destination.

In 1996 the Mu complex was a large and important, but heavily damaged, site. The World Bank's advice on conservation of the Mu Fu emphasized the value of complete and reliable evidence for the work to be undertaken. Because the city was seeking UNESCO World Heritage designation for the Mu Fu complex, high standards for authenticity were especially important.

Figure 4. Lijiang County is home to more than 10 national minority groups.

Correct and authentic conservation was also crucial to ensure that the site could be meaningfully presented to the public.

Architects and archaeologists from eminent research and design institutes in China were brought in to work on the site discovery and design. These professionals ascertained as much information as possible on the compound's site plan, construction techniques, architectural details, and decoration before any demolition or adaptation work was begun. Over a year Mu Fu conservationists used multiple methods for gathering information including:

- Measured surveys of existing buildings and site layout
- Detailed investigations using photography, archaeology, and ground-level examination
- Interviews with Mu family descendants
- Research of historical records including examination of photographic collections, municipal surveys, newspaper articles, family papers, and other public and private archives.

Conservation architects first focused on determining the appropriate "restoration date" for different parts of the complex. Conservation was complicated by the site's age, its degree of deterioration, and the fact that much historic material had been scattered around the complex and built into later structures. Thus, different amounts of information were available concerning each building, making different parts of the site restorable to different dates.

The total budget for conservation of the Mu Fu site was $4 million, with $2.7 million funded by the World Bank loan and $1.4 million funded by a matching grant from the national government. The cost of materials accounted for 60 percent—the largest portion—of the budget (figure 5).

Labor accounted for another 20 percent. Huang Naizhen, director of the Lijiang County Cultural Bureau, managed this large project and reports that he coordinated a work force of 2,800 people, most of whom were local area residents. Of these, 2,200 worked off-site in rock quarries, forests, and factories. Six hundred worked on-site doing everything from wood and stone carving to site preparation and construction. This large number of workers was employed to meet the World Bank's emergency loan requirements for swift project completion.

Plans for the adaptive reuse of the Mu Fu historic buildings are not yet completed. However, new uses for two buildings have been determined. The building once known as Ten Thousand Volumes is to be a library again. Its first floor will be a reception area, and the second floor will house the original collection. The third floor will be set aside for reading and study. The pavilion, once used for formal ceremonial occasions, will be used to present Naxi traditional music. Another building will be furnished with Ming Dynasty period furniture and hung with the Mu prefects' portraits and family trees to present Mu family history to the public.

Figure 5. The Mu Fu site during reconstruction, Lijiang, China.

The World Bank advisors recommended that each building in the complex be given an active use to ensure its maintenance and sustainability. It is of critical importance that the local community be involved in determining these new uses. Historic buildings that perform a useful function and are of value to the community are much more likely to receive proper care and maintenance. Considerations in determining new uses include opportunities for public education, employment, commerce, provision of public services, and the market for tourism.

Conclusion

Today the Old City of Lijiang appears to have substantially recovered from the earthquake. Schools, hospitals, clinics, and factories are functioning again. Chinese officials and the Lijiang community can take enormous pride in what has been accomplished. However, the clear need for further development in Lijiang has identified the importance of future work that combines multiple sectors including community education and development, heritage protection, tourism planning, urban upgrading, and institutional capacity building.

Notwithstanding the project's effective work to conserve the original Old City of Lijiang, there is a need to acknowledge that there is a certain inevitability to future cultural change. Hopefully, the transformations that will occur due to rising standards of living and increased pressures from tourism, among other influences, will recognize the importance of preserving traditions, as well as allowing for change by encouraging tolerance for cultural experimentation and creative adaptation.

Appendix. Lessons Learned: Post-Earthquake Reconstruction and Urban Heritage Conservation

Administrative Management and Coordination

- Heritage conservation requires the effective coordination of government departments that often do not cooperate with one another, such as the Department of Public Utilities, Department of Finance, the Construction Bureau, and the Culture Bureau. Strong leadership and the time required for this coordination must be built into project planning.
- For a consistent and effective strategy to be implemented, all departments and bureaus with responsibilities in historic areas must be made aware of the value of heritage preservation and the importance of adhering to international conservation standards.

Public Involvement

- Local communities should be involved in establishing the goals, strategies, and policies for the identification, conservation, management, and presentation of their heritage resources, cultural practices, and contemporary cultural expressions.
- To preserve and cultivate the public's appreciation of these assets, continued outreach in the form of information and interpretation of the significance and value of local heritage is important.

Upgrading in Historic Cities

- Rebuilding traditional homes without updating basic services such as sanitation and electricity has negative consequences for older neighborhoods in the long term, possibly causing them to be abandoned for newer housing.
- Adding basic services to traditional buildings requires inventive design solutions to avoid unrealistic costs and damage to the historic nature of these structures.
- Historic buildings must accommodate active uses if they are to be maintained. Buildings can be used for education, employment, commerce, public services, or tourism, depending on where the greatest potential for community benefits and heritage conservation lies.
- Infrastructure such as roads, drainage, and power lines in historic cities inevitably needs upgrading if these cities are to continue to offer efficient environments for safe and healthy living, commerce, and tourism. Upgrading must use materials and techniques that are compatible with historic streetscapes.

Historic Site Planning and Management

- Protection of heritage sites for their continued value and use is the ultimate site management goal. A site's physical carrying capacity (number and type of visits that can be sustained without damage) should be determined. Operation and management systems should then be designed to maintain the site at its optimal use level.

- Financial planning should be based on expected income from entrance fees and other related enterprises, as well as subsidies. Long- term operation and maintenance plans based on realistic figures should then be planned.
- All planning for site development and management must be done with an understanding of regional and national policies and priorities. Planned and potential investments in infrastructure, such as roads and airports, are especially important to consider.
- Sites that offer the most educational value to local communities and tourists are based on careful research, authentic development, and engaging presentation. These steps often are ignored in development, much to the detriment of the sites' success.

Tourism Development

- Tourism is likely to be a strong force in most historic cities. It needs to be directed and controlled so that its economic benefits are captured at the local level to preserve the heritage asset and benefit the community equitably.
- When planning for cultural tourism, a multidisciplinary approach is necessary to determine site carrying capacity, project the costs for operation and maintenance, set fees, interpret heritage for visitors, and develop related services. This multidisciplinary approach should particularly involve the Culture and Tourism Bureaus.
- The potential for tourism's positive benefits, as well as its negative consequences on the local population, heritage, and environment must be carefully considered through impact assessments.
- In many historic settings the most unique and valuable heritage asset is the living culture. However, this feature is also the most vulnerable to the negative consequences of tourism development. During tourism planning communities should be enabled to make fully informed choices on the type and level of tourism development in their areas.
- Social carrying capacity for tourism, or the ability of communities to maintain their desired way of life in the face of tourist visits, must govern the extent of tourism development.
- Plans for tourism development at the local level should be evaluated by representatives of the tourism industry for their real potential to attract sufficient visits and spending to justify investments.

World Bank Involvement

- Local project staff need expertise and support from the World Bank in the areas of heritage conservation and management, especially in planning for adaptive reuse of historic buildings, tourism development that maximizes community benefits, and urban upgrading that is compatible with historic areas. ∎

Adaptive Reuse of Mexico's Historic Architecture: Tampico and Tlacoltapan

15

Alfonso Govela

Alfonso Govela is principal partner in Alfonso Govela Arquitectos, Mexico D.F., alfonsogovela@mexis.com

A first basic concept vital in our work in urban historic heritage is that we are not dealing with archeology but with *living cities*. We are intervening not in the preservation of something that is dead and unrelated to us but in a city that is alive and changing.[1] An ironic French intellectual once said that politics is the art of keeping people away from what really concerns them. Our team of architects working on cultural heritage projects takes the opposite view when we intervene in living cities: we encourage as much citizen participation as possible.

Second, an architectural and urban intervention in a living city is directly related to the professional *preconceptions* that we have of heritage, history, and conservation. Thus, addressing our preconceptions is as important as preserving or modifying the physical artifacts or the intangible aspects of culture. We have an important responsibility to permanently question, support, and modify the ways citizens and professionals think about heritage.

The third basic concept is that preservation theory and practice is a relatively *new field*. It has evolved considerably over the past 50 years. Wim Denslagen links the issue of preservation to the distribution of prints and drawings, reminding us of the Society of Antiquarians debate for the restoration of Salisbury Cathedral at the end of the eighteenth century.[2] Until then people had little opportunity to compare any transformation of a historic monument. Since then, some theorists have turned the tables and transformed the monument itself into a living document. Over the last half-century the views and objectives of preservation have changed from isolated objects, or buildings, to central areas of a city, to the broad notion of a whole territory, encompassing different simultaneous moments of history and geography.

Thus, the role of heritage has evolved from a cultural to an economic asset, to become, especially in Europe, an indispensable component in citizens' quality of life. Regardless of ideology, class, or politics, three issues now are accepted throughout the world: *ecology, collective memory,* and *quality of life.* Because these issues cut across whole sections of the population, they have become extremely important to local and global politics.

In what do we intervene? In some countries interventions have been only to conserve facades. This is the easiest to do and should be avoided. We should not restore or preserve only facades; neither should we preserve only whole buildings, which is better than facades only; neither should we intervene only in cities, which is better than in buildings alone. What we should do is promote quality of life and community development.

How do we do this? Some development agencies now are involved in financing.[3] Economists talk about externalities—the impacts that individual actions have on others—but rarely in an urban or cultural context. International development economists are beginning to speak of externalities in the context of the economics of cultural heritage. Fortunately, the concept and the method of calculating cultural impacts as externalities of investment in a country are beginning to be applied to cultural heritage.[4] Architects and urban planners should learn more about economics and demonstrate politically that investment in heritage can be economically and financially sound.

Finally, for whom do we intervene? Citizens have a right to a cultural identity as much as they have a right to health, sanitation, potable water, sewerage, and all the other infrastructure that local, national, and international economic development agencies have promoted and financed all over the world. We should strive for a balanced mix of funds and participants and avoid gentrification. And we should always fight for the right to cultural identity.

To illustrate my points, I will describe experiences in two cities in Mexico: Tampico and Tlacotalpan. Both are river ports on the Gulf of Mexico, one in the northeastern state of Tamaulipas, the other in the southern part of Veracruz.

Figure 1. Customs House, Tampico: overall view after rehabilitation.

Tampico

Very rarely is conservation realized in a rational, sequential, well-planned manner. Nor did conservation happen that way in Tampico. Most of the time it is better if we proceed haphazardly and unplanned while being very alert to the opportunities that crop up as we do things one at a time.

Tampico would hardly qualify as a World Heritage city. Most of the city was built in the early twentieth century, when most of the world's oil came from there. The big oil fields brought plenty of sudden wealth, which manifested in new construction.

Tampico was founded along two rivers. A beautiful industrial cast iron *Aduana*, or Customs House, was built between them (figure 1). It is still in use by the Secretary of the Treasury. Preservation of historic heritage is not the main objective of the Secretary, but the Treasury operates through more than 1,200 buildings all over Mexico, some of which are of historic importance. We were asked to examine Customs House because we had demonstrated to the officials that it would be cheaper to rehabilitate a historic building than to build anew. That caught their interest.

We went through the orthodox program of documenting the building in detail, and we did something that we like to do: we intervened in a historic context. We added new and modern designs. Interventions should not refrain from constructing new parts in old buildings or new architecture in historic areas. However, the proper way to do this is to find the "warp" of the historic "fabric." That is the basic structure through which one

Figure 2. Customs House, Tampico: *Aduana* corridor interior view after rehabilitation.

"knits" each intervention. Using computers, we carefully studied the origins of each "thread" in the existing forms of the building and discovered its "warp," around which we were able to tie the "knots" of a new "tapestry."

We used this principle to design, for example, a new floor to replace one that had disappeared without a trace (figure 2). We were not afraid to reinterpret principles of construction that we saw in the building. We completely restored the structure. New mechanical, electrical, plumbing, and air conditioning infrastructure was installed, hidden from view. While working on the new design for the building, we discovered many local tradesmen and craftsmen who worked in the shipyards. We used their knowledge to restore the architectural details of the building.

After the building was rehabilitated, an unexpected event happened. Tampico is a traditional venue for spring-break vacations for both Mexican and American students. Spring break or Holy Week in Tampico is not holy there at all, because about 200,000 mostly young people go to watch the two-legged monuments on the beach. However, that year 5,000 young people requested permits to visit the Customs House.

Realizing the importance of tapping a collective memory, the manager of Customs quit his job and ran for mayor. He campaigned on restoring the historic center, although such a center did not exist as such. He won.

To concentrate its regional offices in one area, the Treasury then bought another building, the *Edificio de la Luz* (figure 3), just across from the Customs House and near a central square, *Plaza de la Libertad*.

Figure 3. *Edificio de la Luz,* Tampico: View of original porticoes to *Plaza de la Libertad* after Rehabilitation.

Interestingly, both buildings had been bought through catalogues. The nineteenth century may have had more wisdom in terms of pre-fabrication than we have. One could buy buildings by catalogue from Belgium, England, or France. They came unassembled and were assembled in a couple of months. In the United States 100,000 houses were sold by mail order from 1908 to 1940 by Sears, Roebuck, and Company.[5]

We were asked to assist with the second building. We followed the same preservation approach. We searched for the geometry, or "warp" of the building, restored its structure, and introduced new design elements.

After completion of the work, people became aware of the few remaining porticoes and balconies in the downtown square. To some they looked similar to ones in New Orleans, and they were correct. In the nineteenth and early twentieth centuries, commercial agents sold the same add-on architecture all around the Gulf. Many components of historic buildings are not original, and as citizens became very interested in the history of their buildings, authenticity even became a public issue.

In a wise decision to concentrate his efforts, the new mayor decided to work in and around that square. To draw in community participation, it is essential to create a *critical mass of projects.* By that time we could have prepared a complete design for the square and all of its surroundings. However, as professionals we decided not to. *City form is much richer as a collection of successive actions by different people.* Aesthetic coherence probably would have been more appeal to architects, but it would have produced a less vital result.

Figure 4. *Plaza de la Libertad*, Tampico: buildings after rehabilitation.

What did we do for the square? In New York I found a facsimile of one of the original catalogues used by the nineteenth-century.[6] Therefore, we advised the municipality on structural stability and lent the catalogue to the owners, enabling them to rehabilitate their buildings around the *plaza* any way they wanted (figure 4).

Another public space between the *Aduana* and the *Edificio* was transformed. We built a garage underground and a seafood market on top. This building was designed using the prototype of the Customs House. However, the municipality was so invested in publicity and speed that political deadlines destroyed the original project design.

On the one had it is an example of architecture going terribly wrong. On the other it demonstrates an urban participation success. When interventions in historic areas are done correctly, people become deeply interested. In terms of collective memory, when we hit a community nerve, the people move much faster than an architecture firm can respond.

The lesson of Tampico is that the whole process was not planned at all. We started with only one building. Because that building happened to be linked to identity of the whole town, when our design corresponded with, and even exceeded expectations of the community, their reaction was immediate. Politicians immediately became involved. They became very good lobbyists to raise funds from different sources. Some funds were

Figure 5. Municipal Market, Tlacotalpan: aerial view after rehabilitation.

provided by the Secretary of Social Development. Financial agencies for business development were convinced to promote housing. A trust was founded with a revolving fund. Once this started to operate, everything moved very fast. Tampico has a new pride and cultural identity, as well as more tourism and development.

Tlacotalpan

Tlacotalpan is a smaller but more beautiful town. UNESCO recently declared Tlacotalpan a World Heritage city. It is like a tropical Bologna, with columns and arcades in every street.

The Spanish Agency for International Cooperation (AECI) funded the restoration of the market as a key building for the community. The agency asked us to do that project as well as others to rescue the riverfront for public use. The riverfront was overrun with small restaurant shacks. We carried out the restoration according to all the orthodox rules of preservation (figure 5). By finding historic photographs, we did a precise restoration, keeping the original geometry of the structure but adding new structural design according to new building code requirements for earthquakes and hurricanes (figure 6). Along the riverfront we designed a project for a community arcade, a site for public walks and events, as well as an ordered and dignified location for the original restaurants.

Figure 6. Municipal Market, Tlacotalpan: wood structure after reconstruction.

The lesson of Tlacotalpan is that every action has become more difficult as a result of its being in the international limelight. While in Tampico we had only municipal interventions, we were able to move faster and motivate the community. In Tlacotalpan both federal and state authorities have to approve what the municipality or anyone else proposes. It is a town one-twentieth the size of Tampico with numerous new, lengthy processes for historic building permits. It lacks a group of trained administrators and has no way to expedite a productive dialogue among the community members and all of the institutions now involved in the area.

To conclude, I would advise others to be alert to opportunities and not to try to plan everything in advance in a totally rational manner. If we accept a scenario that may be haphazard, unplanned, and totally lacking in order but stay focused on what we can and want to do, we just may touch that nerve of the community. When it is touched, the full community will respond and do exactly what we professionals would love them to do, even though it may be different aesthetically from what we have been trained to design. ■

Notes

1   See I. Serageldin, "Very Special Places: The Architecture and Economics of Intervening in Historic Cities," Culture Unit, Social Development Department, World Bank, Washington, D.C, 1999. Also in this regard URB-AL is a new program created by the European Union to provide grants to subsidize the development of urban and preservation projects. The program involves cities in the European Union and Latin America. It aims to create networks of cities that share similar problems and interests and enable them to exchange useful experiences. Their web site is http://www.urb-al.com

2   W. Denslagen, *Architectural Restoration in Western Europe: Controversy and Continuity*, Amsterdam: Architectura and Natura Press, 1994.

3   See chapters by Rojas; Armaly, Pagiola, and Bertaud; and I. Serageldin in this volume.

4   S. Pagiola, "Economic Analysis of Investments in Cultural Heritage: Insights from Environmental Economics," Environment Department, World Bank, Washington, D.C., 1996.

5   K. C. Stevenson and H. W. Jandl, "Houses by Mail: A Guide to Houses from Sears, Roebuck and Company," National Trust for Historic Preservation, The Preservation Press, Washington, D.C., 1986.

6   W. MacFarlane, "Illustrated Catalogue of MacFarlane's Castings," Glasgow, Scotland, 1882. Copyright Historical Arts and Castings, Inc., Salt Lake City, Utah, 1992. In addition Professor Gomes Da Silva has written a beautiful book about iron architecture in Brazil. Geraldo Gomes Da Silva, *Arquitetura do Ferro no Brasil*, São Paulo: Livraria Nobel S.A., 1985.

16 First Synagogue in the Americas: Kahal Kadosh Zur Israel Synagogue in Recife

Carlos Alberto Vieira

Carlos Alberto Vieira is president of the Banco Safra of Brazil and serves as a consultant to the ITT Group and Ford, Brazil.

At the end of the first half of the seventeenth century, some Portuguese and Spanish Jews expelled from Spain and Portugal immigrated to the Netherlands to escape from Inquisition courts. The Dutch had occupied the province of Pernambuco in northeast Brazil, led by Prince Mauricio de Nassau (figure 1). Thus, between 1630 and 1654 many Jews chose the new territory as a refuge. Since its inception, the Dutch occupation of Pernambuco had the support of the Jewish community from the Netherlands, an enemy of Spain, which in 1580 had gained control over Portugal.

The Jews lived in Brazil in peace until the Portuguese took over Recife and gave them three months to leave the country. Once again about 150 families set out to sea aboard 16 ships. Their intention was to return to Holland.

During their many stops en route north, they started new communities. One ship stopped at Belém do Pará in Brazil. Others stayed in the Caribbean Islands and in countries of Central America.

After many months of storms and diseases, one of the ships, the *Valk*, with 23 Jews on board, was taken by Spanish pirates in Jamaica. Later, those Jews were liberated by the crew of the French ship *Saint Catherine*, which was heading to North America. It was by pure luck that eight months later the Jews who had left Recife arrived in New Amsterdam, a small village with approximately 1,500 inhabitants.

The first Jewish community of North America, the Shearit Jewish Congregation, was founded in September 1654 (5415 in the Jewish calendar). Rosh Hashanah was celebrated in the place where New York was founded.

This history represents not only a hiatus characterized by religious tolerance during the imposition of Catholicism but also the origin of Jewish
survival in the New World.

The history of Jewish presence in Brazil goes back to its discovery in
1500. In Pedro Alvares Cabral's expedition, the commander of the supply
ship, Gaspar de Lemos, was Jewish. Two years later another Jew,
Fernando de Noronha, introduced the first proposal to colonize the new
territory to the King of Portugal, Don Manuel.

The Portuguese Jews, who had emigrated from the Netherlands, established
themselves in Brazil in the peninsula formed by coral reefs—or *arrecife*—
from which the city got its name (figure 2). Initially, they built houses and
sugar warehouses in the village. They built their homes along the same
street. On that street, which came to be known as Rua dos Judeus, or the
Street of Jews, the first synagogue in Brazil and in the Americas was constructed. At that time the Jewish community had 1,200 members.

In a historical registry of the properties in the city the notary Francisco
Mesquita registers the Jewish owners and refers to houses on the even-
numbered side of the road, of numbers 12 and 14, that "served them as

Figure 1. Portrait of Prince Mauricio
de Nassau, who led the Dutch invasion
of Pernambuco in 1630.

Figure 2. An eighteenth-century map of
northeast Brazil indicating early settlements of Recife and Olinda, Pernambuco.

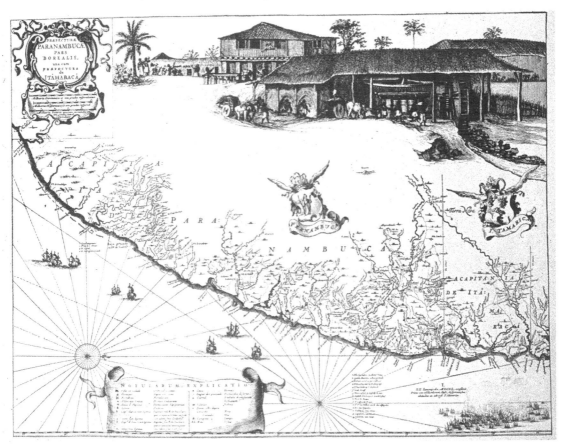

Figure 3. View of the former Kahal Kadosh Zur Israel Synagogue in Recife, built 1640-1641.

a synagogue made of stone and whitewash with two stores underneath."[1] It was named Kahal Kadosh Zur Israel, meaning the "Sacred Community, Rock of Israel." Its construction began in 1640 and was concluded in the following year (figure 3).

After the Dutch were expelled from the village, the houses on Jewish Street were donated to various Portuguese-Brazilian inhabitants. The houses that served as the synagogue were donated to João Fernandes Vieira. In 1679 he donated them to a congregation of Catholic priests. After that they belonged to the Holy House of Mercy. The synagogue, which was identified after research coordinated by historian José Antônio Gonçalves de Mello, has been expropriated and will be registered in the National Monuments listing by Brazil's National Institute for Historic and Artistic Heritage (IPHAN).

At the beginning of the twentieth century the modernization of the historic center of Recife, the port, and its access routes destroyed large parts of the sixteenth-century houses. Maybe not by pure chance, the old Street of Jews, by then called Good Jesus Street, escaped demolition (figure 4). Although they were modernized, the houses still preserve intact their internal walls, constructed more than 350 years ago.

The fact that the Jews in Recife built a street to live on and the first synagogue in the New World justifies all the effort to restore such rich historic references. Not only for Jewish people but also for Brazil and the world, they are symbolic landmarks of survival of a people persecuted for their religious convictions.

The historic restoration of the synagogue's features and its subsequent opening to public visitation are not the only objectives of the cultural project developed by the Association to Restore Jewish Memory in the Americas. The association also plans to create, perhaps on another site,

Figure 4. Street sign on Rua do Bom Jesus indicating its former name of Rua des Judeus (1636-1654).

a repository for archeological research and documents, now scattered throughout the world, that give evidence of the Jewish presence in the colonization of the Americas.

It is not only Banco Safra's foundation Fundação Safra and some financial organizations that are interested in restoring and preserving historic sites of the Jewish tradition. We have the participation of the Ministry of Culture, the City of Recife, IPHAN, and the Jewish Confederation and Federation. We also have the very important participation of the Minister of Culture in Brazil and the federal government, which gives special incentives in terms of income taxes for developing culture and preservation.

One of the amazing archaeological gems discovered in the basement of the two townhouses on Rua dos Judeus—which confirms the existence of a synagogue on the site—is a *mikvah*, a bath in which certain Jewish ritual purifications are performed. A Jewish tribunal has officially recognized the discovery.

Research conducted by archaeologist Marcos Albuquerque of the northeastern university, Universidade Federal de Pernambuco, led to the discovery of the well, practically intact, and the original drains. The *mikvah* in question was filled using pressure from water collected from river wells and channeled to the pool.

Beyond its religious significance, the discovery of the *mikvah* is of the utmost importance for the Jewish community. The findings prove the degree of liberty given to the Jewish community during the Dutch occupation of the province of Pernambuco (1630-1654) and adds to the list of similar mikvah discoveries in Israel (Massada, first century), Germany (Worms, twelfth century), and Spain (Béssalu, fourteenth century).

Other major secular findings were discovered below the two townhouses on Rua dos Judeus (number 197 and 213): eight floors corresponding to the successive land reclamations carried out on the river Beberibe, as well as remnants of an incomplete stone wall that the Dutch had intended to erect to protect the city.

On the first floor of the renovated building a seventeenth-century synagogue will be exhibited for visitors. No religious ceremonies will be held there. The layout will mirror the simplicity of synagogues of the day, consisting only of chairs and the sacred Ark, where the Torah was kept. This stage of the project should be concluded before the year 2000.

The second stage of the project will be marked by the opening of a research and documentation center. Original documents or copies will be brought in from the Netherlands, Portugal, and Spain to form an archive. The objective is to turn Recife, with its already rich religious history and natural attributes, into an international center for cultural information as well as a tourist attraction. Fundação Safra will provide support for the project to restore the Recife synagogue. Under Brazilian Federal Law (*Lei Rouanet*), companies are allowed to invest in cultural projects pre-approved by the Ministry of Culture and receive certain benefits:

- A tax deduction equivalent to 40 percent of the donation, up to 5 percent of income taxes due.
- Companies can calculate the value of the donation or sponsorship as an operating expenditure, reducing taxable income. ■

Note

1   "Inventory of Arms and War Ammunition That the Dutch Left in Pernambuco and in the Constructed or Restored Buildings Listed until 1654."

Part IV

Economic Transition and Urban Heritage Preservation

Editors' Note

Government's role remains essential in the preservation and sustainable use of cultural heritage and historic monuments. Only governments can create the enabling environment for private investment, community action, and individual initiative. In most successful cases over the last decade, national and local authorities made sweeping policy changes to adopt market-driven development strategies to attract long-term investments to historic neighborhoods. Such government intervention is needed to create the public-private partnerships critical to encourage private investment in ways whereby the quality of the public realm as a whole can exceed the sum of its parts.

Michel Bonnette deals with the key strategies for sustainable urban preservation, underlining that successful management of historic cities requires citizen participation in planning and decisionmaking that is fully understood and collectively endorsed. Fundamental decisions on urban conservation are made by local political leaders and are very sensitive to pressure groups. Bonnette suggests that this is part of the process of continuity, a concept that heritage planners and conservationists believe to be a strong basis for good conservation management practices. He suggests that the assessment of the universal value of a World Heritage City or Site is embedded in people's understanding of world history and their identification with it, and their appreciation of the historic and artistic merits of the heritage city. Bonnette proposes a set of working principles for sustainable conservation practice: conservation, valuation, adaptability, continuity, and participation through documentation.

Three chapters assess developments in the historic center of St. Petersburg, Russia. Blair Ruble contrasts St. Petersburg with Leningrad, juxtaposing the imperial capital city with its distinctive baroque city plan and an ensemble of wonderful architecture to the sprawling modern city built during the Soviet period. The subsequent shift in nomenclature from Leningrad back to St. Petersburg poses even greater challenges for those concerned with the preservation of historic and cultural heritage, as well as for those concerned with the fate of the city's residents and its fledgling economy. Victor Polishchuk reflects on the challenges posed by proponents of urban redevelopment and those opposed to new interventions within the boundaries of the historic city. He concludes that conservation should not prevent the emergence of new cultural and architectural expressions in the city. Leonid Limonov describes the process adopted to formulate the Strategic Plan of Development for St. Petersburg, contrasting it with the Soviet planning system. The plan's main objective, he argues, is to foster a favorable business climate that can stimulate economic growth and attract investment. Preservation of the historic center is part of a larger goal of social and economic development.

Rahul Mehrotra examines the dual structure of Bombay, India. Established by the British as a trade center, the unplanned city grew incrementally and impulsively. In the Western section efforts were made to impose a formal structure on growth, with perfectly aligned avenues, restricted building heights, and open public gardens. The Indian section was characterized by chaotic, haphazard growth and overcrowding. This classical dual city structure survived until the 1960s, when the sprawl of the traditional bazaar started to wear down the physical environment of the center districts and public arcades. Mehrotra describes the role of citizens' groups in the preservation of historic buildings, special planning zones, and fate of the bazaars in Bombay's Victorian arcades. He concludes, "The challenge in Bombay is to cope with the city's transforming nature, not by inducing or polarizing its dualism, but by attempting to reconcile the simultaneous opposites, to see them both as valid."

Armaly, Pagiola, and Bertaud use the case of the historic center of Split, Croatia, to research the economics of investing in heritage. Their task was to estimate the benefits from investments in a cultural heritage project and to analyze the project's costs. Contingent valuation surveys were conducted of both tourists and residents to determine their willingness to pay for the improvements to be made by the project. The authors lay out the detailed stream of benefits and costs based on project economic assumptions. To support the project's economic viability study, they also analyze the urban and real estate dynamics. A detailed conceptualization of the model and the preparation of the economic analysis of a project is presented.

Ali Shuaibi examines the impact of 50 years of urbanization and transformations of sacred sites in historic cities of Saudi Arabia. He contrasts the emergence of modernity in a traditional society through the physical changes in Mecca (Makkah Al Mukarramah), Jeddah, and Riyadh, each of which has undergone a different process of transformation of its urban space and modernization of its architecture. He examines the rapid demographic transition, the influx of worshipers to Mecca during the month of Ramadan, and the enormous number of pilgrims who arrive for the Hajj. These present formidable challenges to the preservation of Mecca's sacred heritage and sites.

Saad Eddin Ibrahim addresses the social context, demographic changes, and historical transformations affecting preservation of the historic Cairo. While the population of Greater Cairo tripled in the last century to exceed 10 million people, the city proper grew from two square miles to only six square miles in the nineteenth century with the adoption of European-style urban design. The last 50 years have been characterized by a veritable explosion in both population and surface area, with the expansion and transitions largely determined by internal movements of wealthy and middle-class families into sprawling new neighborhoods, while the low-income workers or "underclass" remain in the historic center. The latter are 40 percent of the urban population. The influences of radical fundamentalism are a serious threat to both the physical and the social fabric of the city. Ibrahim concludes that to attempt historic preservation without understanding the social fabric and involving the people leads to eventual failure. Social inclusion is the key to successful urban development and conservation.

Strategies for Sustainable Urban Preservation

17

Two of the most complex but fundamental tasks in managing historic cities are finding the right approach to urban conservation and ensuring that all the actors involved in the planning and decisionmaking understand and support it.

Writing legislation, making expertise available, and designing and implementing programs are but some of the tools historic city managers and heritage planners can use to support their approaches to urban conservation. The real challenge is to define an approach and have all the actors, from top city officials to local citizens, agree to it and comply with it when they intervene in the city's urban heritage.

This involvement of all actors has proven to be an ongoing exercise, as new people and new trends impact on decisionmaking and change the setting of policies and priorities sometimes faster than one can react to. I remind myself to never underestimate a political leader's capacity to decide against the obvious, and that nothing is more fragile and weak than his or her "strong beliefs." Fundamental decisions on urban conservation are made by local political leaders who are very sensitive to pressure groups and lobbyists. This is part of the game of continuity, a concept we heritage planners and conservationists often refer to as a strong basis for good conservation management practices.

Continuity is a characteristic of the change process to which even historic cities are subject because they are living bodies (figure 1). If we do not agree that historic cities are living bodies and if we do not allow them to change and adapt to new lifestyles and new standards of living, then we sentence them to die, to be disregarded as artifacts of an old age, an exhibit of objects from another era, a museum. Who wants to live in a museum?

The authorities who bear the responsibility for the preservation of historic districts are challenged, and to some extent condemned, to square

Michel Bonnette

Michel Bonnette is an architect and planner, scientific director of the Organization of World Heritage Cities in Quebec, chair of the ICOMOS Historic Towns Committee, and its representative on the ICOMOS International Committee on Historic Towns and Villages (CIVVIH).

Figure 1. St. Petersburg Palace Square, formed by the Winter Palace and the General Staff Building. The uses of this carefully preserved monumental square have evolved. This Sunday basketball tournament organized by the city and sponsored by commercial firms attracts hundreds of athletes and thousands of spectators.

the circle. On the one hand they are asked to preserve the authenticity and integrity of the city's historic fabric and to preserve the structures and events that bear witness to its past. On the other they have to face the pressure of change and allow these objects of memories to be altered and to adapt to better respond to the new needs and realities of contemporary living. To illustrate this dilemma, a Russian friend of mine uses a drawing showing a flying snail.

Imagine the weight of this responsibility on the shoulders of those who are involved in preserving cities listed as World Heritage. This is not just local heritage anymore. It is everyone's common heritage, and our children's and our children's children's heritage, the memory of humankind.

These cities have been listed to be preserved for eternity, and they are now put under the spotlight of the tourism industry. That's good, says one mayor; it creates jobs and brings in new money. With this money we can rehabilitate our heritage. If this scenario works well and brings in a lot of money, then perhaps we can do a little more and make our heritage look even better than it has ever been, beautify it. We can fill in some empty lots with new old buildings or rebuild lost buildings that have disappeared because people at the time, quite unfortunately, did not have our knowledge and our deep understanding of their importance as part of our city's history, says the mayor. Perhaps some of it was destroyed by war or by earthquake or because the symbolism it carried no longer fit the ideals of certain political regimes.

How long will people believe in the preservation of our old cities if we find out that much of the preservation is fake? What will our 300-, 400-, 500-year-old historic cities look like in 100 years if there are no framework or guidelines to govern what can be done to preserve them while keeping them alive and lively?

These guidelines are the components of a global approach to urban conservation. My focus is those that are fundamental to the practice of conservation in an urban context, more specifically, in historic districts.

In most of the many cities around the world that have been designated as historic cities, very few of the local people understand or even have any knowledge of what this concept means. If one asks them to explain how they perceive the historical value of their town and what exactly that designation refers to, one hears many different and sometimes contradictory answers.

Ask the local citizens' committee for safeguarding the historic district and compare its answers to those from the chamber of commerce or the tourist and convention bureau. For the historian the historical value of a site is linked to its significance and its capacity to sustain a community's memory. But the historian may argue that the archeologist is destroying the historical value of a site when he or she is digging down deep to discover and pull out from the soil all its valuable artifacts.

For the entrepreneur the historic city is a work site, and its value rises if there is a great deal to do, whether demolishing, renovating, or building. For the artist the old city with its narrow and uncomfortable streets and dilapidated buildings is a symbol of life and inspiration, a palette of colors, a place for blues.

Owners of historic houses spend their money making sure the boarding, the windows, and the doors of their houses are in perfect shape and look new. Yet when they travel, they take pictures of houses that look actually old.

Where does this historical value lie? Is there only one or are there many? I once was involved in planning for underground parking on a slope. In the middle of the property a chunk of rock stuck out from the grass. Some neighborhood children came to us asking what would happen to their rock. This was their magical rock they said. This was where they held their secret meetings. This rock was meaningful to them and would be forever a part of their childhood memories.

We were giving this piece of property in the city's historic district an economic value that was destroying someone else's feeling of belonging to a city with deep roots in the past. How many of these memory-loaded objects or places are we architects, engineers, and planners destroying every day?

When we contemplate a World Heritage city, where does its universal value lie? The World Heritage Convention says that to be listed as a World Heritage Site, a historic site needs to show universal value. This means that all World Heritage Sites bear witness to our world's history, that each one of them is significant to all of us in understanding the state of our presence on Earth.

That is obvious with the Pyramids, with Rome and Athens, but what about Bergen, Cuzco, or Quebec City? What do they mean to the world? Managing the preservation of a World Heritage city or of any historic city means preserving its value for the next generations to understand and appreciate. It is therefore the first duty of the people responsible to clearly assess and define these values and to share their views on these fundamental matters with those concerned—the local community first, the actors of the conservation process from top to bottom, and the visitors. Only then is it possible to act from a common vision.

When the heritage planner knows which values are to be preserved—the universal value, the national values, the community values—it is possible to secure a long-term vision of the city's historic district's conservation project. This can be achieved only by someone with a great capacity to understand and integrate all aspects of urban life, including a deep concern for expressing the city's past and using it to build its future.

This exercise can be achieved only by someone who thinks very strategically, is very sensitive to the expression of needs and trends, and has a great capacity for leadership to be able to communicate and win over authorities as well as the community to his or her vision. *Vision means both vertical and horizontal integration.*

By vertical integration I mean integrating the concept of and the concern for heritage conservation at all levels of planning and decisionmaking, from the policymaking and strategic planning to the master planning, from neighborhood planning to site planning, to disaster planning, and into legislation, programs, and project design.

Horizontal integration means infiltrating all sectors of urban activity—from politics to social, cultural, and economic development—with a concern for heritage. For optimal stewardship it is a clear target that heritage preservation should become a fundamental component of governmental policies and programs regarding housing, transportation, commercial and industrial development, environment, tourism, recreation, and leisure, not only with respect to historic districts but for the whole city and the whole country.

If one checks the literature pertaining to urban planning in any one historic city and finds the word "heritage" written everywhere, there is a good chance that the concept is well integrated in the minds of the local people and in the city's decisionmaking process. If not, to achieve the vision, there is a need for a set of guidelines. Many rely on legislation, grants, and some technical support.

Although I do not deny the benefit of those tools, I personally argue in favor of setting some tracks for others to follow. This not only guarantees that the vision will be achieved but also facilitates understanding by others of what the conservation project is about, where it is going, and how it is run.

There are many ways to set up guidelines. From numerous charters and recommendations that have been adopted and printed over the past 30 years, I have retained 4 main ideas or principles that I used during the years I headed the conservation program of the City of Quebec, plus one.

1. *Conservation.* In principle, everything included in a historic district should be preserved as is. Like a puzzle, to understand the whole, the pieces are needed. To understand the evolution and history of the whole, all the pieces should remain in the same state as they were when the whole was designated a historic district.

It should be agreed that the first option for any work to be undertaken on any component of an historic district should favor its conservation. This will lead to some difficult decisionmaking. For example, to what extent should a building be renovated? Should all contemporary additions be saved? Can the asphalt-covered cobblestones of the old streets be re-exposed? Should the telephone and hydro lines be kept hanging from leaning wood poles? Should the 1960 rusted commercial signs be preserved as witnesses of a city's past?

The idea of saving everything carries the obligation to debate what can be done with unstable, unaesthetic, and useless structures, as well as how much preservation and restoration work can be carried out on specific structures to secure their authenticity and integrity.

2. *Valuation.* This brings us back to values. Perhaps what is most significant needs full protection and close surveillance during the restoration process. Perhaps less significant structures can be modified to adapt to new uses and new conditions. Perhaps those with very little significance could be demolished to make space for new buildings or for new open spaces. Age, style, artistic qualities, authenticity, integrity, uniqueness, occupation, and state of conservation are criteria that can help to set the value of a structure or a site and to classify it under a category from which it is then possible to set standards for its protection.

3. *Adaptability.* If the historic city is allowed to change, then its individual components must also be allowed to adapt to fit new contemporary living standards. In most countries the interior of private buildings cannot be subjected to any legislation except what concerns the security or health of the inhabitants. Therefore, owners of historic houses that are not listed as individual monuments are free to do as they wish.

Adaptability is then seen as a positive approach to conservation. It offers historic homeowners the capacity for change, while providing an opportunity for some discussion with the conservation staff to avoid unnecessary and sometimes disastrous work on the historic fabric of the house with consequent loss of value.

4. *Continuity.* In the process of change new structures have to be built to fill in empty lots or to replace dilapidated or unrecoverable buildings, and new landscape designs have to be integrated in the historic fabric of the city. Different attitudes are therefore possible, from imitation to contrast, from indifference to harmony, from pastiche to opposition.

Any new building or new landscape design in any historic district should be clearly contemporary aesthetically as well as technically, but historic districts are no place for architectural acrobatics, unless perhaps the architect is Frank Gehry or Antoni Gaudi. New designs should always fit the unique and very delicate settings of historic cities like a glove fits the hand. Any new building or landscape in a historic district should carry the best of its time, as it is going to remain forever, in principle at least, a testimony to the wisdom and talent of the people of its time. What is expected is honest, aesthetically beautiful, and technically clever design.

5. *Participation through documentation.* Finally, I would like to set as one of the fundamental aspects of a good approach to urban conservation the involvement and participation of the local people in the process. Over the last 30 years the concept of monument has grown from the individual building to the historic district to the cultural landscape. Slowly but surely, we will reach the concept of the ecosystem, in which it will become obvious that the preservation of a site, even a city as a historic city, can occur only if it is possible to preserve its environment and all the activities that have traditionally supported the life of the site. Why preserve the fisherman's town if the river is allowed to go dry or if the industrial plant upstream is allowed to pollute the river and kill the fish?

In this more holistic perspective heritage preservation will need to be tackled not only by governments but by all the people. Heritage preservation is changing to be no longer a government initiative but a community project. For this reason it is so important to support a community with the best information available. Citizens can do only as well as they are knowledgeable.

When they are educated in depth about the history and consequent value of their properties and feel well supported in taking up their stewardship, owners of historic properties can be extraordinarily supportive to heritage planners and restoration architects. Documentation is central to involving individual citizens in any urban conservation initiative.[1]

Note

1 The Organization of World Heritage Cities has developed a computer tool called UrbaVista to integrate, disseminate, and network multimedia databases related to the management of urban historic areas. The UrbaVista network is accessible from the OWHC homepage http://www.ovpm.org/ovpm/english/urbavis.html. The organization also is setting up regional secretariats to better link to its membership, which numbered 150 cities in 63 countries in 1998 with an expected 15 new members each year.

18 St. Petersburg's Pasts Compete for Its Future

Blair A. Ruble

Blair A. Ruble is director of the Kennan Institute for Advanced Russian Studies at the Woodrow Wilson International Center for Scholars, Washington, D.C., kiars@wwic.si.edu

On a white night in June St. Petersburg inspires. The neoclassical facades of Peter the Great and Catherine the Great's talented architects bespeak an age long past. Detached from their Imperial purpose, the grand palaces, churches, ministries, and military headquarters that formed Petersburg's monumental core now appear to be cozy and domestic in comparison to so much that has followed since 1917 (figure 1).

Families and tourists mix, munching ice cream cones; clusters of slightly inebriated youth play out the latest mating rituals; pick-up bands perform; and even a poet or two can be heard to shout. A muted northern light magically transforms St. Petersburg into the cities of its past. To walk along a Petersburg canal in June is to be lost in any century but our own. It is to be lost in a "cultural playground."

Monumental St. Petersburg represents the best of planned European urban space. Walking around the historic city on a white night evening, one can believe all the myths about its being "a window on the West," a city of elegance and humanity, the center of Russian democracy and liberalism (figures 2, 3).

One can easily believe that St. Petersburg is a heroic city, staunchly defending Culture and Civilization. The Petersburg Ballet is the best in the

Figure 1. Palace Square in St. Petersburg, a monumental civic space, is defined by the General Staff Building and the Winter Palace. This print depicts the dedication ceremony of the Alexandre I column in 1836.

Figure 2. A protected historic monument, Smolny Convent was built in the Russian baroque style by Italian architect Francesco Bartolomeo Rastrelli, St. Petersburg, 1748-56.

world, its theaters the best in Russia, its poets the primary interpreters of the Russian soul. One can understand how one of those poets, Nobel laureate Joseph Brodsky, when writing about the use of "Peter" as the city's nickname, would say, "This choice of moniker is a further degree of domestication." "Peter," Brodsky wrote, "suggests a certain foreign-ness and sounds congenial." How could one not think about preserving this beautiful cityscape and about viewing the city as an economic asset?

Yet Peter's fragile northern light distorts as much as it illuminates. Nothing in Petersburg is as it seems. In his 1913 symbolist novel named after the city, Andrei Belyi eloquently captured the unique quality of Petersburg light when he wrote, "The streets of Petersburg possess one indubitable quality—they transform figures of passersby into shadows."

Soviet Period

Petersburg is a city of shadows, and those shadows became ever more real during the Soviet period. The city's population declined from 2.3 million in 1917 to 720,000 in 1920 as a result of the Russian Civil War.

Figure 3. A protected historic monument, the Cathedral of Ascension, or the Savior of the Blood, was built in Russian Nationalist style (Revival) by Russian architect Alfred Parland, St. Petersburg, 1883-1907.

Pre-World War I population and economic levels were not re-attained until well into the 1930s, after Stalin launched his national five-year rapid industrialization plan in 1929. But the city that was coming into being was a very different city than what existed before.

Leningrad exploded in the 1930s as peasants fled a countryside devastated by militarized collectivization. They fled into all Soviet cities, into heavy industrial plants surrounding pre-industrial, pre-Soviet cities. By 1939 Leningrad's population stood at 3.4 million. But more important, the single metropolitan area had been shattered. There was no longer a St. Petersburg. There was no longer one city. Indeed, this metropolis came to embrace two quite distinct realities: that of the historic center and the pre-revolutionary values it embodied and that produced it, which became known in shorthand as "Petersburg"; and that of the new Soviet industrial city, which surrounded the historic city and represented all the values of the Soviet Union and rightly came to be called "Leningrad."

The worlds of Petersburg and Leningrad have stood in opposition to one another ever since. That opposition is seen in cultural, economic, and political wars that remained deeply buried under the screen of authoritarian control until the late 1980s, when they burst forth.

The conflict between Petersburg and Leningrad continues to bubble to the surface. It infuses tension into everyday life in the city. This is the point at which practice, reality on the ground, and philosophy meet. It is a battleground that is much larger than local legislation about historic preservation. It is larger than the city itself.

Yes, we need to talk about specific legislation in specific contexts, but preservation often raises issues that transcend the community and the city, and that involve national and international politics as well. Unless we place legislative acts within such larger political context—both national and in some cases international—the legislation will have no impact whatsoever.

The city's Stalinist growth hardly benefited the traditional Petersburg of myth. City planners moved to abandon the historic city altogether for a more grand, neoclassical Stalinist town center to be built on higher ground south of the Neva delta. One can see portions of the city as one drives in from Pulkovo Airport along Moskovskii Prospect, which was built and was the center of the plan. This boulevard was to replace historic Nevskii Prospect as the city's main street.

Post–World War II

The German blockade during World War II ended these plans. By the late 1940s a tattered Petersburg still stood, broken down and impoverished, yet largely intact. Stalinist hostility turned into more benign neglect. Propaganda points could be scored by a Soviet regime seen as reconstructing buildings destroyed by the Wehrmacht a few years before. A new local leadership could care less about the historic city, as it wanted to build a first-rate center of defense industry.

So Petersburg remained, receding ever more into the background of an increasingly provincial Soviet factory town. Leningrad was emerging as predominant.

A turning point came in the battle between Petersburg and Leningrad during the Leningrad Affairs of 1948 and 1949. There were extensive purges against associates of former Leningrad party chief Andrei Zhdanov, eliminating any remnants of an independent local political elite. The new political team was oriented toward Moscow and toward creating defense industries that could support the Red Army. They bound the city's future to the city's heavy industrial plant and to the city's local scientific research centers, which became ever more oriented toward military innovation.

This was a major change in policy, but it is not to be found in any legislation. This was a transformation that very much affected how the city would develop. But once again, such a shift suggests that legislation, although important, is embedded in a much larger context. The result was a new Soviet city appropriately named "Leningrad," a community that was in opposition to everything that Petersburg had stood for.

Leningrad

Frol Kozlov vigorously advocated this new Leningrad throughout the 1950s, initially as local party boss and later as First Deputy Prime Minister of the Soviet Union. He envisioned a local community focused around a handful of technologically specialized defense industries. The city would serve as an innovator and producer of high-quality industrial goods tied to the defense effort. This economy, of course, now lies in ruins, and has undermined much of the city's prospects for the future.

Yet we should not be overly dismissive of Kozlov's vision. By the mid-1970s Leningrad led the Soviet Union on a per capita basis in the annual economic impact of technologies; the number of new types of machines being created; and the number of new, automated production lines. By the early 1980s nearly 10 percent of all new Soviet production technologies were developed in Leningrad.

This Soviet Leningrad imposed an enormous aesthetic cost. The city attracted tens of thousands of migrants from across the Soviet Union to work in Kozlov's new defense plants and research institutes. By 1951 an average of 3.3 families lived in each Leningrad apartment.

Following the lead of Nikita Khrushchev's new housing program in the late 1950s, city officials addressed the housing problems; and they were innovators. They developed industrialized construction techniques that became the model for the entire socialist world. Looking at any Soviet-era concrete apartment block from Prague to Pyongyang, one will see the footprint of Leningrad across the globe.

Once again, these construction plans were not to be seen in legislation; not in legislation as we understand it. Indeed, again, the practice in Leningrad demonstrates the limits of legislation.

Local planners turned to vacant sites beyond the city's traditional boundaries in the search for land for their new housing projects. Over time, as they developed on new land, the city expanded as a coral reef builds up on itself. The city expanded more than 100-fold from a late nineteenth-century walking town of 105 square kilometers in 1917 to a massive metropolitan agglomeration extending over 1,300 square kilometers by 1980.

People eventually followed housing out of the city center. The percentage of the total population of the city living in traditional central districts declined from over 50 percent in 1959 to less than 20 percent by 1980. This is the city that one speaks of trying to restore. Meanwhile, people were inhabiting these new Khrushchev- and Brezhnev-era Leningrad apartments on the outside of the city (figures 4A, 4B).

Tension between these two distinct urban realities simmered under the surface until Gorbachev and Glasnost came along. Pitched battles erupted between everything that traditional Petersburg represented and everything that new Soviet Leningrad represented. This divide rose to the surface in the mid-1980s and would change the course of local history and perhaps national history as well.

Tensions exploded in 1986 as discussions over the quality of urban life began to dominate local politics. In the summer of 1986 the Leningrad

Figures 4A, 4B. Apartment buildings constructed on Vasilyevsky Island, St. Petersburg, in the 1970s and 1980s during the Brezhnev era.

Division of the Union of Architects, which was a monopolistic professional organization for local architects, held a very stormy Congress at which delegates excoriated local leaders for their past mistakes. Local architects used the forum to decry what had happened to the city and to suggest that the only way the city could be changed and salvaged in the future was through the creation of a higher urban planning culture, which could be rediscovered from the traditional core city.

Not only professional architects were involved in this. Politicians and people on the streets also turned a debate over aesthetics and historic preservation into a discussion of the future of the Soviet Union. In March 1987 scaffolding went up around two of the city's most historic hotels—the Astoria and the neighboring Anglatera. From the bar of the Astoria John Reed had watched the Bolshevik Revolution unfold, and in room number 5 of the Anglatera, poet Sergei Yevsenin had committed suicide, writing a last verse in his own blood.

Immediately following the appearance of construction equipment around these two hotels, the local newspapers began to get phone calls asking what was going on. As it became clear what was happening, hundreds, even thousands, of demonstrators began to show up day and night, shouting "Save our monuments, save the history of our city." Out of these demonstrations emerged a vibrant democratic movement, which would eventually bring down Communist power in Leningrad. The genie was out of the bottle. National, local, and international politics began to coalesce in a potent mix around the issue of historic preservation.

What exactly is the meaning of this city of "St. Petersburg?" What is its meaning for Petersburg, and what is its meaning for Russia as a whole?

Post-Soviet Period

The grassroots movement that emerged out of these battles voted every senior Communist Party leader out of office in 1989, an election which broke the back of Communist domination throughout much of the Soviet Union. Since that time Leningraders and Petersburgers have played an important role in liberal politics and democratic politics throughout Russia. Everywhere else, opposition to the August 1991 Communist coup was really much less than it seemed at the time; not so in Leningrad, where one-third of the city's population crowded into Palace Square in front of the Hermitage Museum. August 1991 was a genuine revolutionary moment in this city—it was Petersburg rebelling against Leningrad—and the subsequent renaming of the city was more than symbolism. It was the reemergence of a metropolitan community that had been driven far underground in the recesses of Soviet reality.

These events took on national and international significance as people who participated in that movement, such as Anatoly Chubais and many other reformers who have become familiar to us, emerged to positions of national power. But again, the issue was really politics. It was politics at a national level, at the local level, at the international level that transcended efforts to enact legislation.

Legislation is important but only if it can be enforced. The city's realities are never quite so simple as they appear on a June evening when everybody is enjoying the "cultural playground" of St. Petersburg. They are never so simple as changing a street name or changing the name of a city, because what has happened over the history I have just described is that Petersburg can no longer exist without Leningrad. Its economic base is too small, its population too limited, its physical plant too much in need of extensive repair.

"Petersburg" cannot rely on its own resources, while the Russian national economy has collapsed. "Leningrad," cannot exist unless it can break out of its Soviet mold. Such issues really are not local; they are national. What better model of a post-Soviet future can there be than the starkly beautiful, if decrepit, imperial city lying in Leningrad's midst?

After the hotly contested 1996 mayoral election in which Vladimir Yakovlev, the deputy mayor at the time, defeated internationally known incumbent Anatoly Sobchak, the city moved toward trying to develop the kind of planning structure that would permit the enactment and enforcement of the kind of legislation we are discussing today.

Bridging the Gap between St. Petersburg and Leningrad

Importantly, the city's custodians began to understand that there could be no Petersburg without Leningrad, and vice versa. A slow but steady bridging of the gap that began in 1917 commenced. Planners tried to develop strategies that would meld two very distinct yet entwined urban realities. Their strategies became most apparent in a new strategic plan for St. Petersburg ratified in 1998. That plan came into existence within the framework of the World Bank-assisted project for the rehabilitation of the historic city center. It is very important for understanding what legislation can and cannot do. It provides the context within which the legislation that will determine the details of historic preservation can take place.

As much of an achievement as the city's new strategic plan may be, problems of politics and economic decline remain. The City Council has been rent by factions that do not relate to historic preservation issues but have immobilized local legislative process. The Russian State is weak and collapsing. The Russian national budget is one one-hundredth of the United States' federal budget. Where is the money to undertake all the plans and dreams that can be put into legislative acts?

Legislation is important but it is also necessary to look at legislation in its political and economic contexts. The city's new strategic plan provides a realistic approach to saving the cityscape, to saving that "cultural playground" that everybody can enjoy on a white evening. It points in the right direction in arguing that, to make these plans reality, there needs to be a comprehensive approach. This approach should bring together the old city and the new city, recognize the value of historic preservation while speaking of the importance of a vital metropolitan economy, and provide the basis for melding public and private interests between the local state and the local business community.

At the end of this very tortuous century for one of the world's great cities, the St. Petersburg model underscores the importance of viewing the preservation of historic cities and sacred places as part and parcel of overall regional development strategies. It may be that Europeans will be working 3 days a week with 5-day salaries, but it is unlikely that anybody in Petersburg will receive 5-day salaries for 3 days of work. Indeed, at the moment many people in St. Petersburg receive 3 days' salary for 6 days' work. This is an important reality that underlies the need to try to save historic and sacred places in these sorts of contexts.

None of these trends is exclusive of another. What the muted northern light of St. Petersburg shows is that the shadows can blend. These various components can come together, and the lessons of twentieth-century St. Petersburg become not necessarily what one might think about as one walks around Palace Square on a June evening. St. Petersburg's fate in this new century is about complexity. It illustrates the importance of the historic and the sacred in today's world, while sounding a cautionary note about the limits of the possible. ■

19

Development and Preservation of the Historic Center of St. Petersburg

S t. Petersburg may not be considered a typical Russian city. After all, it was designed and planned by Italian, French, English, and German architects. However, for more than 200 years it was the capital of the Russian Empire.

St. Petersburg is a large metropolis with an estimated 5 million inhabitants. As in any great world capital the city faces difficult challenges. One of these is to find solutions for its future development. Another is how to reconcile new construction and the preservation of its unique ensemble of historic buildings.

St. Petersburg has universal historical and cultural importance not only because of its extraordinary artistic and architectural treasures but also due to its being symbolically the bridge between East and West. The city was founded in 1703 by Peter the Great as a "window to the West" from a country that had been cut off from Europe for centuries. The "Grandfather of the City" selected a strategic location on the mouth of the Neva River delta and the Bay of Finland to build his new capital. The city was laid out as a system of islands and canals, with the civic center built along the waterfront.

The urban scale was monumental, appropriate to such a vast country. The Palace Square was in the center of the Empire's capital. The General Staff building, an architectural complex that housed the High Command of the Army during the Empire, and the ensemble of buildings on Rossi's Street were designed and built by Carlo Rossi, an Italian architect (figure 1). St. Isaac's Cathedral and the Alexandre I column at the Palace Square were designed and built by Auguste Montferrand, a French architect (figures 2, 3). These are only a few examples of the monumental architectural ensembles of historic, cultural, and aesthetic value in the city. Valued by the international community, they are also inscribed on the World Heritage List. We

Victor E. Polishchuk

Victor E. Polishchuk is an architect, planner, and designer; since 1992, he has worked with the St. Petersburg City Administration Commitee for City Planning and Architecture, root@decb.kga.neva.ru

Figure 1. Architect Rossi Street (formerly Theatre Street), laid out by Italian architect Carlo I. Rossi in 1828. The street has long expanses of identical facades on both sides with exceptional proportions built in the neo-classical style.

in St. Petersburg are very cautious in the ways we balance preservation, rehabilitation, conservation, and future development projects.

When looking for solutions or a compromise, I return to my family's experience. Every city, every country has its public sacred sites. On a personal level I have a revered place in my home: the library and my father's desk. A renowned mathematician, he died more than 20 years ago, but I tried to keep all his books and objects in the same position to keep his memory alive. My son is also a mathematician, and my nephew is a physicist. They use my father's books. When they repeatedly did not place them back on the shelves in the same order, I was disappointed and saddened. Finally, after much struggle, I understood that it is more important that these young students read these books than that they keep them in order. Using the books is more important than keeping some semblance of my father's memory.

All cities have similar challenges. How should they combine development and new construction with adequate preservation of historical monuments? How can they save the historical shapes of the past—open space, natural environments, and architectural ensembles—without closing the paths to new culture and new architectural styles?

St. Petersburg was built as the magnificent capital of the Russian Empire. The Baroque and Classical architectural ensembles shaped the image of the capital city of the Tsars. In the late nineteenth century modern architecture, including Art Nouveau and Jugendstil, was introduced and became the first stage of the intervention of new architecture in St.

Petersburg. On Nevsky Prospect, the main avenue, the buildings had always reflected a variety of styles. Another building boom in the last decade of the nineteenth century grew out of considerable economic progress experienced in the city. The city grew rich and industry developed. Urban plots were sold, and new banks, offices, and apartment buildings were constructed. The advent of the market economy and democratic processes in the 1990s have begun to alter the face of the city. The economic upturn is the basis for a renewal process.

The new stage of democratization and reform in Russia is bringing back the town-planning trends that took place at the beginning of the twentieth century. The sale of real estate, including historic buildings, and land parcels; the construction of rental units; and the new development projects create interventions in the historical environment.

A good example is the proposed design of a Swiss business center on the historical Smolny Embankment. In one neighborhood three distinct epochs are unfolding, and three Italian architects will meet. In 1748-64 Bartolomeo Rastrelli erected the monumental ensemble of the Smolny Monastery. In 1806-08 Giacomo Quarenghi built the Smolny Institute. In 1999 Mario Botta designed an ultra-modern complex for a Swiss business center, which was submitted to the town planning council and received a divided evaluation. Many architects in St. Petersburg interpreted this as a positive step forward, overcoming the excesses of conservatism. Others felt that this project would set a precedent toward "the large projects of St. Petersburg" reminiscent of "the large projects of Paris."

As the twentieth century drew to a close, there were no new investments in St. Petersburg and no building boom. For six years I looked out my office window at a cluster of buildings across the quay of the Fontanka River. Most are decaying. Six severe winters have left their traces even on stone and brick. Some builders had intended to "defreeze" one of the sites with the proposed construction of new offices or perhaps a hotel, but the winter of 1999 was too cold and no construction was to be seen (figure 4). ■

Figure 2. St. Isaac's Cathedral built by French architect Auguste Montferrand between 1818 and 1848 is the largest church in St. Petersburg. Built in neo-classical style, it has a Greek-cross plan, and each of its facades features an immense columned portico of Finnish granite topped by a sculpted pediment. The gilded dome was inspired by Western models.

Figure 3. Arched gate toward the Palace Square with Alexandre I column.

Figure 4. Cluster of buildings of an abandoned reconstruction effort on the embankment of the Fontanka River, St. Petersburg, 1999.

20 Strategic Plan of St. Petersburg

Leonid Limonov

Leonid Limonov is director-coordinator of Research Programmes at the Leontief Centre, International Centre for Social and Economic Research, St. Petersburg, Russia, limonov@leontief.ru

The main challenge of St. Petersburg is to attract more economic activities and development, rather than to protect monuments from excessive development. Russian cities have declined and suffer from lack of public funding. Meanwhile, the Soviet arrangement of ascribing responsibility for the wide range of activities related to the preservation of cultural heritage and monuments to the authority of the State has been exhausted and is no longer viable.

This essay reviews three alternative modalities of private investment in monument preservation. In the first model work is done incidentally by the elite, but this is neither sustainable nor profitable investment. The second model is national policy on heritage preservation with state funding or subsidies for state programs. This model also is not sustainable due to financial uncertainties. The third model is to initiate public-private partnerships and attract private investment in more sustainable, long-term cooperation.

Ironically, St. Petersburg is moving from the second phase to the first, rather than to the third. The main challenge is how to promote public-private partnerships in the current environment, in which state funds have dried up and engaging private investment is essential. The future of St. Petersburg's historical monuments and sites is only part of a much larger problem of the deteriorating living conditions and well being of the residents of the City Center and its visitors.

The City Master Plan, prepared during the Soviet period and based on command and control, clearly became inadequate during the economic transition. To promote market-driven development, the City of St. Petersburg needed a new vision and planning and management instruments. A new Strategic Plan was introduced to achieve greater development effectiveness. First it aims to set up partnerships. Second, the plan defines strategic objectives and programs to set priority actions linked to the public investment program (figure 1).

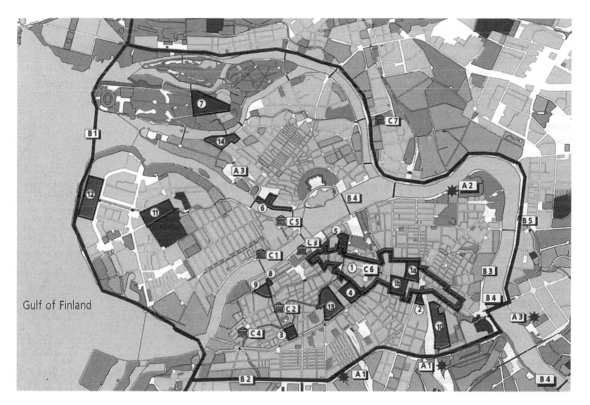

Figure 1. Map of Zones of Urban Development and Reconstruction in the historic center, St. Petersburg, 1997.

The planning process was based on the new principle of involving, to the greatest possible extent, the participation of all stakeholders in working committees. It was developed jointly by the city administration and 250 principal stakeholders, representing a broad spectrum of organizations. A World Bank-assisted project to rehabilitate the historic center helped to generate momentum for a reform-minded group of experts working closely with city officials to prepare the terms of reference for the Strategic Plan for Development of St. Petersburg.

The fundamental differences between the new Strategic Plan and the typical Soviet planning documents are:

1. The Strategic Plan does not contain detailed instructions (assignments) as to who should produce how much of what and for whom. It is a plan of action carefully chosen on the basis of a system of goals adopted by consensus broadly representing the city's community. Each project and measure contained in the plan, whether investment, organizational, legal, or informal, contains indices that make it possible to monitor and evaluate the success of its implementation and its effects.

2. The Strategic Plan is not a long-term planning document. All measures in it demand either immediate or short-term implementation. In this context "strategic" does not refer to the long term but only to importance. The word underscores the fact that the plan is not

Figure 2. Rebuilding the public tram system and preserving historic buildings in the historic center of St. Petersburg, 1999.

all-encompassing but concerns only the strategically most important problems, for which it proposes the most essential actions (figure 2).

3. The Strategic Plan is not a law. From the legal standpoint the Strategic Plan is a contract in which the different branches of power, business circles, public organizations, and others make a commitment to promote jointly realization of strategic projects and other measures. In sum, the Strategic Plan is a contract of public consent, the instrument of an organized community of interests, which includes authorities, business community and city's residents, working through a process of consultations and public hearings with a high degree of transparency.

4. The Strategic Plan identifies a set of priority objectives: cultural and city center revitalization; development of the city, including the seaport, into a transport hub, as a gateway into Europe; economic development through improving the business climate by making regulations and requirements more transparent and facilitating procedures; and public safety, which includes environmental health issues.

In December 1997 the Strategic Plan of St. Petersburg was completed and approved by the General Council, and was officially launched by the city's Legislative Assembly. The main goal of the new strategy is to establish a favorable business climate in St. Petersburg. The plan recognizes that the city's business climate must stimulate economic growth and become the main factor in attracting resources to and investments in St. Petersburg. To transform the business conditions and to make full use of the productive elements of labor, land, and capital, the proposed strategic objectives of the Plan consist of measures aimed at improving:

- Conditions for entrepreneurial activity in a competitive environment
- The local taxation system by lowering tax burden, while collecting more effectively
- Real estate and city planning regulations
- Labor markets and labor relations
- Mobilization of investment funds on the capital markets. ■

21 Bazaars in Victorian Arcades: Conserving Bombay's Colonial Heritage

Rahul Mehrotra

Rahul Mehrotra is the principal of Rahul Mehrotra Associates, architects and urban designers, in Bombay, and founder of the Bombay Collaborative, a conservation architectural practice that consults on historic buildings, rahul@born3.vsnl.net.in

Bombay was not an indigenous Indian city. It was built by the British expressly for trade. Like settlements that are not expected to become large towns, it was not planned. It came into being with every step of its growth being impulsive and incremental. In its form it expressed the idea of the city as a field of human enterprise. The result is that Bombay is many cities—cities within cities that have their own distinct architectural characters. Bombay is a conglomerate of precincts, sacred sites, vernacular architecture, and ethnic neighborhoods.

Structuring the Core

The advantage of this open-ended development was that correction and adaptations could be made to real needs and perceived deficiencies in the physical environment as the city evolved. The most significant such adaptation was made during the late nineteenth and early twentieth centuries when the colonial government reshaped the city through a series of distinct, planned architectural and urban design projects. The old Fort Area of Bombay got particular attention in the renewal process, because besides marking the origin of Bombay as a city, this area had always been the commercial center and is today a symbolic center of the Bombay Metropolitan Region.

The renewal of the Fort Area dates to 1864, when the removal of the fortifications that surrounded the city was finished. Removal of the ramparts symbolized a change of purpose for Bombay, which no longer needed to serve as a land-based defense fort and whose growth as a prosperous trading and manufacturing city had been constrained by the fortifications. Removal also precipitated a strategic plan to restructure the city center

that included widening and improving roads, adding new open spaces, constructing public buildings, and imposing urban design standards.

These renewal efforts projected perhaps the first such urban design gesture in colonial India. At the western edge of the Fort Area, along the Back Bay waterfront, several public buildings were put up on land made vacant by the removal of the fortifications. In fact, the government used every opportunity to use buildings and infrastructure to establish a cohesive urban form that responded to the unprecedented increase in commerce, industry, and political power that Bombay experienced (figure 1).

Figure 1. The High Court and Rajabai Tower, grand public buildings that were built in the neo-Gothic style on land reclaimed by demolition of the fortification.

Dual City

However, simultaneously Bombay was two separate cities—Western and Indian—with parallel residential, commercial, religious, and recreational areas. In these two separate networks of spaces these different worlds existed with minimal conflict. In the Western quarter all efforts were being made to impose a formal structure on the city—reinforcing the axes, controlling building edges and styles, instituting traffic regulations, and encouraging large corporations to open offices (figure 2).

In contrast, the Indian city was characterized by chaotic, haphazard growth and overcrowding. Here, unlike the city center, little control was exercised over the sites being developed for housing or industrial use. Residential, commercial, and religious activity patterns were integrated in a tightly knit urban fabric like a traditional Indian bazaar town (figure 3).

Figure 2. The renovated Fort Area was a transplant of a European model replete with buildings, a bandstand, and a carriage.

Figure 3. A street scene from the native Indian town in Bombay, much like a traditional Indian town. Typical features are the carved awnings and bracket as well as the use of the steps and plinth as a buffer zone between the crowded streets and the private inner realms.

This classical, colonial, dual-city structure survived until the 1960s when the unprecedented scale of distress migration from rural areas to Bombay and other urban centers completely altered the exclusivity of the two domains. The bazaar became an instrument that absorbed migrants, cushioning their entry to the city, and swept across the city—sprawling along transport lines, slopes of hills, underutilized land, undefined pavements, and even the arcades in the Victorian core.

The bazaars blurred beyond recognition the physical segregation of the dual cities. They wove the two worlds together with a system of shopping and recreation spaces that infused their own architectural and visual character wherever they spread. The arcades in particular provided a condition most appropriate for the bazaar. The supporting columns of the arcade gave definition to the amorphous spaces of the bazaar and defined the territory of individual hawkers.

Thus the bazaar—a chaotic marketplace comprised of shops, stalls, and hawkers—can be seen as the symbolic image and metaphor for the physical state of the Indian city. The chaos and apparent disorder of the bazaar is precisely the quality essential for the survival of vending. More importantly, physical proximity of seller and buyer symbolizes positive energy, optimism, and a will to survive outside the official system.

The spread of the bazaar into the Fort Area transformed the intensity and patterns of use there and began to wear down the physical environment

with overlays of an alien imagery and building materials. Today, shrines and stalls abut the splendid Gothic buildings and fill the spaces in their arcades. Overcrowding has altered traffic patterns and made the clarity of the colonial city unrecognizable.

Figure 4. Contemporary view of the Fort Area taken from the Rajabai Tower, 1997. Except for three or four high-rise buildings, the larger urban form and fabric of the Fort Area has remained basically intact.

The physical degradation was accelerated by the imposition in 1942 of the Rent Control Act, which froze rents and gave tenants legal protection. As a result, it became uneconomical for landlords to maintain build ings, which are now subdivided to accommodate the swelling population of the city. Furthermore, the formulation of building regulations such as setbacks and floor-area ratios and their generalization throughout the entire city have resulted in the destruction of the street edge. This has happened in spite of the implicit and explicit rules for building that have been followed in this precinct for the last century (figure 4).

Contemporary Context

Today in the Bombay Metropolitan Region the Fort Area is seen as the city's financial center. This has occurred despite the Bombay Metropolitan Region Development Authority's (BMRDA) aggressive poli- cies to create a polynucleated structure for the region. The state govern- ment's failure to implement this policy of creating "polycentric growth" has accelerated the concentration and importance of the Fort Area as a financial center, with an increasing number of commercial establish- ments opting to be located here. The 1995 BMRDA survey revealed that

100,000 new jobs were created in 23 square kilometers in the southern tip of the city between 1981 and 1991!

Furthermore, with the recent liberalization policies of the government, multinational corporations, especially banks and investment companies, are opting to locate in the Fort Area, usually in historic buildings. The companies acquire and renovate heritage buildings in order to be located in a historic environment, which instantly gives them an identity and a connotation of having been around for a while. Simultaneously, to service the city's global clientele including yuppies and expatriates, art galleries, specialty restaurants, boutiques, and travel agencies are appearing rapidly in the Fort Area.

Meanwhile, with the additional pressure on the southern tip of the city, the infrastructure in the area is being overstressed to the point of collapse—traffic and the physical state of public spaces being the most obvious stressors. Thus, while the Fort Area is becoming a more exciting place to locate in, it is fast deteriorating physically.

In response to this deterioration and the resulting demolition of historic buildings in the 1970s and 1980s, some citizen groups took it upon themselves to list important buildings and petition the government to protect them through legislation. In 1991 the Government of Maharashtra listed approximately 700 buildings, and a draft notification was published. The government list, which recognized and identified primarily individual buildings, did not address safeguarding the physical form of the precinct or the context in which these buildings are situated.

Conservation Legislation

To counter this shortcoming, the Urban Design Research Institute (UDRI) together with the Bombay Environment Action Group (BEAG) lobbied the government and created detailed studies to petition the state government to include area conservation legislation as part of the heritage laws for the city. In 1995 this legislation was accepted—the first in the country in which eight areas were designated and seven additional zones identified for protection, with the Fort Area being the largest (approximately 3.5 square-kilometers).

Interestingly, of 624 buildings in the final list in Bombay, approximately 200 are located in the Fort Area—a third of conservation-worthy buildings in Bombay! Fifty percent of the total number of Grade I buildings and an almost equal proportion of Grade II buildings are in the Fort precinct. In short, the concentration of listed buildings demanded that the Fort Area be treated as a "Heritage Precinct" with a special designation as a Conservation Zone. By protecting the buildings in the Fort, the city administration takes care of approximately half the city's listed stock.

This legislation has been operative for almost four years. Besides the usual grumblings against additional bureaucratic processes, it has drawn virtually no criticism from the builders and landlords. The only criticism, usually voiced informally by citizen groups concerned with heritage and conservation issues, concerns the flexible approach taken toward authentic architectural and material conservation by the implementing authority, in this case the Heritage Conservation Committee, which advises the municipal commissioner.

This contrast between general conservation standards and the "more purist approach" is highlighted by the precedents set by the multinational banks and financial institutions that increasingly locate in old buildings in the Fort precinct. They are committed to the "complete" restoration of the buildings they occupy. In addition, their financial capacities facilitate conservation projects that, unfortunately for the citizen groups, which usually are composed of highly educated upper-income people, are setting benchmarks in conservation standards. This causes the conservation movement to be perceived as elitist and carrying financial implications.

Over the last several years the legislation has been fully understood, and a number of architects and planners have been facilitating implementation of the legislation. Grappling with the transforming nature of the city and the issues related to conservation of sub-areas in the conservation zone have emerged. Besides achieving improvements in the physical state of the environment, these exercises are shifting the debate from architectural conservation to urban conservation—drawing the conservation movement closer to the planning process.

Restoring the Oval Maidan

The first sub-area to undergo such a process was a Grade I open space, the historic Oval Maidan (playing ground), which up to 1996 had been under the jurisdiction of the state government. As this is a city-level open space (used chiefly for cricket), local residents do not feel responsible for its upkeep. The space had deteriorated to a spot for drug dealing, prostitution, and gross misuse. A citizen group, comprising mainly of elderly women residents of the area, petitioned the state government to maintain the space. The state government did not respond, resulting in the citizen group's taking the state government to court. The court ruled in the group's favor and directed the state government to either maintain the space or hand it over to the citizen group. The citizen group took over this space, after which plans were drawn up for the area and to use money raised to fence the space, put up signage, and introduce a walking track, all within Heritage Conservation Committee guidelines. The walking track became the element by which one could then engage the residents of the area to use the space and look after the space. Besides effectively using the legislative and judiciary systems to conserve this space, the one intervention of a walking track connected a whole constituency to this Grade I open space and engaged it in the conservation process (figure 5).

Using Participation to Facilitate an Art District

The participatory approach to conservation in Bombay is exemplified by the Kala Ghoda area. The area derives its name from the statue of King Edward seated on his black horse, although this icon no longer exists in the area. With the support of the UDRI a group of young professionals carried out detailed surveys of traffic, land uses, and gallery spaces. They discovered that this area contained the largest concentration of contemporary art galleries in the country. They formed an association to combine their resources for conservation. The association petitioned the government to officially designate the area an art district. It now hosts an annual art festival whose income is used to improve the area as well as bring attention to its intrinsic values. This process has been successful both in raising money as well as initiating the conservation and restoration of both the public spaces and buildings.

The Art District bought to the public galleries that had been perceived as elitist. Introducing pavement galleries, holding street activities, transforming parking areas into concert spaces with the historic buildings as backdrops created new public space and transitions between existing buildings and the public realms by animating interstitial spaces. It reorganized the environment for a new global culture and the localization of phenomena particular to Bombay. Existing components were conceptualized differently, initiating a process that has become a model for many other areas in the Fort District as well as in Bombay.

In two other projects, the Ballard Estate Area, which is an office district, and the Horniman Circle Area, the formation of associations facilitated people in the areas talking with one another. They pooled their resources to spread improvements more evenly, rather than their being concentrated in small pockets, resulting in a greater impact and well being of the environments.

These four cases in the Fort Area highlight that unless the community is completely engaged in the conservation process, it will not be effective, despite legislation. Similarly, identifying a contemporary purpose or use as the engine to drive this process has been quite successful in facilitating conservation as well as in addressing current realities and issues in these areas.

Specialized Planning Zones

Breaking large conservation areas like the Fort Area into smaller units reduces the number of interests acting on a particular part of the city. This idea of specialized planning zones versus blanket planning ideas for the city is perhaps the most important lesson that the conservation process of the Fort Area has brought to the planning process in Bombay. Using the heritage legislation, 1977 the state government declared the Textile Mill District of Bombay a special planning zone to save the social and physical fabric of this historic district.

This process also brought the fore a fundamental issue of dealing with conservation in post-colonial situations. In these cases the conservation movement invariably grows out of the environmental movement, not out of a cultural desire to preserve historic icons. In fact, for an entire generation of citizens, the Victorian core of the city represents repression and exclusion. The buildings are clearly icons of our colonial past. To others, the historic center is a bit of the city in which the cohesiveness of urban form and the integration of architecture and urban design create a pleasant, or at least potentially beautiful, environment by sheer contrast to the laissez-faire growth that characterizes the contemporary Indian urban landscape.

In this context conservation approaches have to treat their "object" purely in terms of "building and environment as resource," devoid of its

Figure 5. View of the restored Oval Maidan with the High Court in the background, Bombay.

Figure 6. View of one of the ceremonial routes along the Fort Area in which the illusion of the Victorian arcade is basically intact.

iconographic or symbolic content. Many worlds inhabit the same space in the city, relating to it and using it in different ways (figure 6). To facilitate conservation, it is critical that conservation strategies encourage the recycling of buildings. The interplay of this discipline of keeping the external illusion intact while adapting the inside to evolving social needs and contemporary aspirations is worth serious consideration. This process will drain the symbolic import of the edifice while deepening the ties of architecture with contemporary realities and experiences. General architectural interventions can transform a particular urban typology and place it in the service of contemporary life and realities.

Bazaars in Victorian Arcades

The bazaars in Victorian arcades in the old Fort Area are emblematic of this phenomenon. They not only force a confrontation of uses and interest groups but also demand new preservation approaches.

For the average Bombay resident the hawker provides a wide range of goods at prices considerably lower than those in local shops. Thus, the bazaars in the arcades that characterize the Fort Area are thriving businesses. For the elites and for conservationists the Victorian core represents the city center, with icons complete. As the city sprawls outward, dissipating the clarity of its form, these images, places, and icons have acquired even greater meaning for these groups as crucial symbols of the city's fast-deteriorating historic image. Consequently, hawking is deemed illegal by city authorities, who constantly attempt to relocate the bazaars (figure 7).

The challenge in Bombay is to cope with the city's transforming nature, not by inducing or polarizing its dualism, but by attempting to reconcile simultaneous opposites, to see them both as valid. The existence of two worlds in the same space implies that we must accommodate and overlap varying uses, perceptions, and physical forms. For example, the arcades in the Fort Area are a special urban component that inherently possess a capacity for reinterpretation. As an architectural or urban design solution, they display an incredible resilience: they can accommodate new uses while keeping the illusion of their architecture intact.

The original use of the arcades was two-fold. First, they established a definite position in terms of building-street relationships. Adoption of this architectural and spatial element mediated between building and street. Second, they were a perfect response to Bombay's climate: they served as a zone protecting pedestrians from both the harsh sun and lashing rains.

One design solution might be to re-adapt the functioning of the arcades. They could be restructured to allow for both easy pedestrian movement and hawker activities. They could contain the amorphous bazaar encased in the illusion of the disciplined Victorian arcade. With this sort of planning, components of the city would have a greater ability to survive because they could be more adaptable to changing economic and social conditions.

There are no permanent solutions in an urban landscape charged simultaneously with duality as well as rapid transformation. At best, we can constantly evolve and invent solutions for present uses and safeguarding the crucial components of our historically important urban hardware. In fact, "Bazaars in Victorian Arcades" could become an authentic symbol of this preferred reality: an urban landscape that internalizes the past for a sustainable future. ■

Figure 7. View of the Victorian arcade early in the morning. Hawkers' belongings are stored in the boxes.

Economics of Investing in Heritage: Historic Center of Split

22

his chapter chronicles the birth of a project to restore the historic core of the City of Split, Croatia, and the method of preparing the economic analysis of its costs and benefits. An urban and real estate analysis also is included at the end of the chapter.

Split originated from Diocletian's Palace in Split. Built in the early fourth century A. D., the palace is among the best preserved Roman monuments in the world. It has attracted the attention of scholars since the sixteenth century and is listed as a UNESCO World Heritage Site (figures 1-3).

The palace remains the living core of the city. Miraculously, the architectural fabric of the city has never suffered the physical destruction of wars or natural disasters. This fortunate status has resulted in seventeen centuries of building activity during which richly significant architectural structures from all historic periods were erected. The Municipality of Split aims to use the one thousand, seven hundredth anniversary of the palace construction period to undertake an ambitious program of upgrading the City Core. This is being done as a means to improve the quality of lives of the residents and to prepare the city for this new millennium.

Project Genesis, Objectives, and Description

The City of Split is located on Croatia's Dalmatian coast. The city developed within the walls of the palace of Roman Emperor Diocletian and combines Roman, medieval, and baroque architecture. Unfortunately, many parts of the historic core of Split have deteriorated and are in urgent need of repair. Many historic buildings within the core are in poor condition, and some are in danger of collapse. Others are closed to the public. Still others require reconstruction and rehabilitation to reveal their historic and artistic importance or to increase accessibility to visitors. If nothing is done, many valuable historic and architectural monuments will become inaccessible to visitors and lost to future generations.

Maha J. Armaly,
Stefano P. Pagiola,
and Alain Bertaud

Maha J. Armaly is an operations officer in the Infrastructure Sector Unit in the Europe and Central Asia Region of the World Bank Stefano P. Pagiola is an economist in the Environment Department of the World Bank. Alain Bertaud, a former senior urban development specialist at the World Bank, is a consultant.

Facing page. The precinct of the Diocletian's Palace in Split, Croatia. When the Roman Emperor Diocletian left office around 303 A. D., he moved back to his birthplace, where he built a majestic residence in which he lived until his death in 312. As the city around the palace grew, its walls became submerged in a maze of alleys and narrow buildings, 1906 photo.

The Municipality of Split requested World Bank support to rehabilitate the urban historic core of the City of Split. The Bank proceeded to prepare the project in cooperation with the Government of Croatia. The municipality indicated that it wishes to be the direct borrower of the loan, which would be possible provided the government provides a guarantee for the World Bank.[1]

The ultimate objective of the proposed project is to promote an enabling environment for enhanced social, entrepreneurial, and tourist activities in the area. The project would invest in physical improvements of Diocletian's Palace and other significant cultural assets of the city, largely concentrated in the historic core (figure 4). The project cost is estimated at about US$15 million (excluding taxes), of which the Bank would provide $9 million as an International Bank of Reconstruction and Development (IBRD) loan.

The project would pursue two complementary objectives. First, it would support the conservation of cultural heritage assets, including rehabilitation, restoration, and preservation of archaeological sites and historic buildings. Second, it would contribute to the growth of economic activities in the area, such as the creation of new small- and medium-size enterprises and the development of tourism. The extensive program of conservation and restoration in Split's historic core will include:

- Completing the excavation of the cellars of Diocletian's Palace and the restoration of areas that have already been excavated, making the entire substructure accessible to visitors. Work in the cellars will include rehabilitation of the Roman sewer system.
- Undertaking structural improvements to many buildings threatened with collapse, preserving them for posterity, removing ugly scaffolding, and increasing visitor access (figure 5).
- Restoring the South Facade of Diocletian's Palace, bringing to light the original Roman architecture and the medieval wall that was built atop it.
- Making accessible to visitors many valuable collections, such as that of the ethnographic museum.

Project Preparation

In preparing the project, several requirements had to be met and extensive consultation held among specialists from the Bank, conservation specialist institutions, municipal officials, and local stakeholders.

A meeting of the minds was needed to satisfy different view points. The Bank approached the project as a development project that would need to be economically justified and to have a sound financial and implementation plan. Conservation specialists were more concerned with the

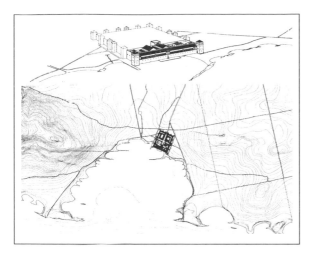

Figure 1. Map of the spatial development of Split, fourth century.

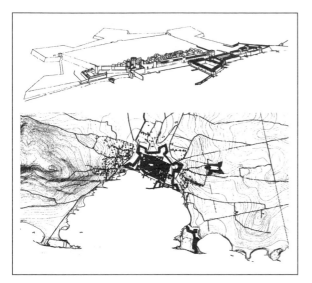

Figure 2. Map of the Split Riva, 1675.

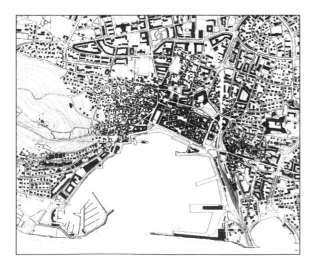

Figure 3. Map of the spatial development of Split, 1985.

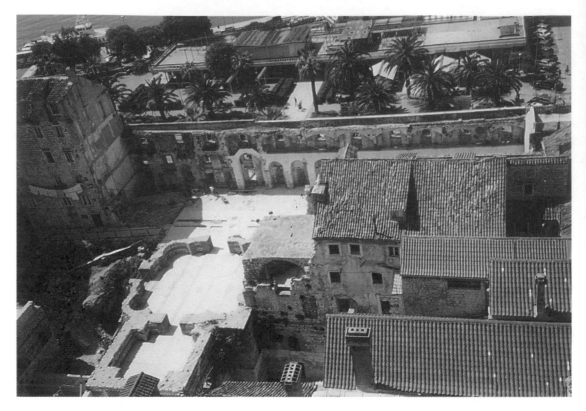

Figure 4. Diocletian's Palace, Split, Croatia, fourth century A.D.: bird's-eye view of interior courtyard.

technical aspects of the project, an area in which the Bank does not have a comparative advantage and relies on partners to provide. Given the historic importance of the area, and the role the historic core plays in the economic and social interactions in Split and the surrounding area, local officials and residents were quite convinced that the project is economically justifiable.

From early in the war in the Balkans, tourism in Croatia suffered, affecting economic and social aspects in the life of every town. The Municipality of Split looked again to the urban historic core to revitalize the city and the population. A social assessment was undertaken that confirmed the population's views with regard to the important role that the historic core plays in their lives. The social assessment also formed the basis for the economic analysis of the project, in that it attempted to measure the value assigned to the improvements planned under the project in the minds of the local population and foreign visitors.

Summary of Benefits and Costs

Costs. The project will undertake a variety of activities designed to conserve and enhance the cultural heritage of the City of Split. The most important component concerns the historic core of the city, which UNESCO has designated a World Heritage city. In Split the project would finance:

- Completion of the excavation of the cellars of Diocletian's Palace and the restoration of areas that have already been excavated, making the entire substructure accessible to visitors
- Structural improvements to many buildings threatened with collapse, preserving them for posterity, removing ugly scaffolding, and increasing visitor access
- Restoration of the South Facade of Diocletian's Palace, revealing the original Roman architecture and the medieval wall that was built atop it
- Construction and rehabilitation of public facilities, making accessible to visitors many valuable collections, such as that of the ethnographic museum.

The costs involved include the investment costs incurred in carrying out the conservation and enhancement, and the additional estimated long-term maintenance costs. In present value the total costs of the Split program come to about US$12.1 million, excluding taxes.

Benefits. This project will generate two major types of benefits:

1. Work on the historic buildings will generate benefits to both residents and visitors. Many of these benefits are intangible—they will increase the overall enjoyment that residents and tourists derive from living in or visiting the site. These intangible benefits will be reflected in observable variables—for example, in higher property prices within the site, higher sales prices for goods sold at the site, increased visitation, and increased tourist spending—but only imperfectly so.
2. Structural work and renovation of existing buildings and construction of new structures will create additional space that will be available for a variety of public and private uses.

Several of the activities will have additional benefits; for example, restoration of the Roman sewer system will have a public health benefit, while structural work on several buildings will improve public safety. Due to lack of time and resources, no effort has been made to estimate these additional benefits.

The most difficult aspect of the economic analysis is to estimate the benefits from the investments being made to improve the cultural heritage of the historic city, since the majority of these benefits are not reflected, or are imperfectly reflected, in market transactions. To undertake this, *contingent valuation* (CV) *surveys* were conducted of both tourists and residents to determine their *willingness to pay* (WTP) for the improvements to be made by the project.

In a CV survey respondents were presented with detailed information on a cultural heritage site and its likely prospects in the absence of intervention. They were then presented with an alternative scenario that explained what interventions were being considered and what their

Figure 5. Conservation of architectural heritage includes structural improvements to buildings threatened with collapse.

likely effect on the site would be. They were asked how much they would be willing to pay for the specified improvements.

This approach enables analysts to focus in very closely on the issue of interest. CV has been used in several previous Bank operations, including notably the economic analysis of benefits to tourists from improvements made in the Fez Medina, Morocco. CV also was used in a previous Bank project in Croatia to value the benefits to tourism of protection and reconstruction measures for coastal forests.

Benefits to tourists. The analysis showed that tourists expressed a relatively high willingness to pay for improvements in the historic core of Split. The mean WTP was about $44, with a 95 percent confidence interval between $37 and $51. This can be compared to the WTP of $70 expressed by tourists visiting the Fez Medina. That WTP should be lower at Split is not surprising since, unlike at Fez, cultural heritage was not the primary reason for a visitor's trip. Visitors to Petra in Jordan pay a $30 per person for visits that generally last a single day.

For the purposes of the economic analysis for Split, a conservative WTP value at the lower end of the estimated range, $35 per person, was used. Since these are benefits to foreigners, however, only the portion that is captured locally should be counted as a benefit to Croatia. For the base case calculations, it was assumed that 50 percent of the benefit was captured locally. By combining these estimates with estimates of the number of tourists visiting Split, the stream of benefits deriving from the cultural heritage improvements could be estimated. Under the assumptions given, an annual income stream of about $5 million would be generated. Assuming it takes five years for the full benefits of the project to be experienced, the value of this income stream in present value terms is about $41 million.

Benefits to residents. The Social Survey showed that residents of the historic core attach considerable importance to its preservation. The Resident Survey quantified this interest by asking residents of the historic core their willingness to pay for the improvements to be made by the project. The results show that residents have a relatively high willingness to pay for improvements in the historic core. The mean WTP for the proposed improvements was $158, with a 95 percent confidence interval of $117 to $198. It is not surprising that the residents' WTP should be higher than that of visitors since:

- It is their own cultural heritage being preserved and improved, so it is reasonable to expect a higher intensity of preferences.
- Residents will enjoy the benefits of the improvements year-round, rather than only for a week or so, as in the case of visitors.
- Some residents obtain at least part of their income from the tourist industry and are likely to benefit monetarily from the improvements. Assuming a WTP of $115, at the bottom end of the estimated range, an annual flow of benefits to residents of the historic core of about $0.25 million will be generated. Assuming that full benefits will be achieved 5 years after the beginning of the project, this represents a present value of $2.1 million. Residents of Split who do not reside in the core itself also can be expected to benefit from the improvements made there. The Social Survey had shown that the historic core remains a principal commercial and recreational center for the city's inhabitants. Since non-residents will have a lower exposure to the improvements made by the project, however, it is reasonable to assume that their WTP for these improvements will be lower than that of residents. Assuming conservatively that the WTP of non-residents would be only 10 percent of that of residents, an additional annual benefit to Inhabitants of Split of $1.7 million would be generated, or $14 million in present value terms. The much larger number of beneficiaries offsets the much smaller levels of benefits per capita.

These results are summarized in table 1. It shows that the estimated net present value of the project, using a 10 percent discount rate, is about US$47 million. The estimated internal rate of return (IRR) is about 50 percent.

It should be stressed that these benefit estimates are *conservative* for two reasons:

1. Conservative assumptions were made in estimating the individual benefits.
2. Several important benefits have not been included. In particular, the benefits obtained by Croatians who are not resident in Split have not been included. Likewise, the individual benefits created by many of the individual sub-components, such as the public health benefit of restoring the sewer system, have not been included.

Because of this second point in particular, actual benefits are likely to be much higher than the estimated project benefits.

Table 1. Estimated costs and benefits of the restoration of historic core of Split							
		Present value of flows (US$)					
		Benefits					
Site	Costs	Tourists	Residents	Other	Total	Net present value	Internal rate of return
Split	12.1	40.6	16.0	3.0	59.5	47.4	49

Main Economic Assumptions

1. That CV accurately captures tourists' and residents' WTP for improvements. Although CV has many of the potential weaknesses inherent in survey approaches, considerable experience in the use of CV methods in the environmental field allows these potential weaknesses to be minimized. The surveys conducted at Split followed closely the recommendations of the U. S. National Oceanic and Aeronautic Administration (NOAA) "blue-ribbon" committee on CV, which is generally considered authoritative on its appropriate use.
2. That tourism will recover to pre-war levels within five years. In areas surrounding Split tourism has already made a substantial recovery, albeit not yet to pre-war levels. Recovery within the city itself is hampered by the poor condition of hotels and other facilities, which were used by refugees. Since a large portion of visitors to Split consists of excursionists from surrounding areas, this is less constraining than it might have been. A resurgence of conflict in the area could affect the recovery of tourism.
3. That a significant portion of benefits to tourist can be captured locally. A number of market mechanisms will come into play, for example, allowing hotels and restaurants to charge a premium

thanks to their location. Entry fees will be charged to some of the new facilities. However, an entry fee to the sites of Split and Trogir as a whole would be impractical. Current law prevents the municipality from imposing a tax; a study will be undertaken of the desirability of such measures.

Sensitivity Analysis and Switching Values of Critical Items

Tourism benefits. The benefits derived from tourism are the most important. These estimates depend on the three sets of assumptions above: the recovery of tourism to at least pre-war levels, tourists' WTP for the improvements made by the project, and the proportion of this WTP that can be captured locally.

1. In the base case, tourism is assumed to recover to pre-war levels within 5 years, which is also the time needed for the project's improvements to be ready. The Split investments have positive net present values (NPVs) even if tourism takes as long as 20 years to recover to pre-war levels. The Split component would be justified even in the absence of any recovery of tourism.
2. In the base case, tourist WTP for improvements at Split is assumed to be $35 per person per visit, which is at the lower end of the 95 percent confidence interval for the WTP estimated in the tourist survey. This is already a conservative assumption. The Split component would have a NPV of $6.8 million even if there were no tourist benefits.
3. In the base case, 50 percent of tourist WTP is assumed to be captured locally. If only 25 percent of this benefit were captured locally, the PV of tourism benefits would be about $21.3 million. The project NPV would fall to $24.5 million, and the internal rate of return (IRR) to 27 percent. As with the previous assumption, the project would still be justified even if *none* of the tourism benefits were captured locally.

These estimates show that the results for the project are extremely robust, even despite major changes in the assumptions regarding WTP and the fraction that is captured locally.

Resident benefits. Since the populations of the cities involved are known, resident benefits depend on only the per capita benefits obtained by residents. For residents of the historic core the base case assumptions for Split take a conservative estimate of WTP of $115, at the bottom end of the estimated range. The assumptions take well below the estimated mean WTP of $158, and an even more conservative estimate of 10 percent of this amount, for other residents. The Split component would be justified on the basis of resident benefits *alone*, with no tourist benefits, if the willingness-to-pay of residents of the historic core were at least $88 per person. If any tourist benefits are received at all, the assumed benefits to residents can fall even further. Tourism benefits would have to be less than a third of those assumed before any resident benefits are needed to justify the project. It should also be stressed that benefits to Croatians who are not resident in Split are not included at all. Even though these benefits are likely to be even lower per person than those of Split residents who do not live in the historic core, the large number of people involved would still result in a significant benefit.

Analysis of the Urban and Real Estate Dynamics of the Project

Despite the stagnation of tourism, real estate prices in the historic core have been increasing. There is apparently a strong demand for office and commercial space. Prices in 1998 reached about US$11,000 per m^2 in the prime location retail areas. These very high prices were confirmed from several sources. By contrast, in some areas of the core, residential prices are declining. This is due to lack of sanitary facilities in about 20 percent of apartments (although water and sewer reticulation is adequate in the area), and the high cost of making major repairs in the city core. However, the current market price of the best apartments should constitute an incentive to renovate the worst structures in the area.

Rent control, still imposed on a number of apartments (about 50 percent of the residential space according to some estimates), is certainly the major hindrance to the private-sector rehabilitation of the worst housing stock. The possibilities of removing rent control or finding compensating mechanisms to enable tenant mobility under rent control are explored earlier in this chapter. If more detailed surveys confirm that 50 percent of the residential stock is under rent control, dealing with the physical decay inherent in rent control may be the major issue confronting the permanent upgrading of the historic core.

During the implementation of the project the Agency for the Historic Core (AHC) should monitor the evolution of real estate prices in various parts of the historic core and identify the number, area, and location of rent-controlled apartments. The choice of alternative solutions will depend in large part on the quantitative aspects of this problem, in particular in the rent differential between controlled and free market apartments. A large differential would enable rent-control tenants to receive adequate compensation for their property interest. A small differential would tend to perpetuate the status quo.

Regulations Affecting the Historic Core

The municipality prefers to preserve the current area under residential use and does not wish to increase the floor space under commercial use (retail and office space), but it has no legal means to enforce this policy. The reason for this preference is to avoid complete commercialization of the historic core, which would deprive it of its lively social character and could increase incidence of unwanted behavior particularly at night when commercial establishments close. However, there is much more demand for office and retail space than for residential use. It is hoped that the general environmental improvements resulting from the project will boost demand for residential use.

Land Use Change Regulations

While it is certainly desirable to maintain a residential population as large as possible in the historic core, it is difficult to do so by regulations alone. Until conditions are created to make the area attractive to a segment of the residential market, slowing down land-use changes by regulations or red tape may not be the best policy. Systematic monitoring of land-use change requests, transaction prices, and rents in the historic core provides enough information to enable the local authority to take an informed decision on the subject of land-use changes. This monitoring should be part of the Geographic Information System (GIS) database planned under the project.

Regulations Affecting Repairs of Public Areas, Signs, Size, and Aspects of Buildings

Regulations concerning the building aspects are considered inadequate and maladapted to market conditions. Although a new set of regulations eventually should be prepared, it is recommended to concentrate on the regulations concerning repairs and maintenance of pavements, placement of electric and telephone cables, openings of retail space entrances and show windows at ground level, and installation of air conditioners cantilevered on street space.

A working group will be constituted by representatives of the Ministry of Cultural Affairs, the municipality, and the district to draft a proposal concerning priority regulations focusing on the topics mentioned above. The working group also will detail the legal steps required to obtain official approval for the new set of regulations. The regulatory proposal will be presented for approval to the relevant authorities during project implementation. The proposed project could provide expert assistance to review the draft regulations and provide a summary of international experience in regulating historic cores in market economies. Approval by the relevant authorities of a set of amended regulations could become a project implementation benchmark.

The proposed project will finance the rehabilitation of a number of historic monuments, improve drainage, and add about 9,600 square meters of floor space to the historic core for cultural facilities. The total cost would be US$15.0 million. The cost of rehabilitation work and drainage is about US$5 million. This cost represents about 2 percent of the total current real estate value of the areas privately occupied in the historic core.[2] The average cost of construction of the new floor space (US$1,000/m² —assuming, of course, that the Emperor Diocletian initial investment is considered a sunk cost) is well below the average market value of floor space in the area (US$1,500/m²). The total cost of rehabilitation, drainage, and additional public facilities construction (US$15 million) represents about 6 percent of the total current real estate value of the privately occupied historic core.

The characteristics of the real estate markets in Split are not yet completely clear. However, the rehabilitation component would produce an IRR of 15 percent if the work resulted in an increased estate value of 2.1 percent over the next 5 years in the city core alone. If we add the cost of constructing new floor space to the cost of rehabilitation, the same IRR of 15 percent would require an increase of 7 percent in real estate value attributable to the project over 5 years. These figures assume that (1) entrance tickets and space rental would cover maintenance only and not contribute to capital cost, and (2) the benefits of the additional new floor space would be entirely captured by real estate values in the core only.

These assumptions on the increase in real estate value that could be attributed to the project seem reasonable. Factors attributable to the projects that may contribute to an increase in real estate value are:

1. The rehabilitation will put to use the only area of the historic core that is obviously blighted. It will remove some of the humidity problems, improve street lighting, and improve the appearance of historic monuments.
2. The rehabilitation of the Diocletian Palace substructure would create 3,800 m² of temporary exhibition space of exceptional quality (the largest usable covered space in the world built entirely in Roman times).
3. The creation of the ethnographic museum and other facilities will increase pedestrian traffic in the historic core, thus increasing the commercial values of retail space and the cultural prestige of the area.
4. The rehabilitation effort together with the new legislation to protect the historic environment will demonstration the local government's determination to maintain a high standard of urban quality in the historic core.

The increase in real estate value depends on the future attractiveness of the area for both commercial and residential use. Commercial use—retail and office buildings—represents about 82 percent of the market value of the core. Recent surveys show that the historic core remains the preferred center for quality shopping and food markets, entertainment, and cultural activities for the Split population. The selection of sites in the historic core by chains of foreign retail franchises confirms the economic vitality of the area and the survey results. The two areas of Split with the highest residential real estate values are located within walking distance east and west from the historic core. These combined factors suggest that an increase in real estate value of 6.6 percent over 5 years in the core only is a conservative scenario. Therefore, the investment in historic preservation made by the municipality seems economically sound. The capital cost might be recovered through tax on business, sales taxes, or increased property tax.

A key factor in the increase of real estate value will be the municipality's ability to maintain and manage the about 9,500 m^2 of public facilities built or rehabilitated under the project. The flow of local, national, and foreign visitors to these facilities outside normal business hours should greatly enhance the value of commercial space. The Agency for the Historic Core (AHC) will begin to monitor the evolution of real estate prices in the area to ascertain the effect of rehabilitation. The municipality may want to use some part of future real estate taxes to finance the routine maintenance of historic buildings for the long run.

The method proposed to calculate the rate of return of the investment in Split is based on the following principles:

1. The rehabilitation component in Split would create tangible and intangible benefits. The tangible benefits would be derived from a direct increase in commercial flows and hence in rents. Most of these benefits will be concentrated locally, although some might incur outside Split. The intangible benefits are generated by an increase in historic knowledge and cultural awareness. These benefits would be spread across Croatia and indeed throughout the world. The calculations of the internal rate of return presented here are restricted to an evaluation of the tangible benefits occurring locally. The other benefits—tangible outside Split and intangible—are ignored in the calculation of the IRR.
2. Real estate prices within the historic core should capture most of the flow of benefits generated from the rehabilitation of cultural monuments, the infill of derelict areas, the drainage work, and the new regulations on street maintenance and displays in public areas.
3. The upgrading or construction of public facilities such as museums, theaters, and exhibition floor space also will generate tangible benefits captured by real estate prices because of the increase in pedestrian traffic and tourism they will generate, in particular outside normal business hours. It is assumed that the sale of tickets and the rental fees of exhibition space would only cover maintenance costs and therefore would not contribute to a flow of tangible benefits. Intangible benefits for these components are probably important. These type of investments are usually justified entirely on the basis of their high intangible benefits. However, in this exercise we found that the tangible benefits of public facilities on real estate values

might also be significant For this reason we have made two calculations of the IRR, one excluding facilities, the other including them, with the understanding that large intangible benefits are not taken into account in the second calculation.

4. Because of the short history of real estate markets in Split and because of the exceptional nature of the investments in historic monument upgrading, it is not possible to predict the effect of the upgrading on real estate prices. However, it is possible to conduct a sensitivity analysis to calculate the IRR that would be produced by different hypothetical increases in real estate prices. A judgment could be made to select the range of price increases that seem "reasonable" and the corresponding rates of return.

The application of this method has been possible because of the detailed inventory and survey of floor space already conducted by AHC. (A detailed map exists for every building at every level). The result of the inventory allows to divide the floor space into seven salable categories disaggregated by type of use and amenity quality. Public facilities and public space have been excluded from the valuation.

The total market value of all the private buildings in the core is calculated by putting an average market price for each of the seven categories of floor space. The rounded value of the private floor space is thus evaluated at around US$250 million.

The total cost of the project Split component, US$15.0 million, is divided into two types of costs:

1. The rehabilitation of cultural monuments, infill of derelict areas, drainage work, and new regulations on street maintenance and displays in public areas repair works (US$5.0 million)
2. Construction and rehabilitation of floor space for exhibition and public facilities (US$10.0 million).

The internal rate of return has been calculated separately for the first type of costs alone (rehabilitation) and for the total cost of the component including the two types of costs (rehabilitation plus new floor space for community facilities). ■

Notes

1 Since preparation of the project in 1998, the Kosovo crisis and government changes in Croatia have affected the project in many ways. In 1999 tourism in Croatia dropped severely. Early readings of the 2000 season and beyond are very positive, and have exceeded the most optimistic expectations. The recent change in the government brought additional enthusiasm and support to the project on the part of the Municipality of Split and the Ministry of Culture. However, given the increasing challenges and priorities of the new government, the project has been postponed. In addition, the project concept and objective may change to increase emphasis on municipal development and capacity upgrading, while keeping the social objective through investments in the historic core.

2 This figure assumes that about 50 percent of the residential space currently under rent control stays that way. If rent control could be progressively removed, the real estate value of the core would significantly increase, but the cost to rehabilitate the former rent-controlled apartments also would also significant.

23 Models of Transformation in Saudi Arabia

Ali Shuaibi

Ali Shuaibi is a partner in Beeah Consulting, an architectural firm in Saudi Arabia, as well as chairman of the Saudi Society for Architects and Planners (Al-Umran) and a member of the Executive Committee of ICOMOS, ashuaibi@hotmail.com

The impact of urbanization and modernization on historic and sacred cities in a developing country such as Saudi Arabia can be understood only when compared to their impacts in developed countries. While the population curve is shooting up in developing countries such as Egypt, Indonesia, or Nigeria, it is virtually flat in developed countries such as Denmark, Japan, or the United Kingdom. This dichotomy reflects the challenge and the interest of the population of both societies. Developed countries have less volatile urban population growth; accordingly, conservation becomes a realistic endeavor. However, for developing countries with massive urban growth, most of their governments' efforts go to address problems of increasing urban population, poverty, and physical change.

Until the 1950s Saudi Arabia was a medieval society. It entered the Renaissance and Modernism only in the last 50 years, after the end of World War II. The transformation of three rapidly growing metropolises in Saudi Arabia, namely Makkah Al Mukarramah, Jeddah, and Riyadh, illustrate some of the issues (table 1).

Makkah Al Mukarramah

Makkah Al Mukarramah has been the spiritual and physical focus of all Muslims at every prayer for the last 14 centuries. It was a holy city even before Islam began. It is a city within a shrine. A prayer in the shrine is equivalent to 100,000 prayers outside. The function of the shrine is to enable pilgrims to circumnavigate the *Ka'bah* (black cube), and to hold collective prayers in circles around it. The population of the city grew quickly in the early centuries of Islam, reaching about 100,000 during the Abbasid dynasty (750-1258 A. D.) It was stable at that number for the last millennium. A comparison between a map of the nineteenth century by Burckhardt and another of 1948 shows that very little change in the historic city had happened until the 1950s.

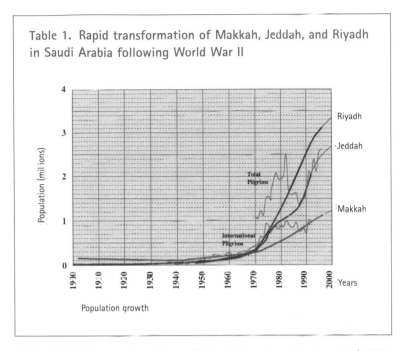

Table 1. Rapid transformation of Makkah, Jeddah, and Riyadh in Saudi Arabia following World War II

Population growth

Makkah Al Mukarramah had beautiful buildings from the Mamluk (1250-1517) and Ottoman (1300-1922) periods (figure 1). The forbidden area dedicated to prayers is known as the Holy Mosque. Historically, secular buildings were built immediately abutting it. Until the Abbasid period, in every cycle of growth the mosque and other secular buildings around it were demolished to allow for expansion. Later, only reconstruction was done by the Ottomans. During these centuries buildings in the city were like trees in the forest, where old ones die and new ones replace them. In the 1950s buildings were hardly older than few centuries, with the exception of columns in the Holy Mosque, which had been retained since the early centuries of Islam.

In the late 1950s with the increase in the number of pilgrims, Saudi Arabia decided to carry out the largest expansion ever for the Holy Mosque, which was in four levels; below grade, main, second, and roof levels. This first modern expansion of the mosque was thought to be sufficient for the coming centuries. But the rapid growth of numbers of pilgrims and local population of the metropolis rendered it insufficient even before it was completed, calling for another round of destruction of the historic buildings to allow for expansion (figure 2).

More than two million worshipers attend prayers simultaneously, and the number is increasing. This historical model of growth was clearly unworkable for the modern phenomenon of continuous growth. A new model was needed. The city found that an integrated mode of expansion is the only viable alternative. This model recommends the retention of the existing buildings of the Holy Mosque. But in the future, every new construction should be a multilayered (storied) development Besides

Figure 1. Makkah is thousands of years old and until the post-World War II transformation had beautiful buildings from the Mamluk and Ottoman periods.

Figure 2. The rapid growth of Makkah called for the greatest expansion in the history of the Holy Mosque. Here the mosque is surrounded by pilgrims arriving for the Hajj.

prayer space, it should include all necessary transport facilities, pedestrian circulation, local services, special uses, and housing. It is hoped that this model that integrates the sacred with the secular will permit future growth and conservation to coexist.

Jeddah

Jeddah was the pilgrims' port until the 1950s, when it became Saudi Arabia's main commercial port. Since that time its population has grown from about 50,000 to more than two million. It was a walled medieval town with high-density, four- to five-story towers, mainly from the nineteenth century. Pressure of the early growth of the city resulted in the demolition of its walls and some buildings to make room for new wider streets or taller buildings. Even though Saudi Arabia does not have a formal policy for historic preservation in urban areas, the city's master plan of the early 1970s called for historic conservation. While the city upgraded the infrastructure and improved the roads and traffic management, it also encouraged property owners to conserve their buildings. The pressure of growth was quickly absorbed in the vast land development away from the historic city, thus contributing to the viability of its conservation scheme.

Riyadh

Riyadh in the early 1950s was a walled desert hamlet built for pedestrians, built entirely of adobe walls and timbered roofs. The walled historic city had a population of about 5,000 inhabitants. The city was the nucleus of the unification of Saudi Arabia, which was ruled over by King Abdul Aziz about 100 years ago. Its population is now about 3.4 million. Possibly ashamed of its modest architecture, coupled with the extreme fragility of its adobe buildings, which required immediate repair after every rain, the city decided to modernize itself. The main mosque and the Justice Palace (Governor's Office) were immediately rebuilt with more durable materials of stone and concrete. Streets were literally cut into the urban fabric. Some buildings gave way to parking lots. Two-story court houses along the newly created streets were replaced by walk-up concrete apartments. In the late 1970s the city realized that it had lost its historic center and was left with a shredded fabric, plagued by traffic congestion. An Italian architect was hired to design a new city center that included a plaza, city hall, and a cultural center. The proposal was rejected because the design ignored the surrounding area and had no circulation plan. My company was hired to create the urban design for the area. Our design included suggestions to:

- Widen the boundary to integrate the area with main roads
- Attempt to restore the traditional fabric

- Preserve the memory of the city by maintaining the original location of all major buildings
- Conserve the fort
- Avoid through traffic
- Create a new network of pedestrian walkways bridging neighboring areas, a plaza, a series of open spaces, and integrating parking
- Integrate parking with shopping and multiple uses at upper levels that include housing and office facilities in a contiguous mass suitable for the hot, arid climate of the city.

By the early 1990s the city had successfully completed the second phase of the design, which included the main mosque and the Justice Palace by Rasem Badran. It won the 1995 Aga Khan Award for Architecture. As a result of this success, the city decided to expand its experiment to include Al Murabba Palace of the late King Abdul Aziz as a gift to its citizens for the occasion of the country's centennial. With Rasem Badran Beeah developed the urban design with the intent to create a cultural center in the area, which will also act as a magnet. The Justice Palace was planned as the administrative center, Al Murabba as the cultural center, and the traditional area between the two centers as the folk and craft center. The Cultural Center included the National Museum by Canadian architects Muriama and Tachima, The King Abdul Aziz Documentation Center (Ad-Darah) by Rasem Badran, and the Library by Omrania. (The urban detailing and landscaping were done by Boedeker and Speerplan of Germany, and the restoration of the existing adobe buildings by Beeah (figure 3)). With this development the city hoped that it had compensated its residents for the lost historic buildings by restoring the values and memories of its historic city.

The three cities in Saudi Arabia each had different functions—the religious capital, the economic capital, and the political capital—in their development and experienced different transformations in their historic centers. Makkah preserved the historic building of the mosque; Jeddah preserved its center; but Riyadh for the benefit of its future population revived the memory of locations, rather than the physical structures. The transformations in the historic centers of these three rapidly developing metropolises provide distinctively different models of intervention for other cities in developing countries. ■

Figure 3. Urban detailing, landscaping, and making foundations and roofs resistant to rain were part of restoring and modernizing old adobe buildings to create a cultural center in Riyadh's Al Murabba palace area.

24 Addressing the Social Context in Cultural Heritage Management: Historic Cairo

Saad Eddin Ibrahim

Saad Eddin Ibrahim is a professor of sociology at the American University in Cairo and chairman of the Ibn Khaldoun Center for Development Studies at the university.

n protecting and preserving cultural heritage and historic cities, it is imperative to consider their social contexts (figure 1). The word "social" in this context refers to patterns of association and disassociation, integration and disintegration, cooperation and conflict, invasion and succession, stratification, and class variables in conflict.

The city is the stage and the reference point in time for all of the society's interactions. The city is defined by population density, the production and accumulation of wealth, and the concentration of wealth and power in a relatively limited space.

Cairo illustrates the complexity of the relationship between urban society and historic places. The concentration of people, power, and wealth represents a focal point in the drama of any city, especially in a historic city like Cairo with over a millennium of uninterrupted human habitation. I am restricting my observations to the Islamic and specifically to the contemporary, reality of Cairo.

Cairo is considered to be a conurbation or an amalgamation of several smaller cities that developed and evolved over the last 1,500 years. In each of these cities the rich lived in the center and next to them lived their soldiers. Cairo experienced successive cycles over that period in which the rich moved from the center to the north or northeast, between the Nile and the Mokattam Hills. For example, the conqueror Amr Ibn-al As built the City of Fustat in 641 A. D., which later was abandoned by the rich, who moved northeast to Al Askar. One hundred years later the rulers moved once again to Katai or Tulun and, finally, to Al Qahira, the Fatimid capital, founded in 969 A. D.

This sequence of moving continued with subsequent moves being less dramatic than these first three moves. The urban expansion gradually

Figure 1. The process of development requires change by which all participate and all benefit. Protecting historic cities such as Cairo requires attending to the social as much as to the physical dimensions.

enveloped the whole area. When the rich moved out from the old rich centers where they had built palaces, they left behind mosques and shrines with beautiful architecture. However, the poor and the down-trodden were concerned with having shelters.

The needy people who moved to the abandoned centers had no means of taking care of the heritage, which was therefore constantly exposed to degradation. However, in inhabited areas the deterioration was minimal so long as the population remained small, as was the case in Cairo until the nineteenth century. In the historic city the population was small, and the geographic patterns of transition stretched over 100 to 200 years, paired with a very limited territorial expansion. For example, the move from Fustat to Askar to Katai to Qahira over 600 years did not expand the urban area more than 2 square miles.

However, at the dawn of the nineteenth century a dramatic change took place due to unprecedented demographic growth, which accelerated in the twentieth century. This growth markedly disrupted the old patterns and cycles.

The new phase of development in Cairo coincided with major changes in the modality and meaning of the social institutions and the social structure. The population was affected drastically, as was the physical urban structure. The disruption was reflected in what demographers call *demographic transition* and the technological transformations of industrialization.

In the twentieth century Cairo's population tripled, to exceed 10 million. A territorial expansion of the city resulted from the increasing needs of the growing population and their new economic activities.

Why did the number of inhabitants triple? The growth was natural, resulting from the number of human beings born exceeding the number dying due to improvements in health conditions and public sanitation. Another contributing factor was migration from the rural areas to the city.

In the nineteenth century the combined urban areas expanded from 2 square miles to 6 square miles. With the expansion, the traditional city centers from Fustat to Katai to Askar to Al Qahira gave way to a modern city built on the banks of the Nile, adopting a European style.

With this transformation came a change not only in the structure of power and wealth but also in the pattern of social classes. In this new Cairo of the nineteenth century the Egyptians adopted European-style cities with broad streets, multi-story buildings, and squares. The Egyptians adopted the vision of Khedive Ismail, a mid-nineteenth century ruler who wanted to imitate Europe in various aspects of life by making Egypt a part of Europe. Khedive Ismail moved the center of power from the Citadel, the seat of power for eight centuries, to Abdin Palace. This move led to the emergence of new quarters such as Zamalek, the Garden City, Maadi, and Heliopolis. These new quarters all developed in the nineteenth and early twentieth centuries.

Another major change happened in the mid-twentieth century, namely, the revolution of 1952. A new class emerged from the 1952 revolution: the middle class. The new middle class intended to make Egypt a modern industrial country, and industrialization became its ideology. A technocratic government and public sector were the means to implement the new ideology.

New quarters were created to reflect the new technocratic and industrial ideology and new perspectives of the ruling class, causing dramatic change. Mohandesseen, a new quarter, reflects the enormous development that started in the middle of the twentieth century and is ongoing. Mohandesseen was named after the engineers who built their houses on a huge expanse on the western side of the Nile River separated from the residential quarter of the nineteenth century. Thus, Mohandesseen was located on the western side of the old City and Nasr City on the eastern side. Nasr City is the product of another big built-up area constructed for technocrats of the new middle class.

During that revolutionary period (1952-70) the city again tripled in size, from 6 square miles to 18 square miles. The trend continued during Anwar Sadat's term and will continue during Hosni Mubarak's term.

Every day the city expands its boundaries. After the term of Gamal Abdel Nasser (1956-70), the rich again opened up to the West. This openness brought back modern Western values, and the rich emulated the suburban life styles of their Western counterparts. In the current phase we discover new areas called Beverly Hills, Dreamland, Golf City, and California. The *nouveaux riches* who emulated the West by moving outside the built space are moving even farther. Thus, the expansion that was 18 square miles in 1970 will reach almost 200 square miles in 2000.

It is hard to imagine a city that expanded from 2 square miles in 1800 to 6 square miles in 1900 to 18 square miles in 1970 to 200 square miles in 2000. A population increase accompanies the territorial expansion— from 200,000 inhabitants in 1800 to 600,000 in 1900. In 2000 the urban population reached over 10 million inhabitants, without counting the 2 million commuters to the city every day.

As the rich flee the center and settle in suburbs, the old city becomes the receptacle for the poor. Increasingly dense settlement, subdivision of old buildings to accommodate expanding families and new immigrants, and new economic activities such as small factories take over the urban fabric of the old historic city.

What are the effects of such population growth and disruption of social structure on the historic city and its sacred places? The spiritual space, the physical space, and the demographic realities are not always in harmony.

A major problem is the very high density of the population in the poorer older historic quarters. The monuments, the shrines with all their sacred scriptures, the physical buildings, and their symbolism and spirituality all are parts of the socio-physical reality.

Today, if people who have the power and wealth have any interest at all in the historic city, it is to move the people out completely and turn it into a museum-like space devoid of people.

But outside of the power in the old center, the rich in the suburbs and the new middle class in Mohandesseen and Nasr City, there are the workers and the proletarian underclass.

The new working class have their own neighborhoods. They are located on the peripheries of the middle class neighborhoods and in the northern part of Cairo and also the southern part, namely, Helwan, home to a large industrial complex. The working class live north or in the vicinity of Zabbaleen.

The working class live in the typical cement-slab housing that one can see everywhere in the world. Such working class housing is fairly crowded, but at least it has basic minimal living amenities.

Then we come to the social formation called the underclass, or proletarians in Marxist terms. It represents the biggest class and is the most threatening to both the physical and the social fabric of the city. The working class and the underclass migrated to the city in huge numbers. The underclass lives in the slums around the city and those slums that are located in the historic city.

The proletarians always existed in the city, but they never exceeded 5 percent to 10 percent of the overall population. In the last three decades their number multiplied so fast that they now represent 40 percent of the city population.

Where did they live? They lived in the City of the Dead, in the historic shrines and historic city of Cairo, on the peripheries of the middle class areas, or anywhere where they found shelters or inexpensive housing. Since most of the historic sites are public places, they moved in, and over time it became extremely difficult to evict them.

The people who reside in the historic cities have been educated and have acquired the expectations of the middle class, but because of the dynamics of the socioeconomic evolution over the last 30 years, they are underclass in terms of their incomes. They have very low-paying jobs or are unemployed. For this reason they are frustrated and discontented. Some have begun to use the symbolic space and a type of religious message to fight the structure of power. Therefore, whether they live in the historic city or in the new suburbs around it, they adopt the religious discourse and the spirit of the historic city to serve their own interests. It is a power game, and increasingly, their feelings are echoed by others.

The physical space of the historic city of Cairo, rich in monuments and history, is engulfed in the sprawling metropolis of new Cairo. Social, economic, and physical dislocation is part of development, but if the changes are not integrated, it is development gone awry. Alienation ensues. Extreme cases of alienation, when manipulated by persons with political agendas, can lead not just to fundamentalism or militant political action but also to extreme terrorists acts such as the murders of innocent tourists in Luxor in the late 1990s. In 6 seconds 6 people killed 60 people and cost the 60 million Egyptian people 6 billion dollars!

Figure 2. The Cultural Park for Children in Cairo designed by Abdelhalim Ibrahim Abdelhalim in 1990. Its design and geometry were inspired by the surrounding monuments.

But, extreme cases aside, the daily life of the old city needs to be incorporated in the future plans of the new city (figure 2). The process of development requires change by which all participate and all benefit. Dealing with historic cities—all historic cities—requires attending to the social as much as to the physical aspects.

To renovate, to protect, to preserve, and to conserve without knowing the social fabric and involving the people often leads to eventual failure.

Therefore, I advocate social inclusion of all classes in the urban development process. ■

Modern mosque designed by Skidmore Owings & Merrill, Manhattan, New York: interior.

Part V

New Approaches to Sustainable Preservation of Natural Resources and Built Heritage

Editors' Note

Part V documents innovative approaches to sustainable preservation of urban built heritage and cultural landscapes as experienced in Brazil, India, Morocco, the United States, and Zanzibar. The deterioration and obsolescence of important monuments and urban fabric has been attributed either to the decline of economic vitality in central cities, the destructive effects of urban-renewal programs, or a combination of inadequate public policies and delivery capabilities. The following case studies suggest a paradigm shift by which the public sector has strengthened its administrative and tax revenue collection capacities and adopted new planning and financing mechanisms for preserving heritage, engaging civic organizations, and relying on market forces. These chapters provide substantial economic and social evidence of preservationists' and experts' contention that historic neighborhoods, cultural landscapes, and monuments are assets that can be economically preserved and effectively used by local communities.

In Brazil, as in most countries, government alone cannot afford to carry the entire burden of heritage preservation. Faced with limited means, governments must focus on ways to mobilize partners from civil society, residents, the business community, and municipal government. Arthur Darling describes the Monumenta *program, launched by the Ministry of Culture of Brazil and assisted by a loan from the Inter-American Development Bank. The objective is to develop a sustainable preservation strategy for federally listed monuments and sites by developing incentive structures for municipalities and the private sector to preserve heritage. The* Monumenta *program assists in the*

*production of special educational materials and awareness-raising activities. Municipal preserva-
tion funds are established in each project city to finance future preservation works. Darling argues
that incentives should be structured to elicit cost-effective proposals, ensure future maintenance,
and stimulate independent action.*

*In the United States the Interstate Highway Act of 1956 marked the beginning of the decline of
downtown areas, or "Main Street." The automobile led to suburban sprawl and the construction of
shopping malls and chain stores far outside the traditional town centers. Residents and businesses moved out of urban centers, taking the tax-base with them. In the mid-1970s, however, the
National Trust for Historic Preservation successfully launched a program for revitalization of
downtown areas in 43 states and Puerto Rico. Kennedy Smith describes the remarkable results of
the Trust's Main Street Program in terms of jobs created, number of buildings rehabilitated, and
total investments made. Smith examines this program for downtown revitalization in terms of its
four main components: design, organization, promotion, and economic restructuring.*

*The case of Ahmedabad, India, a city rich in many ways, but a poor municipality, shows how an effec-
tive team of administrators used innovative financial management approaches to turn around the
Municipal Corporation, improve infrastructure, and preserve the historic city center. Keshav Varma,
former Municipal Commissioner, explains how the new management redefined the public office
mandate, improved tax revenue collection, and gained the confidence of investors and business leaders in the city, which in turn led to a successful issuance of municipal bonds. With this inflow of new
resources city authorities were able to take on a number of urban and heritage preservation projects.
Varma concludes that the key factors in making Ahmedabad a success story were leadership, commitment, passion, and the public's participation in the urban planning process.*

*Charles Birnbaum discusses the role of the National Park Service Historic Landscape Initiative in
establishing standards and guidelines for historic preservation of cultural landscapes in the United
States. Neither technical nor prescriptive, these standards are meant to promote responsible
preservation practices that protect irreplaceable cultural and environmental resources. Birnbaum
discusses important factors to consider in all landscape preservation projects, and establishes
working principles for the rehabilitation of cultural landscapes. These include aspects related to
change and continuity, relative historical significance, the integrity and physical condition of the
site, the context of adjacent areas, archeological resources, biotic systems, management and
maintenance, and interpretation.*

*Maurice Desthuis-Francis contends that most historic districts are preserved and maintained through
market forces, that is, the private sector. International tourism has experienced remarkable growth in
recent years; annual revenues exceed US$500 billion. The International Finance Corporation of the
World Bank Group and other agencies have invested in many cities by funding private investors seeking to improve the tourist industry, often by rehabilitating hotels in historic cities or close to them. The
investment criteria, however, are no longer predicated solely on growth in arrivals. Environment protection is now a priority, to ensure that tourism benefits the local population and helps preserve the
local cultural heritage. Desthuis-Francis examines the case of Stone City of Zanzibar, one of the
tourist destinations that underwent important preservation and regeneration works and is attracting
a new flow of visitors. "Historic," according to the author, no longer refers simply to the passage of
time. "Significance," and not age, is the key criterion to attract tourists to historic areas.*

*Mona Serageldin describes extensive studies of the social and economic circumstances of the res-
idents and the progressive physical erosion affecting the historic heritage and urban quality of life
in the Medina of Fez, Morocco. Initiated by the Government of Morocco and assisted by a small
loan from the World Bank, the project focuses on the rehabilitation of specific corridors, and
improving accessibility to, and circulation of pedestrians and emergency vehicles in, the historic
center. The project also seeks to alleviate poverty through housing improvement activities. Four
different perspectives were used to evaluate the cultural heritage of the Medina: its intrinsic value,
its touristic value, its value for Moroccan cultural identity, and its commercial value as represented by the real estate and economic assets of the site.*

Brazil's *Monumenta* Program: Sustainable Preservation of Historic Cities

25

A s in many countries Brazil's monuments are seriously deteriorated, and the federal government alone lacks the funds needed to preserve heritage. Restoring and conserving these monuments would cost US$65 million a year for 20 years and US$20 million per year thereafter. Brazil's annual budget for heritage restoration is only about US$3 million.

Much of Brazil's built heritage is in urban areas and in private hands. The federal government currently manages this heritage by requiring that all modification proposals be approved prior to execution. However, no norms for preservation exist, and opinions by the regulatory authority are often slow in coming and appear arbitrary. Residents frequently make modifications without filing a proposal, often disfiguring the monument. The *Monumenta* Program, designed by the Ministry of Culture and supported through a loan from the Inter-American Development Bank (IADB), was created to address these problems.

Objective

The objective of the *Monumenta* Program is to develop a sustainable preservation strategy for federally listed built heritage by developing priorities and incentive structures for municipalities and the private sector to preserve heritage, and by educating the public on its importance and care (figure 1).

Priorities

While some Brazilian citizens are willing to pay a great deal to preserve heritage, the majority is willing to pay very little. The *Monumenta* Program believes that successful examples are likely to generate expanded

Arthur Darling

Arthur Darling is a principal economist at the Inter-American Development Bank, where he manages the Monumenta *Program, arthurd@iadb.org*

Figure 1. Church of Sao Francisco de Assis, a federally listed built heritage in historic Ouro Preto, designated by UNESCO as a World Heritage Site.

support, and thus stresses the need for focusing resources on the highest-priority heritage. A strategy focused on sustaining the maximal number of listed monuments should focus on those that are recognized as most important, have the greatest support, and are most susceptible to economic, cultural, and social uses that will support their maintenance. Most of the *Monumenta* Program's resources go to specific work in centers that have been designated as priority areas.

Incentives for Participation

Since the federal government cannot dedicate extensive resources to preservation, it must mobilize as many other groups as possible to participate. Key in the preservation of urban historic cities are municipal governments, which control zoning and provide such critical services as security, trash collection, traffic control, maintenance of public areas, and public lighting. The private sector, residents, and various interest groups also play an important role. The *Monumenta* Program tries to structure incentives to involve all these groups.

Municipalities

To encourage the participation of municipalities containing priority heritage areas, the Brazilian government provides a grant covering 80 percent of the cost of preservation projects; municipalities contribute the remaining 20 percent. Municipalities develop "integrated preservation projects" that they believe will revive the economy of these areas in such a way as to support heritage. This gives the municipality "ownership" of the project. Integrated preservation projects include restoration of listed heritage, repairs to infrastructure that is causing deterioration of buildings (such as poor drainage systems or retaining walls), road access, sidewalks, improvements in public space to make areas more usable and attractive to residents and visitors, improved parking facilities, public lighting, and safety (figures 2, 3).

From the perspective of a development bank, the incentive to municipalities is too generous. The 80 percent grant (free money) may encourage municipalities to over-design projects, include unneeded infrastructure, and generate cost-ineffective proposals inconsistent with the limited amount of federal money available. A better system might be to allow municipalities to compete for funds on a short list of priority historic areas. They would submit grant proposals that include estimates of how much private and municipal counterparts will contribute to the effort. Such a system could lead both to more realistic projects and to a reduced percentage of grant monies from scarce federal funds.

Figure 2. The commercial and residential sector of Corrego dos Contos in Ouro Preto, Brazil, is included in the *Monumenta* Program.

Figure 3. Rua Prudente de Morais, a commercial and residential street in the historic town of Olinda, Brazil, is included in the *Monumenta* Program.

In return for the *Monumenta* Program grant the city makes a commitment to maintain the public space and provide a high level of service (especially refuse collection, security, and public lighting). It also commits to establishing a *Preservation Fund* to pay for maintenance of federally listed buildings that do not generate sufficient revenue to be self-sufficient (such as churches and public office buildings). The Preservation Fund is maintained in a financial institution for 20 years (corresponding to the life of the IADB loan). The fund is fed by a number of sources. First, the municipality must contribute an amount equivalent to the increase in property and commercial service tax generated by the reactivated project area. These amounts are dependent on the success of the project. Since by law municipalities cannot earmark revenues, fulfilling the commitment depends on cooperation by the legislature.

The second source of revenue is repayment of credits that the program makes available to the private sector. Amortization and interest from these credits are to be deposited into the fund and made available for reuse. A third source is revenue from usufruct. In some cases private owners can give usufruct (use of a part or all of a building for 10 to 20 years), and revenues from use go back to the Preservation Fund. Finally, revenue is derived from rental and concession fees from publicly owned buildings or areas that have been restored (rental space, parking fees, concession stands, and admission fees).

Preservation Fund monies can be used only to conserve publicly owned, federally listed monuments. Top priority is given to monuments within the defined project area—a subset of the historic area. If the funds exceed the amount necessary to maintain these monuments, they can be used for other federally declared monuments within the area of influence. As a third priority, the program permits work on other buildings of historic interest within the project area, which can be listed by the state and municipality. If additional funds remain, they can be used to replicate the project in the area of influence.

However, the existence of a Preservation Fund does not guarantee that the areas will be maintained—even if the project stimulates economic recovery. Many municipalities have very poor tax collection systems. Another risk is that local legislatures will not honor the mayor's commitments allocating funds to preservation. A third risk is that the municipalities will fail to fulfill their commitment to collect trash, provide adequate security, and maintain public spaces and infrastructure (none of which is covered by the Preservation Fund).

To address these risks, the *Monumenta* Program established a mixed commission to administer the fund and lobby municipal government. This commission is balanced equally between representatives of the public and private sectors, including residents, business users, and local nongovernmental organizations (NGOs) and universities. Public sector representation includes the national institute in charge of the preservation and the Ministry of Culture. It is not yet clear whether the commission represents a strong enough response to a significant risk.

Private Sector

The key to the sustainability of historic areas is to stimulate economic activity so that people have an economic interest in preserving the area. Private-sector participation is critical.

To encourage private investment, it is necessary to have clear rules about what uses of heritage are permitted and what adaptations can be made to buildings. In Brazil, no such rules exist, nor are there guidelines for maintaining different types of historic buildings and conserving their characteristics. Instead regulators—viewing their role solely in terms of protection and thus taking a very conservative approach—consider each proposal for a change in use individually. The result is a slow and unpredictable process often considered arbitrary, which discourages potential investors.

The *Monumenta* Program is financing the preparation of the needed norms and guidelines and trying to incorporate the notion that heritage is an economic resource. The new framework will help private-sector participants understand how to use heritage buildings and sites in appropriate ways to generate income and revenues.

The program is also investing in improvements in street access, sidewalks, parking, public lighting, trash services, and public safety. The improvements incentivize private investors by making the area more attractive to visitors (potential customers).

The program also provides direct incentives to private owners of historical sites. A targeted credit program finances the restoration of structure, facade, and roofs of privately owned buildings at an extremely low interest rate, which serves as a powerful incentive. Low-income groups have been offered an additional line of credit to adapt houses for small commercial businesses, thus enabling them to repay the credit and remain in the historic area. To ensure that private owners can avail themselves of these opportunities, the program allows owners to give usufruct of part (or all) of restored buildings in payment of the credit. The program then rents out the space to repay the credit. All repayments of credits and revenues from usufruct go to the Preservation Fund.

Civil Society

The program encourages diverse groups (NGOs, universities, and architectural associations) interested in cultural heritage to participate in managing the fund and promoting visits and use of historical sites. The involvement of major corporations is also encouraged through a 70 percent to 85 percent income-tax deduction for contributions to government-approved cultural activities. Corporations also are encouraged to adopt or use buildings for reasons of image and goodwill.

Public Education

Finally, the *Monumenta* Program tries to generate public interest in historical heritage sites and in how to maintain them through education and media campaigns. During project preparation the Brazilian Government carried out an attitude and knowledge survey that indicated general public unawareness of the significance of historic monuments. To inform people of the significance and value of their heritage, the program financed six high-quality documentaries for television and a number of television programs for distance education, to be shown in audio-visual classrooms. Educating the population develops a long-term constituency devoted to preserving the country's heritage.

Alternative Financial Instruments

The strategy used to encourage municipal participation and private-sector involvement in Brazil is not the one the IADB would have preferred, particularly because it does not guarantee that municipal governments will maintain historic areas and use the Preservation Fund in the way specified. The guarantee would be stronger if the federal government loaned the money to the municipality and forgave amortization payments if the municipality maintained the area and use the Preservation Fund appropriately.

The *Monumenta* Program also fails to provide a mechanism to transfer the benefits of success from a historic area in one city to historic areas in another, since the Preservation Fund belongs to the municipality, not to the Ministry of Culture.

Figure 4. Detail of Hotel Majestic renovated under the preservation program in Quito, Ecuador.

A restoration program for the historic center of Quito, Ecuador, addresses these problems. Ecuador's legal system permits the creation of a *mixed public-private corporation*, something not allowed in Brazil. The law also allows the government to expropriate properties. These two legal instruments facilitated the creation of a mixed corporation that could sell property expropriated by the public sector to third parties, something a government agency cannot do. Other advantages of a mixed corporation include its flexibility to enter into contracts without going to public bidding, and the absence of a requirement to pay taxes on profits that correspond to the public portion of its capital. Moreover, it can contract with municipal governments without going through the legal procedures that a private company would face (figure 4).

Another advantage of a mixed corporation is its ability to reinvest its funds where it chooses, solving the transfer problem experienced by the

Monumenta Program. In Brazil the program makes nonrecoverable donations to municipalities. However, if a municipality generates cash flow in
excess of conservation needs, the federal government cannot transfer
the surplus to another municipality for preservation.

The private sector participates in the Quito project in many ways and
without subsidy. First, it is represented on the board of directors, giving
the board a more entrepreneurial focus. The board reviews feasibility
studies and approves projects that are developed either by consultants,
the corporation, or interested private parties. Private capital also can
provide equity capital and participate proportionally in profits from all
the projects, or private partners can make individual investments in
buildings. Private owners can put up the building as their capital contribution, and the public corporation will provide funds to rehabilitate it; or
the private sector can make a cash investment. When the property is
restored and sold, the percentage of profits that correspond to the corporation's investment is reinvested. The public corporation provides
another option for private developers: a developer seeking to restore a
building needs only to have an approved plan. The developer does not
have to participate in the mixed corporation, which permits independent
participation using no public funds.

The incentives to participate in the Quito program are much stronger
than they are in the *Monumenta* Program. First, the mixed corporation is
in the position of a "godfather." It can say to building owners: "Either you
participate, or we will expropriate your building and compensate you for
the market value"—which is low because the area is deteriorated. Private
owners have a strong interest in cooperating. Yet, the participation
scheme reduces the risk to private owners, because the corporation shares
the risk. If the property sells at a loss, part of the loss is at the expense of
the government.

Conclusion

In neither Brazil nor Ecuador can governments afford to carry the entire
burden of monument preservation. Faced with limited means, they must
focus on the most important heritage; establish rules on use and adaptation that reduce the risks for potential partners; and mobilize partners
from municipal government, the private sector, residents, and other
interest groups. Incentives should be structured to elicit cost-effective
proposals, ensure future maintenance, and stimulate independent action.
Initial success will generate more public and private support for the conservation of heritage. ■

26 What Happened to Main Street?

Kennedy Smith

*Kennedy Smith is director of the Main
Street Program, United States National
Trust for Historic Preservation,
Kennedy_Smith@nthp.org*

America's downtowns have undergone three profound retail transformations in the past 50 years. Actually, they have undergone two profound economic transformations; the third is underway. Although this chapter focuses primarily on retail transformations, main streets have more diverse uses than retail only. However, retail uses are what historically made main streets work economically, and, as retailing has changed, the economic foundations of historic main streets have shifted.

Fifty years ago Main Street businesses in downtown areas of United States cities had a virtual monopoly on their community's residents, who could not easily get in a car and drive elsewhere to go shopping. Residents could get most of what they needed locally. If not, they could order things from one of the 50 or so mail-order companies that existed in 1945, or wait until their next trip to a larger town.

With the passage of the Interstate Highway Act of 1956 everything changed. Automobile production spiked, fueled by the post-War economic boom. People could suddenly drive longer distances to buy things. Between 1945 and 1995 the trade area of an average American small town expanded from 15 miles to more than 50 miles. With increased mobility came the ability to live farther from the town center. As people moved out, businesses followed.

Before long the suburban-style shopping mall was born, and the chain-store industry exploded with rapid growth. Shopping malls provided a ready-made environment for chain stores, following fairly predictable sales projections based on the demographic characteristics of middle-income American households. Chain stores located in shopping malls had considerable advantages over Main Street's mom-and-pop businesses. They had home offices with professional economists studying consumers and their shopping habits. They did not need to rely on financing from a local bank to get started. Everything in the store (window displays, background music) was part of a carefully planned formula. Consumers liked chains, and Main Street businesses suddenly had to become more competitive.

This explosion of shopping centers and malls was not a result of sharp increases in population or buying power. Mall management companies and chain stores simply figured that, because of their carefully crafted formulas, they could displace most or all of the sales taking place in existing businesses, the majority of which happened to be downtown. For the first time in Main Street's history, commercial space was being built without regard for whether there were enough retail dollars available in the community to support it.

Chain stores gave America something it had not had before—homogeneity. Unlike Main Street, whose eclectic blend of stores, offices, apartments, and other places was a recipe for uniqueness, malls (and the chain stores they contained) left nothing to the imagination.

Chain stores also gave manufacturers an immense distribution network. The person who figured out how to master this network was Sam Walton, whose company, Wal-Mart, now sells almost 20 percent of all "department-store-type-merchandise" in the United States. By eliminating the wholesaler and using their considerable buying power to dictate terms directly to manufacturers, Wal-Mart, its competitors (K-Mart, Price Club/Costco, and Target), and its cousins, the "category-killers" (superstores that sell only one type of merchandise, such as large-scale bookstores or auto parts retailers) have changed retail pricing in America.

These two transformations—the shopping mall and the discount superstore—have created one of the greatest crises in community economics in American history, because they have built far more commercial space than the country can possibly support. This, more than anything, has caused the economic problems that plague most of America's Main Streets. Our nation has such a glut of commercial space that it would take decades to absorb it all, even if nothing else were built. The U. S. currently has nine times more retail space per capita then it did in 1960. It is the equivalent of about 5,000 vacant shopping mall's worth of *empty* commercial space. Without enough retail dollars to support the amount of commercial space created, someone's commercial space will suffer—and usually it has been the downtown areas (figures 1, 2).

Figure 1. Construction of shopping malls in the U.S. in the 1950s, 1960s, and 1970s created a damaging oversupply of commercial space, emptying historic town centers of businesses and undercutting their economic foundations.

Figure 2. A vacant Main Street building will cost its community more than $250,000 in lost indirect economic activity.

Moreover, many communities make economically foolish choices about the kinds of businesses they recruit and develop. A locally owned business returns more than 60 percent of its profits to the community in which it is located. A chain store, however, returns only about 20 percent of its profit; the remainder typically is distributed to shareholders or invested in corporate expansion (figures 3, 4). Discount superstores return even less economically to the community; estimates range between 5 and 8 percent. Ironically, communities that attract discount superstores in hopes of expanding the employment base or increasing sales and property tax revenues find that they are actually impoverishing themselves. They are shifting jobs and tax revenues from a place already served by municipal infrastructure and services (the town center) to a new place in which services must be expanded or duplicated.

When a downtown is vacant, it is not just struggling or bankrupt businesses that suffer. The indirect economic impact on the entire community is deep and severe. A typical two-story vacant Main Street building, for example, will cost its community more than $250,000 in lost *indirect* economic activity, including diminished property taxes (meaning less money for social services, education, recreation, and other civic priorities); lost salaries and diminished wages; lost advertising revenue; lost loan demand; lost bank deposits (discounters and chains usually deposit their daily till overnight in a local bank but wire it out to their home office the next day); and lost utility collections.

Main Street Program

The Main Street Program was created because of the profound changes that retail transformations were bringing about in America's historic downtowns. In the mid-1970s the National Trust for Historic Preservation's Midwest Regional Office noticed a steadily increasing number of calls from people concerned about their downtown areas. Buildings were deteriorating, and no one knew how to stop the downward cycle. The National Trust put together a demonstration project—the Main Street Project—to find out what was really happening and develop some possible approaches. The new program targeted three Midwest communities and assigned a full-time manager to each city to try to unravel the problem.

Initial analysis showed that previous approaches to downtown revitalization had failed primarily because of one of three factors: they were too narrow in focus (for example, addressing only physical improvements); they relied on the "big-fix" solution *du jour* (the pedestrian mall, convention center, festival marketplace, or marina); or they were the work of either the private or public sector alone.

Figure 3. It takes more effort, planning, and partnering on the part of local and regional governments to develop locally owned businesses than to recruit chain stores. However, locally owned businesses contribute much more to the economic and cultural stability of the community.

Working with the three demonstration communities in the Midwest over three years, the Main Street Project developed a matrix for organizing revitalization activity: the "Main Street Four-Point Approach." It revolves around four broad areas in which work must take place simultaneously and gradually:

1. *Design*, covering all physical aspects of the downtown: rehabilitating existing buildings; building compatible new buildings; improving signs, parking, and public spaces; making window displays and in-store merchandise displays more enticing.
2. *Organization*, which involves building collaborative partnerships among a broad range of public- and private-sector groups, agencies, individuals, organizations, and businesses; mobilizing volunteers to play active roles in the ongoing revitalization process; and obtaining full-time, ongoing professional staff to coordinate the program.
3. *Promotion*, the marketing component of the Main Street approach, involves letting residents, investors, and visitors know what the downtown has to offer.
4. *Economic restructuring*, or strengthening the downtown's existing economic base while finding ways to expand it: conducting retail market analysis to identify market opportunities, strengthening existing businesses, developing new businesses, and diversifying the economic uses of the district's buildings.

The Main Street revitalization process begins gradually, with small-scale, low-cost, but often high-visibility physical improvements and festivals and special events that bring people downtown—not necessarily to spend

Figure 4. A chain store returns only about 20 percent of its profit to the local community.

money but just to have a good time. At the same time the local Main Street organization is learning about the downtown's best market opportunities and developing a solid, realistic, and achievable strategy to strengthen existing businesses, develop new ones, and find new types of uses for downtown spaces. Unused or under-utilized upper floor spaces, side-street locations, or abandoned warehouses or other industrial buildings are of special interest.

During the first few years of the Main Street revitalization program, participants build the basic skills and develop the basic tools they will need to help the program tackle larger challenges down the road. These challenges include, for example, rehabilitating "white elephant" buildings; overcoming regulatory barriers that sometimes make it easier to develop commercial space on strips than in downtown areas; and helping independently owned businesses thrive in an era in which almost 20 percent of all retail sales are made by mail-order. The process never ends and requires full-time management.

The Main Street Program is a truly incremental process of economic transformation. During the first few years of a local Main Street revitalization program a community usually sees only very modest amounts of new investment, but after the third year investment climbs steadily upwards, and eventually plateaus. Today 43 states and Puerto Rico have launched statewide Main Street programs. The program also has served as a model for similar initiatives in Australia, Canada, New Zealand, Singapore, and Venezuela.

The cumulative economic gains these communities have made are astonishing. Through the end of 1999 historic commercial districts participating in the Main Street program had experienced over $12.8 billion in new investment, a net gain of 193,000 new jobs and 51,000 new businesses, and over 62,000 building rehabilitation projects. Most important, every dollar that a participating community spends to support its Main Street revitalization effort is leveraging an average of $38.34 in new investment.

The three most recent U. S. administrations have named the Main Street program as one of the most successful economic development strategies in the nation. However, the program is really focused on *historic preservation*, and it proves unequivocally that preservation is one of the best economic development strategies a community, state, or nation can follow (figure 5).

What Lies Ahead?

In spring 2000 the National Trust surveyed people in the 1,500 Main Street communities to find out what kinds of economic (or other) changes they had witnessed over the past year. More than 90 percent of respondents expressed optimism about their downtowns' futures. They also said that they were experiencing significant increases in professional offices, retail businesses, and housing within their districts. Occupancy levels were higher than in the previous year; retail sales had increased; and more people were attending promotional events and festivals in the town center.

Figure 5. Promotion of local heritage should encompass the business environment as well as the physical environment. Boston, Massachusetts has created a citywide program called "Our Fortune Is Made," highlighting family-owned businesses operated by multiple generations that provide unique products and services.

One of the most amazing trends to emerge from the survey was the rapid growth of "location-neutral" businesses in Main Street districts. A "location-neutral" business is one that can be located nearly anywhere because its customers do not necessarily live in the community. Such companies might be fund managers, publishers, mail order fulfillment companies, consultants, or any of a host of other businesses that, because of overnight delivery services and the Internet, can locate almost anywhere. In increasing numbers these companies are seeking out historic downtowns in which to locate. Among the reasons for this trend are that overhead is usually lower in cities than in strip malls; the buildings are unique; and downtown areas offer walking-distance access to banks, post offices, office supply stores, restaurants, and other services needed by small businesses.

This trend is a true win-win for America's downtown areas. It gives property owners another source of rental income, which makes it easier to afford building rehabilitation and maintenance. By increasing the number of workers in the downtown area, this new trend bolsters the downtown's convenience-oriented businesses; and it puts business owners in close proximity to the services they need. A surprising 84 percent of survey respondents reported that there were more businesses in their districts using the Internet now than just one year ago, which leads to the third retail transformation affecting historic downtowns: the Internet.

Just as shopping malls redefined the relationship between manufacturers and retailers, the Internet provides a new way for retail businesses to reach customers. Unlike the two previous economic transformations, which *hurt* most American downtown areas, the Internet offers new opportunities to expand their sales.

An example is "Nine Lives," a consignment store in a Main Street community in California that sells upscale, second-hand clothing. Using the store's website, customers can indicate what they want to buy, as well as size, color, and other preferences. When new consignments arrive, they are entered into the database and the computer matches merchandise to customer's "orders." Other examples include a business located in downtown Beatrice, Nebraska that recharges toner cartridges for printers and fax machines for customers from several states; a drugstore in downtown Miami, Oklahoma that allows customers to refill their prescriptions online; and a business in Coronado, California that offers specialty merchandise through its website to customers throughout the world.

By enabling people to shop more easily, regardless of where a business is located, the Internet expands a small, independently owned business's market reach from the immediate community to, theoretically, the entire world. Operating a website is much less expensive than mail-order marketing because it eliminates printing and postage charges. This new technology also provides a way for small businesses that might not be able to survive solely from local sales to augment income by finding customers who may never visit their store and thus do not exacerbate downtown parking and transportation problems. For many specialty businesses in particular, increasing sales by as little as 5 to 8 percent can make the difference between remaining viable and failing. The Internet also makes it possible for downtown companies to do business 24 hours a day, 365 days a year.

Obstacles and Challenges

Although most of the communities surveyed by the National Trust for Historic Preservation were optimistic about their downtown's future, obstacles still lie ahead. The regulatory environment often makes it easier to develop commercial and mixed-use space on a strip than on a Main Street. Zoning laws may make it illegal to develop upper-floor housing over a commercial storefront. Inflexible parking regulations can make it difficult to bring some uses downtown, including housing, restaurants, and small-scale industry. Building codes designed to regulate new construction after World War II sometimes make it difficult to rehabilitate downtown buildings for new uses. Financing may not be available for downtown projects, particularly those involving mixed uses (such as ground-floor retail uses and upper-floor housing).

One of the greatest challenges facing America's Main Streets today is complacency. People believe that things are going well enough, so they let things slide and fail to pay attention to the dramatic economic transformations taking place around them. Or people believe that "progress is progress" and that they are powerless to guide the ways in which change and growth occur. Others believe that keeping our town centers and communities healthy is someone else's job. Downtown revitalization is everyone's job. Everyone plays a role in the process, and, ultimately, everyone benefits. As Margaret Mead once said: "Never doubt that a small group of thoughtful, committed citizens can change the world; indeed, it's the only thing that ever has." ■

27 Involving the People and Municipal Bonds in Development and Preservation in Ahmedabad

Keshav Varma

Keshav Varma is sector manager for the East Asia Urban Development Division at the World Bank.

Ahmedabad is truly a unique city, a warm blend of cultural heritage and a modern business center. With its population of 4 million and its 600-year history, Ahmedabad is the premier city of the western-most state of India, Gujarat. The city has been known for its textile industry, its several professional institutes, two of the most prestigious of which are the Indian Institute of Management of Ahmedabad and the National Institute of Design. The old city, formerly the Walled City, prides itself on its wooden houses known as *havelis* with beautiful facades and cool and welcoming interiors.

I had the honor of serving as Ahmedabad's Municipal Commissioner from 1994 to 1997. I joined at a rather intense period when the aftereffects of the plague in nearby Surat were having their repercussions in our city. People were impatient with poor delivery of services and the deteriorating quality of infrastructure. The Municipal Corporation was the obvious target. Corporation staff were demoralized. The challenge was to create hope, pride, and camaraderie (figure 1).

History

Ahmedabad was a rich city with a poor municipal body. It had suffered from cash losses for over two decades. Most of the revenue of the corporation was being directed toward meeting administrative costs and performing minor repairs. The challenge was inviting. The strategy was to create immediate and visible results that would have an impact on the psyche of the citizens and infuse a sense of confidence in the staff. The

Figure 1. An improved public park, Ahmedabad, India.

choice was either to run the city from the cool confines of the Municipal Commissioner's chamber or to move into the streets, meet the people, face the anger, and do something about it. We decided to move into the field and confront the vested interest, the builder lobby, the mafia that was involved in the octroi operations.[1] Within a very short time a computerized management information system was developed that helped tighten the recovery of municipal taxes and octroi. More than 40 Masters of Business Administration, chartered accountants, and engineers were recruited to infuse new blood and a new management culture in the organization. From this success emerged a municipal body that was credible in the eyes of its citizens. The improvement in major roads and lighting; night checking by Municipal Corporation staff and tax recovery inspectors to prevent theft of revenue from the octroi posts by the mafia; and a campaign to keep the city clean and totally free from litter in the congregation areas, especially the night markets, helped create a sense of civic awareness.

Effective Municipal Management

Municipal management is about openness and inclusion. It is like an act in which one has to perform center stage. Progressive municipal management generates outreach and communication and removes the layers of mystery that generally engulf city administrations. We reached out to the press, nongovernmental organizations (NGOs), and professional groups. They responded warmly and strongly because they saw the fabric of the city undergoing a visible change. We reached out to children, politicians, opposition leaders, community groups, and teachers. Our message was, 'This is your city, a city with a great heritage in which you have to do your part to improve your own quality of life and that of the generations that will follow you.' Our message also was that we meant business in terms of our intent to be financially sustainable in all our strategies.

We also made it clear to the staff and to the trade unions inside the Municipal Corporation that the municipal body existed not to serve its own individual ends but to service the people and the city. This is an important message, and if heeded well, creates miracles. Traditionally, city halls tend to be rather inward-looking. They are perceived as corrupt, mysterious, and unresponsive. It is only when the institution turns its face toward the city and starts responding to it that an emotional link is created between the institution and the people. This emotional link is the essence of city management.

We emphasized and worked on this issue. We built on the inherent pride and a traditional business sense of the people of Ahmedabad; we built on the great heritage of the city both in terms of culture and built heritage. We built on the role the city had played when Mahatma Gandhi led the freedom struggle from Sabarmati Ashram in Ahmedabad. Once this emotional partnership comes alive and sublimates itself, city management becomes a joyful adventure of creativity and innovation and an extremely gratifying personal experience.

Within five months the city's overdraft was cleared, and people lined up in overwhelming numbers to pay the tax arrears. Within 3 months the municipal income shot up from 3 million rupees per day to 6 million rupees per day, stabilizing at 10 millions rupees per day. An interesting dimension of this volunteerism was that citizens started removing their encroachments from the city roads. Of course, firm action was taken to clear major city roads from unscrupulous land sharks. The water tariff was raised almost three times, as well as the sewerage and solid waste management charges. There was not a murmur of protest.

In the ensuing three years over 340 kilometers of roads were paved, some of them redesigned to international standards with private sector support. Hundreds of thousands of trees were planted with the help of

Figure 2. A plain strip of asphalt:
CG Road before improvement, Ahmedabad.

corporate entities. Gardens and parks were upgraded, and the water and sanitation system was rehabilitated and augmented (figures 2-4).

The *pols* polio immunization program covering the entire city was successfully carried out.[2] Preliminary medical examinations of 300,000 children in 500 municipal schools were conducted and followed up with the help of three hospitals run by the Municipal Corporation. The Municipal Corporation hospitals were upgraded and technically refined. These hospitals received more than 3 million patients per year, the majority of whom were poor.

The water distribution system was upgraded and organized and indiscipline was firmly curbed. One of the schemes launched at that time was *Parivartan*, meaning "change," an ambitious project focused on slums in the city covering 2,412 locations and 1.2 million urban poor. The idea was an innovative one of creating a triangular partnership among the beneficiaries, the private sector, and the municipal body. The Self-Employed Women's Association (SEWA) came forward to support this initiative, which has now taken root in several slums and is moving ahead steadily. I feel this is one of the few urban slum initiatives that has the capacity of scaling up and should prove to be sustainable.

Once the finances of the Municipal Corporation stabilized, a corporate perspective plan for the next 10 years was built with a total outlay of 7

Figure 3. A more efficient CG Road:
the main commercial street, Ahmedabad.

billion rupees (at that time the rupee was 26 to US$1). We needed inno-
vative solutions to service this and, quite by accident, decided on the
municipal bond. The idea came from Mr. Dave, former Chairman of
United Trust of India, who happened to visit Ahmedabad and spent some
of his precious time with me. He followed up his suggestion by requesting CRISIL, the premier credit rating agency in India, to visit us and
explore the possibility. CRISIL followed this opportunity with great commitment and passion. Their team spent over six months reviewing the
finances of the Corporation and the process of building up the criteria of
credit rating municipal bodies such as ours. After six months we waited
like schoolboys for the results and were elated to learn that the rating
was A+. This rating was received with a great sense of pride and jubila-
tion by the city. What followed was a process of moving towards launch-
ing of a municipal bond, an exercise very ably and professionally supported by a USAID team headed by Earl Kessler and Kamran Khan. The
process took some time getting through the bureaucracy of the State
Government, but finally we ended up with a credit rating of AA.

Interest on the bond was 14.25 percent. The political wing supported the
process, although traditionally municipal bonds are not considered "con-
venient" by politicians and administrators because of the need to be very
transparent and responsive. Bonds create a benchmark in terms of effectiveness and efficiency and, most importantly, they involve the residents
in improving the city's infrastructure.

Ahmedabad began with a small municipal bond of US$33 million, for which the city did considerable advertising. Interested parties began to say that instead of US$33 million, the bond should be issued for US$100 million. This idea generated much support not only locally but also among professionals from Ahmedabad who live in the United States. Moreover, expatriates began returning to the city, investing, buying back *havelis*, and restoring them. Eventually, the bond was completely subscribed, despite the bank's raising the interest rate to 16 percent. The experiment was successful, and it came in handy in financially supporting the water intake line from the Mahi River to Ahmedabad city.

Ahmedabad's experiment came to be viewed as a best practice on solid waste management, municipal credit and finance, and revival of an old city. Just as important, public attitudes and behavior changed, and a real sense of civic pride exists. People in the Walled City feel more integrated in the mainstream of the city. They are changing a 600-year-old city into a productive place. The city is much cleaner, tourism has grown, and epidemics have greatly decreased. Moreover, since 1993, the city has been calm. The communal tension that used to occur there, primarily in the Walled City, has subsided.

Ahmedabad's example has led several other Indian cities to obtain credit ratings, and some are trying to float bonds. The concept is also being promoted in the Philippines and Thailand. The important thing to remember is that bonds should not be seen simply as financial instruments; they should be seen as instruments to bring people together and create partnerships.

Built Heritage

On the side of built heritage, city authorities took on a number of historic preservation challenges: restoration of the Walled City gates, heritage walks, encouragement of community initiatives to protect heritage, adaptive reuse of colonial mansions, and a comprehensive plan for revitalizing the Walled City. One of the main issues was popular involvement to ensure that residents became more aware of their heritage and understood its importance. Laws are not enough. In Ahmedabad builders destroyed a 400-year-old, incredibly beautiful haveli even though the city had issued a stay. Yet there was no outcry from the public.

One of the municipality's first steps was an effort to create awareness and involve youth, encouraging them to think about cleanliness and the potential for tourism. The city brought the private sector, NGOs, and young people together in public meetings to increase their awareness and solicit their support. A local NGO and the Cruta Foundation, which had done similar work in Calcutta, started working to restore one of the havelis. To create a symbol that would attract community participation and bring communities together, city authorities offered a property-tax concession and a

Figure 4. "Corporate citizens" worked to improve parks and gardens, Ahmedabad.

restoration grant to cover the cost of upgrading the building. Eleven *pols* were cleaned up and opened for "heritage walks" by tourists. Residents soon noticed the difference and spoke positively of the effort.

Components of Success

What were the key factors in making Ahmedabad a success story? Leadership, commitment, passion, and popular involvement made the difference. City authorities were determined to turn the situation around. Their efforts and commitment sparked interest and involvement by the private sector and civil society in general—and discouraged criminal activity. Even schoolchildren helped by bringing important environmental messages home to their parents. The municipal bond played a key role, in part because it increased accountability and changed perceptions about city management.

Sitting in my office at the World Bank, I often reflect on my experiences in Ahmedabad. Words like enthusiasm, optimism, hard work, pride, joy, partnerships, commitment, and passion come to mind. People are sick of pessimism and with the tendency, which is one of the biggest problems in India, toward inaction and risk aversion. A city is a living organism. It has a cultural core; it has a professional core; but most importantly, it has a mind and a heart of its own. Municipal management is about stimulating the heart and the mind. Then the rest becomes easy. The success story of Ahmedabad Municipal Corporation is the success story of its people, some of whom also work in the Municipal Corporation, and the joy and pride they take in what they do. ■

Notes

1 Octroi is a local tax levied on all commercial goods entering the city boundaries.

2 A *pol* is a traditional built form in the old city typified by narrow streets and closely built houses. *Pols* were constructed for defense from attack from criminal riots and for community interaction. Many household activities also take place there such as washing clothes and utensils.

28 Treatment of Cultural Landscapes in the United States

Charles A. Birnbaum

Charles A. Birnbaum, FASLA, is coordinator, Historic Landscape Initiative, Historic Preservation Services, U. S. National Park Service, a fellow of the American Society of Landscape Architects, and an instructor for the National Preservation Institute, Charles_Birnbaum@nps.gov

The United States National Park Service Historic Landscape Initiative (NPS/HLI) promotes responsible preservation practices that protect our nation's irreplaceable legacy. This legacy includes three categories of landscape: designed landscapes, such as parks and gardens; vernacular historic landscapes, such as farms and industrial sites; and ethnographic landscapes, such as sacred religious sites and massive geological structures.

In partnership with federal and state agencies, professional organizations, and colleges and universities, the Historic Landscape Initiative (HLI) achieves its goal by developing and disseminating guidelines for significant historic landscape preservation. The potential benefits from landscape preservation are enormous. Landscapes provide scenic, economic, ecological, social, recreational, and educational value. The ongoing preservation of historic landscapes can yield an improved quality of life for all, and, above all, a sense of place or identity for future generations.

Management of Cultural Landscapes

"The Secretary of the Interior's Standards for the Treatment of Historic Properties" and the "Guidelines for the Treatment of Cultural Landscapes" represent important contributions to historical preservation.[1] The "Standards" are neither technical nor prescriptive but rather promote responsible preservation practices that help protect irreplaceable cultural resources. They cannot be used to make essential decisions about which contributing features of a cultural landscape should be retained and which changed. However, once a specific *treatment* is selected, the standards provide the framework for a consistent and holistic approach to cultural landscape projects.

Selecting an Appropriate Treatment

A treatment is a physical intervention carried out to achieve a historic preservation goal. A treatment cannot be considered in a vacuum. A broad array of dynamic and interrelated variables must be considered when selecting a treatment for a cultural landscape preservation project. These include, but are not limited to, the extent of available historic documentation; existing physical conditions; historic value; proposed use(s); long- and short-term objectives; operational and code requirements (accessibility, fire, security); and anticipated capital improvement, staffing, and maintenance costs. The impact of the treatment on significant archeological and natural resources also should be considered in the decisionmaking process.

Preservation Planning

Careful preservation planning prior to treatment can help prevent irrevocable damage to a cultural landscape. Professional techniques for identifying, documenting, and treating cultural landscapes have advanced over the past 25 years, and are continually being refined. As described in the NPS publication, "Preservation Brief 36: Protecting Cultural Landscapes," the preservation planning process for cultural landscapes should involve:

- Historical research
- Inventory and documentation of existing conditions
- Site analysis and evaluation of integrity and significance
- Development of a cultural landscape preservation approach and treatment plan
- Development of a cultural landscape management plan and management philosophy
- Development of a strategy for ongoing maintenance
- Preparation of a record of treatment and future research recommendations.

Recommendations for All Treatment Projects

In addition to the application of the Standards within the general context of preservation, key general recommendations for all treatment projects follow:

- Prior to undertaking project work, research on the cultural landscape is essential. Research findings help to identify a landscape's historic period(s) of ownership, occupancy, and development, and yield greater understanding of the associations that make it significant. Research findings also provide a foundation for educated decisions on project treatment and can guide management, maintenance, and interpretation.
- The goal of documentation is to provide a record of the landscape as it exists, thus providing a baseline from which to operate. All organizational elements (spatial organization, land patterns, views, and

vistas) and features (topography, vegetation, circulation, water features, structures, furnishings and objects) that contribute to the landscape's historic character should be recorded. The level of detail needed depends on the nature and the significance of the resource.

- Assessing a landscape as a historical continuum is critical to evaluating its cultural and historic value. Examining the chronological and physical "layers" of the landscape can help to understand change over time. Based on such analysis, individual features can be attributed to a discrete period of introduction and their presence or absence tied to a given date, thus helping to evaluate the landscape's significance and integrity. Finally, this analysis allows the property to be viewed within the context of other cultural landscapes.

- Preservation planning for cultural landscapes involves a broad array of dynamic variables. Adopting holistic treatment and management plans, in concert with a preservation maintenance strategy, acknowledges a cultural landscape's ever-changing nature and the interrelationship among treatment, management, and maintenance.

Important Factors to Consider

In addition to the considerations outlined above, the following factors also should be considered in all landscape preservation projects.

Change and Continuity

Change is inherent in cultural landscapes, resulting from both natural processes and human activities. Sometimes change is barely perceptible; at other times it is strikingly obvious. This dynamic quality of cultural landscapes is balanced by the continuity of distinctive characteristics retained over time. Despite a landscape's constant change, or perhaps because of it, a property can exhibit continuity of form, order, use, features, or materials. The appropriate treatment of cultural landscapes seeks to secure and emphasize continuity while accepting change (figure 1).

Relative Historical Significance

A cultural landscape might be a significant resource as a rare survivor or the work of an important landscape architect, horticulturist, or designer. It could be the site of an important event or reflect cultural traditions. It significance may derive from local, regional, or national factors. Cultural landscapes may be listed individually or as contributing features in a historic district. In some instances cultural landscapes may be National Historic Landmarks, designated for their "exceptional significance in American history."

Integrity and Physical Condition

Prior to selecting a treatment, it is important to understand and evaluate the difference between integrity and existing conditions. Integrity is

Figure 1. A remarkable record of human occupation exists at Canyon de Chelly National Monument in Chinle, Arizona, and any preservation planning initiative should recognize this long and rich continuum. This cultural landscape represents a vast mosaic of human activity through time, up to the present-day Navajo.

the authenticity of a cultural landscape's historic identity—the physical evidence of its significance. Existing conditions can be defined as the current physical state of the landscape's form, order, features, and materials. The integrity of an abandoned garden may be clear based on its extant form, features, and materials. However, existing conditions may be poor, due to benign neglect or deferred maintenance.

The formal garden designed at the turn of the nineteenth century in Garfield Park, Indianapolis, by pioneer landscape architect George Kessler was in a state of advanced deterioration and in poor physical condition. However, its visual and spatial relationships were virtually intact, as were its character-defining walls, paving, garden objects, and furnishings, thus suggesting that the landscape had a high level of design integrity.

Use

Historic, current, and proposed use of the cultural landscape must be considered prior to selecting a treatment. Historic use is directly linked to significance, while current and proposed use(s) can affect integrity and existing conditions. Parameters may vary from one landscape to another. In one agricultural landscape continuation of historic use can lead to changes in the physical form of a farm to accommodate new crops and equipment. In another agricultural property, new uses might be adapted within the landscape's existing form, order, and features (figure 2).

Figure 2. Acoma Pueblo, 60 miles west of Albuquerque, New Mexico, is one of the oldest continuously inhabited villages in the United States, dating back over 1,000 years. Many of its historic uses are still evident in the traditional construction of adobe-masonry architecture, outside ovens, and outhouses.

Context

The surroundings of a cultural landscape, whether an urban neighborhood or rural farming area, contribute to its significance and historic character and should be considered prior to treatment. The context may contain organizational elements of the landscape (spatial organization, land patterns, views, and vistas) or "character-defining" features (topography, vegetation, water) that fall within the property's historic limits. The context may also include separate properties, beyond the landscape's boundaries, as well as overall patterns of circulation networks, views and vistas into and out of the landscape, land use, natural features, clusters of structures, and division of properties (figures 3, 4).

Archeological Resources

Cultural landscapes may contain prehistoric and historic archeological resources, above or below the ground, or even under water. Such resources include prehistoric mounds built by Native Americans, cliff dwellings, and villages. Historic archeological resources might include features such as a sunken garden, mining camp, or battlefield. These resources not only have historical value, but can also reveal significant information about a cultural landscape. Appropriate treatment of a cultural landscape includes the identification and preservation of significant archeological resources (figure 5).

Biotic Systems

Biotic systems are an integral part of the cultural landscape and must be considered when selecting an appropriate treatment. The significance of these natural resources may derive from their cultural associations or their inherent ecological values. Natural resources form interdependent biotic systems that may extend well beyond the boundary of the historic property. Such systems can include geology, hydrology, plant and animal

habitats, and climate. Some biotic resources are particularly susceptible to disturbances caused by changes in landscape management. Many natural systems, such as wetlands or rare species, fall under government regulations. Since natural resource protection is a specialized field, distinct from cultural landscape preservation, specialized expertise may be required to address specific issues or resources found on the property (figure 6).

Figure 3. At Mount Vernon, Virginia, home of George Washington, the landscape's spatial organization and land patterns within the historic property have been preserved.

Management and Maintenance

Management strategies are long-term and comprehensive and can serve as a means to implement a landscape preservation plan. Maintenance may be day-to-day, seasonal, or cyclical activities, depending on management strategies. Although mowing and weeding, or relaying pavement

Figure 4. Mount Vernon's spatial organization and land patterns within its geographic context also have been preserved.

Figure 5. In recognition of the importance of the archeological resources at the core of the Anasazi complex at Chaco Culture National Historic Park in Bloomfield, New Mexico, every effort has been made to preserve and protect its cultural resources since it was designated a National Monument in 1907.

Figure 6. Invasive plant materials such as Phragmites (tall, reed-like grasses) have overtaken sections of the watercourse along the Emerald Necklace Park in Boston, Massachusetts, diminishing the park's historic character. This interface between the park's natural and cultural values is the subject of discussions for this masterwork of landscape architecture designed by Frederick Law Olmsted, Sr. and his successor firm.

or curbs may appear routine, such activities can have a cumulative effect on the landscape. Therefore, both management and maintenance of cultural landscapes should be considered when selecting a treatment (figure 7).

Interpretation

Interpretation, including guided walks, brochures, and exhibits, can aid in understanding and "reading" the landscape. When considered a management objective, interpretive goals should complement treatment selection, reflecting the landscape's significance and historic character (figure 8).

Special Requirements

Work to meet accessibility, health, and safety requirements is assessed in advance for potential impact on the cultural landscape (figures 9, 10).

Figure 7. Irrigation and other modern turf-management techniques have changed the historic character of the lawn at Scotts Bluff National Monument in Gering, Nebraska. Trees are dying from over-watering, and the manicured blue-grass lawn is distinctly different from its historic appearance.

Figure 8. Franklin Court in Philadelphia, Pennsylvania, had little remaining integrity yet had significant historical associations. The solution including "ghost-ing" vanished historic structures based on archaeological investigations.

Using the Standards and Guidelines for the Treatment of Cultural Landscapes

The "Secretary of the Interior's Standards for the Treatment of Historic Properties" are designed to be applied to *all* historic resource types included in the United States National Register of Historic Places: buildings, sites, structures, landscapes, districts, and objects. "The Guidelines for the Treatment of Cultural Landscapes" apply to a *specific* resource type: landscapes.

Figures 9, 10. The Houghton Chapel at Wellesley College, Massachusetts, was made accessible by regrading over the historic stone steps.

The Guidelines were prepared to assist in applying the standards to all project work involving the treatment of cultural landscapes. They are not meant to give case-specific advice or address exceptions or rare instances. Therefore, it is recommended that the advice of qualified cultural landscape preservation professionals be obtained early in the planning stage of the project. Such professionals may have expertise in landscape architecture, history, or archeology; forestry; horticulture; natural resources; architecture; engineering; cultural geography; or other related fields. Historians generally are part of the specialized team and bring expertise in the history of the landscape, architecture, art, industry, agriculture, and society. Project teams often are directed by a landscape architect with specific expertise in landscape preservation.

The Guidelines apply to cultural landscapes of all types, sizes, and materials. Each section of the publication is devoted to one of four possible treatments: *preservation, rehabilitation, restoration,* or *reconstruction* and contains a set of standards and accompanying guidelines that can be used throughout the course of a project. Each section includes a definition of the treatment and treatment standards and a brief essay that sets out a philosophical framework from which to make educated treatment decisions. The sections are illustrated by case studies that include before and after photographs, historic documentation, plans, sections, perspectives, and other illustrative materials. Exploring one of these treatments, rehabilitation, illustrates how the guidelines are organized and can be applied to a variety of landscapes.

Rehabilitation Treatment

Rehabilitation is defined as the act or process of making possible a compatible use for a property through repair, alterations, and additions while preserving portions or features that convey its historical, cultural, or architectural value. Rehabilitation is recommended when repair or replacement of deteriorated features is necessary; when alterations or additions to the property are planned for new or continued use; and when its depiction at a particular period of time is not appropriate. Prior to undertaking work, a documentation plan for rehabilitation should be developed.

The defining features and materials of cultural landscapes must be protected and maintained during rehabilitation, just as they would be during a preservation treatment. The difference is that a determination has been made that a greater amount of existing historic fabric has become damaged or deteriorated over time and, as a result, more repair and replacement is required. The rehabilitation guidelines allow for the replacement of extensively deteriorated, damaged, or missing features using either traditional or substitute materials. Of the four treatments, only rehabilitation includes an opportunity to create an efficient contemporary use through alterations and additions. Examples would be replacing tillage with permanent grasslands to support a new system of livestock grazing or introducing new turf management to a park's open meadows to support a sports field.

Identifying, Retaining, and Preserving Historic Materials and Features

The rehabilitation process should begin by identifying landscape features and materials important to the landscape's historic character that must be retained. The overall evaluation of existing conditions should always begin at this level. The character of a cultural landscape is defined by its spatial organization and land patterns; features such as topography, vegetation, and circulation; and materials, such as an embedded aggregate pavement (figure 11).

Figure 11. After the significant landscape features associated with the Hokenson Brothers Fishery were identified, a contract with a modern concessionaire was adopted to preserve the former family-owned operation at Apostle Islands National Seashore, Wisconsin.

Protecting, Maintaining, and Repairing Historic Features and Materials

Protection generally involves the least degree of intervention and is preparatory to other work. Protection techniques may include restricting access to fragile earthworks or cabling a tree to protect against breakage. Maintenance can include daily, seasonal, and cyclical tasks and the techniques, methods, and materials used to implement them (figure 12).

Figure 12. In the County of Maui, Hawaii, taro patches, which have often been associated with small hand-cultivated ponds, have come to represent a declining land use. Recent preservation planning efforts to protect these landscape features include the passage of an ordinance granting tax relief to properties in taro production.

When the condition of character-defining materials and portions of features warrants more extensive work, repair is recommended. Guidance for the repair of historic features and materials (such as brick pavements, masonry walls, or wire fencing) begins by recommending the least possible

Figure 13. To repair the fence surrounding Lafayette Square in Saint Louis, Missouri, castings were made to replace a limited number of lost finials along the park's perimeter.

degree of intervention. Such work could include regrading a section of a silted swale, aerating soil, or reclaiming a segment of meadow edge. Repair may also include limited replacement in kind of extensively deteriorated materials or parts of features, or replacement in kind of materials or parts of features lost due to seasonal change (figure 13).

Replacing Deteriorated or Missing Historic Materials and Features

Guidance is provided for replacing an entire character-defining feature with new material, either because the level of deterioration or damage precludes repair or an entire feature is missing. The preferred option is always replacement of the entire feature in kind. Because this approach may not always be technically, economically, or environmentally feasible, the use of compatible substitute materials can be considered. Whatever level of replacement takes place, historic features and materials should serve as a guide to the work. The guidelines never recommend removal and replacement with new material if repair is possible (figure 14).

When an entire feature is missing, the landscape's historic character is diminished. In such a case replacement is always preferred. If historical, pictorial, and physical documentation permits accurate reproduction of the feature, planning, designing, and installing a new feature are appropriate. Replacement could also involve a new design compatible with the remaining character-defining features of the historic landscape (figure 15).

Altering or Adding to Cultural Landscapes for New Use

When alterations to a cultural landscape are needed to assure its continued use, such alterations should not radically change, obscure, or destroy character-defining spatial organization and land patterns or features and materials. Such work may also include the selective removal of features that detract from the overall historic character.

Figure 14. The "repair if possible" principle guided the replacement work in the historic birch allee at Stan Hywet Hall, Akron, Ohio. Dying trees were topped, and basal sprouts were encouraged. Original rootstock and genetic material were preserved.

Figure 15. Rebuilt rustic furnishings in New York City's Central Park match the original features in appearance yet satisfy current maintenance and management requirements.

The installation of additions to a cultural landscape may seem essential for the new use. However, the rehabilitation guidelines stress that such additions should be avoided if possible. They should be considered only after a determination that those needs cannot be met by altering secondary (non-character-defining) spatial organization and land patterns or features (figure 16). ■

Figure 16. The significance of Village of Waterford, Virginia, is conveyed by the integrity of its topography, architecture, hedgerows, and other landscape features. In recognition that development was inevitable, a plan to accommodate limited new residential construction (shaded buildings) while still protecting significant spatial organization and land patterns was adopted.

Note

1 See the standards and guidelines on the National Park Service website at www.cr.nps.gov

Investment Impacts of Tourism in Historic Districts

29

With its ability to quickly generate jobs, foreign exchange, and tax revenues tourism has become a preferred industry in many developing countries. Annual revenues in international tourism exceed US$500 billion.[1] Adding earnings from purely domestic travelers—for many countries, the largest form of tourism—the figure could be 10 times higher. Industry specialists forecast that such figures will triple over the next 20 years. However, tourism is a volatile industry reliant on heavy initial capital expenditure (figure 1).

The International Finance Corporation (IFC) and other international agencies have invested in several major cities in which private investors are seeking to improve the tourist industry, often by rehabilitating historic hotels. The Bristol Hotel in Warsaw, the Hanoi Metropole in Vietnam, and the elegant Polana Hotel in Mozambique are examples of IFC investments in this area. The first new, or rehabilitated, hotel investment often facilitates additional business development by providing an adequate "home base" for accommodations, meetings, and communication. It is also an investment that leverages the formation of many other small and medium businesses in the service sector.

A core issue, not only for tourism, but for most capital investments with a physical dimension is how to achieve an acceptable balance between the positive and negative impacts of a given undertaking and mitigate the worst effects. Such environmental and social dimensions are best debated and reconciled in the political arena, but this is not always possible in early investments in a transitional economy—or when governments lack the expertise to facilitate such debate.

Increasingly, the huge but fragmented global tourism industry is realizing that if its activities harm local ecosystems or societies, they will destroy the very basis on which they are built. "Sustained growth in arrivals is no longer the main criteria," states Eugenio Yunis of the World

Maurice Desthuis-Francis

Maurice Desthuis-Francis is a tourism specialist in the International Finance Corporation, the entity within the World Bank Group that works with the private sector, mdesthuis-francis@ifc.org

231

Figure 1. Detail of the front balconies of the restored Old Dispensary Building in the Old Stone Town of Zanzibar. Serena Hotels, part of the Aga Khan Foundation for Education and Development, is the principal investor in the restoration of the Old Stone Town.

Tourism Organization. "What is needed is a formula to protect the environment, ensuring that tourism benefits the local population and helps preserve the cultural heritage of destination countries." The World Bank Group has joined forces with the World Trade Organization (WTO) and the United Nations Educational, Scientific, and Cultural Organization (UNESCO) to highlight the important, and growing, relationship between tourism and culture. The goal is to promote responsible tourism that meets the requirements of social and economic development without sacrificing environment and cultural heritage.

Old Stone Town, Zanzibar

One of the IFC's hotel investments, beginning eight years ago and operational for the last two years, is in Old Stone Town of Zanzibar. The principal investor is Serena Hotels, part of the Aga Khan Foundation for Education and Development. The Foundation is deeply involved in preserving and restoring Old Stone Town, which despite its name, consists of white stuccoed facades. The Stone Town is Zanzibar's old quarter and has been called "the only functioning historical city in East Africa." It has a rich heritage of a fortress, sultans' palaces, cathedrals, colonial mansions, and a Persian-style public bath. The area exudes a sense that little has changed since 200 years ago, when Zanzibar was one of the most important trading centers in the Indian Ocean region (figure 2).

Public finance is insufficient to bring about the changes to secure the physical integrity of the town. Business—commerce in general and tourism in particular—will have to generate the revenue to provide for and modernize the city's physical infrastructure. Ultimately, private-sector investment, both direct and indirect, must provide for the upkeep and rehabilitation of the historic (as well as the contemporary) city through providing employment and physical space to conduct business and generating public monies through taxation.

But can privatization and the newly embraced tourism rescue Old Stone Town from physical disintegration, or is it still living on borrowed time—despite the existence of a Stone Town Conservation and Development Authority? Authority director Ahmed S. Ahmed stated:

Figure 2. Old Stone Town, Zanzibar.

Before we took over, you'd think twice before going into Stone Town. Buildings were just falling down, especially in the rainy season. We lost lives here in Stone Town. That's when we suggested to the government we should sell some of those buildings to private individuals. This is what saved us because we sold more than 300 buildings, mostly to tenants, at about 20 percent of market value. But our demand was that they should be repaired within two years or we take the building back. It hasn't always happened, but we haven't taken any back.

Outside the commercial private sector, foreign assistance has concentrated on the main historic buildings (the Aga Khan Foundation on a waterfront landmark, the United Nations on the Customs House, and the European Union on the House of Wonders along the seafront). However, there are few funds to restore the bulk of the smaller buildings in private hands. Although individually they are of less historic value than those favored by foreign donors, collectively, the houses fronting the narrow back streets are what make the Stone Town. Will a rehabilitated urban fabric still provide a home and livelihood for those who give it the cultural and contextual meaning that attracts tourists in the first place? Zanzibar is too far from the main feeder markets to be transformed into a museum town.

The IFC hotel investment involves complete restoration of two historic houses to create 51 guest rooms. In operational terms it is the largest hotel in the town. The room capacity of this and other, smaller hotels is complemented by some 15 restaurants acceptable to the international traveler and a plethora of antique, curio, and arts and crafts shops. Taxis and tour operators abound for those wanting to get about the town and island. The airport needs improvement but adequately handles current flight schedules. The more adventuresome can even travel to and from mainland Dar-es-Salaam by high-speed boat.

In short, sufficient tourism infrastructure is in place for Old Stone Town to merit the designation of "destination." In the travel industry Stone Town and Zanzibar are being crafted and molded through multisegmented imagery to be seen worldwide on CNN-TV travel shows, and glossy brochures evoking Zanzibar's color, spices, and other "come-and-discover" features.

Tourists and Historic Districts

As it was a destination previously bypassed by the phenomenal rise in tourism, Stone Town is a time capsule. Political circumstances, ideology, and (too often) war have prevented certain countries or cities from acquiring a tourism industry. Some would argue that, on the other hand, they have escaped the ravages that tourism can bring. Many others have yet to be fully connected to the global transport network, being too remote from the main centers of potential tourists in Europe and the Americas. Hanoi, Maputo, and Zanzibar are examples of newly awakened sleepers, or time capsules. Not long ago Prague fit into this category, but it had the advantage of a more dynamic economy and greater proximity to developed economies. Now Prague has joined the ranks of beleaguered historic cities trying to manage high-density, peak-season tourism.

Where leisure tourism takes root is often indicative of some historic or cultural rapport between the visitors and visited, highlighting the important notion of "destination." These are the places that marketing experts target for potential tourists: the Silk Route, Ruta Maya, the Big Apple, City of Romance (Paris), and Sin City (from Gomorrah to Las Vegas). These are cultural and destination brand names, and thus marketable commodities.

Successful management of historic sites and historic districts depends on revenues. The majority of historic sites are no different from Disneyland or Kruger Park. Ultimately, they must be commercially sustainable without degrading their core asset. They have to manage flows of people in numbers that neither alienate the tourist nor diminish or destroy the objects of attention, be it animals, rides, or people and their way of life. Short of the gifts and endowments that have helped to preserve Oxford and Cambridge, the Vatican, and Mecca, and the state-financed upkeep of public buildings, most historic districts are rehabilitated and maintained through market forces: the private sector. Even state subsidies and grants usually come, in part or total, from the tax base that tourism provides.

It is difficult to cite examples of successfully preserved historic districts in the developing world. There are many examples of conservation and a few of rehabilitation but, especially in urban settings, the success rate is low. Nevertheless, Harold Williams of the Getty Trust has noted in relation to developing countries:

> Particularly in times of dramatic and wrenching social and economic change accelerated by globalization, the well-preserved historic city represents a source of stability, of continuity, of permanence, and of the familiar—of where we've come from and where we are. And it recognizes the importance of public spaces and public life in building a sense of community and of connectedness.

"Historic" no longer refers simply to the passage of time; "significance," not age, is the key criterion to attract tourists to historic areas. Leisure tourism is curiosity, self-education, and a tonic to our every-day experience. It is driven by fashion and purchasing power. It is a very efficient market and can head off in new directions, seemingly forsaking old favorites for no good reason. Creating a destination does not depend on age or beauty but on a cultural interplay between the significance of the site and the perceived needs of the tourist. If the match is positive, investment and tourism will come.

As occurred in Old Stone Town, architects, historians, and politicians can bring to bear the critical skills that encourage, develop, and maintain a historic district. They can be watchdogs ensuring that the fabric remains authentic, and use their ingenuity to accommodate new functions in existing volumes. ■

Note

1   In this calculation business travelers are considered as tourists.

Preserving a Historic City: Economic and Social Transformations of Fez

30

L ike most historic centers in the developing world the *Medina*, or religious center, of Fez, Morocco, is in crisis (figure 1). Despite being on UNESCO's World Heritage List, the city has suffered progressive erosion of its urban quality of life. Although the city appears exceedingly well preserved, the erosion can be seen in the contrast between Fez's vibrant commercial districts and its deteriorating residential quarters. About 10 percent of the latter's buildings are in ruins; 20 percent are dilapidated and on the verge of collapse.

Mona Serageldin

Mona Serageldin is associate director and adjunct professor of urban planning in the Unit for Housing and Urbanization, Graduate School of Design, Harvard University, cuds@gsd.harvard.edu

The City and Its Problems

Fez comprises two districts with a total population of over 180,000. The city encompasses 13,500 parcels of land with approximately 10,000 businesses and 31,500 dwelling units. The Government of Morocco sought the World Bank's assistance to develop a viable strategy to preserve the *Medina*. The Unit for Housing and Urbanization at the Harvard Graduate School of Design worked jointly with the local conservation agency in Fez and in consultation with central and local authorities to formulate a rehabilitation strategy with World Bank staff.

The primary objective of the project is to prevent further loss of the cultural heritage and to valorize the diverse components of this extremely rich urban fabric. The secondary objective is to alleviate poverty. The *Medina* houses a disproportionate number of poor people, most of whom are elderly.

The transformation of traditional handicrafts into partial mechanization has caused a serious pollution problem in Fez. This particularly affects the health of craftsmen who do metal work. Industrial waste from the

Figure 1. Fez, Morocco: aerial view of the historic center.

production process is also highly polluting, particularly chemicals such as chromium, which has completely polluted the water.

Four different perspectives can help to evaluate the cultural heritage of the *Medina*.

1. Its intrinsic value as a recognized cultural heritage site. A contingent valuation method was used to determine the intrinsic value of the *Medina*, in parallel with project appraisal work and based on three categories of foreign visitors: those who had visited Fez; those who traveled to Morocco, but did not visit Fez; and European tourists who had visited neither Morocco nor Fez. The survey quantified the value that these diverse groups placed on Fez's cultural heritage according to what they would be willing to spend, collectively, to save it from disappearance.

2. Touristic value of the *Medina*, which the government has focused on as a potential source of foreign exchange. This is a challenge, because Fez is not a particularly tourist-friendly environment. The

population is very conservative, and their absorptive capacity for foreign visitors is quite limited. Moreover, tourists find the physical environment intimidating, with its dark shadows and tiny alleyways, which architects and designers find breathtaking. Tourists tend to go to Marrakech, completely bypassing Fez.

3. The value of the *Medina* for the Moroccan and Fez populations as part of their cultural identity, which is embodied in the Karaouine Mosque. The mosque is not only a religious symbol and place of learning but also attracts numerous local visitors and pilgrims.

4. The *Medina* has commercial value, represented by the real estate and economic assets encompassed by the site.

The fundamental premise of the proposed rehabilitation strategy is that cultural heritage *other than monuments* should be the focus of this rehabilitation exercise, based on the assumption that monuments can be taken care of through bilateral donations and grants. Thus, the project focuses on rehabilitating the city for local residents, not for tourists or visitors. If the focus were reversed, attention would be paid only to the routes and monuments that tourists visit—never on the core area, which would then be lost.

First Steps

The cycle of deterioration and loss had to be reversed, requiring a thorough understanding of the urban dynamics of this historic setting. In Fez these are particularly complex. Much of the appraisal process was devoted to developing effective methods of documenting, analyzing, and grasping the intricate interplay of factors that would condition the transformation of Fez's built environment.

Despite the overall deterioration, property values in Fez are rising at about 6 percent annually in accessible areas and 3 percent in less accessible areas. Given this high demand and prices, people can profit from real estate if the right conditions prevail. Perhaps the greatest opportunity lies in vacant lots. If a building collapses and the lot becomes accessible, the vacant land can be sold for a much higher price than if the land had a dilapidated building standing on it.

This is an issue with which the conservation agency, Ader Fez, must grapple. As more and more restrictions are imposed on building renovation, authorities must understand that from the viewpoint of the property owner, the cultural heritage building is *devaluing* the property, not enhancing it. The preservation strategy must resolve this dichotomy.

Legal matters also cause problems in Fez—extremely complex tenure and occupancy patterns with layer upon layer of historical primary and secondary property rights. The situation is further complicated by the ownership of *Habous*, or religious endowments established in the Middle Ages to provide public services. In Fez *Habous* own about 40 percent of all commercial property and 30 percent of residential property, making them a formidable actor in the historic centers. Yet they are not particularly interested in cultural heritage, but rather only in ensuring that their assets produce revenue. The owners of *Habous* have made it clear that they are not prepared to invest in property that does not bring them income.

Another issue is the weakness of municipal institutions, which, since decentralization in 1983, have become major actors at the local level. In 1993 a municipal council was created for each of Fez's two districts.

The last factors causing, or contributing to, deterioration are rent control and laws protecting tenants. Since these laws were instituted—particularly a rollback of taxes for lower-income people—dilapidation in the *Medina* has accelerated.

Despite these impediments and the fact that the situation appears very static, to the contrary, the *Medina* area was found to be highly dynamic. One factor is what residents are doing: primarily, installing bathrooms. Bringing water into old structures such as those in Fez often means that humidity and leaking pipes will demolish the structures.

Residents also are subdividing units. The process begins as a temporary measure and then become permanent, built in reinforced concrete. As more and more families are accommodated, the building becomes overstressed. The opposite also occurs. In more accessible areas owners may buy back leases from tenants protected by rent control, consolidate them in one unit, renovate, and move in.

Although the *Medina* has lost many of its middle-income residents, it still compares favorably with other historic centers in the Middle East, North Africa, and elsewhere. The strategy is to encourage these residents to remain in the *Medina* so that it does not become a pocket of poverty. Thus, the project promotes rehabilitation and discourages overbuilding that leads to structural collapse.

Guidelines were devised to allow residents to remodel dwellings and introduce the amenities to which they aspire without damaging the structures. The theory was that since people are undertaking this work illegally in any case, the most effective course of action for the local authority would be to help them renovate more carefully. Such guidelines should be simple, cost-conscious, and enforceable. They present a greater challenge in designated heritage sites, where there is less flexibility in construction norms.

In Fez an exhaustive survey was carried out to rank each building by historical and cultural significance. One way to address the prohibitive cost of rehabilitating to historical or archeological standards is to be more flexible about restoring buildings of lesser significance. Buildings that do not need to be retained with a high degree of authenticity allow for interventions that keep the site vibrant and vital and stimulate the needed turnover. The alternative is gaping holes and collapsing buildings—no matter what their touristic or historical value may be.

Project Strategy

The project estimated that 26 percent of the households in the *Medina* could afford a two-room dwelling, which was the smallest unit for which people are willing to invest. Those who live in one-room dwelling units do not invest because they do not view them as a home. Two-room units, however, inspire investing and remodeling that can be undertaken without outside assistance. Another 20 percent of households required some form of subsidy. Property owners frequently need subsidies to tackle the renovation of historic buildings. The project gave them a 20 percent to 25 percent subsidy on a sliding scale.

The project did not pretend that there could be direct cost-recovery for the investment that the public sector was going to make in the *Medina*. Nowhere has this been achieved in the Middle East or North Africa. In Fez the tenure pattern would completely preclude cost-recovery, since it was not possible even to identify owners, much less collect fees. In Fez less than 7 percent of taxes are collected. It would be fantasy to pretend that it would be possible to collect frontage charges—barring a complete reform of the real estate tax collection system, which is beyond the scope of the project.

The strategy focuses heavily on improving vehicular access (figure 2). Inside Fez with its population of 150,000, there are no fire hydrants or first-aid stations. When people are sick, they must be carried outside in blankets. Those with medical emergencies often die before they can get treatment. The creation of an emergency vehicle road network was identified by the community during Municipal Council meetings as a high priority.

Infrastructure will be repaired along the 14 kilometers of road being repaired, and solid waste collection will become possible for the first time. It will be facilitated by a small vehicle that can navigate the narrow streets and transport the waste to larger vehicles outside the area. This effort will be coordinated with Scandinavian agencies that are overseeing the removal of polluting industries from the city and their relocation to a special industrial zone. Only larger businesses requiring vehicular access are being moved; artisans are remaining. Efforts are also aimed at regrouping nonpolluting industries near access points: to improve vehicular *access* without vehicles having to enter the city.

A program of emergency consolidation of structures will continue, and hopefully be speeded up to prevent the collapse of more buildings. Locating funding for this program is very important, because both outside and inside

Figure 2. Narrow streets and alleys in the Fez historic center.

structural components require strengthening. At present only 15 buildings a year are being worked on. The number needs to reach 30 or even 40.

Finally, the ruins of old buildings have to be cleared. These areas devalue neighborhoods and encourage illegal activities, but could have value to residents once they are cleaned up. The project does not call for displacing people. However, in the longer term market forces probably will cause displacement since many of the structures are overpopulated and dilapidated and sooner or later some of the inhabitants will have to be moved out (box 1).

Assessing Benefits

How can the benefits of a strategy such as that guiding the work in Fez be evaluated? What sort of economic indicators can be used? Benefits must be assessed based on questions such as: What is the immediate impact of these improvements on infrastructure and quality of the public space? This type of development scenario covering both commercial and residential property has been devised for Fez. The economic rate of return was estimated at 13 percent but could vary depending on results on the ground. An estimated 10,000 jobs will be created in construction and public works, mostly in informal building. As people remodel, more activity will be generated and microenterprises will develop due to the high demand for commercial space.

A "leverage ratio" also was calculated. For every dollar of public expenditure the project will leverage three dollars of private investment, and the estimated floor area to be renovated will be on the order of 200,000 square meters. Considerable tax revenue should be generated by both commercial and residential renovation, especially if reforms of the tax collection system eventually are undertaken.

Box 1. Status of project

The project has lofty goals and received a very positive evaluation by the Bank's Quality Assurance Group. Nevertheless, the actual Bank-supported loans (totaling 45 million FF)—one signed by the Government of Morocco and one by the Commune of Fez Medina—will cover only a small part of the overall rehabilitation program. The loans took a longer than average time to negotiate (about one year) and to progress from board presentation to effectiveness (September 1998). Even after effectiveness the first supervision mission did not take place until April 1999 due to delays in undertaking an audit of the executing agency and the new government's subsequent action to remedy the problems emerging from the audit.

The project got underway in 2000, and the president of the Commune of Fez Medina intended to lay the first stone of one the subcomponents of the project, the rehabilitation of Place Boujloud, during that year. Meanwhile, a dynamic new governor undertook to get several Moroccan businesses and banks to donate a number of investments such as the new metal grating on one side of the Medina or the woven cane street coverings that keep the busy passageways cool in the summer months. As expected, businesses and individuals began to acquire and refurbish old mansions and palaces. With the support of the Bank and UNESCO local authorities are planning a major donors' conference in Fez in 2001 to supplement existing commitments and help rehabilitate the adjacent *medina* of Fes Jdid.

Nevertheless, concerning poverty alleviation the larger investments in sanitation and environmental protection that will more directly benefit the poor remain to be started. Contracts for the detailed engineering and supervision of these works are being let. The works should begin in 2001.

It is too early to tell whether the project will fulfill, fall short, or even exceed expectations. So far it has proven to be a very valuable learning experience and remains a centerpiece of the Bank's involvement in cultural heritage/poverty alleviation projects. The level of commitment and political will displayed toward the project by local authorities, the government, and the executing agency are very promising. In the meantime the government has challenged the Bank to provide the closest supervision and support to the project to ensure that it meets its social, economic, and financial goals. Its performance will surely determine the future of such projects in Morocco, as well as support for such projects in the Bank.

Prepared by Roberto Chavez.

This kind of rehabilitated, valorized historic fabric will allow residents of the *Medina* of Fez to fulfill their legitimate aspirations for improved living standards and economic revitalization. ■

Heritage at risk: earthquake-damaged buildings in an Andean village in Ecuador.

Part VI

Technical Applications: Surveying, Valuing, and Documenting Heritage Assets

Editors' Note

In decisionmaking and managing change that affect built heritage, surveying, documenting, and listing are essential activities. Listings and registries are official documents that classify monuments and sites according to specific norms and procedures. However, statutory norms, safeguards, and laws adopted to protect built heritage change over time, as do the listings and inventory procedures. Monuments may be added, re-classified, or even deleted from listings. These changes are based on policy decisions reflecting social, economic, and demographic transformations, which in turn may foster adoption of additional landmarks of historic, artistic, or cultural relevance for listing.

Martin Cherry describes listing as an instrument for managing change to historic buildings in England. A broader, holistic approach to listing historic environments is challenging earlier legislation that protected individual sites and buildings through individual designations. The author concludes that England's listing system is flexible and robust enough to weather the complex adjustments needed.

In Japan the complete or partial dismantling of historic buildings is regarded as an unique opportunity to study building history and old construction techniques. Takeshi Nakagawa examines the detailed records of restoration of built heritage in Japan.

Achva Stein contends that landscapes are a significant arena and one of the ways in which human beings affirm their existential position in the world. Landscapes are manifestations of cultural belief systems; and to document such systems is a complex undertaking. Stein examines the cultural meaning attached to historic and sacred landscapes, and the sacredness of trees.

Budgets often constrain governments' abilities to protect and maintain national monuments. Lauro Lage-Filho and Arthur Darling explain a process to enable public officials to make selections based on a hierarchy of goal, criteria, and alternatives. Based on the Analytic Hierarchy Process (AHP), the method was used to select historic cities for Brazil's Monumenta *Program.*

Dulce Maria Pereira documents the historic roots of Afro-Brazilians and their contributions to Brazilian culture. Brazil has the second-largest black population in the world, after Nigeria; yet this population has been kept silent and disenfranchised. The author describes recent government initiatives to foster social inclusion in Brazil. The Quilombos *program identifies and surveys communities established by former slaves and currently inhabited by their descendants. Its aim is to study and inventory the rich Afro-Brazilian cultural legacy, and to demarcate sites and distribute land titles to residents in the near future.*

Twenty years ago, recognizing the importance of documenting cultural memory, the Center for Jewish Art of the Hebrew University of Jerusalem started a program that assists local experts and organizations to survey and document Jewish heritage in a computerized database. Aliza Cohen-Mushlin examines these activities that have been carried out in 37 countries to survey and document built heritage and artifacts of Jewish communities of Central and Eastern Europe destroyed during the Holocaust.

Marc Grellert depicts the three-dimensional computer reconstruction of synagogues in Germany. The program was initiated by Darmstadt Technical University in 1994. Students and researchers digitally regenerate the destroyed architecture. The aim is to provide an admonition as well as a memorial in connection with the Nazi period, during which nearly 2,000 of 3,000 German synagogues were destroyed.

Bezalel Narkiss examines the most pronounced types of synagogues that have been developed in Jewish communities throughout the world. They are found in the Ashkenazic, Sephardic, and Italian traditions. Most have distinct disposition of the main liturgical elements, or focal points, which are placed in the synagogue's space according to traditional precepts and symbolic meanings.

Harmen Thies explains a methodology to research design called Rissanalyse *("plan analysis"), using two architectural landmarks, the Residence-Church in Würzburg and the "Temple of Jews" in Wörlitz, as examples. This approach gives new insights in the generative and constitutive processes of design used in the early eighteenth century.*

The 13 essays in the chapter by the Center for Jewish Art document Jewish heritage. They address methodological approaches to the analysis of architecture, and the interpretation of the symbols and elements found in religious and secular architecture. Digital reconstruction of synagogues destroyed in Germany as well as in the shtetls *(small Jewish settlements) of Eastern Europe are examined. Also covered are the evolution of the urban fabric of* melah *in Morocco; the legacy of the Jewish presence in the remote Cape Verde Islands; memorializing the Jewish legacy in Germany, Poland, and Greece; sacred spaces in conflict areas; fortress-synagogues; and the wooden sacred buildings of the Ukraine. Bezalel Narkiss stated that the main objective of the Center's research program is to enhance understanding of the Jewish cultural legacy found in so many places and its contribution to the development of art and architecture, for the enrichment of current and future generations.*

Listing as an Instrument in Managing Change to Historic Buildings

31

T he legislation for the protection of historic buildings, monuments, and areas in England has grown up over more than a century.[1] Although the system is generally thought to have served its purpose well, it is in need of an overhaul. A government consultation on this issue was set up in Spring 2000.[2]

Martin Cherry

Martin Cherry is director of National Programmes (Archaeology and Survey) at English Heritage, Conservation, in London, martin.cherry@english-heritage.org.uk

Legislative Framework for Historic Building Conservation in England

The legislation has concentrated on the protection of individual sites and buildings through individual designations rather than on the historic environment as a whole. The virtues of taking a more holistic approach have become more widely recognized in recent years. Government guidance over the last decade or so has increasingly stressed that the historic environment "embraces all those aspects of the country that reflect the shaping hand of human history" from buildings to towns, fields, and barns, hedgerows, walls, and the "semi-natural features which people have also molded (figure 1)."[3]

This broadened approach to understanding and managing the historic environment presents a number of challenges. The first is how to make the best use of existing legislation that was designed with narrower objectives in mind. The second is how to reconcile conservation with the needs of regeneration and development. This chapter is concerned primarily with these issues.

The third challenge, however, is perhaps the greater. As major shifts in England's social and ethnic composition take place over the next generation, ideas of what is significant will change, too. Working definitions and policies intended to protect the historic environment will need to reflect the diverse and often conflicting values that different sections of society ascribe to it. If local and multi-cultural perspectives are not taken into account when making decisions about what to keep and what to let go, more and more people will feel excluded from the "establishment view of heritage." Conservation plans and management guidelines, discussed later, provide one framework for identifying and evaluating the whole range of significances of what survives, a prerequisite for sustainable conservation. Nevertheless, procedures in themselves will not be sufficient to accommodate the diversity of views about what is important. This will require a wider cultural shift in the approaches and working methods of conservation professionals.

Three main heritage designations exist in England.

Figure 1. Swaledale, Yorkshire. The character of areas is defined by innumerable factors such as field boundaries, field barns, woodland, and waste. They are not amenable to individual designations but cry out for a comprehensive historic environmental strategy. This improved agricultural landscape provided for the fast-growing industrial towns of the early Industrial Revolution.

Scheduling

Scheduling is the oldest conservation legislation (1880s) and is concerned with nationally important archaeological monuments and ruined structures that need to be preserved as unchanged as possible. It is a strict regime that requires consent even for repairs and minor works, although some classes of work are exempted. Monuments are scheduled by the Secretary of State for Culture, Media and Sport. His or her powers are discretionary, that is, s/he is not *required* to schedule a monument of national importance and will do so only if scheduling is considered to be an *appropriate* form of protection.

Scheduling is not widely used in historic cities since government policy expects local planning authorities and developers to take full account of the archaeology of urban sites.[4] While not concerned with historic buildings in active use (and houses are specifically excluded) the discretionary element in scheduling which allows appropriateness to be taken into account offers some advantages over listing as an instrument for managing change. There are 18,360 scheduled monuments in England, although the number of individual items contained within these monuments (some of which are very extensive) is in excess of 30,000.

Listing

The backbone of the conservation system, listing was introduced in the 1940s as part of the Town and Country Planning legislation, a quite separate statutory family to the Ancient Monuments Act, which governs scheduling. This is an important distinction because, like the planning system generally, listing is designed to manage (rather than stop) change. It is not about fossilizing historic buildings but seeks ways of keeping them in use while respecting their historic character.

Although listing constraints can be onerous, they are inherently more flexible than scheduling. Consent needs to be obtained only for changes that will affect the building's character. Generally, repair and maintenance do not need permission. To be listed, a building must be of "special architectural or historic interest" (figure 2). Unlike with scheduling, the Secretary of State has no discretion with listing. If s/he is of the view that a building fulfils the criteria, the Secretary has a duty to list it.

In May 2000 the number of entries on the statutory lists stood at 370,742. In fact the number of individual buildings is considerably greater (possibly 450,000), since many items such as terraces or farmsteads may contain many separate addresses or components.

Figure 2. Churchill Gardens, London (Westminster), Powell & Moya, 1946. Current policy for the selection of buildings for listing stresses their importance within the context of their type. Here, a key postwar housing development in London was listed as being among the first and finest of its date.

Figure 3. Housing, Norwich, East Anglia: alterations. While the trend is toward a holistic approach to the historic environment, Conservation Area controls lack teeth, and good runs of modest historic buildings are often debased by cumulative minor changes such as satellite dishes and mock-stone facings.

Conservation Areas

A relative newcomer introduced in 1967, like listing, Conservation Areas nest within the Town and Country legislation. One problem with listing is that it is building-specific and cannot easily help preserve the special character of areas, the relationship among buildings, and the spaces around them. Conservation Areas are broader in that they protect ensembles and the more modest buildings that contribute positively to the character of a place.

However, their controls are less exacting and do not extend to the interiors of buildings, as with listing (figure 3). Recent legal judgments have further eroded Conservation Area controls by seriously limiting the meaning of "demolition." Yet, they have strengths that listing and scheduling do not always possess. Unlike the other designations Conservation Areas are made by local planning authorities and not by the Secretary of State. This locus of control often brings about a closer involvement of local people, especially at the designation stage, when formal public consultation takes place.

Although it has not always been the case in practice, these three designations should be seen as being complementary, bringing the appropriate level of protection to bear on the historic entity in question. Other procedures help protect sensitive historic environments by requiring authorities to take them into consideration when considering planning proposals. For example, supplementary guidance to local plans are regularly reviewed policy statements drawn up by local authorities that cover the whole range of environmental issues. Another procedure is the non-statutory registers of parks and gardens, and of battlefields drawn up by English Heritage.

We come as close as the current situation allows to achieving a coherent and sustainable conservation strategy when (1) the historic environment is researched and characterized, (2) its significance assessed within both local and national contexts, and (3) policies for its management and, where appropriate, protection are written into national guidance and local plans.

Selection Criteria for Listing

The law states simply that to be listed, a building must be of "special architectural or historic interest." No other factors, such as cost of repairs, intentions of the owner, or physical state of the building, can be taken into account at this point. "Interest" includes conventional measures of architectural quality, industrial and technological significance, interest as part of a planned group of buildings, and regional importance. Examples of the last two might be a square or model farmstead, or regional varieties of vernacular techniques or use of materials, respectively.

Interest may also derive from a building's historic association with a famous person or event. Both scheduling and listing designations are made by the government after seeking advice from English Heritage.[5] The terminology used in the different legislation—"national importance" and "special interest"—largely reflects the hands of different drafters at different times rather than a significant difference in intention. Both definitions assume a degree of rarity. The framers of the legislation probably never envisaged the numbers to grow as they have. Government guidance assumed the numbers of listed buildings to decline as a proportion of the total surviving stock as we approached modern times. Rigorous selectivity weeds out the majority of buildings dating from after 1840, and this affects even those that represent the most important phases of our history. For example, of the thousand or so textile factories that survive in Greater Manchester, among the most tangible reminders of the country's leading role in the Industrial Revolution, only 100 (10 percent) are listed.

Relationship between Central and Local Government

Not all listed buildings are equally important intrinsically, and a grading system was developed to help distinguish among them. Grade I listed buildings (about 2.5 percent) are of paramount importance. Grade II (about 6 percent) are of exceptional significance, for instance in regional or technological terms. The rest are graded as lower, and the presumption is that every effort should be made to retain them. The fact that listing assessments are conducted nationally ensures consistent standards across the country. However, a strong body of opinion favors delegating the designation of grade II buildings to local or regional authorities. Doing so may become difficult to resist in the face of the growing trend towards subsidiarity within the European Union.

Routine listed building consent procedures affecting grade II buildings are dealt with generally by local planning authorities, which normally employ specialists to assess proposals for change. Applications for demolition of a grade II building or alterations to buildings in the higher grades are referred to English Heritage, which decides whether to become involved. If English Heritage and the local authority cannot resolve any serious differences of opinion, English Heritage can advise the Secretary of State to take the matter out of the hands of the local authority and deal with it him- or herself through the public inquiry procedures.

This outcome is relatively uncommon, and applications for listed building consent are granted, often after considerable discussion, in over 90 percent of cases. This high percentage is generally seen to indicate the general health of the system. The role of the local government official, usually the historic buildings conservation officer, is to find a way to reconcile any conflict between the need to retain the special architectural or historic character of the listed building with the needs of the owner to keep it in viable use. Negotiation and compromise are the key qualities in the process.

Conservation Practice and Politics

The presumption throughout the process is that if the original use of a listed building is no longer possible, then a new use should be sought. As with all buildings, the long-term future of a listed building is best served by retaining it in use, thereby providing the wherewithal for its maintenance and repair. Sustainability might best be achieved by selling the property to a new owner capable of sustaining it. The listed building consent procedures are designed to manage the process of change that will inevitably affect a living building, especially if it needs to find a new purpose in life. At the point of proposed change all those factors that cannot be taken into account when a building is actually listed can be weighed one against the other. These factors include its economic viability, the structural state of the building and the likely costs of repairs, and general community interests. When all alternative uses have been exhausted, a listed building may be demolished, although permission on economic grounds alone is only rarely given.

The overwhelming majority of listed buildings are fully used and beneficial. Many house-owners know this, and listed building status is often regarded as a *cachet* and selling point. Commercial interests are less easily persuaded of the benefits of listing although in practice they too understand the positive connection between good architecture and good business. In many cities the flagship historic buildings attract the most prestigious and successful occupants. Recent research has shown that listed commercial buildings perform economically as well, and in certain circumstances better, than unlisted ones.[6]

The value of historic buildings to the economic buoyancy of whole areas is now receiving due attention (figure 4). More research is needed to build on important work already done. Much of this has begun to apply the methodologies widely used by economists and geographers in valuing environmental goods, already exploited by nature conservationists to good effect. Increasingly, much of the research is concerned with issues of sustainability.[7]

While the benefits of retaining and enhancing historic buildings and areas long have been recognized as contributing to quality of life, the benefits have been difficult to quantify, and the notion has often appeared fuzzy and unscientific. However, the effects of conservation-led regeneration are measurable, and recent studies have indicated that these benefits may be felt as much in run-down and disadvantaged areas as in the best-known heritage set-pieces.

Indeed, in the former, the impact is normally more dramatic. A recent study commissioned by English Heritage and carried out by the London School of Economics found that every £10,000 invested by that public body on the repair of historic fabric in regeneration areas leverages average almost five times that figure in matching funds from other bodies both public and private (the "heritage dividend"). It also creates 177 square meters of improved commercial floorspace, and delivers one new job, one safeguarded job, and one improved home.[8]

Figure 4. Vittoria and Frederic Streets, Birmingham: view from north. Recent research by English Heritage has established that the historic Jewellery Quarter is one of the most significant light-industrial manufacturing areas of its sort in Europe. Closely packed and still thriving, it demands a holistic management strategy that thinks beyond individual designations to the contribution that all the historic buildings and spaces make to the local economy.

Despite the growing body of evidence that conservation brings economic and social benefits, many remain resistant to the message, particularly in the economic development departments of some local authorities, some major private development companies, and government departments. The government recently commissioned a report on the regeneration of British cities and the reversal of urban decline, which was highly influential. While perceptive and forward-thinking in many ways, it barely mentioned the historic environment and the need to understand it and the potential benefits it can deliver.[9] Placing conservation-led regeneration firmly on all the most influential agendas is still an up-hill struggle, but there are signs that the tide may be turning.

Listing: Obstacle or Enabler?

Listing, along with other conservation instruments, is still seen by many as an obstacle to development. This is particularly the case when a listing order is placed on a building at the eleventh hour after development proposals have been fully agreed and work may have begun on site. This scenario can be avoided in a number of ways. More often than not, frustration with the system on the part of owners and developers is caused by the delays and uncertainties in the consent procedures. The listed status of the building itself is less commonly challenged, and when it is, it usually results from a misunderstanding of the selection criteria or the extent of the listing itself.

The key to removing obstacles is to evaluate the historic significance of the building or site in good time, build these qualities into the development brief, and exploit them as assets rather than liabilities. Such an appraisal is essential from the earliest stages. Underestimating the heritage value of a site and the likely constraints this may involve can lead to unrealistic property prices being paid with all the knock-on effects on returns that this will involve.

A number of procedures can smooth the path towards agreeing a development that is based firmly and realistically on a full understanding of the historic environmental assets of a site. Looking at the process holistically, five key components need to be put in place:

1. Identifying and understanding what is there (definition, analysis)

2. Evaluating the significance of what is there: why and to whom it is important (a different set of activities that looks beyond the physical remains and ascribes values to them)

3. Measuring the fragility or vulnerability of the site to human or natural actions

4. Considering the impact of proposed change and deciding whether to keep, modify, or lose what is there

5. Conserving what is important to pass on to future generations, that is, deciding what, if anything, needs to be done.

The first three of these need to be done first. This is an obvious enough observation but full and timely appraisals of historic sites that may be subject to development are still the exception rather than the rule. The concept of the *conservation plan* has been developed to help provide a methodology that enables a site to be *fully* understood.[10] Full understanding is attained only when the whole range of expertise is utilized: ecologists, archaeologists, architects, museum curators, countryside, and urban and heritage managers, all of whom have different approaches. In addition, their expertise must be combined with a wide-ranging analysis of the values and significance people attach to the site. The latter can be done effectively only by involving all those who have an interest in the site or building in the process of evaluation. In the real world, more often than not the awareness of the need for full evaluations and conservation plans, and indeed the interest and engagement of the public, happen only when there are proposals for change.

It is desirable to have the full understanding of a site's importance established well before the point of proposed change. Should that not happen, there are still mechanisms available that combine the virtues of the conservation plan with clear and practical guidance for future management. *Management guidelines* are designed to provide a greater degree of certainty about the scope for change and allow a more rational and economical approach to complex buildings and sites to be taken by planning authorities.[11] Management guidelines attempt to remove uncertainty and delay from the management of historic buildings without compromising their integrity and special character. The guidelines include three elements:

1. The pre-requisite: a detailed assessment of the historic building or site and its significance. What features are of special interest and which parts are less so? It is important that everyone appreciates what is and what is not important. This will require a degree of public participation for sites that are complex or where there may be competing views of significance.

2. A summary of those works that are unlikely to affect the historic or architectural character of the building and that can be carried out routinely without, in the case of listed buildings, listed building consent. Such work might include most maintenance and much repair, and would establish good practice.

3. An indication of the limits of the possible. Most buildings need to change, and it is important for an owner to know early what sorts of changes are likely to be acceptable. Formal listed building consent would still be necessary for changes that affected the building's special character, not least because the procedure involves the public, who have a right to comment or object. The initial historical assessment already should have established where the dispensable or less sensitive parts of the building are and where new works might be concentrated. It would also define where intrusive and damaging works would not be acceptable.

Conclusion

Considering that there are probably in the region of half a million listed structures in England, the listing system commands a high degree of support. Its inherent flexibility is undoubtedly a factor in that. Flexibility enables a protected building to undergo certain changes to retain (or rekindle) its viability while respecting its exceptional historic or architectural character. Successive governments have reviewed the system and sought to streamline or adapt it in minor ways, but none has embarked on a root and branch reform or contemplated dismantling the procedures that are generally considered to have worked well.

A more holistic approach to understanding and evaluating the significance of the historic environment is gaining ground. If it becomes firmly entrenched in local and regional plans, it may supersede the need for specific designations, although this is likely to be a long way in the future. Some conservation planners and lawyers are already of the view that listing and Conservation Areas should be scrapped and replaced by a requirement to assess the historic importance of every building and area that is subject to change.

Such a seismic shift in policy would require every building, settlement, and landscape to be set in a fully researched context and would demand a significant reprioritization of resources. In a generation's time we may not have the capacity to support conservation evaluations on this scale. In addition, the changing social and ethnic composition of society may result in major, perhaps radical, shifts in the value that people attach to the historic environment. It is possible that the listing system is robust enough to weather changes as it has in the past. Doubtless, procedures such as those discussed in this chapter will strengthen its chances of remaining a key instrument in managing change to historic buildings. ■

Notes

1   The legislation referred to in this chapter is broadly similar throughout the United Kingdom but is enshrined in different statutes and government policy papers. I have not complicated the text by distinguishing among them.

2   The results of the consultation are due to be published by English Heritage in November 2000.

3   "Planning policy guidance note 15: Planning and the historic environment," Department of the Environment and the Department of National Heritage, England, 1994, usually referred to as PPG15.

4   "Planning policy guidance note 16: Archaeology and planning," Department of the Environment and the Department of National Heritage, England, 1990, usually referred to as PPG16.

5   English Heritage is a quasi-autonomous, nongovernmental organisation. It is funded by the Department for Culture, Media and Sport but also raises considerable income from its own historic properties and commercial activities. It is the government's main source of advice on the historic environment and gives substantial grants for the conservation of historic buildings and areas.

6 "The investment performance of listed buildings," English Heritage and the Royal Institution of Chartered Surveyors, London, 1993 and updates.

7 G. Allison and others, "The Value of Conservation? A Literature Review of the Economic and Social Value of the Cultural Built Environment," Department of National Heritage, English Heritage, and The Royal Institution of Chartered Surveyors, London, 1996. See also "Culture Count: Financing, Resources, and the Economics of Sustainable Development. Proceedings of the Conference, Florence, Italy," Government of Italy, World Bank, and UNESCO, Washington, D. C., 2000; and "Sustainability and the Historic Environment," English Heritage, London, 1997.

8 "The Heritage Dividend: Measuring the Results of English Heritage Regeneration 1994-1999," English Heritage, London, 1999.

9 "Towards an Urban Renaissance," Urban Task Force, chaired by Lord Rogers of Riverside, England, 1999.

10 J .S. Kerr, "The Conservation Plan: A Guide to the Preparation of Conservation Plans for Places of European Cultural Significance," The National Trust of Australia, NSW, Sydney, 1996; Kate Clark, ed., "Conservation Plans in Action: Proceedings of the Oxford Conference, English Heritage, London, 1999.

11 "Developing Guidelines for the Management of Listed buildings," English Heritage, London, 1996. The principles set out here apply equally to sites and areas: see "Development in the Historic Environment," English Heritage, 1995.

32 Heritage Surveying and Documentation in Japan

Takeshi Nakagawa

Takeshi Nakagawa is professor of Architecture at Waseda University in Japan, heads the Japanese Government Team for Safeguarding Angkor, and is a member of the Society of Architectural Historians of Japan, naka@mn.waseda.ac.jp

In Japan the complete or partial dismantling of historic buildings is regarded as a unique opportunity to study building history and ancient construction techniques. Japanese records of restoration address two major issues. First, they serve as a primary source of architectural history. Second, the records account for every aspect of the repair project—from construction of scaffolding to the type of joint used in the repair work—which benefits future planning. Based on information contained in the records, it is possible to estimate the costs and time that will be needed for future projects.

During the dismantling of a historic building for restoration, the chief historical architect is expected to be continuously present at the site. Many structural defects or decayed material can be detected in the course of dismantling. The chief architect examines them to determine the cause and prevent further deterioration after the structure has been reassembled.

During the dismantling, after each part has been checked, the architect decides whether it should be kept, repaired, or replaced. Small wooden plates are nailed to each part according to a numbering system established in advance, which might be based on the system used during the original construction. The chief architect first measures each part, then carefully investigates the wood, labeling each piece and trying to identify the district from which the lumber originated.

The architect also examines tool traces to learn how the part was processed, and checks pressure marks to determine whether the part had previously been removed from the structure or used in a different position. Finally, the chief architect searches for inscriptions and studies relevant architectural techniques, such as well made joints.

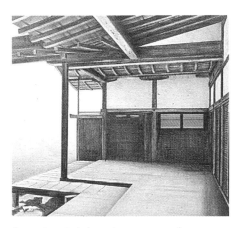

A study of Asian documents about construction during corresponding periods for comparable structures in the same district helps the chief architect study the history of the building in detail. Architects sometimes also use X-ray or infrared photography if further analysis is required. After the dismantling and investigation phases are completed, the architect can classify each part by type and age, providing a clear conception of the structure's development and how its state has changed.

Figure 1 (left). Onjo-Ji-Kojoin Temple Guest House, Kyoto, 1603, pencil drawing.

Figure 2. Katura-villa, Kyoto, seventeenth century.

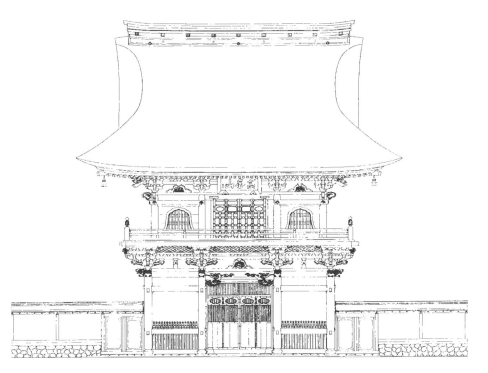

Figure 3. Tennei-ji Temple, Tokyo, 1759: front elevation.

The custom of publishing reports about restoration works started well before World War II. The first record dates from 1925. Since then 1,586 reports have been published. Today 300 copies of each report are published and distributed to conservation architects, design institutes, and

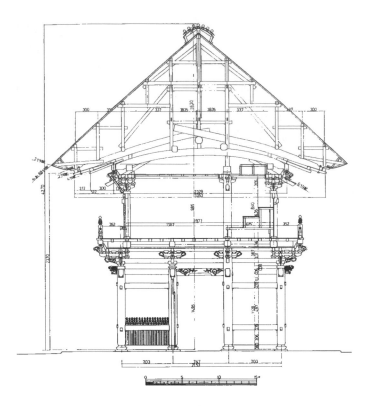

Figure 4. Tennei-ji Temple, Tokyo, 1759:
cross section.

major libraries throughout Japan. Copies also are sent to the Central Authority for the Preservation of Cultural Properties in Korea and the People's Republic of China. Publication expenses for these records are included in the overall budget of the restoration project.

All the records combined provide a detailed account of all aspects of the project. The first information recorded relates to the work schedule, budget, and extra work at the site, including construction of the site office and scaffolding. Next the building and its history—based on evidence found during the work—is documented using text, diagrams, drawings, and photographs. High-quality drawings show the state of the building before and after repair. Japanese preservation architects use the traditional ruling pen with twin steel chop blades that hold the ink and traditional brushes for details. These drawings, in traditional Chinese ink, are of a quality rarely seen elsewhere today. All the prescribed photographs and the main and detailed drawings published in the records are kept by the Agency for Cultural Affairs, while photographs and sketches prepared during the work are normally retained by the owner of the building. These records should be placed in the archives of a public institution and made available to researchers. In Japan the detailed reports and records are published for experts and the Architectural Institute of Japan and cannot be acquired by the Japanese public. ■

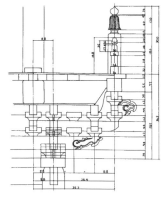

Figure 5. Tennei-ji Temple, Tokyo, 1759: detail.

Preserving the Cultural Significance of Landscapes

33

According to an ancient Hebrew proverb, human beings affirm their existential position in the world in three ways: through their relation to themselves, to one another, and to "place."[1] The place—the landscape—is the arena in which the other relationships are given form and exhibited. For precisely this reason landscapes should not be viewed as objective realities but as manifestations of cultural belief systems.

Documenting these systems is complicated and needs to be clearly defined. Muddled understanding can result in turning any landscape into a theme park devoid of sacredness and meaning, save temporary commercial value. The differentiation between "landscape" and "garden" needs to be understood, since the phrase "historic and sacred landscape" is used to describe places ranging in scale from a sacred tree to a large ecological system.

Gardens are created by human beings for productive, recreational, or spiritual purposes. Landscapes are not created, nor are they a result of a premeditated, designed gesture. Rather, they are the result of human activities on the land, manipulating the physical environment surrounding human settlements. They are mosaics that reflect a location's natural resources, the culture of human habitation, and the interaction among these forces. Variations in the assumptions regarding landscapes or gardens, which influence the process of documentation, usually arise from cultural attitudes toward work and leisure and the schism between culture and nature.

Landscape types range from primordial to restored. Some are consecrated by a religious institution; some became sacred as a result of habitual visitation. Documenting landscapes can illustrate the conceptual framework that needs to be considered and may suggest ways to undertake a more fruitful reconnaissance to obtain information needed prior to initiating site restoration and rehabilitation.

Achva Benzinberg Stein

Achva Benzinberg Stein is director of the Landscape Architecture Program, North Carolina State University, achva_stein@ncsu.edu

Sacred Trees and Historic Plants

From the beginning of recorded history, people have venerated plants. The healing power of plants, trees, shrubs, groundcover, and the flowers they produce has created a world of lore that connects people to their sacred plants. The strength of beliefs in the sacredness of trees can be seen in the Middle East, where the worshipping of trees has been forbidden since the beginning of monotheism, yet persists to today. Their usefulness for human survival and their age are other reasons that trees are venerated (figure 1).

Figure 1. Sacred tree inside a shrine, upper Galilee sources of the Jordan River, Israel.

Figure 2. Sacred tree and a shrine, Beith Hanania Galilee, Israel.

Plants do not grow in isolation. A tree or group of shrubs is a mini-ecosystem composed not only of the main species but also of the surrounding wildlife. Efforts to protect a specific sacred tree must extend to the system in its entirety, thus creating an "island" biocommunity.

Anecdotal information is often the best source for documenting this information. Stories told by those who live in the vicinity may reveal important facts, such as the approximate age of the tree, the origin and nature of specific species cohabiting the site, and the plant's healing properties. Such facts can help to ensure proper conservation measures. Older generations steeped in tradition may know about the sacred tree —but rarely does the younger generation (figure 2). Information concerning collected stories and other scientific data needs to be recorded and exhibited. An exhibit located in the vicinity of the site may reveal additional information by stirring visitors to reminisce.

Following the tradition of visiting a site on specific holy days is a valuable ritual, as it allows the fauna and flora to recover from human disturbance and thus to survive over time. Even in a limited system, differing claims on the land by culture and nature create a schism: cultural claims are often detrimental to a living object of veneration.

Canal Cities in China and Dhal Lake in Kashmir

Aquaculture as a way of life was common on all continents where environmental conditions necessitated it. It now takes place in very few areas—primarily in Asia, with a few remnants in Central and South America and Europe. The canal cities of the lower Yangtze River are an example of a historic landscape in which culture and nature have been intertwined to provide sustainable living environments (figure 3). On a far more limited scale Dhal Lake in Kashmir exemplifies an aquaculture that has been maintained and continues to operate (figure 4).

These landscapes provide a wealth of practical and scientific knowledge. The current trend of attracting the people off the land into factories and

Figure 3. Tong Li Canal city zone of habitation, China.

Figure 4. Vegetable farmer and his product, Dhal Lake, Kashmir. The vegetable grows on floating beds.

service industries in metropolitan areas thousands of miles away gradually destroys such historic landscapes. Lacking workers to produce and maintain the delicate processes, the landscapes deteriorate immediately, and production of food and other necessities quickly declines. These, in turn, cause additional human displacement.

Furthermore, until a sophisticated and very costly infrastructure can be installed to replace the existing biotic system, the use of chemicals increases exponentially and renders the entire riparian environment unfit for human use. Sometimes, even living in proximity to the waterways becomes hazardous as a result of polluting fertilizers, insecticides, and waste chemicals from households and factories.

The knowledge needed to maintain these systems is being lost as the older generation passes away. Their information represents sound scientific knowledge based on thousands of years of observation and trials and plays a key role in cultural rituals that have held communities together. The additional source of income from tourism, which could have helped sustain such landscapes, is also lost forever. Restoration of such landscape cannot be achieved by highly localized work. The entire watershed area must be restored and maintained.

The foothills of the Himalayas, which sustain Dhal Lake in Kashmir, are being rapidly deforested. Deforestation is creating an immense erosion problem and causing siltation at the mouths of rivers and flooding in the valley where the lakes are. Recent flooding patterns in China are directly connected to the same process of deforestation and lack of groundcover protection. The human and economic losses are enormous, and the new landscape is devoid of meaning and content. In cases of productive historic landscapes clearly there is no conflict between preserving the ecosystem and conserving cultural values. They form overlapping systems that serve as illuminating examples of how beneficial such relationships can be.

Entire ecosystems, not merely a particular site and its components, must be documented. Such work should include data on the physical resources of the watershed area as well as the social and the economical interrelationships.

When recording the process of production and landscape maintenance, special attention should be paid to the tools used. The use of heavy equipment and machinery to achieve a rapid result is likely to compromise the integrity of the structure. Using the correct tools has become an accepted practice in restoring artifacts and historic monuments. It is time to extend such understanding to the preservation of historic landscapes.

Palmeries of Morocco

In Morocco's oases the traditional irrigation system, built long ago, has enabled people to survive and flourish for centuries. This underground system of deep wells and canals created a carefully crafted ecosystem. The landscape was composed of three tiers of planting: palms provided shade to more delicate fruit trees, which, in turn, eased the heat for vegetables and herbs. People preserved the hydrological cycle through the migration of settlements to new locations, thus enabling the resources to replenish themselves (figure 5).

Today most of these oases have become monocultures of date palms. The ancient irrigation system has been neglected in favor of modern pumps, which boost production for a short time but deplete water resources. The nature of settlements has also changed, becoming fixed as a result of access to water (figure 6).

The restoration and preservation of oases should begin with an understanding of the entire agricultural life-cycle as well as the impact of a periodic hiatus in productive use. Knowledge of water collection and distribution techniques, so necessary throughout the arid world, requires careful documentation. Equally important is the dissemination of such information to appropriate political stakeholders. Understanding of the validity of maintaining such systems from an economic point of view will gain force as governments begin to change their accounting systems to reflect the loss of natural resources.

Twentieth-Century Sacred Fields

Among the sacred landscapes of the twentieth century are what can be called "killing fields"—where nations shed their own blood and that of their enemies in the name of nationalism, ideology, and persecution. These are not established, maintained cemeteries. They are open fields, concentration camps and forced labor sites, or railroad tracks and

Figure 5 (left). Traditional palmeries, Draa Valley, Marrakesh, Morocco.

Figure 6. Contemporary palmeries, Efrud, Morocco.

Figure 7. The Golan is a politically sacred landscape, a disputed land, and a battlefield.

Figure 8. The sources of the Jordan River are wetlands and politically sacred land.

borders separating political entities (figure 7). These fields tell conflicting stories; some are shared stories among former enemies. They are the monuments to the "unknown civilians." The need in such places is not to memorialize brutality but to commemorate life and celebrate the sharing of human emotions and experience. Such landscapes are not preserved to protect nature and wildlife, or for leisure and recreation. Their sole purpose lies in their sacredness as a symbol of the human souls destroyed in search of identity (figure 8). In my opinion documentation should not dwell on who or how it happened, since this will perpetuate hatred and revenge. Instead, documentation should stress the "sacredness of the void." How to maintain these voids without institutionalizing them as war monuments or cemeteries falls in the realm of public art. ■

Note

1   In Hebrew the term *Makom* ("place") has several connotations. One meaning is in some way equivalent to the concept of *genius loci* (spirit or sense of place). Another is a synonym for "God." A third is the concrete term referring to a specific geographical location and the natural forces operating there.

Establishing Priorities for the Preservation of Historic Cities

34

S ince the early 1990s the preservation of cultural heritage has received increased attention from many countries and multilateral institutions, including the World Bank, the Inter-American Development Bank (IADB), and the United Nations Educational, Scientific, and Cultural Organisation (UNESCO).

Budget limitations necessitate the establishment of priorities for preservation activities, a process that is always controversial because of the large number of stakeholders with conflicting objectives. To establish priorities, it is essential to represent all legitimate interests and views and achieve consensus. Brazil's Ministry of Culture went through such a process to decide which historic cities would benefit from a preservation loan from the IADB.

Method

The method used in Brazil is based on the Analytic Hierarchy Process (AHP), developed by Thomas Saaty, which enables decisionmakers to represent decisionmaking as a hierarchy of goal, criteria, and alternatives (table 1).[1] The hierarchy, or decisionmaking model, can have several levels. The goal is the first level; criteria used to judge the merits of the alternatives appear in subsequent levels. The final level of the hierarchy contains the alternatives to be considered.

A facilitator helps decisionmakers to build the hierarchy, orienting discussion about the goal, the criteria, and alternatives. After decisionmakers approve the hierarchy, the facilitator helps them to establish (a) the relative importance of the criteria in terms of contributing to a higher-level criterion (or goal), and (b) the relative preference for the alternatives in regard to each criterion at the level immediately preceding the alternatives.

Lauro Lage-Filho and
Arthur Darling

*Lauro Lage-Filho, an expert in decision support, is a consultant to the Inter-American Development Bank, laurol@iadb.org
Arthur Darling is principal economist at the Inter-American Development Bank, arthurd@iadb.org*

Table 1. Analytic Hierarchy Process decisionmaking model

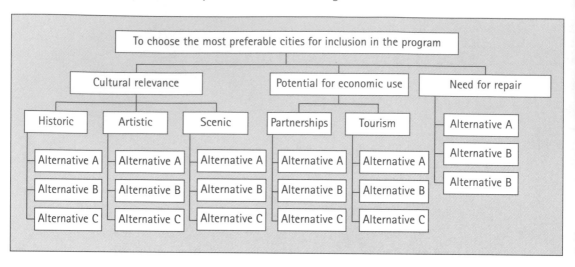

Establishing Priorities

The establishment of priorities for the selection of Brazilian historic cities to be financed by the IADB loan was undertaken by high-level officials from the Ministry of Culture and the National Institute for Historical and Artistic Patrimony (IPHAN). It was carried out in two distinct phases.

Phase I

Initially the facilitator introduced participants to the method and to "Expert Choice" (EC), the computer program used to implement the method.[2] Second, participants structured a decisionmaking model using cultural, political, economic, social, and technical criteria to establish priorities. Next, the participants incrementally tested and improved the decisionmaking model, sometimes working in small groups to further define the criteria and evaluate their relative importance. At the end of phase I the participants approved, by consensus, the final decisionmaking model (table 2).

To test the validity of a *preliminary version* of the model, the officials selected four cities for comparison: Antônio Prado, Ouro Preto, Porto Seguro, and Salvador. Using EC, they compared all sets of alternatives (Ouro Preto vs. Salvador, Ouro Preto vs. Porto Seguro, Ouro Preto vs. Antonio Prado, Salvador vs. Porto Seguro, Salvador vs. Antonio Prado, and Porto Seguro vs. Antonio Prado) for each criterion (for example, historical relevance and artistic relevance) to establish a ranking on that particular criterion.

Table 2. Structure of the decisionmaking model for assigning priorities

Criterion	Sub-Criterion	Weight (%)
Cultural relevance		38
	Historic	15
	Artistic	11
	Scenic	4
	Ethnographic	4
	Archaeological	4
Potential for economic use		19
	Potential to form partnerships to maintain the area	6
	Potential for private participation	3
	Interest and capacity of users to contribute to maintenance	3
	Potential of municipalities to provide required urban services	3
	Unoccupied space available for use	2
	Easy accessibility for cars	1
	Potential for cultural tourism	1
Urgency of intervention		16
	Exposure to risk (environmental, predatory tourism, poor conservation techniques, developers' pressures)	9
	State of conservation	5
	Compatibility of present use with conservation	2
Cost of intervention		11
	Complexity of intervention	5
	Magnitude of intervention	5
Potential for social improvement		9
	Potential for educational benefits	3
	Potential to improve living conditions	3
	Potential to generate employment	2
	Other positive impacts on the area	1
Local political support for heritage conservation		7
	Political will and capacity to manage heritage	3
	Interests in conflict with preservation	3
	Existence of lines of credit and incentives for conservation	1
		100

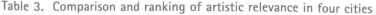

Table 3. Comparison and ranking of artistic relevance in four cities

The comparisons for artistic relevance are described in the first part of table 3, which shows the pairs of comparisons in lines numbered from 1 to 6. For each line the black bar is next to the preferred alternative, and the ratio between the lengths of the black and gray bars indicates the degree of preference for that alternative. It can be seen that Salvador was found to have somewhat more artistic relevance than Ouro Preto (line 1). Both Ouro Preto and Salvador were found to have considerably more artistic relevance than either Porto Seguro or Antonio Prado (lines 2, 3, 4, and 5). Porto Seguro was judged to have somewhat more artistic relevance than Antonio Prado (line 6). The second part of table 3 shows the ranking resulting from those comparisons.

When the comparison process was completed, the EC program calculated a global ranking aggregating rankings on all criteria (table 4).

Table 4. Global ranking of the alternatives (all criteria considered)

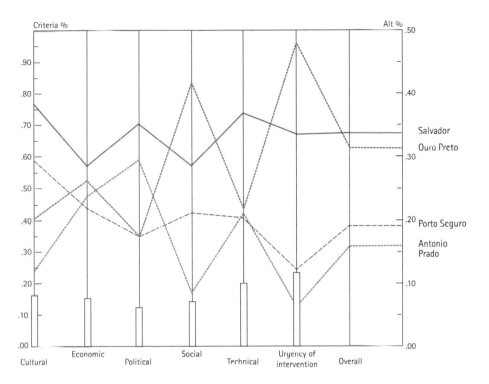

Table 4 shows that Salvador was ranked first. It was judged preferable to other cities on all criteria except for social benefits and urgency of intervention. Ouro Preto was judged preferable to other cities in regard to both social benefits and urgency of intervention; it was ranked second. An increase of the importance (weight) of cultural or political factors would increase the preference for Salvador over Ouro Preto.[4] If decisionmakers were to decide that social benefits or urgency of intervention were more important, then Ouro Preto could become the preferred option. To allow decisionmakers to explore changes in the weighting of criteria, Expert Choice includes sensitivity analysis options that show the effects on preference for the various alternatives.

Reviewing the outcome of the test application, some participants observed that they expected Porto Seguro to be much closer to Ouro Preto than the graph in table 4 shows. The search for an explanation helped the group to refine the preliminary model. The refinement included a slight change in the structure of the model, more precise definition of some criteria, and changes in the weights of the criteria. Table 2 portrays the final version of the decisionmaking model.

Phase II

When phase I was completed, IPHAN's Regional Coordinating Offices supplied information to be entered into the decisionmaking model, leading to the generation of regional priorities. Next, a panel formed by IPHAN's regional coordinators and high-level officials discussed, adjusted, and approved the regional priorities. Finally, the group used the decisionmaking model to establish national preservation priorities for the 54 historic cities considered (table 5).

Table 5. Top 20 historic cities

Priority	Site	Score	Priority	Site	Score
1	Salvador	0.787	11	Santa Cruz Cabrália	0.663
2	Olinda	0.764	12	São Cristovão	0.663
3	Porto Seguro	0.728	13	Praça XV	0.658
4	Mariana	0.724	14	Parati	0.657
5	São Luís	0.715	15	Cachoeira	0.655
6	Ouro Preto	0.705	16	Tiradentes	0.626
7	Bairro do Recife	0.688	17	Brasília	0.622
8	Diamantina	0.682	18	Igarassú	0.621
9	Alcântara	0.682	19	Petrópolis	0.606
10	Serro	0.675	20	Corumbá	0.599

Results and Lessons Learned

Brazilian and IADB authorities analyzed and approved the proposed priorities. They selected six of the first seven cities listed in table 5 to be financed under the US$100 million *Monumenta* Program for the preservation of historic cities.

Important lessons were learned during this exercise in establishing national priorities. Among them was a realization that including outside experts—such as historians, economists, and tourism experts—would help the panel by offsetting regional interests and providing complementary knowledge. It was also determined that some criteria had little power to differentiate alternatives and thus could be eliminated from future versions of the decisionmaking model.

Conclusion

The method, which had been successfully applied on several previous occasions at the IADB, proved to be appropriate to establish priorities for the preservation of heritage sites.[4] It focused discussion on relevant concepts, allowed consideration of stakeholders' interests and viewpoints, and provided the basis for transparent decisions. Overall, the approach improved IPHAN's decisionmaking process for allocating resources and should increase the credibility of that agency with organizations that fund its budget. ■

Notes

1   T. Saaty, *The Analytic Hierarchy Process*, 2d ed. (Pittsburgh: RWS, 1990).

2   "Expert Choice," Version 9.5. Expert Choice, Inc., Pittsburgh, Pa.

3   The scale appearing on the left side of the graph (table 4) gives the weight of the various criteria (represented by the vertical bars over the criteria's names). The scale on the right side measures the preference for the alternatives (represented by the lines associated with the alternatives' names).

4   L. Lage-Filho, "AHP at the Inter-American Development Bank," in E. Forman, *Decision by Objectives* (forthcoming).

35 *Quilombos:* Preserving Afro-Brazilian Roots

Dulce Maria Pereira

Dulce Maria Pereira is president of Fundação Cultural Palmares, Ministry of Culture, Brazil.

Although Brazil's national culture has deep Afro-Brazilian roots, the importance of this historical contribution has not been fully appreciated or acknowledged.[1] Until recently, Afro-Brazilians were systematically excluded from the economic development paradigm. After 350 years of existence, slavery in Brazil was abolished in 1888. However, the development doctrine of the early Republican era specifically excluded Afro-Brazilians, who at the time were over half of Brazil's population. Instead, reflecting the mindset of the times, the Brazilian delegation to a world conference in London in 1914 stated that Brazil would become "white" within 100 years.

Beginning in the 1920s, this attitude was substituted by an official myth of "racial democracy," which put forth the notion that, given the country's high degree of miscegenation, racial discrimination does not exist in Brazil.

Today Brazil has the second-largest black population of any country in the world—only Nigeria's is larger—yet this population has been kept pervasively silent, invisible, and disempowered.

What would Brazil be without *feijoada*, the national dish? What would Brazil be without samba, *capoeira* (martial arts), *maculele* (a dance)? Without its spirituality, art, and cosmology, all of which are permeated by the values and contributions of Afro-Brazilians? Most of those who have produced this culture have not been entitled to enjoy the wealth they have generated, nor has the legacy of sacred sites and material references of their ancestors been preserved. The negative consequences of this political attitude toward human development—combined with prejudice, discrimination, a skewed legal system, and difficult access to education, jobs, and land—have yet to be evaluated and these injustices mitigated.

In the aftermath of political liberalization in the 1980s and the struggle for civil rights, which included many black movements, a new Brazilian Constitution was adopted in 1988. Among other things the new document recognized the legitimacy of many *Quilombo* communities: settlements and areas occupied, without tenure, by independent, self-reliant communities of Afro-Brazilians, descendants of runaway slaves. The constitution states: "The definitive property rights of the descendants of Quilombo communities who occupy *Quilombo* lands are recognized. It is the responsibility of the State to issue respective land title."

In 1995 newly inaugurated President F. H. Cardoso called for the creation of a task force to draft public policies to promote social inclusion in Brazil. His central message was that the goal of national development could not be achieved if racial or ethnic discrimination forced nearly half of the Brazilian population to remain at the bottom of social and economic ladder.

The longstanding myth of Brazilian racial democracy was challenged. This exclusionary attitude had sapped the energy and self-esteem of a large segment of the population, denying the nation a genuine vision of its own identity. Unable to celebrate and enjoy its cultural diversity, Brazil was incapable of establishing mechanisms to promote harmonious social and cultural development.

The new political attitude has made Brazilians cognizant not only of the great cultural and historic wealth with which the nation is endowed but, above all, of the considerable human potential being wasted because of persistent biases and lack of multicultural awareness.

The Ministry of Culture is now trying to raise popular awareness of Brazil's multicultural and multiracial reality, so that the nation can better understand its history and heal the scars of historic injustices. This change in attitude of both government officials and scholars has provided an essential impetus by recognizing the importance of preserving Afro-Brazilian cultural traditions, including historical sites and communities.

Throughout Brazil examples of Afro-Brazilian cultural artifacts are numerous, including sacred places, religious sites, historic monuments, and towns. Until recently, this patrimony was not considered significant, nor was it registered or protected by national laws. The first Afro-Brazilian monument to be included in the National Listing—which contains about 1,000 protected sites and monuments—was the Casa Branca, in Salvador, Bahia, which was inventoried and designated as National Patrimony in the mid-1990s.

The Fundação Cultural Palmares is a not-for-profit organization linked to the Ministry of Culture and in a working partnership with a number of government and nongovernmental institutions. It has been charged with restoring and revitalizing specific historical and ecological sites of Afro-Brazilian origin. One of its principal programs is to identify, map, and inventory the *Quilombos* (figure 1).

Figure 1. *Quilombos*—land demarcation and regularization of land titles—has started. It will benefit about 80,000 people living in 130 communities.

For many years it was believed that only a few *Quilombos* remain and that they are isolated communities. Recent studies, however, have identified at least 800 distinct areas, with about 2 million inhabitants. To protect this fundamental Afro-Brazilian heritage, sites must be properly identified, mapped, registered, protected, and restored. The *Quilombos* have been recognized as a special category of historical site: residents will be granted rights to the land and to the historical patrimony, which includes cemeteries, pillories, mills, churches, and warehouses. Archeological work is just beginning in selected areas. Important information is being assembled from different sources; documents are being collected throughout the world; and oral reports are being recorded. Significant cultural artifacts, many of which were brought to Brazil by enslaved Africans, have been found at many religious temples or sites. A comprehensive databank, the National Information and Reference Center on Afro-Brazilian Culture, has been organized and will be built in Brasília to house the documentation and research. Afro-Brazilian places of worship and religious expression (of *Candomblé* and other faiths) constitute key sources of information. Some institutions are building museums and organizing Internet linkages to the Reference Center.

In addition to preserving and revitalizing Afro-Brazilian sacred sites and religious practices, an important part of the Foundation's program is devoted to the study of the distinct languages spoken by the *Quilombos*' inhabitants. This should ensure better understanding and preservation of many traditional healing practices and cultural and spiritual expressions. Traditionally, *Quilombos* have had a strong link with nature, which forms an integral part of their cosmology and an essential element of their religious practices. These communities are not exploitative and extractive of the natural environment. To them nature and the environment do not represent limitations but, rather, are seen as a source of livelihood opportunities.

In the process of organizing the National Center of Information and Reference on Black Culture, diverse cultural traditions—visual arts, music, dance, crafts, and culinary traditions—have come to light. Projects developed with the communities aim to promote these cultural expressions and products in the cultural market.

Preserving the historical sites established by Afro-Brazilians gives Brazil an opportunity to move away from the perverse tradition of exclusion by redressing historic injustices and reconnecting with national identity and spirituality. For Brazilians their homes, the ceremonies surrounding food preparation, raising children, and even song and dance are associated with the sacred. Because they are linked to Brazilian legacy and imagery, they bring people closer to the Divine. People who cherish such references and respect others and the natural environment will be able to coexist in peace. ■

Note

1 Christine M. Smyrski-Shluger assisted in preparing this chapter.

36 Cost-Efficient Virtual Preservation of Synagogues

Aliza Cohen-Mushlin

Aliza Cohen-Mushlin is director of the Center for Jewish Art at the Hebrew University of Jerusalem.

At one time the focal point of every society was its religious buildings, where community life and spiritual life were centered. Unfortunately, the twentieth century has witnessed upheavals that have intentionally destroyed national cultures, targeting the buildings sacred to them. To sustain stability in these volatile societies, we must reaffirm the integrity of these sacred places and their roles in the cultural memories of their peoples.

Many international bodies are aware of the urgency to preserve what remains of these structures and are willing to help by providing financial aid and specialists. In addition local governments and cultural bodies have been mobilized. We are recommending that systematic and detailed documentation of buildings and neighborhoods be an integral part of the initial stage of these efforts.

First, in these times of limited resources, it is impossible to physically reconstruct and renovate all the historic sites and sacred buildings that are deteriorating due to natural or human causes. To set the criteria for choosing which buildings or sites are to be reconstructed, it is crucial to have systematic documentation that gives information on a building's present condition, its original form, the different stages of past reconstructions, and the history of the building and its community.

Second, buildings that cannot be renovated due to limited resources or other considerations can be kept alive by documenting them in plans, photographs, descriptions, and three-dimensional computerized models. In this way the memory of the community who used the building also is preserved. This documentation can serve as the basis for a wide range of educational programs to enhance cultural awareness.

A third important aspect of documentation should be the involvement of local architects and students. Exposing the young generation to their own history will encourage the awareness, respect, and sense of responsibility necessary to preserve the sacred places of the communities who lived there.

Documentation and subsequent virtual preservation are especially important for regions in which a minority culture no longer exists due to migration or annihilation. A case in point is the Jewish people, who were dispersed from Middle East throughout the world to Europe, North Africa, Asia, the former Soviet Union, and the Americas. In the twentieth century we have witnessed the destruction of most of their communities, with no custodians to safeguard the remaining material culture.

Twenty years ago the recognition of the importance of documentation in the preservation of cultural memory led Bezalel Narkiss to establish the Center for Jewish Art at the Hebrew University. By creating a visual record of the Jewish heritage throughout the world, the Center retains the memory of what cannot be preserved physically. Often, the documentation in the Center is the last evidence that a Jewish community once existed in a place.

To date, the Center has documented in 37 countries and has entered thousands of objects in its computerized database, the Index of Jewish Art, from coins to synagogues, ritual objects, illuminated manuscripts, to ancient art and modern Jewish fine art. The Index is the largest resource of Jewish visual culture and is used by museums, educators, researchers, students, architects, and conservationists throughout the world.

The Center began documenting synagogues in the early 1990s when the borders of Eastern Europe opened. There we discovered numerous synagogues and sites that had survived the ravages of the twentieth century, many in a state of ruin or converted to other purposes with no extant architectural plans. Since then, the Center has worked tirelessly to document over 400 synagogues in Asia; North America; Eastern, Western, and Central Europe; and the former Soviet Union.

A detailed study of a synagogue is done in stages. A team of architects is sent to the site to measure, sketch, and photograph the structure. In addition, a detailed textual description is written, following to a questionnaire developed by the Center. Research is conducted in local archives to obtain historical data on the community and the synagogue. Cultivating relationships with local institutions, museums, and universities wherever possible is essential to our work. We have been especially successful in working with local architects in the Belarus, Lithuania, and Ukraine, and architectural students in Germany.

The resulting architectural plans, photographs, and descriptions are then used to build three-dimensional models of each synagogue through a computer-aided design program. These models enable researchers and educators to follow the different stages of reconstruction and renovations, as well as make comparative studies. These models can also be used for educational purposes in CD ROMs, thus providing visual aid to reconstruct Jewish life and culture.

Some of the best preserved synagogues are found in Spain. They date from the thirteenth and fourteenth centuries and were, paradoxically, preserved because they were turned into churches, some even before the expulsion of the Jews in 1492. The earliest synagogue in Toledo was built in 1205. It has a central nave flanked by two aisles. Confiscated in 1411, during the sixteenth century it was turned into a convent, St. Maria la Blanca. The horseshoe arches and capitals are typical of the local style in the twelfth and thirteenth centuries.

Also typical of local contemporary style is the private synagogue of Don Samuel Halevi Abulafia, the treasurer of King Pedro the Cruel, built in Toledo circa 1357. The single hall is decorated with fine stucco work in the Mudejar style. The king confiscated the building when he executed Abulafia. In 1492, at the time of the expulsion it was given to the Order of Calatrava, and in the eighteenth century the building became an oratory, dedicated to Nuestra Senora Del Transito. It is now a Jewish museum. The tradition of fourteenth-century Mudejar decoration persists in synagogues outside of Spain up to this very day. For example, in the private synagogue of the merchant Saadon in Fez, Morocco, built in 1920 and still active, the walls are covered with rich stucco decoration. The Torah Ark is on the eastern wall, and the reader's desk is placed opposite it, attached to the western wall. By contrast, the synagogue Em-Habanim, also in Fez, became a private apartment, and the Torah Ark is now a kitchen cupboard.

On rare occasions synagogue buildings that were used for other purposes were reconverted to synagogues. An example is the 1907 synagogue in Kuba, Azerbaijan in the Caucasus Mountains. It was turned into a textile factory during the Communist regime. Recently, when some members of the community became more affluent, they donated money to renovate it (figure 1).

However, most synagogues confiscated during the Communist era are still being used for other purposes. One example is the large Ashkenazi synagogue in Baku, Azerbaijan, which at the beginning of the twentieth century became a Yiddish, then a Russian, theater. Another example is the synagogue in Privolnoe in South Azerbaijan, which was confiscated in 1936 (figure 2). The synagogue is still a cowshed; the Jews who live in the area have no other synagogue and are praying in a private room.

In Georgia, also in the Caucasus Mountains, the situation is no better. In the town of Kulashi a complex of three synagogues stands abandoned because the entire Jewish community has left for Israel. The interiors with

Figure 1. Kusari Synagogue, Kuba, Azerbaijan, 1907: exterior. Renovated as a community center in 1997.

all the furniture, books, and empty Torah cases are there, untouched, as though a ghost community were still praying there.

In 1988 the Center documented synagogues in Bulgaria. The 1850 synagogue in Pazardzik is similar in style to the local church and is kept in good state of preservation because it was turned into a coffeehouse. Unfortunately, this is not the case for other synagogues in Bulgaria, such as Samakov of 1881 and Varna, also of the nineteenth century, which are deteriorated (figure 3).

In small hamlets in Ukraine, where no Jews exist, magnificent fortress synagogues of the seventeenth and eighteenth centuries stand as witnesses to a once rich and lively culture. The building of Satanov is one example out of 200 hundred extant former synagogues (figure 4). It was built in the seventeenth century as a fortress synagogue, with thick walls

Figure 2. Balashov Synagogue, Privolnoe, South Azerbaijan, ca. 1900: north façade. Synagogue is now a cowshed.

Figure 3. Sephardi synagogue, Varna, Bulgaria, late nineteenth century: interior of the destroyed west view.

to protect the Jewish community from local wars and pogroms. There are stairs leading to the roof protected by a parapet with loopholes and underground passages designed for flight. We do not know how often it was used for defense.

Figure 4. Fortress synagogue, Satanov, Ukraine, 1716: exterior, east façade.

Another synagogue of 1718 in the hamlet of Berezhany had a large hole in the wall when we first saw it in 1991 (figure 5). The Conservation Department of West Ukraine warned us that it might collapse, as indeed it did two years later (figure 6). Due to lack of funds, nothing could be done to physically save the building. However, the Center for Jewish Art, together with the West Ukraine Conservation Department, initiated a project to document Berezhany and other endangered synagogues in the Ukraine: to measure and photograph them, draw architectural plans with detailed descriptions, do archival research on the community and different restoration stages of the building, and construct three-dimensional computer models (figure 7).

Berezhany made us aware of the disastrous conditions of abandoned synagogues all over the world. Since then, we have been documenting in different countries with the help of our four architects, cooperating with conservation departments, local architects, and local schools of architecture.

An example of virtual preservation through documentation is a partially destroyed synagogue in the Ukraine. Located in the city of Brody, the

Figure 5. Synagogue, Berezany, Ukraine, 1718: exterior, 1992 photo.

Figure 6 (above). Berezany synagogue: as it appeared in 1994.

Figure 7 (left). Berezany synagogue: three-dimensional computer model.

synagogue was built in 1742. From the measurements and architectural drawings of facades, sections, and details of spatial elements (figure 8), we constructed a three-dimensional model of the original building (figure 9). In addition it comprises what we know of various stages of reconstruction throughout the ages. For example, the original women's section was on the ground level on the south, and a later women's gallery was built In the west.

Virtual preservation is an ongoing process involving archival research, which sometimes uncovers old plans and photographs. Our documentation comprises a short history of the place and the community and a detailed description of each part of the building, going from the general to the particular. Each document has an "identity card," which includes information on the location, the place, the name of the site, the date or period, and the architect, if known.

Figure 8. Brody Synagogue: south facade, 1995 drawing.

Figure 9. Brody Synagogue: exterior, southeast view showing women's section, three-dimensional computer model.

The data are entered in a specially designed template of the computerized Index of Jewish Art, with retrievable fields common to other objects documented in the Index. Furniture is also described, such as the Torah Ark, where the Torah is kept, and the *bimah*, where it is read; and the seating arrangement of the participants, which may vary in different communities. Moreover, if the synagogue is decorated with stucco or wall paintings, the scenes and decorative elements are described, and when possible, cross-referenced.

For example, one common subject used to decorate synagogues and ritual objects is the Sacrifice of Isaac. In the restored synagogue of Lancut in Poland, this scene adorns the canopy of the *bimah*. This subject adorns other objects that have been documented in the Index of Jewish Art. The Index lists the single episodes in a given narrative and their various iconographical components, with the relevant literary sources. This facilitates the retrieval of other objects with similar or varied iconography: a prayer book from Germany of 1300, a nineteenth-century ritual plate from Lvov, or a painting by Chagall. They all depict variations of the same subject.

For comparative study, objects of ancient art, architecture, manuscripts, ritual objects, modern art, and funerary art can be retrieved through common fields or through the subjects that adorn them. Thus, the documentation of synagogues throughout the world is only part of an all-encompassing project, which aims to document the entire visual culture of the Jewish people and virtually preserve it on computer for posterity.

In the present circumstances the virtual preservation of a culture is by far more feasible than its physical preservation, especially where buildings are concerned. Documentation should be the first step in setting criteria for the physical preservation of a building. However, when funds and other considerations do not allow the latter, documentation can be used to preserve the building virtually. The entire documentation and research of the Index of Jewish Art is done by graduate students of the Hebrew University as part of their curriculum. These talented and motivated teams of researchers are the main resource of the Center for Jewish Art, which has facilitated the documentation of tens of thousands of objects in 37 countries at minimal cost. Moreover, a younger generation of educators and scholars is emerging, steeped in the knowledge and understanding of its culture and heritage.

Six years ago we started a project with our German partner, Professor Thies, involving his students of Architecture at Braunschweig University. As part of their curriculum the students were asked to identify, measure, and make architectural plans of former synagogues, which are now used as dwellings, storerooms, or restaurants. Sixty-five students were involved in the first project, which was completed, and 165 students are participating in two concurrent projects, together with the University Architectural School in Dresden and the Bauhaus in Weimar. Our collaboration helps to preserve our common heritage. We hope that other countries will soon join in, for time is of the essence. ■

37 Computer Reconstruction of German Synagogues

Marc Grellert

*Marc Grellert is assistant professor,
Computer-Aided Design, Architecture
Department, Darmstadt University of
Technology, Darmstadt, Germany,
grellert@cad.architektur.tu-darmstadt.de*

The Darmstadt Technical University's team began the reconstruction of three Frankfurt synagogues in 1994 and completed the work in 1997. Because of our political interest; the positive experiences gained from this project; and the great interest shown by the public, the Jewish community, and survivors; it was our desire to expand this project to 15 more synagogues.

Since the Darmstadt Technical University's budget contains no line item for them, expanded special projects are dependent on grants and private donations. At this point the reconstruction of five more synagogues is guaranteed. The synagogues of Hannover, Cologne, and Plauen are being sponsored by the German Ministry of Education. The synagogues of Munich and Nuremberg are being sponsored by the local municipal governments. The Frankfurt project resulted from studies of the Nazi period, from the interest in its architecture, and the uses of computer-aided design (CAD) (figure 1).

Figure 1. Virtual reconstruction of the interior of a destroyed synagogue.

Figure 2. Virtual reconstruction
of synagogue built in neo-classical style.

The idea for this project came after a 1994 arson attack on a Lubeck synagogue. The intention is to visually regenerate the destroyed architecture
and to provide an admonition as well as a memorial in connection with
the Nazi period. The university team wishes to send a signal against
racism and anti-Semitism as well as pay tribute to the historical architectural importance of the synagogues.

These political aspects hold true for the entire project. The additional
objectives of the entire project are to give a representative overview of
the architecture of nineteenth- and twentieth-century synagogues. We
want to convey three-dimensional impressions of an almost unknown
architecture and contribute to educational and commemorative work for
use in schools, universities, and museums.

The university team is planning to produce a documentary film and a new
web site covering the entire project and combining the computer simulation of the synagogues with testimonies of survivors and background
information about architectural monuments, the Third Reich, and Jewish
culture. The intention is to provide an incentive, particularly for the
younger German generation, to reflect on this period of German history
(figure 2).

Selection Criteria

The team selected synagogues using architectural criteria. We chose
large cities with the expectation that the political aspect would reach
more people. The synagogues selected are from the nineteenth and
twentieth centuries. The oldest synagogues—small buildings—extant in
Germany date back to the Middle Ages and are located in important
cities. Pogroms during that period led to an expulsion of the Jewish

Figure 3. Virtual reconstruction
of the synagogue, detail of figure 3.

population from almost all cities. At that time most Jews lived in small towns and villages, and the architecture was accordingly modest in scale. The buildings were inconspicuous and resembled private homes.

During the Enlightenment (eighteenth century) Jews were allowed to return to the cities. The synagogue in Karlsruhe (1792) was the first inner city temple synagogue. With the beginning of equality for the Jews, migration to the cities by Jews increased. This resulted in the need for larger places of worship. The social status of Jews then made it possible to erect prestigious buildings for large congregations. The architectural style reflected social status and the way the Jewish community saw itself. This was the birth of large synagogues in Germany.

Styles

Three different styles of nineteenth- and twentieth-century synagogue architecture centuries can be distinguished:

1. Oriental, which emphasized the independence of the Jews. The synagogue of Kaiserslautern is a good example.
2. German Romanesque, which emphasized the affiliation of the Jews with the German nation, for example, the synagogue of Munich (figure 3).
3. Contemporary or regional styles, for example, the neo-classical synagogue of Berlin, Kottbusser Ufer, and the Bauhaus synagogue of Plauen (figure 4).

Because of the different architectural styles, synagogues from this period have no uniform look or characteristic feature. However, the inner room of every synagogue has characteristic features: the Torah Ark, the *almemor*, and the spatial separation of men and women.

The arrangement of these elements determines the interior architecture of the synagogue. In the Orthodox liturgy putting the Torah Ark on the east wall and the *almemor* in the middle of the room creates an architectural tension between these two poles. In the nineteenth century a new liturgy—the liberal liturgy—arose. In these synagogues, in which the *almemor* is placed near the Torah Ark, the emphasis is on the longer axis of the building.

The history of these synagogues stopped on November 9, 1938 on *Reichskristallnacht.* On November 9 and 10 not only were synagogues destroyed but also more than 100 Jews were murdered, many injured, thousands of stores plundered, and 20,000 to 30,000 Jewish men deported to concentration camps.

More than 2,000 of the 3,000 synagogues in Germany were destroyed during the Nazi period, almost all of them in the larger cities. The synagogues had characterized the cityscapes. What reminds us of the synagogues today? Hardly anything is left.

Regeneration

The sources for the Frankfurt reconstruction were blueprints, descriptions of the buildings, contemporary drawings, and photographs. And, very special for the project in the other five cities, there are eyewitnesses, persons who survived the Holocaust and possibly can provide missing information. However, due to the advanced age of the survivors, only a few years at best remain to gather this invaluable information. ■

Figure 4. Virtual reconstruction (wire frame) of a synagogue built in neo-classical style.

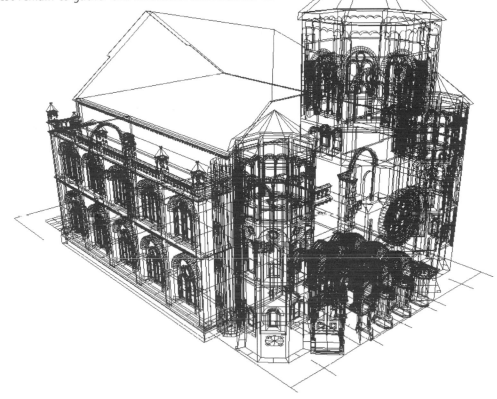

38 Preserving Jewish Heritage

The Center for Jewish Art
of the Hebrew University
of Jerusalem

T he Center for Jewish Art of the Hebrew University of Jerusalem sponsored a day-long roundtable to review and discuss current scientific research on Jewish-built heritage in Central and Eastern Europe and North Africa. The following 13 essays address both conceptual and technical issues. They include, on the one hand, methodological approaches for the analysis of floor plans and volumes, and on the other, interpretations of the symbols and elements found in religious and secular architecture.

Among the topics is the virtual reconstruction of Jewish synagogues destroyed during World War II in the major cities of Germany and synagogues and dwellings in the *shtetls*, or small towns of Jewish settlements, of Eastern Europe. Other essays show how documents and typological and historiographic references have been used to reconstruct historic buildings and places created by communities no longer in existence. Also brought to light are the evolution of the urban fabric of *melah* in Morocco, the legacy of the Jewish presence in the remote Cape Verde Islands, examples of reutilized synagogues in Germany and Poland, sacred spaces in conflict areas, and the wooden sacred buildings of the Ukraine.

Discussion focused on the analytical methods, based on geometry and comparative architectural systems, used to analyze the design and construction of churches, mosques, and synagogues, highlighting common and differing features. Professor Narkiss concluded the roundtable by reiterating that the main objective of the research program conducted by the Center for Jewish Art is to enhance understanding of the Jewish cultural legacy found in so many places and its formidable contributions to the development of art and architecture. The results of these studies will enrich the education of future generations.

Melah of Morocco

Considerable research has been devoted to Jewish settlements known as *melah* within Arab-Islamic cities in Morocco and other Muslim countries. The study of *melah* begins with a given dwelling unit and proceeds to look at both continuity and piecemeal, or limited, transformations introduced through this unit into the urban fabric over time. Architectural monuments are part of this fabric but may not be subject to similar transformations. Studying the fabric of the *melah* derives from an interest in understanding the daily lives of ordinary people, which would affect the quality of life in the settlements and adjacent neighborhoods. Working on two levels of scale—first, on individual buildings and second, on larger areas, or clusters, of dwellings—offers important clues about the inner logic of the spatial transformations of the subdivision modules, known as *taddarts*, typical of all North African cities.

The old *melah* of Essaouira, a city founded in 1765 and formerly known as Mogador, had a large Jewish population. It provides many examples of well-preserved residential dwellings organized around courtyards. Studying and comparing the floor plans and sections of these dwellings and the typical processes of reconstruction provide ample understanding of the original dwelling types and the variations introduced over time. The individual variations contribute to the creation of new ideas about how to organize living and working space and the relationship between the interior (private, family) space and exterior spaces facing yards or streets. The evolution and growth of the dwelling's interior, often encroaching into public space, usually were a result of adaptations of the ground floor space for commercial purposes, or expansion of residential space to accommodate more than one family.

The evolution of residential dwellings provided essential elements for special buildings such as synagogues, mosques, churches, and hospitals. These structures derived directly or indirectly from the evolution of the house, which tended to become more and more specialized over time until it was no longer a dwelling but had acquired a special function.

This raises the questions as to whether Morocco's Jewish architecture reflects a specific, or unique, lifestyle or way of defining space. Research into this question, including houses and the urban fabric of the Islamic world in North Africa and Morocco, spanned 10 years and extended to Spain and Italy. The research concluded that Jewish settlements in North Africa and Morocco were devoid of such specificity; instead they were able to integrate perfectly with local culture. Yet many researchers are convinced that life in the *melah*—the customs, habits, and behaviors of its inhabitants—was different from life in Islamic or Christian communities. Defining these differences, however, calls for more than an architectural study.

Attilio Petruccioli

Attilio Petruccioli is professor of architecture and editor of the IED Journal of the Islamic Environmental Design Research Center, Como, Italy, petruccioli@yahoo.com

Architectural Analysis Based on a Scaled Geometric System

Hans-Martin Mueller

Hans Martin Mueller is an architect
and teaches at the Technical University
of Braunschweig, H-M.Mueller@tu-bs.de

In the past research for rules in architecture led to totally different methods, each with its own subjective aspects. One architectural methodology was the derived from other branches of knowledge, such as investigations and observations of social circumstances and political processes. Applying ideological doctrines and subjective interpretations to architecture was bound to cause prejudice and misjudgment, at least sometimes.

Another methodology of the past was concerned mainly about the results of designing. The process of designing was ignored.

Therefore, despite totally different outcomes, the history of architecture very often meant a history of perception as well. Often the evolution of design from early ideas during the conceptual phase to the final elaboration of three-dimensional models was largely excluded from scientific research. The formation of architecture as a matter of individual effort played a subordinate role.

In the late 1920s and early 1930s Hans Sedlmayr introduced an innovative method of analyzing architecture based on describing elements and units, using a study of Borromini's architecture as the vehicle. He divided the entire structure of a building into distinct elements and then resynthesized the building by describing the constituent elements. His method led to scientific research on the rules of thinking and of organizing thought as a means of interpreting the resulting architectural object.

In the mid-eighteenth century Vico and Herder had discovered common worlds of imagination in individual human beings based on a common platform, such as the same language. The comparability of thought of various individuals was built on a similar organization of reasoning. This hypothesis led to the research into the rules of thinking and thence into the rules of the resulting products.

In 1979 predicated on this concept that thinking has an inherent order, Harmen Thies introduced a new method called *Rissanalyse* (plan analysis).[1] He applied this new methodology to interpret the generation of architecture, which he believed occurs in an ordered sequence of steps and phases. Whereas Sedlmayr's method of structural analysis differentiates the constituent elements, Thies' *Rissanalyse* describes the absolute relationship among different units through reconstruction.

Recognition of the inner logic of the design—that is, the architects' own rules of expression and formal style—means that it is no longer open to interpretation but is a demonstrable series of decisions made by the architect while planning. Thus, the research and its results are detached from the researcher. This method eliminates interpretation of objects based on personal experience and subjective points of view.

For example, comparing architectural principles made it possible for Thies to solve the authorship of Würzburg Cathedral Residence-Church, a long-standing controversy in research on Baroque architecture in Central Europe, in favor of Balthasar Neumann. Thies has also proven the effectively of Rissanalyse in his research on Michelangelo's designs of the Capitol Hill in Rome. The method has made it possible to induce the organization of constitutive elements in the overall design statement by the architect.

The sequence of interpretation begins with the concepts of the basic design program and the language used. Associations and external motivations are examined as well. The results of the design and the components of its internal order are expressed in a system of drawings. The scaled drawing, a two-dimensional projection, is a description of the entire, projected three-dimensional architecture. In the past the method was used effectively in numerous attempts to analyze the geometry of medieval as well as Gothic architecture. However, there was no clear evidence for the rational shaping of elements and for combining these elements in units in a defined architectural form. Today, a number of monuments have been successfully interpreted using this methodology.

Synagogues and Dwelling Houses in the Shtetls of Podolia, Poland

Early in the eighteenth century, after Polish control was restored in Eastern Podolia, Jews settled in the towns of this region, forming *shtetls* ("small towns" in Yiddish). The Podolian *shtetls* inherited the spatial grid of the old sixteenth- and seventeenth-century fortified urban settlements, which had survived many destructions and restorations (figures 1, 2). Well-preserved Jewish settlements in the vicinity of Vinnitsa in Eastern Podolia, Ukraine, provide the essential elements required to study the architecture of Eastern European *shtetls*. The architectural monuments of Podolian *shtetls* are of the utmost importance for studying the culture of Ashkenasic Jewry of Eastern Europe.

From the late eighteenth to the early twentieth centuries, urban centers of these small trade towns were populated exclusively by Jews. A stone synagogue building of the fortress type constructed just after the foundation of Shargorod in 1589 gives evidence of the important role that the Jewish community played in the town. Until the early twentieth century, traditions of folk architecture remained alive in Podolian *shtetls*. Their architectural environment corresponded to the traditional lifestyle of the Jewish community, which had been predominantly trade and craft

Alla Sokolova

Alla Sokolova is an architect in St. Petersburg, Russia.

Figure 1. Schematic town-plan
of Shargorod:
1. Synagogue building
   of the fortress type, 1589
2. St. Florian Roman Catholic
   parish church, 1593
3. St. Nicholas Monastery,
   founded in 1782
4. Non-preserved building
   of the Russian Orthodox church
5. Stone palace within the castle
   walls, 1585
6. Market storehouse and shops
7. Synagogue building,
   late nineteenth century
8. Jewish cemetery.

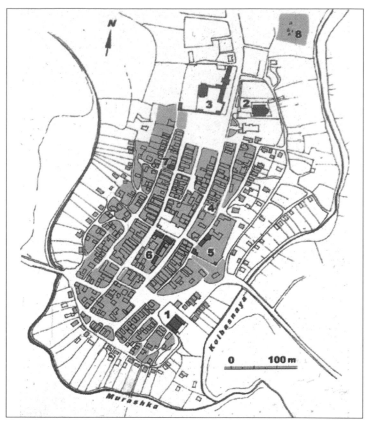

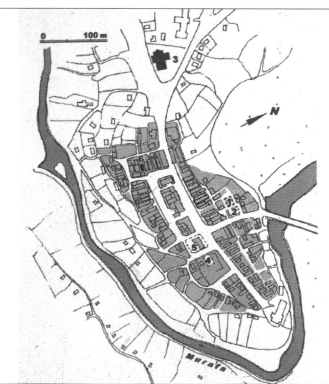

Figure 2. Schematic plan of Cherinvtsi:
1. Position of the oldest stone
   synagogue (fragments of its stone
   foundation preserved to the present)
2. Position of the synagogue building
   with adjoined houses of worship,
   late eighteenth-early nineteenth
   centuries (information about these
   buildings was taken from interviews
   with local inhabitants)
3. St. Nicholas Roman Catholic cathedral,
   1640
4. Non-preserved Russian Orthodox church
5. Location of non-preserved market
   storehouse
6. Synagogue building, late nineteenth
   century.

oriented. The layout of the *shtetl* of Shargorod, for instance, was formed along a system of small marketplaces attached to a pair of parallel market streets, each of which was the extension of a trade route through the built residential and commercial areas. The rural areas were very close to town borders, a characteristic of the small, urban settlements of Podolia.

The towns' layouts remained almost unchanged during the eighteenth and nineteenth centuries because the stone buildings, such as a synagogue and a Roman Catholic cathedral, had escaped demolition during the late seventeenth century. Those that had been left in ruins were rebuilt on their original sites. Thus, it is conceivable that the synagogue of Shargorod, erected in 1589, was rebuilt on the same site in the early eighteenth century. Although the synagogue building sustained some losses during World War II, on the whole it has been preserved. Its function, however, was changed during the Soviet era, when a juice factory was installed in the building. The factory is still operating.

The study of these heritage sites—the architecture of the Podolian synagogues and the traditional Jewish houses in Shargorod—constitutes an important reference for understanding community life in the *shtetls* of Podolia. The Center for Jewish Art of the Hebrew University of Jerusalem has studied and documented the synagogues of Shargorod, Satanov, and Chechelnik (figure 3).

Well-preserved Jewish *shtetl* houses, some from the late eighteenth century, have important typological features drawn from medieval European culture. A traditional *shtetl* house was a multi-functional building that combined in itself trade, cottage-industrial, dwelling, and household rooms. The layout of the *shtetl* house corresponded to the compact arrangement of *shtetl* town blocks (figure 4). Housing construction

Figure 3. Synagogue in Chechelnik: western facade with main entrance, 1996 photo.

Figure 4A. Shargorod. Frame house on stone basement, late eighteenth century. The house has a preserved glazed veranda, which is used for creating a *sukkah*—a provisional hut, covered by branches—for celebrating the festival of *Sukkoth*. This structure has a remarkable ceiling with a hatch, which could be closed from the top by removable wooden boards. The tradition of having such small structures continued to exist in Podolia until the beginning of the twentieth century, 1998 photo.

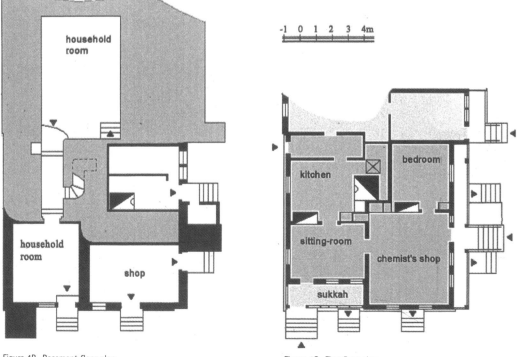

Figure 4B. Basement floor plan.

Figure 4C. First floor plan.

customs that have been preserved give evidence that definite principles of architectural arrangement of the buildings were included in the traditional culture of Podolian Jews. A few traditional *shtetl* houses with glazed balconies and remarkable roofs, used for creating a *sukkah*, have been preserved and also have been studied by the Center. The tradition of maintaining such small structures continued in Podolia until the early twentieth century. Unfortunately, today these heritage monuments are not being adequately preserved.

Recovering Jewish Heritage in the Cape Verde Islands

The story of Jewish migration from Morocco to the Cape Verde Islands will be told as part of a project to celebrate the historic and cultural legacy left by the community, which is inextricably linked to its Moroccan origin. The primary goal of "The Jews of Cape Verde Project: Preservation of Memory" is to investigate the role, and honor the memory, of the many Sephardic Jews who traveled to Cape Verde in the nineteenth century. The project will restore four small Jewish cemeteries and create educational documents based on oral and archival research. The mounting of an unprecedented photographic exhibition at a Jewish museum in the United States, which would also travel to other countries, is also envisaged.

By preserving collective memory, we preserve the past in order to create the future, and cemeteries can be seen as quintessential repositories of collective memory. From the Hebrew and Portuguese etchings on the tombstones in the cemeteries, we know that the majority of Jews in Cape Verde came from Morocco, mainly the Mogador district (now known as Essaouira), Rabat, and Tangiers.

In 1975 after successfully winning independence from Portugal, Cape Verde became a sovereign country. As a result of nearly 500 years of Portuguese colonial rule, Cape Verde is predominantly Roman Catholic. Nonetheless, evidence shows that from the period of the Spanish and Portuguese inquisition through the nineteenth century, Cape Verde was a haven for Jews fleeing religious persecution or for those emigrating from Morocco seeking greater economic stability. The settlers landed primarily on the islands of São Vicente, Santo Antão, Boa Vista, and Santiago and proceeded to engage in international commerce, shipping, civil service, and other trades.

Because a majority of the settlers were male and their numbers were few relative to the Catholic majority, widespread intermarriage diluted an already tenuous affiliation with Jewish customs and rituals. Nevertheless, the descendants of these families speak with pride of their Jewish roots and are dedicated to the exploration, preservation, and magnification of the memory of their forebears. Because of patrilineal descent, generations of offspring continue to bear such typical Sephardic names as Auday, Benollel, Benros, Benathar, Benchimol, Cohen, Levy, Pinto, and Wahnon (figures 5, 6).

The resurgence of interest in Jewish heritage prompted a group of these descendants in Cape Verde to press for the restoration of Jewish cemeteries and the creation of a permanent archive (figure 7). To this end groups of descendants in Cape Verde, Lisbon, and the United States have begun to work together. They are forming a nonprofit organization based in Washington, D.C. to raise the funds necessary to underwrite the

Carol S. Castiel

Carol Castiel is a writer and consultant, Washington, D. C., ccastiel@aol.com

Figure 5. Headstone of Moises Auday, d. May 9, 1886, in the Jewish section of the Christian cemetery in the capital city Praia, São Tiago, Cape Verde. The Hebrew inscription reads: "The tombstone of the grave of the lamented young man Moises Auday, who went to his eternal reward not in his proper place or time on the eve of Monday, 15 Iyar [a month in Hebrew] 5646. May his soul be bound in the bond of eternal life."

Figure 6. Brothers Antonio and Firmino Benros at the home of Firmino in the interior of the island of São Tiago, Cape Verde. They were the descendants of the Benros family from Tangiers, Morocco, who originally settled in the islands of Santo Antão and São Tiago.

Figure 7. The small Jewish cemetery in Boa Vista illustrates the danger of what can happen to other historic headstones if immediate action is not taken to restore and preserve the cemeteries from the elements.

various components of the Jews of Cape Verde Project, including interviewing elderly descendants, collecting photographs and artifacts for the exhibition and archive, and publishing research findings.

The Governments of Cape Verde and Morocco have enthusiastically endorsed the project not only to honor shared history but also to promote bilateral economic development. In addition to recreating and documenting this lost chapter in Jewish-African history, the Jews of Cape Verde Project will contribute to Cape Verde's economic development by encouraging cultural heritage tourism, which will stimulate employment in related industries and generate much-needed foreign exchange. Not coincidentally, ecotourism is a top development priority for Cape Verde's government.

In addition to its historical, economic, and aesthetic benefits the project demonstrates interracial and interfaith tolerance. Moroccan Muslims, whose society exemplifies Islamic tolerance, together with Cape Verdean Catholics, who take pride in their Jewish heritage, could provide inspiration to others around the world working toward religious pluralism. In addition, contemporary efforts at building good relations between North African Muslims and Jews, on the one hand, and Jews and blacks, on the other, can only be enriched by the historical example of trialogue on the Cape Verde Islands among Sephardic Jews, who shared the fruits of Moroccan Islam with Africans introduced to Catholicism by Portuguese sailors.

Homes in Sacred Spaces: Reused Synagogues in Germany

Since 1994 the Institute of Architectural History at the Technical University of Braunschweig in Germany, in cooperation with the Center for Jewish Art in Jerusalem, has been working to document synagogues in Germany.[2] The work began with a survey of synagogues in Niedersachsen (Lower Saxony). Since 1997 it has continued in Sachsen-Anhalt, through the generous support of the Alfred Freiherr von Oppenheim-Stiftung. In 1999 documentation started in Sachsen and Thueringen (Saxony and Thuringia), parts of the Neue Bundesländer, the former German Democratic Republic, with the support of the German-Israeli Foundation.

The aim of the research is to produce a catalogue covering all of the former synagogues, cemetery chapels, and ritual baths for each region. These catalogues will contain the precious synagogues of rich communities, as well as the poor, smaller houses of the rural communitiesæall buildings, destroyed or existing. Together the catalogues will provide a complete overview of the Jewish architectural heritage in each region of Germany. This documentation will become part of the Jerusalem Index of Jewish Art at the Center for Jewish Art in Jerusalem and can serve as a basis for further research.

Synagogues in Germany represent a type of architecture that deserves special attention in regard to its history, especially in the German context. Contrary to the popular supposition that after *Reichskristallnacht* in 1938 no synagogues remained in Germany, approximately half of synagogues are still standing. While the great buildings of the capital cities were largely devastated, only the interiors of the smaller synagogues in towns and villages were destroyed to be modified for other functions. Many of the smaller structures survive.

The buildings are testimony to Germany's rich Jewish heritage—its development and repression—as well as reflections of the way that Jewish communities in Germany saw themselves. Synagogues and other Jewish ritual buildings have to be seen as important parts of the stylistic development of German architecture. To let these remaining examples vanish unidentified means to erase the memory of what happened. The project involves reawakening peoples' awareness. Whether they are interested or antagonistic, they are forced to revisit the past.

The synagogues often represent a problem for those charged with protecting them. Because of conversions, the original shapes of the former ritual buildings have disappeared almost completely. Including them on a list of buildings to be protected seems questionable when the buildings do not differ from others in their neighborhoods. Yet they represent an important link to Germany's rich Jewish heritage.

Katrin Keßler and
Ulrich Knufinke

*Katrin Keßler and Ulrich Knufinke are architects and teach at the Technical University of Braunschweig, Germany,
katrinkessler@yahoo.com*

The first task is to locate the former synagogues. In Sachsen-Anhalt, for example, about 50 synagogues were in use in 1938; 19 have survived, along with 3 ritual baths and 8 cemetery chapels. Forgotten former synagogues were rediscovered in over 20 villages. Most are synagogues that were sold by the Jewish community during the nineteenth or early twentieth centuries. In small towns and villages the Jewish community declined as a result of rural exodus; in larger towns it expanded and needed more spacious synagogue buildings. The old synagogues were often sold to Christians, who converted them long before *Reichskristallnacht.* In the literature such buildings are mentioned only rarely, and it is difficult to find references to them.

The actual state of the 19 former Jewish ritual buildings in Sachsen-Anhalt is very diverse: only two are still being used for their original purpose. Two of the buildings are used as museums, and the rest serve as homes, churches, or warehouses. The same is true throughout most of Germany.[3]

Some of the buildings documented by the Institute for the History of Architecture in Braunschweig years ago have already changed, and the original structure or even traces of original paintings have been lost. There is no way to save all former synagogues in their original condition. Sometimes the project arrives too late, and a building has been rebuilt or destroyed without any documentation, leaving no possibility of reconstructing the former shape. This is why documentation projects are so important.

Because of the reduced number of Jewish communities in Germany, there is no need for a large number of synagogue buildings. The only way to preserve the structures is to re-use them. While not every former synagogue can be reconstructed to its former shape and converted to a museum, the buildings can be preserved and documented—hopefully before their conversion—to draw conclusions about the building, the architect, and even the community. The buildings must be at least preserved virtually, to prevent their falling completely into oblivion.

Thus it is necessary to take detailed measurements of the buildings, produce scaled drawings, and document the buildings through photographs. The shape, structure, and materials have to be described exactly. This information will be important for an investigation of the building concerning its origin and historical development. The project also tries to find original drawings, historical pictures, or reports of people who remember the former shape of the building. These varied sources enable a visual reconstruction of the synagogue that, depending on the material found, is more or less detailed.

It is also necessary to link the history of the building to the development of the community. This can give valuable hints and help to understand decisions made by the architect or the community. The project works cooperatively not only with architects, but also with historians, archives, museums, and institutions for building preservation. By synthesizing this historical and architectural material, we can trace the history of the building. At the end we can make assumptions about the architect's intent and why a particular style or type of structure was chosen or what examples were followed.

The documentation is carried out by about 160 graduate students of architecture from the universities of Braunschweig, Dresden, and Weimar in teams of two or three students per synagogue. These students are not Jewish; therefore, they have to learn about Jewish culture, German-Jewish history, and the historical development of synagogues. Of course, they learn not only about Jewish culture but also about their own past.

Although most reused and rebuilt synagogues and cemetery chapels are in a poor state, they must be seen as historical documents. Like every historic building they reflect the life of their builders, users, and reusers. Documentation of such historical source material is important not only for the history of architecture but also for a society seeking and commemorating its own history and culture. Many synagogues and other places have lost their religious functions, perhaps forever. Reconstruction of the buildings in their original shape would appear to be useless and often impossible. Thus, the documentation of these buildings helps to recognize the original meaning of what are now restaurants, workshops, and homes. In this way they are preserved as documents of Jewish culture and history in Germany as well as remarkable, but often forgotten, examples of the history of architecture.

Several examples of reused synagogues documented during project work in North and East Germany since 1994 illustrate the current condition of these buildings and the process of documentation and reconstruction. They also show a nearly forgotten part of the German-Jewish cultural heritage that still can be found and that should be recognized.

Egeln, Sachsen-Anhalt

The synagogue of Egeln, a small town in Sachsen-Anhalt, East Germany, was built in 1853. Since 1938, after the Jewish community was forced to sell the synagogue, it has been used as a residence. Many changes were made, and it is hard to imagine its original appearance. Only a special form of pediment distinguishes it from other houses of the town. In the town archive no original drawings or other sources for a reconstruction of the synagogue's original shape were preserved. One photo ca. 1900 shows the building indistinctly. By analyzing the scaled drawings of the present state, the old photo, and some similar synagogues of the area, it was possible to reconstruct the original building.

Norderney, Niedersachsen

The synagogue of Norderney, an island in the North Sea, is an exceptional building in several respects. As far as we know, it was the only synagogue in Germany built for a vacation community and was used only during the summer. Many Jewish guests, such as Franz Kafka, visited the island, famous for its healthful climate, and some of them founded a society to build a synagogue. In 1878, with permission from Emperor Wilhelm II and the help of many wealthy and influential donors, a small and unpretentious building was erected. The architect was probably Edwin Oppler, one of the most important German-Jewish architects in the second half of the nineteenth century. This building is the only one of his many famous synagogues that still exists. In 1933 Jews were forbidden to enter Norderney. The synagogue was no longer used for services, so it was sold. After many alterations and additions it is now used as a restaurant. Nothing remains of its former shape or original purpose.

Halle, Sachsen-Anhalt

In 1926 the Jewish community of Halle, a city in East Germany, opened a new cemetery next to the municipal cemetery Two years later a new ceremony hall was consecrated. It included a prayer-room, rooms necessary for the ritual washings of the dead, and offices. The hall was demolished during *Reichskristallnacht* and in 1942 was transformed into a home for the elderly Jewish population. Many older people were forced to live there under poor conditions before being deported to Theresienstadt. Originally, the building was an important example of late expressionistic architecture. A pattern of brickwork covered the facades, which together with the triangular roof-windows, gave the building a unique appearance.

Wilhelm Haller was one of the architects of that time who tried to find his own style by adapting fashionable elements and older traditions. Influences from German expressionism, art deco, and Bauhaus-functionalism, as well as reminiscences of neo-Moorish eclecticism characterize his projects for Jewish sacred buildings during the 1920s.

Synagogues of Poland

Ongoing research on Jewish culture and heritage in Poland supported by the Jewish Historical Institute indicates that before the war over 3 million Jews lived in over 1,000 communities in Poland. Several thousand synagogues (*batei-midrash*) and various houses of prayer must also have existed. In 1947, when just over 100,000 Jews were left in Poland, only 38 synagogues and several dozen Houses of Prayer served their needs (figure 8).

No information documenting the number of synagogues that survived the war is available. During the post-war years the remaining Jewish communities were unable to oppose the dismantling and destruction of the surviving synagogues, which were no longer in use. Without the assistance of Polish art historians and conservationists it would have been impossible to save many of the synagogues that we admire today. It is clear that, beginning in the nineteenth century, these structures were considered by both Polish and Jewish scholars as part of the Polish landscape.

In 1953 an initial list of 25 synagogues that survived the war was issued. They were documented and photographed by a commission of the Institute. Some of the listed monuments have been lost since the inventory was made, as is the case of the cemetery adjacent to the synagogue in Klimontow (figures 9, 10). However, a number of significant monuments were comprehensively documented, redesigned, and restored by State Business Workshops for the Conservation of Monuments. The official list of architectural landmarks published in 1964 referred to 72 synagogues in Poland. A more recent book refers to 320 Jewish heritage sites in 240 localities.

Eleanora Bergman

Eleanora Bergman is director of the Jewish Historical Institute, Warsaw, Poland.

Figure 8. Nozyk's Synagogue, Warsaw, 1902. It is the only one in operation of the over 400 houses of prayer that served the Warsaw Jewish community until World War II, 1995 photo.

Figure 9. The cemetery by the synagogue in Klimontow existed until 1962, pre-1962 photo.

For research purposes the Institute collects information on the synagogues and cemeteries of the entire former Polish Jewish world, now part of Lithuania, Byelorus, and Ukraine. The Institute does not simply evaluate synagogues. Rather, they are treated as material evidence—all too often the only evidence—of the existence of the Jewish community in a given place, making them of unquestionable historical value. However, staff conservationists carry out an architectural and artistic evaluation of the synagogues. All of the 140 designated landmarks protected by law have been documented and recorded on standard inventory cards. Today this documentation is considered inadequate. How to update and improve the quality of the information contained in the inventory merits closer examination.

In 1991 the Institute began a cooperative relationship with the World Monuments Fund, which recommended that the Institute establish priorities and prepare a list and description of 10 important synagogues in a state of decay and in danger of destruction. The purpose was to select one synagogue building for restoration, sponsored by the World Monuments Fund. In cooperation with M. and K. Piechotkas the Institute identified 13 synagogues, and the World Monuments Fund selected the Tempel of Krakow, built in 1862 and rebuilt to its present size in 1894 and 1924. Thanks to many private donations, the efforts of the City of Krakow, and especially the generous grants from the Getty Foundation, preservation work is almost completed (figures 11, 12).

The Kupa synagogue, also in Krakow, is a community treasure. Built in 1647 and rebuilt in 1834, until recently it was used as a workshop by a tailors' cooperative. The Kupa synagogue is being restored by the Citizen's Committee for the Protection of Krakow's Historical Monuments. These synagogues belong to the Jewish community. While after restoration the Tempel will serve a religious purpose, the community has yet to find a function for the elaborately decorated Kupa synagogue, which was extensively damaged during the war. The structure is listed by the World Monuments Watch (figures 13, 14).

Other synagogues studied include those of Piotrkow Trybunalski, Orla, Chmielnik, Rymanow, Wodzislaw, and Dabrowa Tarnowska (figures 15-17). Some of these buildings were constructed in the early seventeenth century. Most reveal a host of similar problems, including a dearth of resources for conservation and lack of an effective management strategy for preservation. The key issue is their future use. Some experts maintain that all synagogues of artistic value should be turned into museums (figure 18). This may seem unrealistic at present. However, the idea merits further consideration if the synagogues are to be incorporated in a network of regional heritage resources as part of a proposal to establish a Jewish museum in Warsaw to celebrate the 800 to 1,000 years of Polish Jewry.

Figure 10. Synagogue, Klimontow, built in the 1850s. Restored on the outside in 1980s, 1996 photo.

Figure 12. The Tempel Synagogue, Krakow: the ceiling restored, 1999.

Figure 11. The Tempel Synagogue, Krakow: general view, 1996.

Figure 13. The Kupa Synagogue, Krakow: general view, 1996.

Figure 14. The Kupa Synagogue, Krakow: detail of ceiling painting under restoration, 1999.

Figure 15. Piotrkow Trybunalski, The Mala (Small) Synagogue, now a children's library. Decoration of the Holy Ark, late eighteenth century: detail after conservation, 1995 photo.

Figure 16. Synagogue, Rymanow, late eighteenth century: general view, 1996 photo.

Figure 17. Synagogue, Rymanow: paintings in the interior of 1920s, 1996 photo.

Figure 18. Synagogue, Rymanow: paintings in the interior of 1920s, 1996 photo.

One proposal suggests marking the exterior of all synagogues with granite tablets provided by the government-funded Remembrance Foundation. These markers would serve an important function not only for visitors from abroad but even more for the local population. The latter now thinks of these buildings as cinemas, warehouses, libraries, sport facilities, or whatever else they may have been turned into in the post-war years. According to Jewish law, only a few specific uses for inactive synagogues are forbidden. Synagogues not being used as such are not considered sacred places. When this status is understood and respected by the non-Jewish public, it becomes a matter of culture and sensitivity, not of religion. The status of Poland's former synagogues is a central issue with which experts are trying to come to terms.

Fortress Synagogues in Eastern Europe

Surveys indicate that, in addition to their religious use, some synagogues were "fortress-synagogues" with the added function of defense. The fortress-synagogue buildings first appeared in the sixteenth century in Polish and Ukrainian towns during a time of extensive town building on the eastern border of the Polish-Lithuanian commonwealth. Jews became an important element in this unstable and dangerous area, which was frequently invaded by Turkish, Russian, and Walachian troops. Jews provided both numerous settlers and financial support for the growing towns. Most of these towns and cities were established at the initiative of private magnates, independent of the Christian clergy, who had insisted on the anti-Jewish limitations of the old, crown-ruled cities. This private-sector genesis provided better conditions for synagogue construction and increased donations and tax exemptions, which met the needs of the growing Jewish communities.

The Jewish community and synagogue buildings became significant elements in the cities' defense systems. Jews participated in military obligations hand in hand with other religious communities and institutions. In accordance with town planning schemes developed in the fourteenth century, the sacred buildings were located close to the city walls. One aspect of Jewish ritual, however, contradicted the defensive function of synagogues. The custom of individual prayer using personal prayer books demanded enhanced lighting of the prayer hall through extensive glazing. This made synagogues vulnerable elements in the city's system of defenses. The need for fortifications was reduced with the development of military technology, especially artillery.

The first synagogue recognized as a fortress was the Old Synagogue of Kazimierz in Krakow, rebuilt in 1570 (figure 19). The building features an attic wall with loopholes, decorated with round arches. Clearly, these elements were borrowed from military architecture and are commonly

Sergei Kravtsov

Architect Sergei Kravtsov teaches at the Center for Jewish Art at the Hebrew University of Jerusalem, Israel.

Figure 19. The Old Synagogue, Kazimierz, rebuilt in 1570.

found in fortified buildings such as castles. In general the exterior elements of the fortress-synagogue are powerful buttresses and windows placed high above ground level.

Baroque development in the seventeenth century resulted in alterations. First came changes in the character of the skylight used in fortress-synagogues. A second tier, placed above the arched bend of the attic wall, became more common. Elements added later, such as rows of obelisks and watch towers, were borrowed from seventeenth century military architecture. A detailed comparison of synagogue-fortresses in Sokal (figure 20), Ostrog (figure 21), Husiatyn (figure 22), Luboml (figure 23),

Figure 20. The old synagogue, Sokal, early seventeenth century.

Figure 21. Synagogue, Ostrog, first half of the seventeenth century.

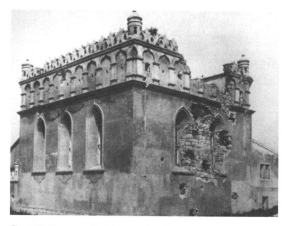

Figure 22. Synagogue, Husiatyn, seventeenth century.

Figure 23. Synagogue, Luboml, seventeenth century.

Figure 24. Synagogue, Zolkiew, 1692.

Figure 25. Synagogue, Brody, 1742.

Zolkiew (figure 24), Brody (figure 25), and Szarogrod (figure 26) highlights the particular features of their defensive walls: loopholes, the shape of the saw-tooth lines, and the layout of their attics.

Figure 26. Synagogue, Szarogrod, eighteenth century.

During the eighteenth century the design language of fortress architecture became a recognizable feature of synagogue architecture in the Ukraine. Although the military function was no longer relevant, this language was used continuously in the nineteenth- and twentieth-century architectural forms of traditional synagogues, and eventually penetrated the architecture of Hassidic communities. The influences of the nineteenth-century fortress synagogue in Belz can be found in the Bnei Brak and Jerusalem synagogues built in this century.

The Jewish Quarter and Synagogue of Veroia, Greece

Elias Messinas

Architect Elias Messinas, an associate of the American Institute of Architects, Washington, D.C., is adjunct lecturer in the Architecture Department of Technion Institute of Technology, Haifa, Israel, and author of The Synagogues of Salonika and Veroia (1997).

Efforts are being made to preserve the Jewish quarter and synagogue of Veroia, a small town in the northern province of Macedonia, Greece, not far from Salonika. Like Corinth, Athens, and Philippi, Veroia and Salonika were among the few cities visited by St. Paul the Apostle in the first century A.D. The Jewish community of Veroia, which received St. Paul in its synagogue, was a Romaniot community. Unlike the Sephardic communities, the Romaniots had been present in Greece since ancient times. Sephardic Jews settled in Salonika and Veroia in great numbers after the fifteenth century when they were fleeing Spain and Portugal. Greece at that time was part of the vast Ottoman Empire.

Houses in the Jewish quarter are well preserved. The buildings were densely built around open courtyards that are almost triangular in shape (figure 27). The clustered dwellings formed a protective wall around the

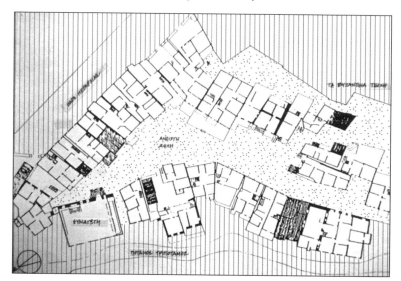

Figure 27. Plan of the Jewish quarter, Veroia.

courtyard. Access was controlled through two gates, closed at night and on *Shabbat*. This introverted, defensive structure is very common to the Jewish and Greek quarters in northern Greece. It also is often found in other cities of the Ottoman Empire built between the fifteenth and nineteenth centuries. Synagogues and churches were part of the urban fabric of the quarter, rather than freestanding buildings.

This defensive typology changed in the middle of the nineteenth century after the Tanzimat Reformations took place in the Ottoman Empire, giving equal rights to non-Muslim subjects. Henceforth, Jews moved freely and were no longer restricted to the confines of the Jewish quarter. Before World War II about 460 Jews lived in the Jewish quarter of Veroia. In May 1943, 424 Jews were arrested in the synagogue and deported by train to concentration camps. Refugees and peasants soon took over the houses in the Jewish quarter (figure 28).

As occurred elsewhere in Greece, after a short reorganization, the Jewish community of Veroia became inactive in 1970, leaving the synagogue and the cemetery unattended. These monuments, like many others throughout the country, are of unquestionable importance to Greek-Jewish heritage. They mark the history and legacy of a vibrant community that once prospered in northern Greece, thriving on the heavily used trading route that connected Constantinople (Istanbul) with Europe.

Figure 28 (left). House in the Jewish quarter, Veroia. The Hebrew inscription reads, "If I forget thee, O Jerusalem," and the date is 5619 (1858).

Figure 29 (top). Synagogue of Veroia prior to its exterior renovation in late 1999-2000.

Of the 100 synagogues that existed before World War II, today, more than 50 years after the Holocaust, the synagogues of Veroia and Monastirilis (in Salonika) are the only two remaining (figure 29). In recent years the author has worked to gain the preservation of Greek-Jewish heritage considerable international attention and funding. The Getty Grant Program has been providing essential support for the conservation study of the synagogue in Veroia. A fundraising campaign was organized, and an exhibition on the history and legacy of the Jewish community of Veroia was planned for September 2000, when restoration of the synagogue was to be completed (figure 30).

The Government of Greece was one of very few in the world to return most property confiscated from Jews to its rightful owners or their descendants. The properties included private homes, synagogues, cemeteries, and religious schools. They had been used by private individuals, the Greek army, the Red Cross, banks, and other organizations but were returned to the local Jewish communities. Synagogues and cemeteries belonging to communities that dissolved or became inactive in the 1970s were entrusted to a central Jewish body in Athens.

Figure 30. Scaffolding during the exterior restoration of the synagogue.

However, centralized management of small synagogues and cemeteries scattered throughout the country became inefficient, resulting in decay, private and municipal encroachment, and often in demolition, as occurred with important synagogues such as Didimoticho, Xanthi, and Komotini as recently as the 1980s and 1990s.

Figures 31A, 31B. The Jewish cemetery of Veroia immediately after World War II and in 1994.

Similar conditions have arisen in Central and Eastern Europe. After the war, in lieu of legal recourse over lost properties, Jewish organizations often reacquired synagogue buildings and cemeteries. In Veroia the Central Jewish Board made arrangements with the municipality to take on the responsibility of preserving and maintaining the synagogue. In exchange, the board offered the municipality the large Jewish cemetery of Veroia to be developed into athletic facilities (figures 31A, 31B). A small monument incorporating some marble tombstones was erected on the edge of the Jewish cemetery as a reminder of the land's original use.

Sacred Sites in Conflict Areas: Synagogues in Bosnia, Croatia, and Serbia

Ivan Ceresnjes

Architect Ivan Ceresnijes, head of the Jewish community in Sarajevo during the war, is working on a project to document Jewish heritage in Bosnia, Croatia, and Serbia, supported by the Center for Jewish Art.

Throughout history the Balkans have been divided among multiple spheres of influence: Roman and Greek, Eastern and Western Christianity, Christian and Muslim, Ottoman and Hapsburg, Soviet socialism and Western democracy. Within this framework diverse peoples nurtured their identities and traditions, creating strange alliances or bitter divisions among themselves and among the powers that temporarily controlled the territories. With the end of World War I, when Serbs, Croats, and Slovenes were unified in 1918 by the Corfu Declaration, different ethnic and religious groups found themselves living in a highly diverse worldænationally, ethnically, and religiously. This social convergence lasted for 72 years. The war that began in 1991 was a consequence of long-repressed nationalisms and resulted in the emergence of five new states.

Fewer than 6,000 Jews remain in the former Yugoslavia. Like the entire country, the Jewish community was once defined by its unique combination of Eastern and Western traditions. Vibrant populations of Sephardic and Ashkenazic Jews coexisted with their Christian and Muslim neighbors. This unique culture has never been systematically studied, and its remnants are disappearing rapidly. Particularly between 1945 and the civil war in the 1990s synagogues were destroyed, sacred objects were looted, and land mines were placed in cemeteries.

Sephardic Jews expelled from Spain and Portugal in the fifteenth century settled in the Ottoman Empire, which benefited from their erudition and their knowledge of economics and the manufacture of arms and ammunition. Jews in the Ottoman Empire had a special status and were treated equally to all Muslims. In the sixteenth century Sephardic Jews began to settle in Bosnia-Herzegovina, mainly in Sarajevo. With the occupation of Bosnia-Herzegovina by the Austro-Hungarian Empire a substantial number of Ashkenazic Jews came to the region. Educated and trained in economics, they promoted industry, and their scholarly achievements were notable. Meanwhile, Sephardic Jews continued their traditional occupations of foreign trade and crafts.

The mixture of nationalities and religions side by side encouraged the development of lifestyles respectful of others' needs. Public buildings, churches, mosques, and synagogues were constructed in a small area in which the sights and sounds of worship often disturbed worshippers of other faiths. However, living in close proximity taught people to be tolerant and respectful of one another.

The Center for Jewish Art-supported survey project to document Jewish heritage has identified a number of important Ashkenazic and Sephardic synagogues in need of conservation and repairs. However, some of the

Figure 32 (top right). The Old Temple
(Il Kal Vieju), Sarajevo, Bosnia/Herzegovina,
1581: exterior.

Figure 33 (top). The Old Temple, Sarajevo,
presently the Jewish Museum: interior.

Figure 34 (above). The Old Sephardic
cemetery, Sarajevo, 1630.

Figure 35 (right). The Great Sephardic
Synagogue (Il Kal grandi), Sarajevo, 1930:
one of the biggest synagogues in the
Balkans, interior.

synagogues and cemeteries have been converted to other uses, as in the
case of the Old Temple (in Ladino Il Kal Vieju), built in 1581, renovated after
being damaged by fire in 1697, and again in 1788 (figure 32). It is now a
Jewish Museum, forming part of the City Museum in Sarajevo (figure 33).
The old Sephardic cemetery was bisected by the construction of railroad
tracks; today only the upper half of the plot remains a cemetery (figure 34).
As in the case of the Great Synagogue of Sarajevo, among the largest synagogues in all the Balkans (figure 35), a magnificent building with a neo-
Moorish façade (figure 36), most synagogues were demolished or stripped
of their original function or identity. The synagogues of Dubrovnik and

Figure 36 (top left). The Great Sephardic Synagogue, Sarajevo: exterior.

Figure 37 (top right). The synagogue in Dubrovnik, Croatia, built in 1300, a synagogue since 1508: interior.

Figure 38 (above). The synagogue in Split, Croatia, 1500: interior.

Figure 39 (right). The synagogue Subotica, Serbia/Vojvodina, 1902: used today for cultural activities.

Split, built in the fifteenth and sixteenth centuries respectively, were severely damaged during the wars and subsequently rebuilt by the community (figures 37, 38). However, in the wake of the Holocaust, the small but vibrant Jewish communities who played an important role in the political, economic, and cultural history of these places almost disappeared.

The fate of Jewish heritage and Jewish communities in the former Yugoslavia are inextricably linked. After the Holocaust the buildings slowly fell into decay. Some buildings were sold by survivors to local municipalities. However, with the onslaught of the civil wars in the 1990s all preservation work halted. In cities in which synagogues were neglected during and after the wars, individuals and communities often came forward to rebuild them and fight to preserve the wealth of cultural heritage (figure 39). Preserving Jewish heritage in the former Yugoslavia is a significant task, both to celebrate the memory and to mark the legacy of the thriving Jewish communities for the benefit of present and future generations.

Wooden Sacred Buildings in the Ukraine

Ivan Mogtych

*Ivan Mogtych is director of the
Conservation Department
of Western Ukraine.*

Between the sixteenth and twentieth centuries in the Ukraine followers of the Christian Byzantine faith used Ukranian churches for their spiritual rituals, while Jews and Poles built synagogues and Catholic churches. These last two types of structures were built according to traditional, local techniques, which as a rule emphasized a large central nave with almost square plans and a high framework. Windows were situated high above the ground, and the buildings were covered with a vault, hipped roof, or cupola. Another local tradition was to place the altar in the eastern portion of the plan and make the main entrance either from the west or the south.

Although the wooden sacred buildings were based on masonry prototypes to a significant extent, they were strongly influenced by traditional Ukrainian architecture. Closer examination reveals the following features or distinctions:

- Ukrainian churches are characterized by one or many hipped roofs.
- Catholic churches reveal one or two towers, usually located on the western portion of the building.
- Synagogues are cubic frameworks with massive roofs in several tiers. While Ukrainian churches were built primarily in open fields, amid trees, or on hillsides distant from villages, the Ukraine's Catholic churches and Jewish synagogues were built in densely populated town centers, as can be seen by synagogues in the villages of Bukivets and Velyki Komiaty. Churches with towers over the vestibule appeared as a result of policy decisions on how to design Ukrainian churches. Often, during reconstruction of older structures, this feature would be added. However, even under these circumstances folk masters created veritable masterpieces, such as Lukovytsia in 1658 and Serednie Vodian, the oldest preserved church in Ukraine, which dates from 1428 and received its tower in the late eighteenth century.

Byzantine influence also can be noted in the Ukrainian churches. The characteristic centrality of their plan and architectural details clearly influenced the way later Catholic churches and Jewish synagogues were built in the Ukraine. Another common feature is the adoption of characteristic Baroque fenestration and doors in churches and synagogues rebuilt in the seventeenth and eighteenth centuries. As part of efforts by the West Ukrainian Restoration Institute to identify and preserve churches and synagogues, a catalog was published that documents about 200 preserved objects—about one-third of all heritage preserved in Ukraine—including the existence of three wooden synagogues.

Notes

1   See chapter by Harmen Thies in this volume.

2   For synagogue architecture in Germany see H. Hammer-Schenk, *Synagogen in Deutschland Geschichte einer Baugattung im 19 und 20, Jahrhundert (1780–1933)*, (Hamburg, 1981); or H.-P. Schwarz, ed., *Die Architektur der Synagoge* (Frankfurt a. M., 1988); and A. Cohen-Mushlin and H. Thies, eds., *Synagogenarchitektur in Deutschland vom Barock zum 'Neuen Bauen'* (Braunschweig, 2000).

3   For other Geman federal states see, for example, U. Dinse, *Das vergessene Erbe. Jüdische Baudenkmale in Schleswig-Holstein* (Kiel, 1995); or T. Altaras, *Synagogen in Hessen – Was geschah seit 1945?* (Königstein i. T., 1988); and E. Pracht, *Jüdisches Kulturerbe in Nordrhein-Westfalen*, vol. I (Köln, 1997).

39

The Synagogue and Its Sacred Space

Bezalel Narkiss and the Index of Jewish Art

Recipient of the 1999 Israel Prize and founder of the Jerusalem Index of Jewish Art, Bezalel Narkiss is the Nicolas Landau Professor Emeritus of Art History at the Center for Jewish Art at the Hebrew University of Jerusalem.

This brief outline of the development of the synagogues through the ages is typological rather than historical.[1] Unlike the churches, mosques, and possibly other sacred temples all over the world, which have only one clear sacred focal point, the synagogue has two. One is an Ark, *aron* in Hebrew.[2] It is a sanctuary, *heikhal*, in which the Holy Scrolls of the Torah are kept. The other focus is a reader's desk—*teivah*, *bimah*, or *migdal*—a tower from which the Torah is read. Historical documents do not indicate specifically where each focal point should be placed. Only synagogues themselves, and at times the knowledge of tradition, guide us in exploring the placement of these two foci.

Ashkenazic Tradition

In the medieval Ashkenazic culture in the German countries the placement of the Ark and the *bimah* seems quite clear For example, in the thirteenth-century Altnueschule Synagogue in Prague the Torah Ark is raised a bit, looks like a single cupboard, and is built into the eastern wall facing Jerusalem (figure 1). The *bimah* with its reading table is placed in the center of the single hall between the two supporting pillars.

In Prague, as well as in other early surviving synagogues from the eleventh through thirteenth centuries, the *bimah* was surrounded by a fence, as in Worms or Krakow. The seating in these synagogues is around the *bimah* and along the walls, an Ashkenazic tradition. This Ashkenazic tradition may have continued in East European countries up to the eighteenth or nineteenth century. The typical nine-bay synagogue in Poland, Galicia, or Belorussia exposed a central *bimah* surrounded by four pillars, which supported the roof. An example is the eighteenth-century synagogue in Lancut, Poland, which has wall paintings from the twentieth century (figure 2).

The elaborate Torah Ark can be seen from between the opposing columns, as in the nineteenth century at Wlodawa, Poland (figure 3). The seating in these synagogues is also along the walls and around the *bimah*.

Figure 1. Altnueschule, Prague, thirteenth century: interior facing Ark.

The Ashkenazic synagogue in Plymouth, England built in 1762 has a similar placement of Ark, *bimah*, and seating. The *bimah* with a desk for the reader of the Torah and the cantor was joined with the elaborate Torah Ark structure, as in the late-nineteenth century Szeged Synagogue in Hungary. It was only during the late nineteenth and early twentieth centuries due to the influence of the Christian churches that the theater-like seating arrangement was introduced in modern sumptuous synagogues.

Sephardic Tradition

In synagogues of the Sephardic culture, which started in Spain and continued in the lands of the Sephardic diaspora, the two focal points are somewhat unclear. The Toledan El Transito Church was built around 1357 as the private synagogue of Samuel Halevi Abulafia, advisor to King Pedro the Cruel. There is an indication of where the *heikhal*, the sanctuary, an enlarged Ark, must have been—facing southeast toward Jerusalem—but no trace of the *bimah* (figure 4).

Figure 2. Synagogue, Lançut, eighteenth century: interior with *bimah* surrounded by pillars.

The *bimah* with the reader's desk for reading the Torah may have been a wooden tower-like structure to climb to, *migdal* in Hebrew, like the Muslim *minbar*, which may have been placed anywhere within the prayer hall. The *migdal* is depicted in an illuminated manuscript, the "Sister to the Golden Haggadah" of the fourteenth century from Barcelona. The masonry of the Torah shrine may indicate a proper structure for this purpose (figure 5). The triple-arched entrance of the *heikhal* in El Transito was probably blocked when the synagogue was confiscated during the fifteenth century by the Catholic Church to become a Christian prayer hall.

In excavations led by Spanish archaeologists in 1987, the outline of an entire *heikhal* room was found behind the triple-arched entrance, indicating an entirely different structure from the traditional Ashkenazic synagogue.

Figure 3. Synagogue, Wlodawa, nineteenth century: interior facing Ark from central *bimah.*

Indeed, such *heikhal* rooms have been found in synagogues of the dispersed Jews from Spain as late as the eighteenth-century synagogue at Mondovi a Piemontese, Italy (figure 6). The Torah Ark itself is gone. It still exists in the *heikhal* room of the eighteenth-century Provençal Synagogue of Carpentras. It is a movable Torah Ark on wheels, which is taken out at the appropriate time, whereas other Torah scrolls are left on the shelves within the *heikhal* (figure 7). The appointed scroll is then taken to the fenced *bimah* at the center of the hall to be read.

However, in Carpentras there are two reader's desks, or *teivot*, as the desk is called locally. The other *teivah* is placed in an upper gallery to the west under an impressive baldachin, which is reached by a staircase from the main hall (figure 8).

Figure 4. El Transito Synagogue, Toledo, 1357: interior toward Ark.

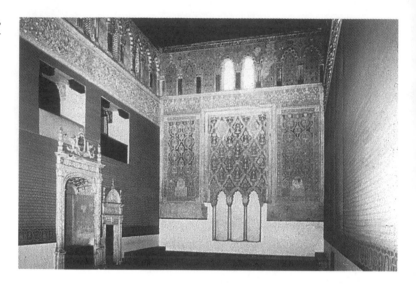

Figure 5. "Sister to Golden Haggadah" Synagogue, Barcelona, fourteenth century: interior.

Figure 6. Synagogue, Mondovi, eighteenth century: interior of Torah Ark.

The seventeenth-century synagogue of the neighboring Provencal city of Cavaillon has a similar structure in the gallery on top: a baldachin over a *teivah* with stairs leading up to it. Below the gallery are two movable Torah Arks on wheels, which are taken out of the *heikhal* room. They are empty since the synagogue is no longer active.

Two *teivot*, one in the center and one above, can be seen in typical Sephardic synagogues all over the world. One, in an eighteenth-century synagogue in Bursa, Turkey is called *Gerush*, which means "expulsion" in Hebrew. It is possible that they all used a lost Spanish model (figure 9).

This custom existed as far as away as Kadavumbaghum Synagogue in Cochin, India. One such synagogue, partly destroyed, has been reconstructed in the Israel Museum in Jerusalem at the instigation of the Center for Jewish Art researchers. Two *teivot* in a similar arrangement also can be seen in the 1863 Sephardic synagogue in Akhaltsikhe, Georgia, in the former Soviet Union (figure 10).

Figure 7. Synagogue, Carpentras, eighteenth century: interior, Torah Ark on wheels.

Figure 8. Synagogue, Carpentras, eighteenth century: interior facing upper *teivah* on the west.

Figure 9. Gerush Synagogue, Bursa, eighteenth century: interior with two *teivot*, one in the center and one in the gallery.

Figure 10. Great Synagogue, Akhaltzikhe, 1863: interior facing two tevot.

Figure 11. Synagogue, Vitorio Veneto, 1701: interior facing the Torah Ark.

It is possible that another arrangement of the two focal points existed in Spain, one opposite the other, as in the Sweeri Synagogue in Tangier of Spanish Morocco in the late nineteenth century. The *heikhal* sanctuary occupies the entire eastern wall while the *teivah* is opposite on the western wall.

Italian Tradition

The double-pole arrangement is typical of Italian synagogues, such as the one built in 1701 in Vitorio Veneto, Italy. It has been reconstructed in the Israel Museum in Jerusalem (figure 11). The reader's desk is in the west of the synagogue towards the sumptuous Torah Ark in the east. The seats are arranged along the walls, and above them is the lattice work partition of the women's gallery.

The Scuola Grande Spagnola in the old ghetto of Venice from either 1635 or 1655 was attributed to the architect Baldassare Longena (1598–1682). The elongated hall has seats along the walls and in the women's gallery above. The baldachin is over the *bimah* on the west side. The ground plane exposes the two-pole arrangement of the Scuola Grande Spagnola very clearly (figure 12). Like most synagogues in the old ghetto of Venice, the Scuola Grande Spagnola is located on the third floor of the building, unobtrusive to strangers. There is a debate on the origin of this two-pole type.

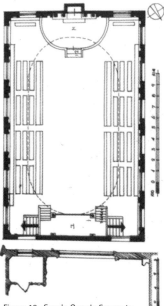

Figure 12. Scuola Grande Spagnola, Venice, 1635 or 1655: ground plan

The fourth-century synagogue of Capernaum in the Galilee exposes no fixed point for either the Torah Ark or the reader's desk, and its entrance faces Jerusalem (figure 13). Since the Torah had no built Ark in Capernaum, it could have had a wooden one, possibly on wheels, similar

Figure 13 Synagogue, Capernaum, fourth century: aerial view.

Figure 14. Synagogue, Capernaum, fourth century: capital with movable Ark.

to one depicted in a stone relief from Capernaum (figure 14). It is known as a *teivah* in the Mishnaic and Talmudic literature and also could have been stored outside the building. A reader's desk, or *bimah*, may have been a wooden structure in the center of the hall, as is known to have existed in the large synagogue in Alexandria.

The idea that the two-pole arrangements derive from early synagogues in Palestine cannot yet be substantiated. However, later the place of the Ark is clearer, as in the sixth-century Beth Alpha Synagogue from Palestine, which has a special place for the Torah Ark in a large apse facing Jerusalem. It should be stressed that, outside Palestine, as early as the middle of the third century the Dura Europos Synagogue on the Euphrates River had a built niche as a Torah Ark in the center of the Western wall facing Jerusalem (figure 15). Could a different system have existed outside Palestine, and could Babylonia have had a different tradition than that of Palestine? It is possible, but not yet established.

Figure 15. Synagogue, Dura Europos, 244 A.D.: interior, western wall with Torah niche.

To sum up, of the several types of synagogues that developed in Jewish communities all over world, the most pronounced types are the Ashkenazic, the Sephardic, and the Italian. These types may have influenced one another throughout history and may have created local subgroups. Finally, they all may have derived from early Jewish types in ancient Palestine or Babylonia. ■

Glossary

Apse
: Latin, *apsis*. A semi-circular or polygonal recess, arched or dome-roofed, especially in churches, and later in synagogues.

Aron
: "Ark" in Hebrew. It is the sanctuary, or *heikhal*, to contain the Torah.

Ashkenazi
: In the Bible Ashkenaz was the grandson of Japheth (Genesis 10:2-3). Since Japheth was considered the father of European nations, Ashkenaz's name was taken to mean the Jewish communities of Germany, France, England, the Netherlands, and Eastern Europe.

Bimah
: Literally, "platform." In the Ashkenazic synagogue a raised platform on which a desk is placed. The Torah scrolls are placed on the desk while they are being read.

Heikhal
: Literally, "sanctuary." In Sephardic synagogues it is the Torah Ark, which can occupy up to the entire wall that faces Jerusalem.

Migdal
: Literally, "tower." It is the name medieval Sephardic communities gave to a high *bimah*.

Minbar
: A high pulpit in a mosque with steps leading up to it.

Sephardi
: Sepharad, an unknown country mentioned once in the Bible (Obadia 1:20). It was considered to refer to the Iberian peninsula. Hence the Jewish communities were of Portugal and Spain were called Sephardim.

Teivah
: (plural: *teivot*) Literally, "box." The name given to the *bimah* in Sephardic synagogues.

Torah
: Literally, "Pentateuch," the five books of Moses in the Bible. For the synagogue the Torah is written by hand on a continuous parchment scroll, wrapped around staves, and placed in the Torah Ark, or chest. Each week a different portion of the Torah is read.

Notes

1 The work in this chapter is not entirely my own. I have used a great deal of research done at the Index of Jewish Art by my students and colleagues. I cannot acknowledge them all here because they were too numerous but I am calling it work of the Index of Jewish Art.

2 For specialized terms see the Glossary at the end of the chapter.

40

Analysis and Reconstruction: The Residence-Church in Würzburg and the "Temple of Jews" in Wörlitz

T his chapter focuses on methodological questions using two seemingly unrelated examples of central European sacred architecture. The first example is Balthasar Neumann's Roman Catholic Residence-Church in Würzburg, constructed between 1732 and 1743 (figure 1). The second is the so-called Temple of Vesta (or "Temple of the Jews"), the neo-classical synagogue situated between the famous park and the small town of Wörlitz designed by Friedrich Wilhelm von Erdmannsdorff and constructed after 1789 (figure 2).

To study such architecture, we must distinguish the specific sequence of research steps that are repeated in every case and are necessary proportions of any meaningful scientific investigation. These steps are an inversion of the generating processes and moments that underlie almost any realized architecture:

1. There must be an idea or concept of design, usually based on functional, economic, and constructive propositions; a short description; a reference to built examples; or a small sketch. A number of generative suggestions and moments, as well as the limiting conventions and restrictions, should be described and combined here.

2. A system or set of plans has to be generated, visually describing the conception of the building by measured and well-defined drawings, or orthogonal projections known from the beginning of architecture. This system of measured plans is obviously indispensable when

Harmen Thies

Harmen Thies is a professor at the Technical University of Braunschweig, Germany.

Figure 1. Residence-Church, Würzburg, Balthasar Neumann, 1732-43.

Figure 2. Neo-classical synagogue, the "Temple of Vesta," Wörlitz, F. W. von Erdmannsdorff, 1789.

realizable architecture, including early historic divisions of labor and the necessary organization of the building site, is to be generated.

3. Only then can the third step—the building itself—be realized in exact accordance with the "model" described in step two. This process (and its sequence of steps) can be compared with the analogous process of generating music. The notation of tones, intervals, and sequences in music—that is, the score—corresponds to the system of plans in architecture.

The history or science of architecture—and topics related to it—should be considered an inversion of the generating process described here. To document, survey, and measure architecture is to retrace the process from step three to step two: from material realization to its representation in architectural drawings. Analysis of the system of plans moves from an exactly described model of what has to be done to its initial conception and basic design. We call this *Rissanalyse*, the systematic analysis of measured architectural drawings. After several studies we are convinced that such analysis can offer insights into generative processes that the conventional comparison of images, elements, and details cannot supply.

Analysis of plans provides reconstructions of architecture—not of structural images but of the generating processes. Reconstruction is a virtual "re-designing" and "re-building" enhanced by the understanding and comprehension that has been acquired through this process of study.

Plan analysis offers interesting possibilities for the specific tasks of documentation and survey. There are more than constitutive elements and generating moments to discover. It is possible to proceed further by integrating a building in the history of architecture and by discussing its position within a well-defined system of architectural values. Würzburg and Wörlitz may provide some suggestions.

Würzburg Residence-Church

The Würzburg Residence-Church was conceived and designed by Balthasar Neumann with the evident intention of making this sacred space appear as an autonomous, independent structure that exclusively follows its own laws of figuration. A contemporary engraving shows the structure and space of the church hidden behind the walls and facade of the residence. The castle can be seen as a box-like house, which contains the totally different structure of the church.

Although church and castle were designed and built simultaneously—according to designs and plans supplied by Neumann—neither structure seems to acknowledge the other. Plan analysis reinforces this impression. Closely related to Neumann's individual mode of design, this architectural relationship reveals the extremely interesting genesis of the structure.

A ground plan (figure 3) and two sections (figure 4)—signed by Neumann—have been preserved. They show different stages of the design but are closely related. The ground plan and its plan analysis reveal a combination of well-defined circular and oval units, each carefully and exactly measured, which should not be confused with triangulation or quadrature. During analysis it is easy to recombine the fundaments and reproduce the structure, thus understanding its features and qualities.

The geometry and measurements of the two sections make it possible to recreate the ground plan (figure 5) from the beautiful drawings signed by Neumann. The sections reveal the ground plan positions for the structurally decisive columns. Analogously, but far superior to the preserved ground plan, the reconstructed, impressive combination of units give us a richer understanding of Balthasar Neumann's architecture and its characteristic elements.

Step-by-step demonstrations of the generative process are based on analyses of both the preserved and the reconstructed ground plan. They show that Neumann started with positioning simple circular groups, shifted up and down along the main axis. He then combined this first group of identical circles with larger overlapping ones to create finally five units, which became elements of the realized architectural structure.

Figure 3 (top left). Residence-Church, Würzburg, unsigned plan, B. Neumann, realized 1732–43.

Figure 4 (top right). Residence-Church, Würzburg, B. Neumann January 26, 1732: cross-section.

Figure 5. Residence-Church, Würzburg: vaulting.

The complex figuration analyzed corresponds precisely to the visual effect of the actual vaulted architecture of this church. Independent, perfect and self-explanatory, this piece of architecture is a work of art of the highest order (figures 6, 7).

"Temple of Jews"

While quite different and visually less complex, the Wörlitz synagogue (figure 8) nevertheless is an astonishing and sophisticated architectural work. Here, too, plan analysis can offer revealing insights that go beyond collected sources and historical facts, the establishment of typologies, and the critical comparison of images. The survey, measure, and reconstruction of plans is indispensable because the original plans have not been preserved. In 1789 Prince Leopold Friedrich Franz von Anhalt-Dessau together with his friend, architect Friedrich Wilhelm von Erdmannsdorff, conceived of this building as the unifying element to the prince's famous English park, begun about 20 years before and one of the first to be laid in Germany.

Contemporary descriptions refer to this architectural structure as the "Temple of Jews" and simultaneously as a neo-classical "Temple of Vesta." Use of both nomenclatures is well established. Round, centralized, and ordered as it appears, this building has numerous elements in common with the early imperial *tholos* in Rome, to which the name and image allude.[1] In Prince Leopold Franz's time this Roman temple did not show the originally free-standing columns, but rather a cylindrical wall with engaged columns. While the *tholos* in Rome has 20 columns and the probably better-known Tivoli *tholos*—likewise called a Vesta Temple—has 18, the temple in Wörlitz has 12, which were transformed into pilasters.

Although the typology of Central European Ashkenazi synagogues does not generally employ cylindrical ground plans, there is no doubt that Prince Leopold Franz and his architect von Erdmannsdorff decided to erect a new synagogue for the Wörlitz Jewish community. Situated in the center of the basement of the building is a *mikvah* (ritual bath) (figure 9). The inner structure and furniture, destroyed by the Nazi government in 1938 but documented in photographs and plans, were arranged to meet the demands of function and liturgy. These include two entrances, a women's gallery, a *bimah* (reader's desk) in the center, and a Torah Ark within a wall niche (figure 10).

In this case, too, plan analysis offers additional insights (figure 11). In Würzburg the complex but materially present and always visible structure supplies important allusions to its genesis. Wörlitz reveals its structure only after reflection and experimentation. In Würzburg the plan analysis is confirmed by the Neumann plans and by the building itself. In

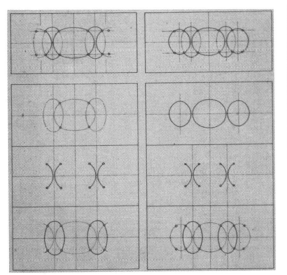

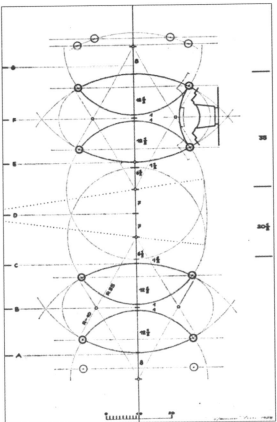

Figure 6 (above). Residence-Church, Würzburg: composition of "units": January 26, 1732 plan left; realized plan right.

Figure 7 (right). Residence-Church, Würzburg: analysis of the reconstructed plan, B. Neumann, January 26, 1732.

Figure 8. Synagogue in the park, Wörlitz, F. W. von Erdmannsdorff, 1789.

Figure 9. Synagogue, Wörlitz, *mikvah* in the basement structure, 1998 photo.

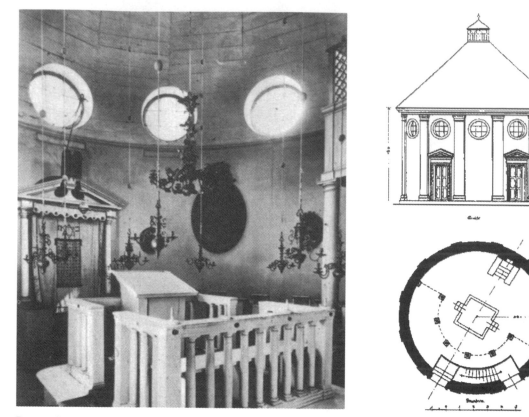

Figure 10. Synagogue, Wörlitz, F. W. von Erdmannsdorff, 1789: interior, destroyed 1938.

Figure 11 (right). Wörlitz, synagogue, F. W. von Erdmannsdorff, 1789: drawings.

Wörlitz, on the other hand, original or at least contemporary plans of the synagogue are lacking; only the external masonry and the roof are really preserved. In this situation the plans had to be measured and re-designed.

One may wonder why there are 12 pilasters surrounding the circular wall of outer building at regular intervals, while the inner structure, destroyed in 1938, is arranged according to a decagonal plan. It is difficult to combine these two plans—dodecagon and decagon—symbolizing, it should be assumed, two different but equally constitutive moments of this architecture.

First, the cylindrical rounded wall with 12 pilasters and a greater circle that fixes the main features of the structure must be isolated. Inscribed within is a hexagon with 12 axes constructed of equilateral triangles. Evidently, the dodecagon, its angles, and its 12 axes determine the positions of the outer order.

Interestingly, the decision is not to arrange the inner columns in accordance with the geometry of the dodecagon following the positions of the 12 exterior pilasters but to establish the quite different geometry of a decagon. The six columns originally supporting the women's gallery, lost today, were set on the corners of this decagon. Simultaneously, six of the

10 columns formed a semicircle, apparently in accordance with the central position of the *bimah* and the lateral axis of steps leading onto its platform.

Doubling the number of geometrically fixed axes or positions—12 becoming 24 and 10 becoming 20—establishes the possibility of combining these different figures and architectural units. They have 4 as a common number: 5 parts multiplied by 4 makes 20; 6 parts multiplied by 4 makes 24. If we concentrate our attention on the central cross-axes, plan-analysis and built architecture show this. Only along the axis lines do the two different geometries and architectural units cross and link. The main axis goes through the men's entrance, *bimah*, and shrine. The lateral axis bisects the room and fixes the steps onto the *bimah*. Finally, the women's entrance, which is linked to the surrounding dodecagon rather than the central decagon, determines the exterior order and appearance.

Plan-analysis tries to go one step further. At the moment it is only a hypothesis; new measurements will have to confirm it. As we have seen, the dodecagon originates from a hexagon, created by combining 12 equilateral triangles, which together form a Star of David. Constitutive for these 12 triangles is an inner circle and its radius, identical with the triangle-sides. The same circle must now be put into the center to construct the decagon of this complex plan-configuration.

The decagon-circle and the Star of David reveal a common origin that is linked by the cross-axes. Evidently, this structure offers a vast range of possible interpretations too numerous to be fully discussed here. ■

Note

1   *Tholos* are circular, beehive-shaped tombs, also called dome tombs, belonging to the late Helladic period.

Afro-Brazilian mosque in Western Africa, built by former African slaves. Many former slaves returned to Africa after the abolition of slavery in Brazil, bringing with them cultural influences acquired while building baroque churches in Brazil.

Part VII

Preserving the Sacred Sites and Cultural Roots

Editors' Note

The chapters on North American indigenous culture and the traditional ritual of Kuarup *among Brazilian indigenous people reflect a common perspective that nature and the natural landscape are part of the spiritual endowment of these peoples. For the indigenous people of the New World, the whole Earth is a sacred place. These groups believe that forces within the Earth need to be cared for and managed to maintain balance between the community and nature. Patricia Parker's overview focuses on the spiritual symbols vested in the natural landscape by indigenous people in various parts of the United States. The integrity of a sacred place must not be altered by activities such as clear cutting timber or mining. Many indigenous people consider their sacred sites private and do not wish to identify them on paper because, once the information is given to a government agency, it is subject to public scrutiny under the Freedom of Information Act. Without this confidential information, however, it is difficult for government agencies to protect such sites.*

Indigenous peoples' sacred sites require clear policy regulations and enforcement of laws that can effectively prevent encroaching commercial activities. Accommodating the traditional uses of sacred sites while protecting them remains a very complex cross-cultural issue. Marcos Terena focuses on the importance of land for the indigenous people of Brazil. Without territories that are vast enough to support their economic, social, and cultural ways of life, it is impossible for them to maintain spirituality and the ceremonial rites of passage for each phase of life. In the great ceremony of

Kuarup, *which symbolizes the passage of sadness over a period of one year, the whole village invites all the other communities for a final lament for the deceased. This ceremony affirms the value of life and continuity of the community. The community is able to celebrate its traditional Kuarup because their preserved lands are legally demarcated by the federal government and the rituals are not disturbed by outsiders. Terena concludes that throughout the colonization process, "the white man, in his ignorance, considered the indigenous peoples an obstacle to development, savages, or even beings without souls. But now we understand much more that the power doesn't lie in the man-made machines but inside each of us."*

In his chapter on sources of Axum's sacredness Joseph King examines the centrality of the Ethiopian Orthodox Church and the memories and legends that Axum evokes. An ancient biblical association is the layer on which Axum's sacred and cultural values are built. Another important layer can be found in the role of Axumite civilization in the history of Ethiopia's national identity. The symbols of political and religious power are manifest in the town's role as a capital of the ancient Axumite empire. The St. Mary of Zion church, built in the fourth century, is a repository of a variety of objects and treasures that hold strong religious and cultural significance. Among the most valuable is the legendary Ark of Covenant, the box built by Moses to carry the Ten Commandments. The Ark is believed to have been brought to Ethiopia by Menelik I, the son of King Solomon and Queen of Sheba. In 1998 with the assistance of the World Heritage Fund, ICCROM, and the World Bank, the government initiated a participatory conservation planning strategy for Axum. The main objectives were the retention of local residents in the old town Axum, the identification of the most valuable archeological sites in need of protection, and an inventory of traditional houses in the old town.

Vivian Mann covers the art of convivencia *("living together" in Spanish), eight centuries during which close interaction of cultural elements were filtered through the collective consciousness of Muslims, Jews, and Christians in medieval Spain. Similar interwoven cultural relationships existed between the Muslims and Jews of Morocco in the eighteenth and twentieth centuries. Mann examines the aesthetic aspects of art, including development of Jewish iconography and the genesis of cultural roots. The written records from the Aragonese archives of the last three centuries of Jewish life in Spain, and written accounts of Jewish activity under Islamic rule from Cairo's Ben Ezra Synagogue in Fustat, provide the basis for this study. Convivencia in Spain ended with the fall of Granada and the expulsion of the Jews in 1492. From this point the highly educated and skilled Sephardic refugees enriched the native Jewish communities of the Ottoman Empire and North Africa. In these realms Jews and Muslims lived together until mid-twentieth century.*

Laurent Lévi-Strauss examines the importance of the non-built sacred places. The World Heritage List contains 100 historic cities and about 200 entries referring to sacred places. The widespread representation of these categories demonstrates that they are at the very core of the concept of cultural heritage, serving as strong roots of people's identities, and are the basis of the definition for any culture. Lévi-Strauss describes UNESCO's past campaigns to safeguard, reconstruct, and conserve world heritage at risk. He asserts that historic complexes are faced with acute problems of physical conservation, internal balance, and functioning. The fundamental tasks are the development of social and economic life of the city, the management and preservation of a decent standard of living for the population, and the maintenance of the integrity of the historic fabric. It is necessary to study each case with diligence to determine the unique and specific ways to approach it. Lévi-Strauss concludes, "At a time when social diversity is everywhere leading to fragmentation, it is only this cultural memory that will maintain the indispensable social bonds that enable a mosaic of people with different origins and cultures, and of different generations, to live together."

Sacred Sites in Traditional American Indian Culture

41

To many American Indian people, and to indigenous people generally, the whole earth is a sacred place. These people believe that the forces within the earth need to be cared for and managed to maintain balance and harmony within the community and among peoples.

American Indian people see nature and the natural landscape differently than do non-Indian people. For example, there is a rock that to some non-Indian people is simply an interesting outcropping, but to Wintu artist Frank Pena it is known as a Bag of Bones. Indian people literally see human bones inside the rock. To the Wintu it is a sacred site, but to non-Indian people it is invisible.

To most Americans and people all over the world, the Grand Canyon in Arizona is an astonishing geological feature of beauty and power (figure 1). However, to eight American Indian tribes the Grand Canyon is an origin site—the strata in the canyon walls are not geologic features but are symbols of the various worlds through which the ancestors traveled on their journey to enter the world we now inhabit.

The Sandia Sand Bars are sacred to the people of the Sandia Pueblo. For hundreds of generations people have descended from the pueblo on a ritual trail to the Rio Grande, where they conduct annual ceremonies that renew the world and renew the spiritual energy of the pueblo. This site was determined eligible for the United States National Register of Historic Places due to its significance to the ongoing cultural tradition of the Sandia people.

A particular island in Chúúk State in the Federated States of Micronesia is also an origin site (figure 2). The culture hero Sowukachaw created Chúúkese society on the knob on top of the mountain. The knob is seen by the people as the head of an octopus, which spreads its tentacles over thousands of square miles in the Pacific, connecting the high islands

Patricia L. Parker

Patricia L. Parker is chief of the American Indian Liaison Office at the United States National Park Service, Pat_Parker@NPS.gov

Figure 1. Grand Canyon is a sacred origin site for several tribes.

with the low islands of Micronesia and uniting the people who inhabit all of those islands into a single social unit.

Many sacred sites are natural features. The human hand is generally absent. It is the *mind* of human beings that gives these places their spiritual significance.

Canyons are often origin sites and are sacred to American Indian people. Spencer Canyon in the Grand Canyon is sacred to the Hualapai Nation in Arizona. Tahquitz Canyon is the site at which the blue comet emerged, allowing the entrance of the Cahuilla Indian people from the underworld to the present world, where they live near Palm Springs in California.

Water sources, particularly isolated sources such as oases, often are sacred sites to American Indian people. They are important particularly to nomadic people as places to gather annually. Often these water sources are inhabited by spiritual beings.

Waterfalls, too, are often sacred sites. American Indian tribes have fought many battles in the United States courts to try to stop hydroelectric projects, which harness the power and the forces of waterfalls that tribes believe need to be free. River courses themselves are often sacred sites and at the very heart of American Indian cultures. Rock outcroppings along the Plumas River mark the places where the creator stopped on his journey from the underworld as he created the Wintu people in California.

Fire, too, has sacred power. On the Big Island of Hawaii the goddess Pele spews lava into the sea.

Similarly, geysers have power. To non-Indians a geyser in Yellowstone National Park is an interesting hydro-geological feature. To the Shoshone Indians it is a sacred site.

Black Mesa overlooks the San Ildefonso Pueblo in northern New Mexico. It is a sacred site to the Pueblo people, who continue their traditions in the central square in San Ildefonso, where they do the deer dance.

Pictographs play an ongoing integral role in the cultures of the American Indians, such as the Navajo and the Pueblo in the American Southwest.

Burial sites are always sacred places to American Indians, as are the ruins of the ancestors. One of the major intellectual shifts in the last 15 years in the United States concerns the human remains of American Indians. In the past it was accepted by the non-Indian community that archaeologists could scientifically disinter Indian skeletons, study them, and keep them in museums forever for future study. Now legislation requires federal agencies and museums to inventory their collections to determine the cultural affiliations of human remains, to notify the tribes

Figure 2. On Chúúk Lagoon travelling toward the Outer Reef.

with whom these remains are culturally affiliated, and to assist tribes in repatriating them so that they can be reburied. Other countries are considering similar legislation.

Some sites raise the troubling issue of boundaries. For instance, stones mark the vision quest sites of men from the Nez Perce tribe in Idaho. These are places to which, under the tutelage of their mentors, individual Indians go to seek spiritual guidance as they journey through life. Usually these places are not marked. In the case of the Nez Pierce they are marked by stones. But what constitutes the site? How does one draw a line around it? Where are the boundaries? Is the site the stone marker? Is the site the viewshed—every place that the person could see? What are the responsibilities of federal agencies in managing these kinds of places when they are located on federal land?

A circle makes up the sacred Medicine Wheel in northern Wyoming, which is used by many Indian tribes on the Northern Plains (figure 3). The United States government, in this case the Forest Service, and a coalition of Indian tribes have come together to develop a management plan for this location. The plan guides the Forest Service in respecting the values and the traditions of the American Indian people who still use it.

Devils Tower National Monument, a volcanic monolith, is a sacred site to more than 20 different Indian tribes. Over the last decades it also has become a very popular site for rock climbers, who like to scale the tower. American Indians use this area, particularly during the summer

Figure 3. The Medicine Wheel in Wyoming is a designated National Historic Landmark. While it was nominated as an archeological site, it is also a sacred site used by the tribes of the Northern Plains.

months around the solstice, for the sun dance and other religious ceremonies. Climbing is very disturbing, distracting, and, from their point of
view, sacrilegious. The National Park Service tried to accommodate the
need for privacy and quiet by requesting that climbers not use the monument during June. The agency's authority to make this request was
upheld by the U. S. Tenth Circuit Court of Appeals in 1999. This decision
was upheld by the U. S. Supreme Court in March 2000.

A similar situation exists at Ayres Rock, Uluru-Kata Tjuta National Park,
in Australia, where aboriginal people object to tourists climbing on their
sacred site. The park and the aboriginal people are trying to educate the
public regarding their concerns.

Bear Butte in South Dakota is a state park while it continues to be used
by American Indian people as a ceremonial site.

Battlefields are also sacred sites. For 120 years after the battle of the
Little Bighorn, in which the Cheyenne and the Sioux tribes defeated
General George Armstrong Custer and his troops, the Little Bighorn
Battlefield National Monument was interpreted by the National Park
Service as a memorial to the United States government soldiers. Only in
the latter 1990s has it become an area in which American Indians com-
memorate their victory and the interpretive story at the park has been
broadened to include the views of both sides (figure 4).

The San Francisco Peaks are sacred to the Hopi and the Navajo. They are one
of the four sacred mountains that contain the great Navajo Reservation.

Sites are sometimes sacred for the resources that they contain. Tule
marshes are sacred to the Indians of central California. They are home
to water fowl and to the tule used in making rafts and houses and for
many other purposes. For example, a slope in coastal California is a
place on which California Indian basket makers gather their materials.
Gathering itself—taking the willows—has religious connotations.

The resurgence of Indian basketry in California, Nevada, Washington,
and Maine is one of the great examples of a cultural renaissance in
American Indian communities at the close of the twentieth century. The
federal government must take action to ensure that Indian people have
access to the materials they need to continue these important cultural
traditions, especially when these materials are on federal land.

Wildlife is important to Indian sacred sites. A creek in Pohnpei in the
Federated States of Micronesia is sacred because it is home to particular eels, which are the ancestors of a clan.

As a result of the history of the United States government and American
Indian relations, most of the sites that are sacred to Indian people are
on public lands. The sites are not on Indian reservations themselves. An

Figure 4. The Cheyenne and Sioux celebrate the anniversary of the defeat of General George Armstrong Custer.

exception is Taos Pueblo in New Mexico. It is a World Heritage Site, and the Pueblo manages its own sacred sites there. Ladders rise from a sacred kiva, a ceremonial structure that is usually circular and partially underground. Signs warn tourists to stay away.

Helkau National Historic District in northern California was the site of a disagreement between Indian tribes and the United States Forest Service. Chimney Rock is one of the most sacred sites within the historic district. A group of tribes led by the Karuk alleged that a road proposed by the Forest Service to open an area to logging would disturb their ability to worship at Chimney Rock. Such a disturbance, they argued, was an infringement of their right to freely exercise their religion, which is a right guaranteed to all Americans by the First Amendment to our Constitution.

The Supreme Court found that the Forest Service did have the discretion to build the road, but also encouraged the Forest Service, and the United States government in general, to find ways to accommodate religious practices by American Indians on public land.

The use of many American Indian sacred sites requires solitude and meditation while looking out over vast distances. Land managing agencies struggle with how to accommodate these needs on land open to the public. Many of the sites have viewsheds that now look out over a tremendous amount of clear-cutting. In some cases altering the appearance of a sacred area can be very disruptive and disturbing to American Indian people. However, often it is the land itself that is sacred, and the integrity of a sacred place is not altered by activities like clear-cut timbering.

For example, Mount Shasta in northern California is a sacred site to several tribes in California and Oregon. As part of the review process for a proposed ski resort, the Keeper of the United States National Register of

Historic Places was asked to determine whether or not Mount Shasta was eligible for the national register. The Keeper determined the entire mountain, from foot to peak, was eligible.

There was intense public interest, and the Keeper requested public comment. The Keeper made an on-site visit to Mount Shasta and observed development, including clear-cutting. On the basis that the integrity of the site had been compromised, and to the consternation of the tribes, he revised his decision and found only a certain small area on the mountainside eligible for the National Register and therefore protected under Federal law. Part of the area considered eligible includes Panther Meadows, where a sacred spring is located.

From the perspective of non-Indian people, the whole mountain was not worthy of protection because the mountain had been disturbed by logging and other development. It lacked "integrity," a threshold element needed for a place to be determined eligible for the National Register. However, from the point of view of the tribes, what was really significant was the mountain itself. Logging and development did not affect its "sacredness" nor its "integrity." We are struggling wit h the application of the concept of integrity as seen from different cultural perspectives in the United States.

Kaho'olawe, a Hawaiian island, is sacred to Native Hawaiians, who used it for centuries for ceremonies until it became a bombing range for the United States Navy. It is now being restored at great cost and in consultation with Native Hawaiians. Dangerous and toxic materials are being removed. The island is being rehabilitated and is now used regularly by Native Hawaiians.

Most sacred sites of indigenous American peoples are not readily recognizable to non-Indians as sacred sites and are rarely documented. The nature of sacred places is learned over the generations as elders pass the history and traditions on to future generations (figure 5). The only way that non-Indians can find out about them is by consulting with Indian people, either in an office, in the field, or in their homes.

The National Park Service faces particular cultural difficulties when it seeks to protect Indian sacred sites and to accommodate traditional religious practices on public lands. To protect a site, whether it is on the World Heritage List or the U. S. National Register of Historic Places, requires providing detailed documentation. Those preparing the nominations must document the reasons a site is important, which means we have to ask Indian people for information, or they must volunteer it. Often such information is private and secret, not to be made public.

Non-Indian people can take pride in building a case for significance, building detail upon detail, argument upon argument. Indian people do

Figure 5. Knowledge of sacred places is passed through generations in Northern Alaska and elsewhere.

not want to do this. The fact that something is sacred is part of their culture. It is private. They do not want it on paper, and they also do not want to have to prove it. An Indian youth could never ask an Indian elder to prove something. Elders do not have to explain. They know. In many ways the concept of documentation, which comes out of the European intellectual tradition, works against American Indian cultural traditions.

In the United States we have an additional problem in collecting confidential information from Indian people about sacred sites, because once information is given to a government agency, it is available for public scrutiny under our Freedom of Information Act.

This problem is emerging as we carry out our responsibilities under our Native American Graves Protection and Repatriation Act. Agencies like the National Park Service have collected information from American Indian people to determine the cultural affiliation of human remains and associated grave goods held in museums and collections. This information was needed to identify to whom such things should be returned. Now scholars and others want that information. The Indians do not want it made public because to them it is a private matter concerning the return of their ancestors. Over the years I have come to realize that there are inherent conflicts between the non-Indian's need for documentation and keeping sensitive information confidential in the United States.

Figure 6. The National Park Service faces particular cultural difficulties when it seeks to protect Indian sacred sites and to accommodate traditional religious practices on public lands.

The National Park Service also has difficulty in accommodating the use of sacred sites by traditional Indian practitioners when those sites are on public lands (figure 6). Trying to accommodate traditional ceremonial uses by closing public lands to others is very difficult. The agency was sued at Devils Tower National Monument, mentioned above, because a group of non-Indians claimed that by asking climbers not to climb during the month of June, the National Park Service was "establishing" religion, which is prohibited by the First Amendment to the United States Constitution. The court eventually found that a voluntary closure was within the legal discretion of the National Park Service.

We also tried to close an area of Glen Canyon National Recreation Area in Arizona at Rainbow Bridge, which is sacred to the Navajo people, to enable Navajo traditional religious practitioners to conduct their ceremonies in private, away from the public eye. The courts prohibited us from doing that in another case that went all the way to the Supreme Court. We have placed a sign in the area asking visitors not to approach or walk under Rainbow Bridge in respect for Native American religions and, as a result, again are being sued for "establishing religion."

The most recent tool that we have to help us protect American Indian sacred sites is an executive order that President Clinton signed in the mid-1990s. It directs federal agencies to accommodate access to, and the ceremonial use of, public lands by traditional American Indian religious practitioners. But even in this new executive order "sacred site" is defined in a very non-Indian way. Sites must be discrete, bounded areas that make sense to federal officials. But, as noted earlier, many sites sacred to Indian people were never meant to have boundaries drawn around them. Thus, for the United States government, accommodating the use of American Indian sacred sites and protecting them remain very complex cross-cultural issues. ■

42 Traditional *Kuarup* Rituals of Alto Xingú, Pantanal, and Southwest Brazil

Marcos Terena

A founder of the Brazilian Ministry of Culture as a special advisor addressing indigenous matters, Marcos Terena is head of cabinet of FUNAI (National Foundation for Indigenous Peoples Affairs) and a member of the Intertribal Committee.

I am a son of the Terena people of Brazil. We in Brazil recently commemorated 500 years of Western civilization, but those also have been the centuries during which we, the indigenous people of Brazil, were silenced in the name of the new civilization.

My people never had coins or money until the white man came. Then we suddenly realized that we were a poor people. We, the Indians or indigenous peoples, were always thought of as being impoverished and an obstacle to development. I pray to our creator, the great spirit that created all of us, that a new age is to come in which we also will be considered part of the development equation.

My wishes are that the international development banks continue their functions of development and searching for financial gains, but also that we should seek social gains. This development should be a road to peace and harmony among people. Culture will play a great role in this process.

For many years, long before the white man crossed the great river of the Atlantic in his canoes to invade our lands, our people were fully integrated with the earth, the waters, and the environment, as part of the life system created and governed by the Grande Ituko-Oviti, the all-mighty creator.

In Brazil 215 indigenous groups have survived in diverse settlements. Through their ceremonial songs they keep alive their languages and cultures. Each time the first cry of a newborn child breaks the forest silence, their hope for the indigenous way of life is renewed.

For indigenous peoples land is life. Without territories large enough to support their economic, social, and cultural ways of life, it is impossible to maintain spirituality and the ceremonial rites of passage for each phase of life. These rites begin when one is a child and continue as one develops into an adolescent, to the time that one becomes an adult, when one is strong, vigorous, and ready for the art of living, to the time that one becomes an elder, when one reaches the phase of life with diminished physical stamina but enormous spiritual strength and ceremonial knowledge.

This knowledge is symbolized for the Bororo Indians by the Onca (the Jaguar); for the Terena Indians by the birds; for the Guaraní by the sky and the land; and for the Kuikuro and the other people of the Alto Xingú in the Brazilian Amazon by the trees and the rivers.

In the region where Brazil borders Bolivia and Paraguay, my people the Terena have coexisted with the new settlers for over 100 years. Through their elders and their women the Terena communities seek to preserve their traditional spirituality, despite the fact that they possess a very limited territory, splintered into tiny islands. Villages are tiny, ranging from 70 to 4 hectares in size.

One can still hear the *Canto do Pagé*, the shaman's chant. This traditional wisdom is divided into specialized knowledge: the medicine man, the seer, the one who can speak with nature, and the spiritual traveler who can fly like the wind.

A few years after the white man arrived, he brought his religion and his churches, but the Great Ituko-Oviti never abandoned the Terena people, and it is easy to see why not. First, because even though the territory was limited, his people still live on the land. Second, the sacred chants are still sung, and the prayers are still offered in the traditional languages through the appropriate ceremonies, and not just on important religious holidays or on the weekends.

Another people who have been in contact with the white man for more than a century are the Guaraní, who have endured physically, culturally, and spiritually. Their survival was totally incomprehensible to the white man, since the Guaraní are not materialistic and they use their land only to derive their spiritual and physical sustenance. According to their belief system, they are traversing a virtual corridor that crosses the southwest of Brazil, through Bolivia, through Paraguay and Argentina, all the way to Uruguay, in search of a better world.

Their tradition also knows the song of life and their hopes are sung in the chants of their elders, children, men, and women. With their maracas they gather to dance in a circle every dawn and every dusk. They believe that if there were no more Guaraní to shake the maracas in a circular motion, the earth would fall into disequilibrium and it would be the end.

Another people lives in the most central part of Brazil along the banks of the Xingú River, covered by the great forests of the Brazilian Amazon. Many different groups live here but one stands out—the Kuikuro, who practice the great ceremony of the *Kuarup*. It could be compared with the Catholic funeral mass, *missa de 7o dia*, but here it is an integral part of village life.

The *Kuarup* symbolizes the passage of sadness over a period of one year, from the loss of the deceased to the following year when the family—the village—invites all the other communities for a final lament. A tree trunk is adorned with the most beautiful decorations, feathers, and weapons of war. This genuine funeral feast lasts for three days and takes place every year before the spring in August.

In the Kuikuro universe of traditional wisdom, the *Kuarup* ceremony emphasizes respect for the "other," respect for the deceased. This vitally important funeral feast affirms the value of life and the continuity of the community (figure 1).

The community is able to continue practicing its traditions because its lands are legally demarcated by the federal government. Consequently, it can practice its ceremonies in privacy without the simplified and impoverished "folklorism," which is so common among the Western "interpreters" who still speak on behalf of the indigenous peoples as if they were the great specialists, instead of letting the Indians speak for themselves and be themselves.

The *Kuarup* takes place in the center of the village, where the decorated tree trunks have been placed (figure 2). Here the women lament all night long, their cries interspersed by the shaman's chants to liberate the spirit of the one who has died. The spirit of the deceased enters the tree trunk, which is taken the next day by the warriors and thrown into the waters of the rivers so that the spirit may become free for its new life.

All the other villages celebrate on the morning of that day with a new joy, singing, playing communal games, and exchanging food in a sacred

Figure 1. Dance of the *Kuarup*, Kuikuro Tribe, Alto Xingú, Mato Grosso State, Brazil.

ceremony. The ceremony affirms the true equilibrium between life and death as an integral part of the life of the indigenous people and, certainly, all of humanity.

Perhaps in the process of colonizing, the white man, in his ignorance, considered the indigenous peoples an obstacle to development, savages, or even beings without souls. But now we understand much more. The world of the white man needs an integration that strengthens not only the muscles, that demonstrates not only the technical knowledge of how to clone living organisms, that does not demonstrate the false smile of happiness. It needs the integration of solidarity and brotherhood to substitute the monetary greed that enriches the few to the detriment of the many. We, the indigenous people, have wisely preserved our codes of conduct of how to coexist with one another free of prejudice.

No value would be worth anything without the power of the Spirit or Great Creator, and this power is not to be found in the man-made machines but inside each of us. ∎

Figure 2. *Kuarup* ritual, Kuikoro Tribe, Alto Xingú, with author, Mato Grosso State, Brazil.

43 Sacred Spaces and the Search for Authenticity in the Kathmandu Valley

Eduard F. Sekler

Eduard F. Sekler is professor emeritus of Architecture at Harvard University and a leading expert on architectural preservation.

The important realization is spreading that historic preservation must be treated as an integral part of sustainable development.[1] Development "which meets the needs of the present generation without compromising the ability of future generations to meet their own needs"[2] clearly cannot refer to material needs alone but must equally include the needs of the spirit. Historic preservation addresses the latter in a powerful manner, while frequently beautifully satisfying certain material needs. This holds true for all countries, but it can be observed with special clarity in several developing countries, among them the Kingdom of Nepal.

Issues of Authenticity

Some aspects of the Kathmandu World Heritage Site demonstrate the need to observe a methodological caution when applying the term "authenticity" to sacred places. In such cases one must distinguish between the *religious* authenticity and such other authenticities as those of *form*, *material*, and *urbanistic* context.

Nepal, a country in and at the foot of the Himalayas, was opened to travelers from the industrialized, West with its orientation toward secular progress only in 1951. By contrast, at that time Nepal's cultural center, the Kathmandu Valley, was still paradigmatic of a way of life in which the concept of the sacral interacted with all important human activities and concerns, as it was the case during the Middle Ages in the West. For this reason even today, half a century after the opening of the Kathmandu Valley, it still provides many examples for the variety of meanings the term "sacred place" may signify. What is considered sacred may be not only buildings and sculptures for worship but also simply a corner in a traditional house, the auspicious paintings on a facade that are renewed every year, the small area in a court or lane marked by a symbol, an entire site, special features in the landscape such as mountain peaks or the confluence of rivers and, finally, the entire Valley itself.

All this however is slowly—or at times quickly—affected by the impact of modernization and the social changes in its wake. As the traditional belief systems become weaker and economic and social pressures stronger, the partial or total secularization of once-sacred places seems unavoidable. This process has momentous consequences for the preservation of the Valley's exceedingly rich cultural heritage, its landscape, its buildings, and its urban spaces. In the Valley's *Protective Inventory of 1975* no fewer than 888 individual monuments, 34 monument zones, and 32 preservation districts are briefly described and classified, which gives an idea of the magnitude of historic preservation needs.[3]

From time immemorial the Valley was famed for its natural beauty, which, according to a legend in the *Nepala-mahatmaya*, attracted the god Shiva to stay in a forest of the Valley as Pashupati, lord of the animals.[4] This, in the mind of the Hindu believer, is one of the reasons for the sanctity of the Valley, where the sanctuary of Pashupatinath memorializes the god's stay (figure 1). Today there can still be magical moments, when the Valley shows itself at its best with its meandering rivers, terraced rice fields, flowering trees, groves of tall bamboo, and forested hills against a backdrop of distant white peaks. Houses and hamlets, strategically placed on less fertile land here and there, still fit harmoniously into the landscape, although disturbing encroachments become more frequent every year. Everywhere shrines and temples, stupas, and other memorials of a sacred presence demonstrate the close interweaving of religion and life in this culture.

When in 1979 the Kathmandu Valley was inscribed in the UNESCO list of World Heritage Sites, seven distinct monument zones were singled out as forming the World Heritage Site. Each zone has the character of a sacred place, but in each changes happened that jeopardized the formal and material authenticity of the site. However, in all cases the authenticity of the site's religious function remains intact. An analogous dichotomy can be observed in many places outside the seven individual zones, not only in settlements but also in the landscape.

One of the best places to view the often disturbing changes in the landscape is the hilltop of Svayambhunath, from which the all-seeing eyes of the Buddha watch over the Kathmandu Valley. Unfortunately, around the stupa more buildings were placed than the filled hilltop could carry,

Figure 1. Pashupatinath precinct with the main temple and the stairway to the sacred river Bagmati.

and severe landslides were the consequence. Svayambhunath, like Pashupatinath, stands at the mythic origin of the Kathmandu Valley. Here, according to the Buddhist version of the foundation myth, the Bodhisattva Manjushri came to worship the primordial Buddha's miraculous light-emanating lotus flower, the Svayambhu (the self-created, self-manifest), but was unable to do so because of the surrounding lake. With his sword, used otherwise to cleave asunder the clouds of ignorance, he cut an opening through the southern hills at Chobar, thus draining the Kathmandu Valley.

Chobar is the most dramatic incident of the desecration of a once-sacred landscape by a badly conceived industrial installation. The site where the sacred river Bagmati leaves the Valley and Manjushri's sword cleft the rock was hallowed by a temple at the water's edge, set next to the well-tended rice fields. It is one of the four Ganesha temples, which protect the Valley from their four comers (Jal Binayak, Surya Binayak, Chandra Binayak in Chabahil, and Ashoka Binayak near Hanuman Dhoka).[5] After development aid in the form of a cement factory was placed near the temple, the site changed from what once was a favorite picnic spot of the local population to a wasteland covered by fine whitish dust. Owing to severe pollution, the river, too, no longer invites admiration but repugnance.

What Svayambhunath is for Newar Buddhists, Pashupatinath is for the many Hindu pilgrims who come every year to the banks of the river Bagmati to worship Shiva.[6] The large crowds who attend the festival of Shivaratri or arrive on other occasions, often staying for days, contribute to the deterioration of the natural and built environment. Here, as at other parts of the World Heritage Site, one faces the problems that occur when the demands of an authentic religious group contradict those of historic preservation with its quest for authenticity of material and form. The Pashupati complex is under the jurisdiction of its own religious authority and of a separate development trust, which prepared a master plan for it. The Department of Archaeology, which elsewhere is responsible for World Heritage Sites, here has less influence when projects are undertaken. As a consequence problems may occur, and some restoration work may be carried out in a manner open to criticism.

The second great center of Hindu worship in the Valley is the sanctuary of Changu Narayan, dedicated to Vishnu.[7] Like Svayambhunath it is superbly located on a hilltop, from whence the golden roof of the main temple can be seen from afar, and there are superb views towards the Himalayan peaks and into the Valley. Comparable to the two previously discussed World Heritage areas, it comprises an entire precinct that combines significant natural features with precious human-made objects such as very early sculptures of the highest quality. Looking across the Valley toward Ichangu Narayan in the west and knowing there exist the strategically placed other Vishnu temples of Shikara Narayan and Bisankhu Narayan,[8] one again is made aware of the sacred character of a landscape that is guarded not only by Ganesha but equally by Naryan (Vishnu).

The fourth religious complex of the Kathmandu Valley World Heritage Site is the great Buddhist stupa of Bodnath, the foremost pilgrimage center for Tibetan devotees.[9] As can best be discerned in an airview, it is a built mandala, overwhelming in its large physical size, which originally created a striking contrast to the small houses ringing it. In 1978 the stupa, seen from a distance on its three-story podium, towered above the houses. In 1991 the stupa was no longer so visible and imposing as in earlier years because tall buildings, many of them Tibetan monasteries, had been built all around it. In close proximity the most conspicuous atrocity yet to be perpetrated was under construction when I last visited the site in December 1998—a gigantic hotel block. In this case a truly comprehensive, critical design review by the bank or banks that financed this monster could have made a great contribution toward safeguarding the historic character of this part of the World Heritage Site.

Paradoxically, Bodnath has been spoiled by its success. Because of its popularity among Tibetan pilgrims and others, ample means became available for what those in charge considered improvements. Around the circumference of the stupa, where the visitors perambulate past innumerable prayer wheels in the low boundary wall, obtrusive tall steel masts replaced the slim bamboo culms that in the past were used to support prayer flags. A monumental entrance gate in painted reinforced concrete was put up, where there had been none before. But worst of all, thanks to the business initiative of shopkeepers and landowners, many old houses around the sanctuary were replaced by tall, deep buildings with shops and shopping arcades on the ground floor. Unquestionably, the religious authenticity of the stupa is as intact as ever, but the urbanistic, formal, and material authenticity of its setting has been lost for good.

The pressures of changing economic and social conditions at work at Bodnath are equally, if not more strongly, felt in connection with the three urban monument zones of the World Heritage Site, the *Durbar* or palace squares, in the towns that once were the capitals of three small kingdoms, Kathmandu, Bhaktapur, and Patan (figures 2, 3). These Durbar Squares are places of great religious significance because of the divine nature of kingship in Nepal, and because the numerous sanctuaries and religious images assembled in them vouchsafe divine protection. Moreover, at their outskirts Bhaktapur and Patan are encircled by sanctuaries of protective goddesses: the Ashtamatrika and Navadurga (figure 4).

The Durbar Squares enjoy a reasonable amount of maintenance and preservation but suffer greatly from encroachment by adjacent tall

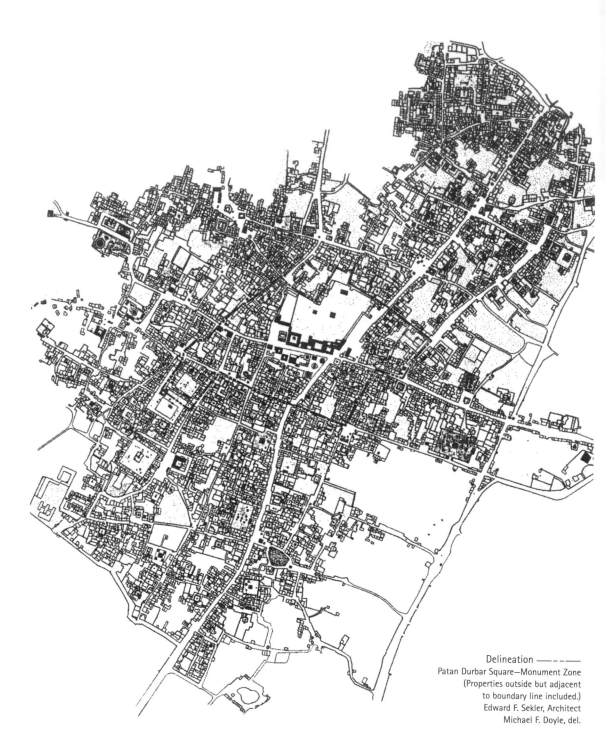

Delineation —— —— ——
Patan Durbar Square—Monument Zone
(Properties outside but adjacent
to boundary line included.)
Edward F. Sekler, Architect
Michael F. Doyle, del.

Figure 2. Patan Urban Preservation District.
Base map after the protective inventory
of the historic center of Patan city.

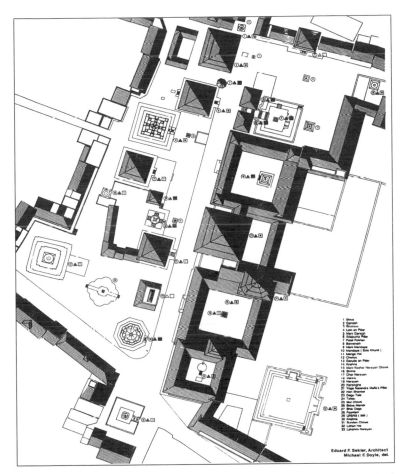

1 Shiva
2 Ganesh
3 Bhimsen
4 Lion on Pillar
5 Hari Ganesh
6 Garuda on Pillar
7 Fatal Pokhari
8 Bhimsen
9 Hari Mandapa
10 Mandapa (Sola Khutti)
11 Manga Hiti
12 Chaitya
13 Garuda on Pillar
14 Krishna
15 Mani Keshar Narayan Chowk
16 Shrine
17 Char Narayan
18 Vishnu
19 Narayan
20 Narsingha
21 Yoga Narendra Malla's Pillar
22 Hari Shanker
23 Degu Tale
24 Talaju
25 Mul chowk
26 Bidya Mandir
27 Bhai Dega
28 Fountain
29 GRAINS (Mill)
30 Krishna
31 Sunder Chowk
32 Lohan Hiti
33 Lakshmi Narayan

Eduard F. Sekler, Architect
Michael F. Doyle, del.

Figure 3 (left). Patan Durbar Square
Urbanistic Conservation and Design Study:
enlargement of the central square
in figure 2.

Figure 4. Kathmandu Durbar Square
monument zone: partial view with
the Maju Deval temple in the center.

Figure 5. Kathmandu Durbar Square
monument zone: partial view with
the Bhagvati temple and, behind it,
the Degutale temple.

Figure 6. Bhaktapur Durbar Square
monument zone: partial view with
the rebuilt octagonal Cyasilin Mandapa
in the background.

buildings. Since these squares have a great deal in common, I will deal in detail with only one of them, Patan Durbar Square (figures 5, 6). Before doing so, however, I want to present one telling example of the way religious authenticity may continue while material and formal authenticity are lost.

In 1985 I took my first photograph of a small ruinous Shiva sanctuary next to a *Sattal* (resthouse) on the road to Panauti. Here, as on so many occasions, unhampered plant growth had ruined it. When I came again that way in 1991, I was happy to discover that the little building had been restored, although plant growth had set in again. By 1994 the plant growth had become a real menace once more. Three years later, all that remained of the building were wall fragments and the sacral Shiva *lingam*, freshly painted as evidence of ongoing worship despite the lack of the built sanctuary. Its functional, religious authenticity was untouched by the loss of its shelter, the formal and material authenticity of which was gone. "But we can rebuild it," the then-director of the Archeology Department said to me as we gazed at the scene.

That brief statement taught me a lot about the way cultural tradition influences concepts of authenticity in different parts of the world. Yet I

Figure 7. Patan UNESCO World Heritage site: the ruinous Radha-Krishna temple.

Figure 8. Radha-Krishna Temple after its restoration by the Kathmandu Valley Preservation Trust.

do not believe that in cases in which the survival of an authentic religious function exists, one should argue against the search for authenticity of form and material. To do so would ignore the complexity of legitimate interests that interact in a society. Not only scholars who are concerned about the value of surviving monuments as veridical sources of historic information, but also ordinary citizens may care about historic monuments and sites, and not for religious reasons only. The artistic and scientific value of an element from the past may be of little or no interest to many inhabitants of the Kathmandu Valley, but they will care about some aspect of its use value, particularly in connection with tourism. They also will care about its historic value if we take that term in its widest possible sense that includes the commemorative value with its evocation of personal memories and associations. The sense of memory and the sense of place and belonging still appear to be strongly anchored in the culture of the Valley as constituent elements of its identity. Cultural identity, however, in this context must not be misinterpreted in a spirit of radical nationalism.

Cultural Identity

There are many ways in which a cultural identity is formed and maintained. Much of what happens in the process has to do with the intangible cultural heritage of a body of traditions and usage, rites, poetry, song, and dance. A great deal of all of this is passed on orally through generations. Consequently, its survival is always threatened. Moreover, in tourism-oriented countries like Nepal, the temptation becomes great to replace what once were genuine manifestations of a living culture by purely profit-oriented, spurious reenactments.

By contrast, the tangible cultural heritage has the great advantage over its intangible counterpart that with proper care it will remain authentic over centuries. As long as historic monuments remain without falsification and misleading imitations, they will, even in a neglected state, create a sense of continuity that is an essential part of cultural identity.

Thus, in the historic conservation and restoration work done by the Kathmandu Valley Preservation Trust, which I had the honor of chairing from its foundation in 1990 until 1996, in the Patan World Heritage Zone we have observed what is generally considered the best practice when aiming for authenticity. We meticulously research and document a building like the Radha Krishna Temple prior, during, and after any intervention (figures 7-11). We respect the authenticity of material, form, and technique of the old building and avoid replacing lost carved elements when there is no unequivocal evidence of what had existed. Any replacements are dated inconspicuously.

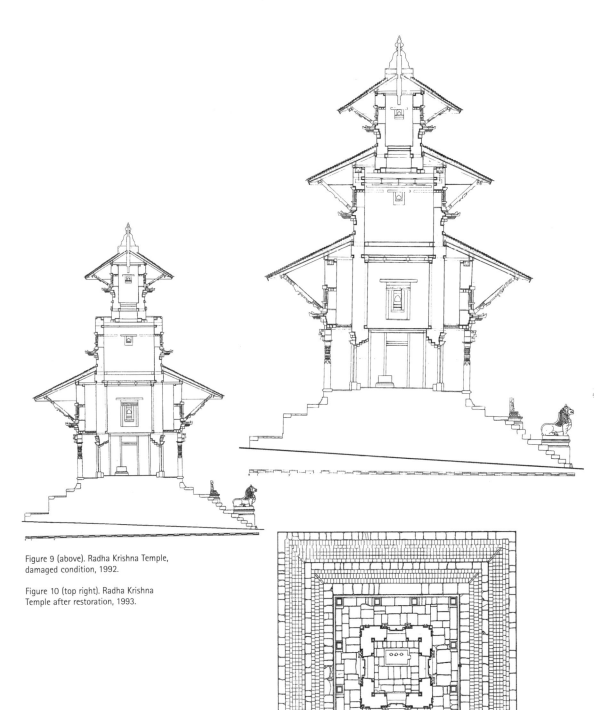

Figure 9 (above). Radha Krishna Temple, damaged condition, 1992.

Figure 10 (top right). Radha Krishna Temple after restoration, 1993.

Figure 11. Radha Krishna Temple, ground floor plan, existing condition, 1992.

By experience we have become convinced that it is essential to involve the local community in the conservation activity, even if it is by nothing more than a comparatively small financial contribution. Finally, we are training young local professionals in the hope that some day they will take over the work of preservation.

The tangible heritage of buildings and other elements of the environment has a facticity that affects a viewer in a unique way because it engages his or her total sensuous perception in a process that makes time visible and links historic time with personal time. This can be experienced most convincingly during a visit to the sacral historic urban space that I present as a concluding example: Patan Durbar Square. It is the center of the historic part of Patan, a town sanctified and ritually imbedded in a protective network of stupas and sanctuaries by a process that includes yearly processions and circumambulations.

The Square[10] has been praised by many authors in the most enthusiastic terms, beginning with the seventeenth-century Nepalese poet Kunu Sharma, who rhetorically questioned: "Isn't it like a piece of heaven?"[11] The urbanistic historic conservation study done over several years by Michael Doyle and myself revealed that the impressiveness of this urban space derives from several mutually enhancing factors.[12]

1. Even though it is of comparatively small objective size with a maximum length of some 500 feet, it appears monumental when entered from its comparatively narrow approaches. Some of these are still, as originally, lined by typical Newar townhouses, rarely more than two or three low stories high. Today this is changing as buildings are replaced or heightened, jeopardizing the original monumentality.

2. The more than 30 palace buildings, temples, and other historic monuments in Durbar Square form an exciting three-dimensional composition. It seems to be ordered by a system of underlying geometric order and cosmic orientation toward the highest visible peak in the far distance, Shivapuri.[13]

3. Several historic monuments are of high artistic quality and well preserved, including the remarkable Krishna Temple of 1637, built in stone after models from north India.

4. The powerful overall effect is enhanced by statuary in front of temples and parts of the palaces as well as by richly carved decoration, polychromy, and gilding.

The sacral character of this space is borne out by the daily rituals of worship at some of its temples, by yearly ritual dances, and by documents from the past that record encounters of Malla kings with their divine counterparts. In Patan Durbar Square in the late afternoon, when the setting sun spreads a golden glow over the palace facades, the many-roofed temples with their gilt pinnacles, and the distant

Himalayan peak in the north, one can still see the seventeenth-century king Yoganarendra Malla on his column in perpetual adoration of Taleju, his tutelary deity. One need not share the old king's belief system to understand how such a powerful environmental experience, when nature interacts with art and architecture, can transport the viewer beyond the realm of the purely material. Indeed, the great historic monuments in the Durbar Square, so inseparably linked to their setting with its truly cosmic background of high mountains, offer the possibility of an authentic spiritual experience to those who come seeking it. ■

Notes

1 The author gratefully acknowledges the assistance of his wife Mary Patricia; Michael F. Doyle, American Institute of Architects; Erich Theophile; and Professor Michael Witzel in the preparation of this chapter. Text copyrighted by Eduard F. Sekler.

2 World Commission on Environment and Development, *The Brundtland Report: Our Common Future* (Oxford, UK: Oxford University Press, 1987).

3 C. Pruscha, *Kathmandu Valley: The Preservation of Physical Environment and Cultural Heritage: A Protective Inventory*, vols. I and II (Vienna: Schroll, 1975).

4 J. Acharya, *The Nepala-mahatmaya of the Skandapurana* (Jaipur: Nirala, 1992), 15.

5 N. Gutschow, *Stadtraum und Ritual der newarischen Städte im Kathmandu-Tal* (Stuttgart: Kohlhammer, 1982), 21.

6 A. Michaels, *Die Reisen der Götter: der nepalische Pashugatinatha Tempel und sein Umfeld* (Bonn: VGH Wissenschaftsverlag, 1994).

7 J. Lidke, *Vishvarupa Mandir; A Study of Changu Narayan* (New Delhi: Nirala, 1996).

8 Gutschow, *Stadtraum und Ritual der newarischen Städte im Kathmandu-Tal*, n. 4, p. 21.

9 Gutschow, *Stadtraum und Ritual der newarischen Städte im Kathmandu-Tal*. Stuttgart: Kohlhammer, note 4, p. 96 ff. See also Ulrich Wiesner, *Nepal* (Ko1n: Dumont, 1977), 117 ff.

10 A. Saphalya, *Art and Culture of Nepal: An Attempt toward Preservation* (Jaipir: Nirala, 1991), 87 ff.

11 M. Slusser, *Nepal Mandala* (Princeton, N. J.: Princeton University Press, 1982), 204.

12 E. F. Sekler, "Proposal for the Urbanistic Conservation of Patan (Lalitpur) Durbar Square as a Monument Zone," Graduate School of Design, Harvard University, Cambridge, Ma., 1980.

13 Sekler, "Urban Design at Patan Darbar Square, " in N. Gutschow and A. Michaels eds., *Heritage of the Kathmandu Valley* (Sankt Augustin: VGH Wissenschaftsverlag, 1987), 3-17.

44 Axum: Toward the Conservation of Ethiopia's Sacred City

Joseph King

Joseph King is program coordinator for Africa 2009, a project for the conservation of the Immovable Cultural Heritage in Sub-Saharan Africa, at the International Centre for the Study of the Preservation and Restoration of Cultural Property (ICCROM) in Rome, jk@iccrom.org

Almost any text that describes the city of Axum describes it in terms of being Ethiopia's sacred city.

Sources of Axum's Sacredness

Axum's sacredness derives in large part from its centrality to the Ethiopian Orthodox Church through the presence of the Saint Mary of Zion church complex. More than this, there is a melange of values existing in Axum that make it important not only from its religious and spiritual significance but also from its key role in the national identity of Ethiopia, which goes back to its most ancient legends. In essence layers of important values have been built up over time in Axum. These values were recognized as being of "outstanding universal value" by Axum's placement on the UNESCO World Heritage List.

Axumite legends go back to biblical times, to the time of King Solomon and the Queen of Sheba. It is an Ethiopian belief that the Queen of Sheba came from Ethiopia and that her son, fathered by Solomon, returned later to Ethiopia to establish the ruling dynasty. This fascination with the Queen of Sheba is manifest today in the popular names of a few of the historical monuments. In particular, the Dungur Palace archaeological site (figure 1) is popularly known as the Queen of Sheba Palace (although it probably dates to the early centuries A. D.), and the Mai Shum, a manmade pool of water, is known as the Baths of the Queen of Sheba. She has, in fact, become a potent symbol of the importance of the town. This ancient biblical association is the layer on which Axum's sacred and cultural values are built.

Another important layer can be found in the role of Axumite civilization and history in Ethiopia's national identity. This is amply demonstrated by

Figure 1. Dungur Palace Archaeological Site, Axum.

the rich archaeological heritage that has been found in and around the town over time. The built heritage includes palaces (the Dungur Palace mentioned above is one), tombs, and houses, and there is also numerous movable heritage such as coins, pottery, and stone inscriptions. These remains testify to the importance and power of the Axumite civilization.

Probably the most potent symbols of that history, however, are the amazing carved stelae found in the central stelae park of the town. Although there are many hundreds of simple stelae in and around the town, six large, intricately carved ones were erected, probably around the fourth century A. D. These stelae are cut from stone monoliths. Their quarrying, carving, and erection represented an astonishing feat of engineering for their time. The carving represents multi-storied buildings complete with false doors at the base and rows of windows above. Only one of these remains standing at Axum (figure 2). The largest (33 meters tall and 520 tons) lies in pieces on its side. There is some question as to whether it was ever completely raised or it fell and broke during its erection (figure 3).

One of the stelae was carried to Rome during the rule of Mussolini, where it stands today in front of what is now the United Nations Food and Agriculture Organization (FAO). Recently, the Italian government began the process of returning this stelae to Axum. The International Centre for the Study of the Preservation and Restoration of Cultural Property (ICCROM) was involved in this process on the scientific side, working on cleaning and consolidating the stelae and conducting a study as to the possible means of transporting it back to Axum.

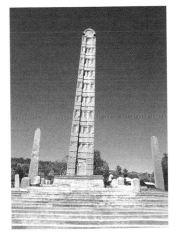

Figure 2. Standing stelae, Axum.

Figure 3. Fallen stelae, Axum.

It is believed that at least some of the stelae served as funerary monuments. Tombs have been excavated beneath some of them, and altars can be found at the base of the carved stelae. These findings link the stelae to the religious life of Axumite civilization.

Symbol of Religious and Political Power

The layer of values related to Axumite civilization and history is also manifest in the town's role as capital of the ancient Axumite empire. It was from here that kings were crowned and from whence they ruled the vast surrounding territory. This importance was retained even as Axum declined late in the first millennium and the capital moved to the southeast. Until the last ruler, Haile Selassie (the 225th direct descendent of Menelik I), Ethiopian kings always returned to Axum for their coronation, as it was a potent symbol of the power of both the monarchy and the church.

Christianity was adopted in Ethiopia in the fourth century by King Ezana. Previously, polytheism predominated in the region, although there was also an ancient strain of Judaism present (represented by the Falashas). Sometime between the fourth and sixth centuries, an important church, St. Mary of Zion, was constructed at Axum which almost 200 centuries later continues to serve as the spiritual center of the Ethiopian Orthodox Church.

The current church site is more than just a single church building. It is a compound containing churches constructed during different periods, as well as other important buildings. The first church, built sometime between the fourth and sixth centuries, is now a ruin. Tradition has it that it was destroyed in the ninth century by Queen Gudit. The older of the two churches still standing dates from the seventeenth or eighteenth century and is similar to construction found at Gondar to the southwest (figure 4). This church, still in use, may be entered only by men. A

Figure 4. St. Mary of Zion Church building, seventeenth or eighteenth century, Axum.

modern church and tower was built by Haile Selassie in the 1950s as a contemporary symbol of the church and monarchy and accommodates both men and women. Although the modern building is felt by many to be a disturbing element in the historical landscape of Axum, it now must be seen as an important part of the historical continuum of the site, especially since there is no more monarchy in Ethiopia.

Within the church compound the church treasury is the repository a variety of objects of both religious and secular value such as crowns, religious texts, illustrations, crosses, and umbrellas (used in religious ceremonies) (figure 5). Many of these objects hold a strong religious significance, and some are still in use. It is important to emphasize the need to look across the range of cultural heritage. The movable heritage found in the treasury is an integral element to understanding Ethiopian culture and both the movable and immovable heritage must be addressed in an integrated fashion.

It should be mentioned in this context that the Ethiopian Church is one of the main holders and custodians of cultural heritage resources in the country. This includes both moveable heritage mentioned above, and also immovable heritage such as church buildings and monasteries. Therefore, the Church is a very important partner in any attempt to conserve cultural heritage of Ethiopia.

The church treasury contains one other object that is of the utmost value to the Church and is the main reason for which Axum is considered sacred. This object is the Ark of the Covenant, the box built by Moses to carry the Ten Commandments after they were brought down from Mount Sinai. The Ark is mentioned many times in the Bible before the time of Solomon. After Solomon, however, mention of the Ark virtually stops. According to one of their sacred texts, the Kebra Nagast, Ethiopian tradition has it that Menelik I, the son of King Solomon and the Queen of Sheba, brought the Ark to Ethiopia during his lifetime and that it has resided in Axum ever since. The Ark itself is not allowed to be seen by anyone. In fact, the only one who can see it is the guard whose job it is to stay with the Ark at all times. Not even the priests of the church are allowed in. The Ark is kept in the treasury building in a special room above the rest of the treasures. The presence of the Ark in Axum is really central to the belief system of the Ethiopian Orthodox Church, and replicas can be found in the "Holy of Holies" of all churches in the country.

Turning from the physical and historical importance of Axum, mention should also be made of the spiritual values of the population living there. They have been described to me as being conservative, not in the political sense but from the point of view of their deep religious faith and the value that they hold for their heritage. One can sense this spirituality in walking around the town and talking with the people. It has

Figure 5. Interior of the church treasury, Axum.

been said that the sacred can exist within the everyday actions of people, and this clearly applies in Axum.

Finally, another contributing element to Axum's importance should be pointed out: the fabric of its townscape. This fabric serves as a context for the historic and spiritual elements within its midst. The stelae, archaeological sites, and churches are an integral part of the urban fabric of Axum. Axum was declared a World Heritage Site in the late 1970s. As part of its favorable evaluation, the International Council on Sites and Monuments (ICOMOS) specifically mentions Axum's historic urban character in addition to its monuments. That urban fabric has certainly undergone changes in the past 100 years, but it retains some of its important vernacular characteristics. The value of this townscape must be considered an important element in the complete understanding of Axum's importance as a sacred site.

Conservation Planning for Axum

In 1998 the World Bank, in partnership with ICCROM and the World Monuments Fund undertook a mission to Ethiopia to develop a "Learning and Innovation Loan" (LIL) for Cultural Heritage. One of the components was to be concerned with what was referred to as "site planning" in Axum. The main focuses of this project were to:

- Examine the current state of conservation of the archaeological sites, stelae, and other monuments
- Carry out conservation work as necessary
- Develop preventive maintenance plans
- Develop a better system of visitor management, interpretation, and presentation of the sites.

This last aspect is very important because of the desire to do a better job of explaining and presenting Axumite culture to both foreign tourists and Ethiopians. This element would also be important if there is a desire to increase tourism revenues. As part of this effort there is also a plan to design a new museum for the town. This is a priority that has been identified by the regional government of Tigray. The current museum is much too small to display all of the rich treasures unearthed during archaeological digs in the area. In addition a need is felt to expand the collection to include aspects of Axumite culture other than archaeology. This new museum also could serve as a center for community cultural events.

Another aspect of the project would be an inventory of the old town. A preliminary inventory has been carried out identifying 312 traditional buildings. There is a need, however to do a more thorough job of documenting these important vernacular buildings. At the same time, to build up a complete picture of the old town, it will be necessary to document the type, scale, and condition of even the newer buildings.

All of these activities are important aspects of the work that needs to be carried out in Axum, but they are only part of the larger picture. The themes underlying this chapter are conservation and continuity. They imply that any work must be based on the principles of conservation of the heritage values of the town (including religious ones), and on the concept of avoiding radical changes in the monuments and town fabric. At the same time we must ensure continued active use of the town by residents in a way that provides an acceptable quality of life for them.

Previous planning efforts for Axum did not take these principles into account. Some years ago a master plan was developed that drew a line around the historic part of the town and left it blank. The feeling was that its historic status meant that there could be no development or improvement within this area. In response to the desire of residents to upgrade their quality of life (provision of water and sanitation), a plan was drawn to relocate approximately 65 percent of the population away from the old town. This plan would have created unsustainable conditions for the old fabric and, rather than promoting conservation of the town and its values, probably would have caused the old town to rapidly fall into decay.

Fortunately, the people of Axum were not happy with the plan, and as a result the government of Tigray convened a meeting of all stakeholders to discuss the matter. Participants at this meeting included representatives of the region, the CRCCH, the local population, and the church. The recommendations that came from the meeting included:

- People living in the old town of Axum should not have to be relocated away from the old town to meet their development needs.
- An inventory of possible archaeological sites (both above and below ground) should be carried out to identify the most important areas to be protected.
- An inventory of traditional houses located in the old town should be carried out.
- The master plan (Axum Development Plan) should be amended in consultation with relevant authorities to include the old town, especially in regard to the provision of adequate infrastructure.
- Local residents and professionals should be trained in methodologies to identify local historic sites.
- The CRCCH should develop "guidelines" or "regulations" for rehabilitation and new construction in the old town.

These recommendations are quite specific and are aimed at conserving the heritage values, while allowing development and improvement in quality of life. The World Bank project would fit into these larger goals and should be seen as one part of an overall coordinated effort to improve conditions in Axum.

Axum is a living city, and to ensure continuity, we must ensure a well balanced life in the town. This means a new master plan that takes into account:

- The infrastructure needs of the people
- Guidelines for growth that allow people to pursue their wish for economic development within the context of the historic town they wish to protect
- A means of ensuring that a dialog continues with the people of Axum and all of the other stakeholders.

Only in this way will we ensure the proper balance between development and conservation, a balance that protects the heritage values of this very important World Heritage Site and allows for a better standard of life for its residents. ■

References

Aalund, F. 1985. "Ethiopia: Master Plan for the Preservation and Presentation of Cultural Heritage." UNESCO, Paris.

Angelini, S. 1971. "Ethiopia, The Historic Route: A Work-Plan for the Development of the Sites and Monuments." A technical report. UNESCO, Paris.

Angelini, S., and Mougin L. 1968. "Ethiopia, Proposals for the Development of Sites and Monuments in Ethiopia as a Contribution to the Growth of Cultural Tourism." A technical report. UNESCO, Paris.

CRCCH. 1993. "Action Plan for Ten Years: International Campaign for Safeguarding Principal Monuments and Sites in Ethiopia." CRCCH, Addis Ababa (unpublished).

Gaidoni, B. G. 1970. "Ethiopia, Cultural Tourism: Prospects for its Development." A technical report. UNESCO, Paris.

Hancock, G. 1993. *The Sign and the Seal.* London: Mandarin Paperbacks.

Hirsch, B. 1996. "Monitoring Report on Six Ethiopian Cultural Heritage Sites." A technical report. UNESCO, Paris.

Pankhurst, R. 1982. *History of Ethiopian Towns: From the Middle Ages to the Early Nineteenth Century.* Wiesbaden: Franz Steiner Verlag.

Phillipson, D. W. 1998. *Ancient Ethiopia, Axum: Its Antecedents and Successors.* London: British Museum Press.

Phillipson, D. W. 1994. "The Significance and Symbolism of Aksumite Stelae" in *Cambridge Archaeological Journal* 4 (2): 189-210.

Phillipson, D. W., ed. 1997. *The Monuments of Aksum.* Addis Ababa: Addis Ababa University Press in collaboration with the British Institute of Eastern Africa.

The Art of *Convivencia* in Spain and Morocco

45

Vivian B. Mann

Vivian B. Mann is an art historian and curator, and the Morris and Eva Feld Chair of Judaica, Jewish Museum, New York.

Earlier in the twentieth century historian Americo Castro used the term *convivencia* (literally, living together) to denote the interaction of cultural elements that were filtered through the collective consciousness of Muslims, Jews, and Christians in medieval Spain.[1] Thomas Glick has commented that the cultural interaction among the three ethnic groups of Spain reflects "a concrete and very complex social dynamic" and was the process by which cultural traits of the "other" were adopted by the two remaining groups.[2]

This description of *convivencia* must be modified somewhat in regard to the art and material culture of medieval Spain. The Arabs who conquered much of the Iberian Peninsula in 711 A.D. brought with them traditions of craftsmanship and of artistic achievement of the highest order. As a result their architecture, architectural decoration, calligraphy, and textiles became accepted models of excellence. This was true even after the *Reconquista*, or Christian Reconquest, had reclaimed many areas of the peninsula. One example, at the highest level of Christian patronage in Spain, was the burial of the kings and queens at Burgos in clothes fabricated of Mudejar textiles, that is, textiles made by Moors living under Christian rule.[3] Christian clergy also wore vestments made of Islamic silks (figure 1).[4]

Another example of the regard in which Islamic art was held by Christians and Jews is their adoption of Muslim types and forms for their own purposes. The very beautiful stucco work in the Cordoba Synagogue, dated by inscription to 1314/5 (figure 2), is similar to the stucco in the fourteenth-century Convent of Las Duenas in the same city and to fifteenth-century stucco designs in the Alhambra Palace In Granada, which are based on thirteenth-century Nasrid types.[5] Islamic decorative arts also were highly valued. Muslims brought the art of lusterware to Spain, and the ceramics they produced were imitated by both Christians and Jews.[6]

Similar, interwoven cultural relationships existed between the Muslims and Jews of Morocco in the eighteenth and twentieth centuries. (The

Figure 1. Chasuble, Spain, fifteenth century: fragment.

Figure 2. Synagogue, Cordoba, 1314/15: interior.

Christian population of Morocco disappeared at the time of the Arab invasion in the eighth century, with a small Christian element reappearing only with the establishment of foreign protectorates in the nineteenth century.) This paper will explore aspects of *convivencia* in the visual arts of both Spain and Morocco, concentrating on relationships between the dominant artistic culture of Muslims and the arts practiced by the Jewish minority.

The roles of Jewish artists and artisans in Morocco are matters of recent memory and easy to reconstruct. They specialized in metal-smithing, jewelry, the weaving of gold cloth, and the fabrication of gold thread, braid, and ribbons. It is more difficult to understand the place of Jewish artisans in Spain. Aside from illuminated manuscripts and wedding contracts, only 11 works can be attributed to Jewish ownership in Iberia, and their authorship is uncertain.[7] All date from the last three centuries of Jewish life on the peninsula when the *Reconquista* was in full swing. The written records referring to Jewish artists are all from the Christian north. For example, those from the archives of the Kingdom of Aragon record names of Jewish silversmiths and painters of retables for Spanish churches.[8]

The Aragonese archives also document the existence of a synagogue of silversmiths in the city of Saragossa, which implies that Jewish silversmiths and goldsmiths were particularly numerous there.[9] Papal bulls forbade Jewish goldsmiths and silversmiths to manufacture church vessels such as crucifixes, sure evidence that Jews were actively producing Christian ceremonial art.[10] A responsum of Rabbi Solomon ibn Adret (1235-1310) provides evidence for the participation of Jewish women as weavers in the artistic life of medieval Spain.[11]

Written accounts of Jewish artistic activity under Islamic rule come from Jewish sources: one is the Cairo Genizah, a repository of discarded texts found in the Ben Ezra Synagogue in Fustat. Most of these documents date from the eighth to eleventh centuries and stem from the Islamic countries in the Mediterranean littoral and the Fertile Crescent. An eleventh-century receipt for a shipment of various types of rugs from Cairo to Kairouan includes the earliest mention of prayer rugs (*sajjada*).[12] Jewish familiarity with this Muslim art form may have inspired their adaptation as synagogue furnishings. A fourteenth-century responsum of Asher ben Jehiel[13] tells of congregants in a Toledo synagogue who hung prayer rugs with images of the *Kah'ba* on either side of the Torah ark (figure 3).[14] After a discussion of the iconography of the works and the function of prayer rugs in Muslim ritual, Rabbi Asher reviews the etymology of the word *sajjada* and concludes that a work made for Muslim worship had no place in a synagogue.

The aesthetic appeal of rugs could not be denied. Another group of congregants asked Asher's son, Judah, if a prayer rug could remain in the

Figure 3. Prayer rug with *Kah'ba*, Western Anatolia, early eighteenth century.

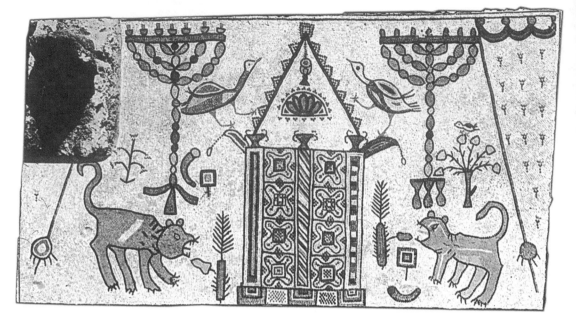

Figure 4. Synagogue mosaic, Spain, fourteenth century.

Figure 5. Synagogue, Beit Alpha, ca. 527: detail of mosaic floor.

synagogue if the central motif were modified and flowers were substituted.[15] The only Jewish rug to survive from medieval Spain is a fourteenth-century example, now in Berlin, whose long narrow shape suggests it was used for sitting, one of the functions of rugs mentioned by Asher ben Jehiel (figure 4).[16]

The main motif, a gabled shrine with horns is unknown in Islamic art, but appears on the mosaic floors of ancient synagogues, for example, at Beit Alpha dedicated ca. 527 (figure 5). Similar portals appear on extant Coptic textiles and in Hebrew manuscripts. Either type of work could have served as a model for the Spanish rug maker.[17] Although the Jews of Spain adopted the art form of the knotted pile carpet, whose techniques and compositions had been developed by their Muslim neighbors, this rug is evidence that they also had developed a specifically Jewish iconography for it.

An interesting question is the relationship between the arts of Morocco and those of Spain during the Middle Ages. The movement of people back and forth between the two countries is well known. The conquest of Spain in 711 was followed by the Almohad invasion of the eleventh century, and that of the Almoravids in the twelfth. Refugees from Spain fled to Morocco with the ascendancy of the Almohads. Perhaps the most famous among the refugees were Maimonides (1138-1204) and his family. The massacres of 1391 led more Jews to escape southward; they were followed by many of those expelled in 1492.

These back and forth migrations had consequences for the artistic development of both countries. One result was the continued use of medieval Spanish textile patterns in the weaves produced by Jews in northern

Morocco, where most of the peninsular refugees settled (figures 6, 7). It is possible that the transmission of patterns was a function of the desire to preserve cultural traditions. However, a reading of sources indicates that Jewish involvement with medieval Spanish textiles went beyond mere use. The responsum of Spanish rabbi Solomon ibn Adret (1235-1310) mentioned above considers the question of whether it was proper for Jewish women in Toledo to be weaving silk textiles whose designs included crosses.

> Those images of crosses that women weave in their silks made for non-Jews should be forbidden. Nevertheless, they can be deemed permissible because non-Jews do not worship their deity in this way. The women make nothing with their looms but designs that are like drawings for aesthetic pleasure....

Although medieval Spanish weaves are well-known in textile literature, the fact that Jewish women were involved in their manufacture is unrecognized. This responsum must be joined to other texts indicating that during the Middle Ages Jews traded textiles throughout the Mediterranean world. Thus, Jews were involved with many aspects of textile production in medieval Spain. It may have been the depth of their experience in the production and marketing of these luxury silks that facilitated the transfer of specific patterns to Morocco.

Other types of works made in Spain were shipped to North Africa. There is a famous instance of the preservation of a major example of medieval Spanish marquetry, in Morocco. An inlaid mosque pulpit or *minbar* that was commissioned from craftsmen in Cordoba by the Almoravid sultan Ali ibn Usuf ibn (r.1106-42) for the Kutubiyya Mosque he built in Marrakesh is preserved in Morocco (figure 8).[18] It is an intricate example of the art of inlay that was created out of wood and ivory. Along the sides, strapwork

Figure 6 (above). Textile, Spain, fifteenth century.

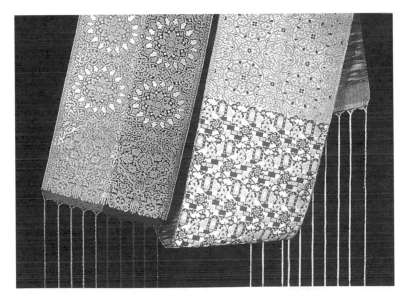

Figure 7. Belt, Fez, nineteenth-twentieth century.

bands separate intricately inlaid small panels. The risers of the staircase are inlaid to form arcades of horseshoe arches, and the sides of each step were once surmounted by finials. This superb example of marquetry may have been modeled on the *minbar* made for the Great Mosque in Cordoba in the tenth century that was destroyed in the sixteenth century.

Although no patently Jewish-owned marquetry objects are extant, one was depicted in the Barcelona Haggadah, an illuminated manuscript of the second quarter of the fourteenth century.[19] In a genre scene preceding the main text, a congregation is shown in a synagogue venerating a Torah scroll, which has been raised by the sexton, who is standing on a *minbar*-type platform (figure 9). The scroll is contained in a rigid cylindrical case

Figure 8. Kutubiyye Mosque, Marrakesh, 1125: *minbar* (after Al-Andalus)

known as a *tik*, which appears to be composed of wood and ivory squares inlaid in a checkerboard pattern. The adoption of a type of decoration developed by Islamic artists for a specifically Jewish object, the cylindrical case for the Torah scroll, is an interesting example of *convivencia*.

This particular type, the cylindrical book box of inlaid wood, had an interesting afterlife in the Ottoman Empire. In 1492 the Jews were expelled from Spain. Their gold and silver were confiscated, including those of synagogues. Ceremonial textiles were burned to extract the bullion from metallic embroideries. But the Jews were allowed to leave with their manuscripts, including Torah scrolls. Many emigrated to the Ottoman Empire, whose Sultan Bayezid (1481-1512) "took pity on them, and wrote letters and sent emissaries to proclaim throughout his kingdom that none of his city rulers may...refuse entry to the Jews or expel them. Instead, they were to be given a gracious welcome...."

During the late fifteenth and sixteenth centuries numerous Jews had daily contact with the Ottoman court as physicians. One of the earliest was Yakub Hekim, who served Mehmed II (1451-81) as chief physician of the palace. Moses Hamon (1490-1554) served both as doctor and diplomat to Sultans Selim I (1512-20) and Suleyman the Magnificent (1520-66). Joseph of Naxos (d. 1579) became a diplomat and governor under Selim II (1566-74). Another group of Jews having access to the court were vendors such as Esther Kyra, who exerted political influence during the reigns of Suleyman the Magnificent, Selim II, and Murad III by virtue of her relationships with women of the harem.

The Jews who immigrated to the Ottoman Empire brought with them the knowledge of technologies hitherto unknown in the Sultans' realm. The manufacture of cannons and gunpowder, the art of printing, and new

Figure 9. "Synagogue Scene," Barcelona Haggadah.

techniques for manufacturing textiles are three examples. Might not the Sephardim who came to Istanbul have brought with them examples of wood inlay, which had become a highly developed art form in Spain? The inlaid *tik* known from the Barcelona Haggadah could explain the sudden appearance of a new form of Koran box in Istanbul at the beginning of the sixteenth century: a polygonal container with a domed top, all of inlaid wood. The first was made for Bayezid in 1505/6 to house an early 30-volume Koran (figure 10).[20]

Sultans of the sixteenth century followed suit, commissioning polygonal inlaid Koran boxes with domed tops for their religious foundations. No need to postulate foreign sources for

Figure 10. Koran box of Sultan Bayezid, Maker: Ahmed b. Hasan Kâllibî, Istanbul, 1505/06.

the new combination of form and technique; the models may have been close at hand in the inlaid wood *tikim* brought from Spain. Based on similar occurrences between Jews and their rulers elsewhere, one might speculate that the Spanish refugees paraded a Torah in its case before Bayezid. The result was the transmission of a new form of book case from medieval Iberia to an Ottoman Empire poised on the threshold of a century of greatness in the arts.

This example of Spanish artistic influence on the Ottoman empire is clear-cut. In contrast, the direction of influence is not at all clear when considering the arts of Spain and Morocco. Arcades of horseshoe arches, to cite but one example, define the naves of thirteenth-century synagogues in Toledo and Segovia, but these arcades appear in twelfth-century North African mosques and the later, mud-built synagogues of southern Morocco.[21] Was this building type taken to Spain by its Arab conquerors or brought from Spain by refugees?

Convivencia in Spain ended with the fall of Granada and the expulsion of the Jews in 1492. The highly educated and technically skilled Sephardi refugees enriched the native Jewish communities of the Ottoman Empire and North Africa. In these realms Jews and Muslims lived together until the mid-twentieth century. The partnership was not an equal one, but under the conditions defined by ruling Muslims acting in accord with the Koran, Jewish minorities were creative artists and artisans. ■

Notes

1 T. Glick, "*Convivencia*: An Introductory Note," in V. B. Mann, T. F. Glick, and J. D. Dodds, *Convivencia: Jews, Muslim and Christians in Medieval Spain* (New York: George Braziller, 1992), 1-2.

2 "*Convivencia*: An Introductory Note."

3 C. H. Carretero, *Museo de Telas Medievales: Monasterio de Santa María La Real de Huelgas* (Madrid: Editorial Patrimonio Nacional, 1984).

4 On this fragment of a chasuble see *Convivencia*, cat. no. 109.

5   J. D. Dodds, "Mudejar Tradition and the Synagogues of Medieval Spain: Cultural Identity and Cultural Hegemony," Convivencia, 122.

6   Convivencia, cat. nos. 78 and 86, figure 66.

7   V. B. Mann, "Sephardi Ceremonial Art: Continuity in the Diaspora," in Crisis and Creativity in the Sephardic World 1391-1648, ed. B. Gampel (New York: Columbia University Press, 1997), 282-91.

8   A. B. Martínez, "Pintores y Orfebres Judiós en Zaragoza (Siglo XIV)," Aragón en la Edad Media (Saragossa: 1989).

9   A. B. Martínez, La judería de Zaragoza en el Siglo XIV (Saragossa: 1988), 162.

10 S. Grayzel, The Church and the Jews in the Thirteenth Century, ed. K. R. Stow (New York and Detroit: The Jewish Theological Seminary and Wayne State University Press, 1989), 276, 280-82.

11 S. ibn Adret, Teshuvot uShe'alot le-haRashba (Rome, 1470).

12 R. Ettinghausen, "The Early History, Use and Iconography of the Prayer Rug," in Prayer Rugs, exhibition catalogue (Washington, D.C.: The Textile Museum, 1974-75), 15.

13 Asher ben Jehiel emigrated from Germany to Toledo in 1304, served as the community's principal rabbi, and died there in 1327.

14 A. ben Jehiel, She'elot uTeshuvot le-haRav Rabeinu Asher (New York: 1954), vol. V:2.

15 J. ben Asher, Zikhron Yehudah (Jerusalem: 1972), no. 21.

16 Convivencia, cat. no. 107.

17 For a Coptic textile with the image of a portal with paneled door see L. Woolley, "Pagan, Classical, Christian," Hali 48 (1989), 29, and figure 9; for the manuscript see B. Narkiss, Hebrew Illuminated Manuscripts (Jerusalem: Encyclopedia Judaica and the Macmillan Company, 1969), pl. 1a.

18 See Al-Andalus, cat. no. 115.

19 On the manuscript see B. Narkiss, Hebrew Illuminated Manuscripts in the British Library (Oxford and Jerusalem: Oxford University Press, 1989), cat. no. 13.

20 For other examples see F. Cagman, The Anatolian Civilisations III: Seljuk/Ottoman (Istanbul: Turkish Ministry of Culture and Tourism, 1983), cat. nos. E19, E75-76, E147-50.

21 Dodds, "Mudejar Tradition and the Synagogues of Medieval Spain," 116-18.

Russian orthodox church, Novgorod, Russia.

Sacred Places and Historic Cities: Preservation Governance and Practicalities

46

N on-built sacred sites are an extremely important subject to which sufficient attention has not been paid. I will consider sacred sites in the context of historic cities.

On the World Heritage List more than 100 sites are historic cities, and perhaps more than 200 are sacred places. It is amazing to acknowledge that these two categories are so widely represented, as if they are at the very core of the notion of cultural heritage, at the roots of people's identity, and at the basis of the definition of any culture.

The visible differences between historic cities and sacred places are length (large/small), components (complex/simple), function (secular/spiritual life), and status (profane/sacred). However, beyond these differences are deep ties that bind them, specificities that make them different from other categories of properties and to which special attention must be paid when we have to preserve or restore them.

For more than 30 years the United Nations Educational, Scientific, and Cultural Organisation (UNESCO) has contributed significantly to activities designed to safeguard historic cities. UNESCO has endeavored to link the restoration of monuments to the revitalization of historic urban centers as well as to safeguard and restore different kinds of sacred monuments.

Many on the long list of UNESCO international safeguarding campaigns have addressed historic cities and sacred places. Examples include the City of Venice (figure 1), the monuments and temples of Nubia, the Stupa of Borobodur, the temples of Sukhothaï, the Medina of Fez, the

Laurent Lévi-Strauss

Laurent Lévi-Strauss is deputy director of the Division of Cultural Heritage, UNESCO, L.Levi-Strauss@unesco.org

Figure 1. Venice, one of the world's most popular tourist destinations and a World Heritage Site: view of the canal and a row of vernacular architecture that has been preserved.

Old City of Sana'a, the megalithic temples in Malta, and the Jesuit missions of the Guaranís in Argentina, Brazil, and Paraguay.

Recently, UNESCO also intervened for restoration work in the Great Mosque in the Old City of Sana'a; in the Synagogue Ibn Danan in Fez; and, thanks to the generosity of the Japanese Government, in Probota Monastery in Romania.

Today historic urban complexes are faced with acute problems of physical conservation, internal equilibrium, and functioning. Studies have highlighted the indisputable link at the design and planning and the implementation stages between two fundamental tasks. These tasks are the preservation of the urban and architectural heritage, and the development of the economic and social life of the city. Both are needed to facilitate the balanced management of the built area and ensure not only the material foundations of a decent standard of living for the population but also the integrity of the historic fabric.

Reconciling the location of historic cities or quarters and sacred sites with the demands of urban development represents a major challenge. My focus in this chapter is one aspect of the governance for preservation that appears to UNESCO as important, based on our experiences around the world.

A main error in urban restoration and rehabilitation projects, which occurs too often, is the temptation to apply imported models to urban identities of another culture.

Over 100 historic cities and urban centers have so far been recognized on the World Heritage List. However, this all-embracing term, "historic urban center," covers a wide range of specific cases, each with its own distinct identity. These identities are even more dissimilar than the cultures and forms of urban life that have created them. It would be simplistic and extremely dangerous to take the view that certain models or processes of conservation, restoration, or rehabilitation can be universally applied, and that approaches that have produced desirable results in some cases can be equally successful at all these differing sites.

During the 1930s the Chicago School of Sociology, which had a leading role in the development of urban studies, said that each city is a kind of "state of mind" for its inhabitants. Sacred places, by definition, also bear a sort of state of mind.

The existence of this "state of mind" requires from us particular caution and special attention before undertaking any kind of intervention. Historic cities and sacred sites cannot be addressed by merely adding functionalities: the means with which to live, to work, to rest, to learn, to enjoy, or to pray. These quotidian needs could be enhanced simply by providing such facilities as water, electricity, and sewerage. With these two categories of cultural properties, however, the whole is much larger than the sum of the parts.

Historic cities and sacred places are not only built by human beings but also experienced by them. Beyond their functions, they can survive only if the ways of life, values, norms, and representations that they bear are also respected (figure 2).

The local experience requires an original complex composed of the urban forms themselves and their very strong images in the minds of their inhabitants. These images are the reason that an inhabitant can be so closely attached to all of his or her city's elements and their articulation, which are linked to all the individual's daily movements.

Figure 2. Gate to the *souk*, Fez *Medina*.
The cultural center is also a vibrant commercial and tourist destination.

One of the bases of a collective identity is the "visible character of the
place," understood as concrete evidence of the representations and projections that it needs to see itself existing.

This visible character of place presents a challenge for the local society
but also for the external society. If the latter wants to seek inside the
historic city or a sacred place a sort of organized and constructed vision
of culture, it must allow the inhabitants to take care of the historic city
or sacred place and delicately adapt it to socioeconomic evolutions.

It is artificial to try to separate a building from its environment because the
building belongs to its environment, structures it, and gives it life. The continuum between building area and urban zone must not be ruptured; otherwise, the historic structure loses its coherence as well as its authenticity.

The context and values of restoration of sacred places are much more
specific than the technical work to carry out such restoration. There is

no difference in the skills and techniques to restore a church, a mosque, a Buddhist temple, or a historic house or a castle. In 1998 when we wanted to restore an old synagogue in Fez, we hired the same team of craftsmen specialized in sculpted plaster and mosaics who had carried out the restoration of the Dar Adyel Palace. For the structural restoration of the great mosque of Sana'a, we used the team of civil engineers who previously had worked on historic houses.

The main differences between the restoration of a sacred and a secular site are the question of ownership of the property and the attitude of the community of local believers. These two differences are also often the source of difficulties regarding sacred sites.

When we have to restore a palace, a castle, or an archeological site, the property generally belongs to the national state or the municipality. Under these conditions intervention generally is not difficult. However, sacred sites still active generally belong to a religious entity; for example, in the Muslim world to the *Waqf*, or sometimes, as in the case of the Ibn Danan synagogue in Fez, to numerous members of the large family who have inherited the building. These situations can sometimes dramatically complicate obtaining the agreement of all stakeholders.

For example, in the case of the recent restoration of the Ibn Danan synagogue, which was made possible by the generous contribution of the Danan family itself and the World Monument Fund, UNESCO had to set up an agreement involving the representatives of the Danan family, the Directorate for Cultural Heritage of the Moroccan Ministry of Cultural Affairs, the Council of Jewish Communities, the community of Fez, and the Judeo-Moroccan Heritage Foundation. As usual, the role of UNESCO was to assume responsibility for the scientific management of the restoration and to guarantee the safeguarding of the monument's authenticity.

In the case of the extensive ongoing campaign to restore the Angkor temple complex in Cambodia, the issue is no longer the character of sacred places—some of the temples are still in use. Rather, challenges arise due to the size of the site, the number and importance of the buildings, and the number of partners willing to cooperate in this huge, long restoration project. For this purpose UNESCO has set up an International Coordination Committee, co-chaired by Japan and France, which ensures good coordination of the activities and use of the funds provided by the numerous donors, which include countries as well as nongovernmental organizations (NGOs).

In the case of a well-known site such as Angkor, the question addressed to UNESCO is not only to coordinate works and funding and to ensure the scientific quality of the works using internationally known experts. It is also to address issues such as tourism development, hotel construction, establishment of a master plan, and zoning for the development of the site. In other words UNESCO's tasks include all of the protective measures that have to be set up parallel to the restoration work itself. Prevention of archeological looting and illicit trade are at the core of UNESCO's priorities.

Another difficulty encountered in the restoration of sacred places is the attitude of the local believers. In certain situations the believers are full of goodwill to safeguard and want to restore their sacred sites by themselves. However, as they have no knowledge about what the restoration of a historic building is and what is required for the preservation of the authenticity of the monument, they themselves sometimes spoil the integrity of the monument instead of preserving it.

We have, unfortunately, a long list of sacred places that have been irreparably damaged by the use of concrete, the replacement of original sculpted elements by new ones, and the inappropriate use of adornment, such as marble. It is here that we encounter one of the major difficulties in preserving authenticity in historic buildings, because sacred places are also living places in which people worship.

In Europe, as elsewhere, even the minimal cohesion essential for all social life is under threat. Some of the causes of this loosening of social bounds are unfortunately too easy to identify. They are to be found in the creation of public spaces that are devoted almost entirely to traffic and parking and offer no opportunity for the normal development of social life and citizenship. These automobile-focused public spaces negate the past and a place's identity. They stem directly from a *tabula rasa* approach that ignores history, forms of social organization, ways of life, and their symbolic representation in the physical world, as well as from the destruction of the collective memory that they contain. They originate in the failure of a functionalist and technocratic approach to urban planning to recognize the cultural distinctiveness of different communities, and in the attempt to impose the same norms, values, and standardized solutions everywhere.

Instead, we need to seek solutions that are the very opposite to this negation of place, to this concept of space both anemic and amnesiac, based on the principle of a supposed universal rationality. However, experience shows that the success of any urban development project is due primarily to the fact that its guidelines are drawn from the specific circumstances of the place in question and that it rejects *a priori* solutions and favors an empirical approach rooted in concrete reality rather than one based on deduction and abstraction.

Conclusion

From a purely technical point of view I would like to stress that there is no specificity or universal formula for the restoration of sacred sites in an urban context. The primary challenge is to address the intangible values that the site represents for the local population. These sites very often enshrine a large part of the cultural identity of a local group. Thus, the attention that must be given to them is much broader than the technical aspect alone.

As for the historic city itself, the sacred places bear norms, values, representations, and identity for the local population. There are no ready-made, universally applicable formulas to preserve and restore them. On the contrary the need is to study and understand each situation as a unique one, with specific solutions and ways to do the job. This necessity confirms that our work is not only technical but also fully belongs to the social and human sciences.

The urban societies of the twenty-first century will be able to survive only if they continue to find ways to develop and function within a framework of common references, that draw not only on their social diversity but also, and perhaps mainly, on the depth of the cultural memory contained within each city itself. At a time when social diversity is everywhere leading to fragmentation, it is only this cultural memory that will maintain the indispensable social bonds that enable a mosaic of people with different origins and cultures, and of different generations, to live together. ■

Standing stelae, Axum, Ethipia.

Part VIII

Partnerships in Action

Editors' Note

The authors examine practical experiences in which myriad multilateral agencies, nongovernmental organizations (NGOs), local and national governments, and communities have worked together to protect historic cities and heritage. A common thread is the quest to integrate skills and resources into collaborative action to preserve built heritage and promote cultural diversity in a sustainable manner.

Lawrence Hannah describes a new strategic partnering approach adopted for the post-conflict reconciliation and peace efforts in Bosnia-Herzegovina. The efforts to rebuild the old town and the bridge—built in the fifteenth century— were integrated with a long-term concern for lasting peace and sustainable preservation management of the common heritage. Hannah describes how the partnership, which included the local community, national and regional governments, UNESCO, the Aga Khan Trust for Culture, World Monuments Funds, the World Bank, and bilateral donors, was formed. The International Committee of Experts, organized by UNESCO, continues to provide local and national authorities with technical assistance for the reconstruction.

Eduardo Rojas looks at private sector involvement in recent revitalization efforts in select historic cities in Latin America. He draws lessons from preservation projects executed with assistance from the Inter-American Development Bank in Cartagena, Colombia; Recife, Brazil; Quito, Ecuador; and Montevideo, Uruguay. Rojas asserts that attracting the private sector to the domain of preservation of historic centers hinges upon strong public leadership, willingness of the public sector to provide a stable regulatory environment, and the commitment for a long-term and significant public investment program. To remedy the short supply of long-term financing and managerial capacity in the region, appropriate reforms and institutional development are needed. Rojas concludes with the examination of public and private roles in historic center preservation.

Harold Williams stresses the need for the incorporation of a cultural dimension in the sustainable development paradigm. We have only recently come to understand the need to preserve historic city centers for their human dimension. The conservation of historic centers is a collective obligation that compels us to understand tradition and cultural diversity and to combat a sense of transience, lack of belonging, or lack of community. The author describes the collaboration of the Getty Conservation Institute with urban conservation plans in Quito, Ecuador, and in Ouro Preto, Brazil. Sustainable development was understood not only in the economic sense but also was integrated with the cultural dimension. Williams concludes that in a globalized economy, the distinctness of a given place —its character, history and culture—assumes greater significance in attracting both financial and human investment.

Marilyn Perry looks at corporate support provided for cultural heritage preservation. There are no replacements for the unique sites on the World Heritage Watch list; yet cultural sites and heritage monuments suffer from neglect, natural disasters, mismanagement, excessive development, mass tourism, and armed conflict. With limited funding and expertise, we are forced to ask: What is to be saved? How? What roles should different actors play? Perry describes the pioneer role played by the Kress Foundation, and later by the World Monuments Fund, in granting funds for the conservation of endangered heritage. The WMF has effectively mobilized and encouraged corporate partnerships, and generated well over US$30 million for the conservation of endangered heritage sites and monuments, thus becoming a vital tool in the struggle to protect our cultural legacy.

In spite of a hostile legal and fiscal environment that provides no tax incentives, private individuals and corporations invested nearly US$200 million for development of culture in Spain in 1998. According to Luis Monreal's chapter on corporate contributions for culture, foundations invested an additional US$350 million in cultural, scientific, and environmental programs in the same year. Monreal describes the activities of Fundación la Caixa of Barcelona and its partnerships with the public sector in organizing the 1992 Olympics. He also highlights the remarkably successful impact on the revitalization of the old industrial center that the construction of the Guggenheim Museum Bilbao has had.

The Partnership for Mostar

47

Lawrence M. Hannah

Lawrence M. Hannah is an economist at the World Bank and has worked more than 20 years in urban development; he leads the World Bank's Mostar Cultural Heritage Project.

The city of Mostar, whose name means "bridge-keeper," was an established community at a strategic crossing of the Neretva River before the Ottoman conquest of Bosnia-Herzegovina nearly 500 years ago.i It was, however, the construction of what became known as Stari Most, the Old Bridge (1557-66), by the order of Sultan Suleyman the Magnificent that secured the city's economic importance and came to symbolize the area's long-term stability. According to records, the bridge replaced an earlier wooden structure. The Old Bridge was built between two existing medieval towers but in a style and scale that reflected the riches of the Ottoman state and the Sultan's desire to spread Islamic culture and architecture (figure 1).

The Old Bridge soon became the anchor for urban development in Mostar. However, this entire area of the city with its distinct ethnic neighborhoods and architectural icons in such close proximity represents the historic coexistence of this society. The prosperity of the period when the bridge was built accelerated the creation of the rich urban fabric of Mostar, including many of the lasting physical features of the city. Alongside the existing towers and military fortifications, the bridge became the focus for the bazaar which, together with other public and religious buildings, created a commercial center that has endured until today.

The durability and prominence of the bridge in the historic core came to symbolize the multicultural environment of Mostar in which all major religious communities co-existed. Shared history and culture were reflected in the shared neighborhoods and symbols. The war in the 1990s, however, reminded us of the fragility of these arrangements and the difficulty in rebuilding them.

As much as Mostar had been a symbol of harmony and tolerance before, the recent war demonstrated all of the opposite characteristics of the city. Mostar's people and economy suffered disproportionately. Industrial production fell to only a fraction of pre-war levels. Unemployment became and remains high. Living standards have been dramatically

Figure 1. This sixteenth-century stone bridge linked the steep banks of the Neretva River until its destruction in 1993, Mostar.

reduced. The destruction of the bridge on November 9, 1993 under-scored the intense animosity and length that partisans would go to inflict damage on each other. Even when the peace agreement was signed in 1994, Mostar remained a divided city because of the passions both Bosniaks and Bosnian Croats felt for the city (figure 2).

The signing of the Dayton Accord in 1995 laid the groundwork for sta-bility in Bosnia-Herzegovina and in Mostar. By June 1996, all local res-idents (including absent refugees) participated in elections for a unified municipal government in Mostar, where an elected Bosnian Croat and a Bosniak alternate in the post of mayor and deputy mayor. Almost five years later, today there is a local government in Mostar in which the leaders act in unison on behalf of all Mostarians, not as representatives of their own ethnic or religious factions.

The political changes made possible the Mostar project. In 1996 the elected bipartisan local government cooperated with local and interna-tional institutions to generate a reliable professional network and a sound agenda for revitalization of the historic core of Mostar. On this foundation the present partnership and project were built.

In its strategy to assist Bosnia-Herzegovina, the World Bank highlight-ed the need to move from a program based on post-conflict recon-struction to one that supports sustainable growth. World Bank president James D. Wolfensohn, linked well these two ideas in his remarks to the Symposium on Preserving the Architecture of Historic Cities and Sacred

Figure 2. Temporary bridge over Neretva River, Mostar, 1999 photo.

Places, held in Washington, D.C. in 1999: "...I kept trying to say to my colleagues that if [we] are talking about building international architecture, it has to be built on structure, on governance, on justice, on legal systems, on social systems, but it also has to be built on history and culture."

The objective of the project supported by the World Bank and others is to improve the climate for reconciliation among the peoples in Bosnia-Herzegovina by recognizing and rehabilitating their common cultural heritage in Mostar. Reconciliation among the peoples is a clear prerequisite for economic revitalization and social cohesion in post-conflict Bosnia-Herzegovina. This strategy determines all aspects of the project: the choice of physical components, the implementation method, and the way the supporters of the project work together. By promoting reconciliation and mutual respect for a common heritage, the project attempts to reinforce prospects for a lasting peace, which is a prerequisite for any form of sustainability. This objective has created and inspired a unique cultural support partnership that includes the local community, national and regional governments, individual bilateral donors, UNESCO, the World Monuments Fund (WMF), the Aga Khan Trust for Culture (AKTC), and the World Bank.

World Bank support for the project was approved in 1999. The project includes reconstruction of the Old Bridge including the Tara and Halebija Towers, restoration of selected monuments in the historic district of the city, and preservation of the old town's historic character through a series of neighborhood initiatives including the adoption of architectural guidelines. The bridge complex was chosen as the centerpiece of the project because it represents the historic core of Mostar and is a symbol of the multicultural heritage all three peoples of Bosnia-Herzegovina.

Admired for its technical perfection and beauty, the bridge is considered an architectural masterpiece. It consists of one stone arch with a span of about 30 meters at a height above river with a low water of approximately 20 meters. Tenelija, a local limestone, was the main building material, and the only fasteners in the bridge were internal iron clamps held in place by poured lead once the stones were in place. Under the reconstruction project the decision was taken to produce an exact copy of the original bridge with stone from the original quarry.

To promote a more strategic development of the city, the monuments component of the project pays attention to the overall plan for the old city in addition to supporting the rehabilitation and adaptive reuse of damaged monuments and historic buildings. It accomplishes the former through preparation of an overall plan as well as regulations and guidelines for the preservation and restoration of structures in this area. A forward-looking scheme for maintenance and management of the old city has also been developed. During the project donors are asked to consider supporting monuments from a list of about 15 damaged structures in historic areas on both sides of the river that have been identified as pilots under the project (figure 3). The neighborhood component attempts to preserve the historical character of the old town through a series of local investment initiatives in infrastructure and public spaces as well as through the adoption of regulations for this quarter of the city.

The partners for Mostar did not wait to start working on these issues until the World Bank decided to provide loan funding. In fact, all three principal partners were already long active in Mostar on related individual programs. In 1997 AKTC in partnership with WMF created a field office in Mostar staffed with Bosnian professionals who prepared restoration plans for the old city. With their own funding they restored a number of structures and organized broad planning exercises between foreign professionals and the local community to build awareness of and consensus on what needed to be done. AKTC/WMF also trained a team of local craftspersons to be able to work according to international technical standards.

UNESCO had taken a particular interest in the bridge and had already drawn international attention to its importance in this historic city. In 1997 it prepared a rehabilitation plan for the Old Town that was adopted by the City Council in 2000. UNESCO is restoring several important monuments in the Old Town area, included the Crooked Bridge over the Radobolje, traditionally regarded as the model for the Old Bridge. UNESCO played a particularly important role in organizing an International Committee of Experts (ICE), who have met five times in

Figure 3. Aerial view of old-town Mostar. At the center the temporary bridge over Neretva River and on both margins damaged stone structures.

Mostar to review and make recommendations on the restoration process of the bridge complex.

The decision to support a major effort such as reconstruction of the bridge became the opportunity for all actors to work together. Coordination and synergy were the major reasons for this collaboration, but it also created a critical mass for these efforts to maintain and strengthen programs and to attract new support to the project. In fact, the European Commission and the governments of Italy, the Netherlands, and Turkey already have made major donations. Nevertheless, significant additional support is still required to complete the project.

As mentioned, the partnership in this case serves several purposes:

• It recognizes and integrates the ongoing efforts of several agencies that were already working on preserving the Mostar's cultural heritage.

• It makes use of the relationships and contacts of all partners in publicizing and seeking support for the project. A common fundraising campaign is in place.

• It uses the special talents of each partner to guide the implementation of the project.

A special feature related to the last point is the role that the UNESCO-organized ICE plays in safeguarding the technical and historical integrity of the reconstruction of the bridge and towers. The partners work closely with a Project Coordination Unit (PCU), which represents the city on all aspects of the project and professionally interacts with the partners and the community. In fact, the PCU has become a model of how cultural heritage of the city need not turn into ethnic heritage of any one group. A special feature of the partnership is that it makes more funding opportunities available to potential supporters: support can be given directly to the city, to any of the partners, or through the World Bank in trust for use on any project component.

Despite some delays in getting started, the project has progressed well since the World Bank loan became available. The main preparation activities for the bridge and towers component have been to investigate the condition of the destroyed bridge, to assess the materials used and available for construction, and to produce a design that can be used to solicit tenders from builders to reconstruct the bridge. One of the first actions was to recover the bridge's original stones from the water. This was done by the NATO Stability Force (S-FOR). Tests on these stones revealed a rich story about the construction of the bridge 500 years ago, including proof of where the stones were quarried and physical evidence of exactly which tools were used to cut them. More importantly, the tests enabled the investigators to better understand how and why the bridge was built as it was. Unfortunately, the examination of the stones from the river led to the conclusion that few if any could be used in their original position in the reconstructed bridge due to both physical and water damage.

The challenge of the investigation has been to understand and prepare remedial actions for damage from both the destruction of the war and from almost 500 years of weather and erosion. Special geological and materials investigations of the foundations and the remaining portions of the bridge have revealed how both questions need to be addressed. The materials under and behind the foundations will be stabilized, while special underwater walls and reinforcements will be built to protect against future river erosion. The original design of the bridge was exactly replicated by a process known as photogrammetric studies and by structural calculations that permit known measurements to be combined with previous studies and pictures to form a complete and fully detailed modern specification of the bridge.

All of these activities are coming together in the form of final designs and bidding documents, which will permit contracts to be tendered for the bridge and towers. Present scheduling suggests that the foundations are to be built during the summer of 2001. The main span of the bridge should be constructed during the following summer. The two towers should also be completed by the time the bridge is finished. Along with the monuments and neighborhood components this symbol of the cultural revival of Mostar is expected to support reconciliation in Bosnia-Herzegovina.

To sum up, the support for cultural heritage represents not only a new method for the World Bank to support its clients' development objectives but also a new and effective model for donors to work together. ■

Revitalization of Historic Cities with Private Sector Involvement: Lessons from Latin America

48

C reating an enabling environment for private-sector involvement in historic preservation in Latin America and the Caribbean poses several challenges.[1] Nonetheless, in the 1990s the Inter-American Development Bank (IADB) approved several loans in this field in response to a growing interest among clients, particularly some municipalities, in investing in the preservation of urban heritage sites.

The countries of Latin America and the Caribbean possess a rich urban heritage, including historic cities. These settlements retain their original structure, monuments, and residential architecture representing specific periods in the evolution of urban construction.

Heritage is embedded in the urban structure, that is, in the street layout and land-use patterns that remain to this day and the magnificent public spaces in which many important events of the countries' histories took place. Impressive monuments synthesize many cultural influences— notably, architectural styles fashionable in Spain and Portugal and the construction techniques and decorative styles of indigenous cultures. Most important is the use-value of historic centers, which contain commercial and domestic buildings from different phases of city growth that can be returned to full use and represent valuable capital.

This heritage is deteriorating very rapidly. The causes are well known: rapid population growth and the horizontal expansion of cities that has pushed development to the fringes and emptied historic centers of activity. Abandonment leads quickly to deterioration.

Eduardo Rojas

Eduardo Rojas is an architect and principal urban development specialist, Sustainable Development Department, Inter-American Development Bank, Eduardoro@iadb.org

Rapid urban growth also changed the way public spaces are used. Although abandoned by wealthier residents and most dynamic economic activities, the historic centers of many Latin American cities retain importance for low-income populations, who use the deteriorating buildings and public spaces for residential and service purposes. Moreover, modern transportation makes intense use of the narrow colonial streets, contributing to pollution and the deterioration of buildings.

Notwithstanding this bleak picture, there are signs of hope. Communities are increasingly concerned about preserving their urban heritage and are promoting conservation efforts. Governments are increasingly assuming responsibility for promoting and financing preservation. Three phases can be distinguished in the evolution of concern for urban heritage preservation in the region.

Three Phases of Preservation

The first phase is often characterized by pressure from cultural elites for preservation legislation, resulting mostly in isolated interventions to benefit specific monuments financed by private philanthropists. Most preserved buildings are devoted to public uses—a strategy that often leads to unsustainable conservation. Significant investment is often made in the same buildings over and over again, due to lack of maintenance and inappropriate use (figure 1).

Figure 1. Salvador, Largo de São Francisco, Brazil. Public sector investment rehabilitated public spaces, monuments, and residences in the Pelourinho, the historic center of the city.

Latin America is now involved in a second phase of preservation, in which governments are assuming responsibility for conservation. National and municipal governments are adopting a leading role. They not only are improving legislation but also are establishing public institutions to deal with conservation and allocating public resources for conservation work. This government involvement creates a host of new problems, mostly related to lack of continuity of conservation efforts due to budgetary constraints and the volatility of public resources. Nevertheless, despite its limitations, this phase has brought about significant conservation programs that have preserved part of the region's urban heritage.

The IADB's major policy concern is that the conservation process, as currently organized and financed, is not sustainable in the long term and represents a heavy burden on public-sector budgets already strained by the need to solve the problems of poverty.

The IADB would like to see the region move toward a third stage in the conservation process, in which the preservation of historic heritage becomes the concern of the whole community, including the private sector. To this end good enabling legislation must be enacted, and fruitful collaboration between the public and private sectors encouraged. The long-term sustainability of urban heritage preservation will be achieved when buildings and public spaces are being used properly, and all social actors are collaborating in this endeavor.

The IADB has developed strategic approaches to promote sustainable urban heritage preservation in Latin America. To better visualize the development potential of these approaches and understand the problems they raise, two projects follow that demonstrate the IADB's approaches in action. The objective of these IADB-financed projects is to propel urban heritage conservation into the third stage of development described above: involvement of all social actors. This objective is complemented by the idea of integrality: urban heritage preservation must be part of the recycling of the areas in which historic monuments are located and be a component of the efforts to inject new dynamism into historic centers.

Incentivizing the Private Sector

The use of heritage as a catalyst for urban rehabilitation is attempted in these projects by promoting regulations and incentives for the private sector to undertake much of the work, that is, by creating the enabling environment. To identify the conditions under which the private sector engages in urban heritage reservation, we investigated a few cases in the region in which this has taken place, or is occurring now (tables 1, 2).

Table 1. Theoretical public–private relationships in historic center preservation

Preservation activities		Free market		Incentives		Association		Public intervention	
		Public	Private	Public	Private	Public	Private	Public	Private
Private functions	Building management								
	Marketing								
	Building rehabilitation								
	Financing								
	Land consolidation								
	Economic development								
Private functions	Direct subsidies								
	Tax incentives								
	Preservation of heritage sites								
	Improvement of public spaces								
	Improvements of infrastructure								
	Revitalization plans								
	Preservation regulations								

Source: E. Rojas, *Old Cities, New Assets: Preserving Latin America's Urban Heritage* (Washington-Baltimore: Johns Hopkins University Press for the IADB, 1999), 34.

Table 2. Actual public–private relationships

Preservation activities		Cartagena		Recife		Quito		Salvador	
		Public	Private	Public	Private	Public	Private	Public	Private
Private functions	Building management								
	Building management								
	Marketing								
	Building rehabilitation								
	Financing								
	Land consolidation								
	Economic development								
Private functions	Direct subsidies								
	Tax incentives								
	Preservation of heritage sites								
	Improvement of public spaces								
	Improvements of infrastructure								
	Revitalization plans								
	Preservation regulations								

Source: Rojas, *Old Cities, New Assets,* 35.

Cartagena, Colombia

In Cartagena, Colombia, there has been a convergence of interest among economic and cultural elites in preserving the walled city. The cultural elite is interested in protecting the monuments, while the economic elite seeks to take advantage of restored monuments and public spaces to restore residences and create a privileged environment for vacation and leisure. In Cartagena, public and private preservation activities are completely separate, except for certain tax incentives created for conserving historic buildings (figure 2).

Figure 2. Magnificent privately restored residences line Calle Ricaurte in the core of the historic center in Cartagena, Colombia.

Recife, Brazil

The municipality of Recife in Brazil is promoting private-sector investment in rehabilitating the Bom Jesus area near the port (figures 3, 4). In Recife the public sector undertook private-sector functions such as rehabilitating buildings and marketing them among private tenants to demonstrate the viability of commercial projects in the historic center. A high level of public intervention was a necessity due to the extreme deterioration of the historic center when conservation efforts began (figure 4). The Brazilian city of Salvador da Bahia also has experienced positive public intervention. In its case the public sector has taken total responsibility for preservation efforts. The State Institute for Culture took on the management of rehabilitated buildings along with more traditional public responsibilities such as planning and executing improvements to public spaces. The Institute even organizes cultural events to attract tourists to the historic center.

Figure 3. On Bom Jesus Street in Recife, Brazil, the City Colors project financed by private philanthropy rehabilitated the facades of many buildings helping to eliminate the image of decay and abandonment that the historic center had prior to the rehabilitation program.

Figure 4. Polo Alfândega, a historic center of Recife, Brazil, is part of the *Monumenta* Program, assisted by an Inter-American Development Bank loan.

Quito, Ecuador

An IADB-supported project in Quito, Ecuador, was designed to promote public-private partnerships to rehabilitate the vast stock of historic buildings located in the old city center. The IADB began with a theoretical model of the likely relationship between public and private actors in urban heritage preservation. At one extreme are cases in which there is no direct interaction, and each sector focuses on its specific functions. These cases can be called "free market": the public sector defines the rules and regulations; the private sector undertakes rehabilitation activities. At the other extreme are cases in which, to accelerate the process, the public sector carries out all the functions—from establishing rules and regulations to rehabilitating and selling or renting buildings. Intermediate cases might be those in which the public sector provides subsidies to promote private investment or undertakes investments in partnership with the private sector (figure 5).

Even in Quito, however, where the IADB project was designed to exemplify the best theoretical assignment of responsibility between public and private interventions, this did not occur in practice. The public sector went much further than expected toward investing in the rehabilitation and marketing of buildings to demonstrate the viability of many types of projects and attract private investors.

Public–Private Partnerships

Promoting private investment in historic centers in Latin America requires strong public sector commitment, both to preserving urban heritage and to providing sufficient resources to do so. Public commitment is demonstrated by the ability to design and implement conservation plans and enact conservation legislation that provides a stable regulatory environment for private investment. Another demonstration of public commitment to preservation is sustained investment in infrastructure and improvement of public spaces. Moreover, the public sector must be willing to share some of the risk with the private sector. Public-private partnerships seem to be one way to achieve the latter. The IADB is promoting this approach, taken from a successful experience in Barcelona, Spain, and successfully transferred to the project in Quito.

Figure 5. Independence Square in Quito, Ecuador. Improvements in the public spaces greatly enhance the attractiveness of the historic center for private investors. On the left the Hotel Majestic rehabilitated by the Quito Historic Center Company under a partnership with private hotel operators.

Public-private partnerships enable the public sector to provide comfort to private investors at two distinct levels.

1. Stability of the regulatory environment. Investors always fear the risks associated with entering an area with an unknown future. A good regulatory environment gives them some level of comfort.

2. Pioneering investments by the public sector. The demonstrated viability of investments in untested markets breaks an important barrier for private investors.

Another factor promoting sustainable private investment is the control of land speculation. In contrast to increased activity in historic centers, land price increases resulting from the retention of land outside the market will make private investment nonviable or more risky.

Another consideration is the social impact of investments in central areas: gentrification. Inasmuch as land prices and property values reflect increased demand and private investment, gentrification represents a measure of success in the rehabilitation of historic centers. Nevertheless, it is important to mitigate the negative impacts of gentrification on low-income households. Promoting low-cost housing can be an important tool, the effectiveness of which depends on the existence of an enabling environment for housing finance in the country. Such an enabling environment is not always present in Latin America. Support also can be provided for traditional crafts and other economic activities that benefit from being located in deteriorated centers but are usually expelled as a result of rehabilitation and preservation projects.

Two project examples provide insight into the problem of attracting private investment into urban heritage preservation. The first is the historic center of Quito, which is a World Heritage Site. The second is the central railway station and surrounding area in Montevideo, Uruguay, which is a National Historic Site. These projects represent two complementary approaches to involving the private sector in urban heritage preservation projects.

Historic Center of Quito, Ecuador

Quito is the capital of Ecuador. A very important religious center during the colonial era, the historic center contains a rich urban heritage represented by many religious and public buildings from the seventeenth, eighteenth, and nineteenth centuries and a sizable stock of domestic architecture, mostly from the late nineteenth and very early twentieth centuries. Quito's historic center faced classic deterioration problems. Dynamic activities fled the center during the decades of high urban growth (1960s-1970s). The public sector postponed investments in the historic center to accommodate demands from fast-growing areas in the north and south of the city. Meanwhile, reduced rents and real estate sales discouraged private investment in the center. Low-income families occupied the area, subdividing private residences to fit their needs, and public spaces were taken over by informal commercial and service activities. The infrastructure deteriorated, and the whole area entered a vicious cycle of abandonment and decay.

The municipality of Quito requested IADB financing for an investment program aimed at reestablishing in the historic center a sustainable balance between activities that could benefit from being there and the existing stock of buildings and public spaces. These considerations led to the design of integrated and multidimensional interventions framed in a long-term perspective of the area's development potential.

Three components of the investment program were financed by the IADB. The first was geared to generate externalities that would attract private investment, such as making the area more accessible, rehabilitating public spaces, constructing new parking areas, and generally improving environmental conditions. The second component supported the creation and operation of a mixed-capital company owned by the municipality and a nongovernmental organization. The IADB loan provides capital to the company to undertake joint-venture investments with landowners or private investors. The third component is a social development program designed to support the social groups that are benefiting from the historic center and to mitigate the negative effects of gentrification. The program invests in low-cost housing and promotes crafts and traditional economic activities in the historic center.

The results so far can be seen in improved public spaces around the rehabilitated monuments. Other accomplishments include improved accessibility, better parking operated by the private sector, and, above all, a changed investment climate in which the mixed-capital company is finding partners to undertake innovative investments. Among the latter are rehabilitated office space, new hotels operated by a private company, and new retail spaces in commercial buildings rehabilitated after many years of decay. Other rehabilitated buildings have been leased or given in concession to the private sector.

The mixed-capital company uses these management strategies when it seeks to retain some control over the tenants who come into the rehabilitated buildings (for instance, to prevent uses that would harm the buildings or would not contribute to the diversification of land uses sought by the rehabilitation program). Rehabilitation of low-income housing for sale to former tenants, who receive up-front subsidies from the central government and loans from the public housing bank, is also taking place.

Historic Central Railway Station in Montevideo, Uruguay

The project in Uruguay addresses a situation in which a valuable monument was at risk. The central railway station of Montevideo, including a terminal building declared a National Landmark, lay almost abandoned, subjecting the surrounding neighborhood of La Aguada to urban blight. The terminal building was poorly maintained, because railway passenger service no longer operates in Uruguay. The station is an architecturally valuable building built in the late nineteenth century and is located just six blocks from the central business district of Montevideo, facing the harbor.

The project proposed for IADB financing includes rehabilitation of the terminal building as a combined cultural, commercial, and recreational complex; and development of the railway yards for mixed residential, service, and commercial uses. These investments are expected to act as a catalyst for the rehabilitation of the surrounding districtæa role reinforced by investments in infrastructure and public space improvements.

Public resources are being used to conserve the terminal building's shell (structure, roof, and facades), to ready the building for private bidding for a concession for the railway building and yards. These investments are geared to create favorable conditions to attract private investors to the rehabilitation or redevelopment of properties in surrounding *La Aguada*.

Among the lessons to be learned from these experiences is that attracting the private sector to invest in historic centers is possible in Latin America, but the conditions under which this objective can be attained are very specific. They include strong public leadership, demonstrated by willingness to provide a stable regulatory environment and a commitment to undertake significant investments for extended periods. Also required is public-sector willingness to enter in partnerships with the private sector, thus sharing risks (and benefits). Critical macroeconomic conditions for success include the stability of key variables, such as low inflation and steady economic growth to fuel private demand for rehabilitated space in the historic centers. The availability of long-term financing is another crucial ingredient.

To propel urban heritage conservation toward sustainability requires a profound change in attitudes and values. First, the valuation of urban heritage by communities must change and be expressed by a willingness to invest in heritage preservation. Second, the social actors concerned must adopt conservation as a shared objective and be willing to give up short-term gains to reach long-term objectives. Private and public actors must be willing to accept the greater risks involved in preservation, as compared to investing in green-field projects. Risk management is a very critical element to be considered when drafting legislation and designing public interventions. Involving the private sector in the preservation of urban heritage in Latin America and the Caribbean requires a long-term commitment of resources and managerial capacity: goods that are in short supply in the region but can be procured if appropriate reforms and institutional developments are put in place. ■

Note

1   The information and opinions contained in this text are those of the author and do not represent the official policy of the Inter-American Development Bank.

Historic Cities: The Sense of Place, Sacred and Secular

49

W e are committed to sustainable development, but it is difficult to imagine development truly being sustainable without the appropriate incorporation of the cultural dimension. How to inculcate that concept into the culture of a national government or a development institution is a challenge unto itself.

I had an opportunity some years ago to visit a developing country that was enormously proud of what it had accomplished economically. I was very impressed by a large group of very bright young technocrats, all with advanced degrees from the best American universities, and witnessed extensive economic development.

On returning to the States, I wrote a glowing memorandum on my experience. When I got to the section that addressed prognosis, however, I was very troubled because, for example, sheepherders were now stevedores. The sense of community of the rural part of the country was gone, and the people had not become integrated in the urban scene. Many of the religious rituals and symbols that had kept the country together seemed to have been eliminated in the interest of freedom and progress. My prognosis was that the progress that had been made in that country would not last. And, indeed, less than half a decade later, it was gone.

Conservation of cultural heritage of the historic city is inevitably essential to sustainable development. It recognizes the importance of cultural continuity and of human history in nourishing social cohesion, a sense of self, of belonging, and of place in a context within which to understand the past and to contemplate the future. Particularly in times of dramatic and wrenching social and economic change accelerated by globalization, the well-preserved historic city represents a source of stability, of continuity, of permanence, and of the familiar. It is a witness of where we have come from and where we are. It recognizes the

Harold Williams

Harold Williams is president emeritus of the J. Paul Getty Trust, Los Angeles, California, is a member of the United States President's Committee on the Arts and Humanities, and was designated as an Officier dans l'Ordre des Arts et Lettres by the French government.

Figure 1. Historic and cultural landscapes, such as the Lake Gardens on the outskirts of Shanghai, China, provide public space for public life, which builds a sense of community and connectedness with cultural heritage.

importance of public spaces and public life to build a sense of community and connectedness.

However, it is only recently that we have come to recognize the need to preserve historic cities for their human dimensions. One of the great challenges of cultural conservation is how to deal with historic city centers today. How to balance the legitimate needs of a contemporary urban population with the preservation of a city's historic fabric. How to reconcile conservation with sustainable urban development.

Pollution eats away at historic buildings. The requirements of modern services such as water, electricity, and sewerage conflicts with the desire to preserve the historic integrity of streets and structures. Migration of rural residents to the urban centers leads to an increasingly large and increasingly poor population in the historic core.

The global trends of redevelopment to increase density, to modernize accommodations, to industrialize, and to capitalize on investment return have contributed to an unprecedented loss of historic fabric in past decades. Yet, the conservation of historic centers is not a luxury. It is a part of a collective obligation to understand and preserve history, tradition, and cultural diversity; to combat a sense of transience, of a lack of belonging or lack of community (figure 1).

The challenge is not only how we preserve architectural artifacts or preserve history, but also how we can conserve urban neighborhoods for human purposes. To quote from the European Charter of the Architectural

Heritage, "[T]he past as embodied in the architectural heritage provides a sort of environment indispensable for a balanced and complete life. It is a capital of irreplaceable spiritual, cultural, social and economic value."

To conserve a historic community poses challenges unequaled in cultural heritage conservation. It is beyond the need to conserve building and objects. One needs a total or holistic approach involving not just technical expertise but the recognition of a larger social, cultural, and environmental context in which the work must take place.

Unlike museums, in which the past is there to see but not to touch, historic cities are places in which life continues to be lived, in which cultural heritage is not protected behind barriers, in which it is part of a populated community making its living and making a life. Through historic conservation we have the opportunity to enhance or, perhaps better put, for the first time to provide a quality of life for the growing populace who lead an ever more dismal existence in a rapidly deteriorating urban environment.

Historic centers are cultural centers, not simply collections of structures. Their history and their people give them meaning. Conservation of historic centers and districts seeks ways to ensure that the full range of qualities that give a place a particular character—its history, its buildings, its open spaces, its traditions, its cultures, and its social life—are kept alive for its inhabitants 'and for future generations.

Development of historic centers cannot be stopped, nor should it be, particularly when it improves the physical and social environment of a city's inhabitants. Conservation of historic centers should not seek to halt change, but rather to manage it and to shape development so that the culture and character of a city are retained.

Just as every place is unique, there is not a single prescription for how to deal with historic centers or districts. The means will depend on the specifics of the locale. What works in one region may not be practical in another.

However, what is clear and what is important, wherever the place, is the need to preserve the everyday culture as well as the physical fabric, which means to value and preserve the characteristics of the existing population and its cultures. To do so, we must involve the people who have a vested interest in the planning for development and change. The community is the ultimate guardian of a historic place. Conservation programs cannot succeed or be sustained without ongoing, organized commitment and support from the community. The involvement of the residents, that sense of partnership and participation, is essential if a center is to maintain its unique character while renewing its vitality.

Safeguarding historic centers is most effective when there is a true partnership among all the interested parties—the community, the local government, the business sector, and the national government. This partnership needs to be nurtured with programs to build awareness of the value of conservation, including its economic, social, and cultural benefits.

However, those who control the futures of historic centers usually think in economic, not cultural or social, terms. The renewal of the economic base, the increase in the investment, and the revitalization necessary to fund and maintain the restoration are essentially economic activities, because historic cities are an economic resource. The economic benefits of historic preservation are significant. Urban conservation programs can strengthen economic development and stimulate new investments. Recognizing the interests of those in control, it may be that the most persuasive case for preservation of the historic city can be made in economic terms. In those terms historic essence is maintained and respected.

The Getty Conservation Institute has collaborated with municipalities in urban conservation projects in Quito, Ecuador, and in Ouro Preto, Brazil (figure 2). Early in each project, public surveys were conducted to determine what the public expected, how the public and the community defined the importance and significance of their historic center, what it

Figure 2. Ouro Preto, Brazil: a harmonious hillside development with a baroque church on top.

meant to them, and how to plan for its future. The Getty then proceeded to develop a plan, working with the full support of the government of the municipality, its civic and business leaders, and the community at large.

As for so many historic cities, one of the attractions of both cities is tourism, one of the world's largest industries and one often viewed as a panacea for urban ills. As elimination of the barriers of time and space makes the world truly more global, the distinctness of a given place—its character, its history, its culture—assumes greater significance in attracting both financial and human investment. The preservation of historic cities provides an opportunity for a locale to develop and maintain a competitive advantage over other historic places.

Cities that demonstrate their historic richness are more appealing to those with capital who seek attractive locations and, of course, to tourists and visitors. Yet, the historic assets of a city are liable to deteriorate through increasing population and the pressure for new forms of development.

People like visiting historic districts and cultural sites and are doing so in impressive numbers. There are tremendous and sustained local benefits if tourism opportunities are well conceived and well managed. But as with the use of any resource, there is a thin line between proper use and exploitation.

The group tours and visitors who are attracted in search of new historic experiences do produce a major dilemma for historic cities: how to manage the conservation of the physical fabric while accommodating the pressures associated with an expanding range of tourist activities and functions, as well as maintaining the city and enabling it to develop as a place for people to live and to work.

In many historic cities, we find over-consumption of local infrastructure, a conflict between historic buildings and the demand for land, growing social conflict between visitors and residents, and negative environmental impacts of tourism. To ensure the sustainability of the historic city requires regulation and management of the physical, cultural, and social fabric in which the uniqueness and economic success of the historic city is grounded.

While concepts of sustainability and sustainable development are well established in purely economic terms, the cultural dimension needs to be fully integrated in the planning and development process in historic cities. Without that dimension development is not sustainable. ∎

50 Cultural Institutions: Between History and the Avant-Garde

Luis Monreal

Formerly director of the Getty Conservation Institute, Luis Monreal is director general of Fundacio la Caixa, Barcelona, Spain.

Some cultural institutions and the private sector, through cultural initiatives and activities financed on its own, can catalyze historic cities. Some museums have potential in terms of cultural identity to be instruments for interpreting a city and to be catalysts of urban rehabilitation.

I define the "history" in my title as that period in which all cultural institutions were state-run, and "avant-garde" as the new phase in which no cultural institutions are state-run. The vision I present is kaleidoscopic and comes from my experiences in Spain.

As a result of our short experience of democracy in Spain since 1977, many interesting things are happening in culture, and many people from abroad are looking at our experience. In the context of the young Spanish democracy three factors are significant:

Politics. With democracy a central state is decentralized into regional governments.

Culture. Under dictatorship Spain was a monolithic state. Now, culturally, Spain has disintegrated in the recognition that since the Middle Ages it has been a multicultural, multilingual state composed of several historic nations: Navarra, Castille, Leone, Catalonia, the Basque, and others. This is a fundamental new factor for cultural development and for the treatment of cultural identity and cultural heritage in my country.

Economics. The development of the gross national product and the ensuing economic bonanza that touches all classes and creates a very powerful middle class. That results in the very active presence of economic agents—corporations—in financing culture.

Why Corporations Contribute to Culture

In 1998 corporations in Spain invested approximately $200 million in culture. More surprisingly, they invested this amount despite a very hostile legal and fiscal environment with no tax incentives.

If one is going to ask a Spanish corporation to finance a project, it is important to know why it would invest in culture. My interpretation is that these corporations do not work like the corporation I work for—with a genuine interest in the common good. The former give money for cultural affairs because they want to compete favorably in the market.

Today it is very difficult for a consumer to distinguish among products and services, because in industrialized countries modern firms all produce goods and services of even quality. So what can make the difference in the market? The difference is that a corporation or a firm that has a foundation and gives money away is, in the mind of the consumer, acting for the common good.

In 1998 Spanish corporations gave $200 million to culture and cultural affairs in Spain. On top of that, in the same year foundations invested the equivalent of $350 million more in cultural, educational, scientific, and environmental programs.

Activities of Fundacion la Caixa

In 1999 our foundation had a budget of $150 million, which came from a net profit from our savings bank in 1998 of $730 million after taxes. This very improbable situation was the result of a number of circumstances that statistically had no chance to happen.

A small savings bank founded in the nineteenth century married with another savings bank founded at the turn of the century. Together these two nonprofit banks became the largest savings bank in Europe. It controls a holding with toll freeways, gas companies, water distribution, and telephone companies. At the end of 1998 it had $730 million net profit after taxes.

I am in charge of this nonprofit bank's foundation, which is charged with distributing this money to social and cultural affairs. To see how, first it is interesting to see the evolution of our budget in the last few years because the budget grows more quickly than the inflation.

In 1993 we had a budget of $55 million, and in 1999 we had a budget of around $150 million. Where does this money go? Social programs receive almost 40 percent of the total budget, and science and environment get 6-7 billion Spanish pesetas. One-hundred-and-fifty pesetas is equal to one U.S. dollar, so 7 billion pesetas is the equivalent of approximately US$30 million.

What is the profit of that investment? In 1998 an audience in users of services and visitors to exhibitions was slightly over 8 million people, in a country of 35 million inhabitants. This is the reason that this corporation invests money in this kind of exercise: because it will benefit a number of people who in the end probably will open an account with us.

These activities, particularly the cultural activities, of this foundation catalyze cultural activity in all types of cities. In 1998 we had activities in over 640 localities and presented 273 different exhibitions in the country. We produce between 60 and 70 new exhibitions each year, and some of these exhibitions travel to historic cities, or to all kinds of cities, for 1 or 2 years. We are probably one of the largest producers of art, history, science, and environmental exhibitions in the world.

This type of activity–and this is what is original in our country–is conducted by a private, nonprofit bank, but most of these activities, particularly in the social field, are undertaken in a symbiotic collaboration with the central or the local administrations in the country.

We have an enormous flexibility. We are at the same time a grantmaking and an operating foundation, and we can work in synergy with the public sector, something which is totally unheard of in most countries. In addition these synergies between the public and the private sector explain one of the largest urban rehabilitation operations ever undertaken in past years: the urban renewal of Barcelona for the 1992 Olympics.

This urban renewal had very important and fundamental cultural aspects, among them the construction of a new contemporary art museum by architect Richard Mayer. The public sector invested the equivalent of $30 million and the private sector in excess of $6 million.

Economic Contributions of the Guggenheim Museum in Bilbao

The most recent experience our foundation had was the construction of the Guggenheim Museum in Bilbao. This was another improbable success. All the conditions were there for the project to be a failure. First, the initiative came through two improbable partners. On the one hand was the Guggenheim Museum in New York, with Thomas Krens, who was traversing the world trying unsuccessfully to sell a Guggenheim franchise. On the other hand was the strongly nationalistic Basque country's government.

Both personalities got together, struck a deal, and had the wisdom to appoint Frank Gehry as the architect. They gave him a site that was a derelict, early twentieth-century building in the center of the city, something that merited rehabilitation but was by no means a unique site.

Frank declined this choice and insisted on another site by the river, under the bridge and next to the railroad. Both the Basque government and Thomas Krens felt that Frank Gehry was crazy. However, as they had agreed upon him as an architect, in order not to break the deal, they agreed. It is the most incredible location ever.

Gehry created something that must be praised. He created a contemporary building that works as the best preservation tool for the city of Bilbao. In all cases I believe that creativity is the best tool for preservation (figure 1).

However, the Guggenheim Museum has made something better than that for Bilbao. The museum has become an excellent business. During the first 12 months of operation the Guggenheim Museum received 1,300,000 visitors, which makes it the second-most visited museum in Spain, after the Prado. Entrance fees at the Guggenheim are expensive, so the museum collected 741 million pesetas, or almost $5 million. Total operating costs in the first 12 months were $22.5 million, and the income generated by the museum approached 67 percent of that total (figure 2).

This is income distribution. The Basque government had invested only 33 percent. The remainder for the first 12 months is already a profit generated by the museum. But there is still better news. Bilbao, which used

Figure 1. General view of the Guggenheim Museum Bilbao. The museum has served as a magnet for international tourism to Bilbao and the Basque region. According to a visitor survey, more than 1 million people (79 percent of all visitors) travelled to Bilbao expressly to see the Guggenheim Museum Bilbao.

Figure 2. Entrance to the Guggenheim Museum Bilbao. The museum succeeded in realizing the model of a public-private cultural partnership. With more than 9,000 individual members and 100 corporate members, the museum has established the largest membership program of any museum in Spain.

to be a very unattractive city, has become a weekend destination for Spaniards and Europeans in general. Twenty-seven percent of the visitors are foreign. One out of three visitors to Bilbao for business spends one day of his or her trip visiting the Guggenheim Museum.

The U.S. firm Peat Marwick prepared an interesting report on the impressive economic impact of the Guggenheim Museum in the Basque economy. The existence of the Guggenheim Museum added a value of $160 million to the local economy during the first 12 months. This figure represented 0.47 percent of the gross national product of that region. This amount generated added value by maintaining 3,816 jobs, which in turn represented 0.5 percent of total employment in the Basque country.

The investment has been around $150 million, including in the area of $105 million for the building and the rest for the collection. As to how that is amortized, the existence of the Guggenheim Museum in Bilbao has generated a tax income for the local government—in corporate taxes, in value-added taxes, and in income tax—of $3 million per year. Thus, the city will very soon recover the investment. It is a good business, particularly during that time, in which interest rates in Spain were low.

Some things that apply to Bilbao, to Barcelona, and to the museums cannot be measured in a cost-benefit analysis. These museum projects are catalysts of change in the urban environment. They help to develop public opinion in favor of cultural heritage. They help to develop ideas of conservation and preservation. The combination results in a sense of urban pride and a sense of belonging, in other words, social cohesion, employment equity, partnership, and participation. ■

The Role of the Private Sector in Cultural Heritage Preservation

51

I n the built world, meaning resides in unique places. Humankind's passage through history is memorialized in the ancient ruins, the sacred and secular buildings, the townscapes and cityscapes, the monuments and gardens and cultural landscapes that survive to us from the past. There is no substitute for the experience of the real place: a 9,000-year-old life-size carving of giraffes in Niger, the ruined columns of Greek city on the Black Sea in Ukraine, Mayan hieroglyphs in the jungles of Mexico, or the historic heart of George Town in Malaysia, to cite a few examples from the World Monuments Watch (see below). As nothing else can, such places resonate with the human lives that proceeded ours, their hopes and beliefs, and the shape of the worlds they knew.

Marilyn Perry

Marilyn Perry is president of the Samuel H. Kress Foundation, and chairman of the board of the World Monuments Fund, www.worldmonuments.org

Yet our relation with our historic heritage is far from easy. Cultural sites around the globe suffer the consequences of social and financial neglect, natural disasters, mismanagement, excessive development, mass tourism, and armed conflict. Limited resources of funding and expertise impose difficult questions of gain and loss. What is to be saved? How? What roles should be played by international agencies, governments, concerned citizens, and organizations within the private sector?

My intention is to look at the last of these categories, the private sector, and to describe the evolution of the international preservation movement from this vantage point. I describe the work the Samuel H. Kress Foundation and the World Monuments Fund. Both organizations share a long-term commitment to the preservation of architectural heritage internationally, and both have seen their programs evolve in response to the needs of the field.

Kress Foundation

Established by the five-and-dime store magnate Samuel H. Kress in 1929, the Kress Foundation has a long and distinguished record of support for the cultural heritage of Europe. In the United States it is perhaps best known for the great Kress Collection of European Old Masters, distributed to the National Gallery of Art and 90 other American institutions, and for our program of Kress Fellowships for young art historians and art conservators. Other funding is granted for resources of art historical scholarship, art conservation, the display of European art, and the preservation of European monuments.

Seventy years ago Samuel Kress's first major act of philanthropy was a munificent personal donation to the Italian State for restorations in several provincial cities. For his generosity he received a coveted royal decoration and national esteem as an American Maecenas. As the work progressed, Mr. Kress took a special interest in the recovery of the vast Ducal Palace in Mantua, and during the 1930s the most brilliant Renaissance rooms of the Gonzaga court were conserved at his expense. The relationship of generous foreign patron and grateful local authorities was typical of the philanthropy of the day.

In the post-war reconstruction of Europe the Kress Foundation sponsored the rebuilding of the Ponte della Trinità in Florence and the Gothic cathedral of Nuremberg. Other field projects in the same period—the late 1940s and 1950s—included Byzantine frescoes and mosaics in Istanbul, the splendid Renaissance sculpture of the Tempio Malatestiana in Rimini, and Marie Antoinette's rococo boudoir at Versailles. Although the sites were geographically widespread, the unifying element was their recognized artistic quality.

World Monuments Fund

Opportunities for international philanthropy for cultural heritage were significantly advanced in 1965 when the World Monuments Fund (WMF) (originally the International Fund for Monuments) was founded by Colonel James A. Gray. An electrical engineer and inventor from San Francisco with a distinguished war record as a paratrooper, Col. Gray had retired from the United States Army to live in Italy. Intrigued by the static problems of the leaning Tower of Pisa, he became aware of the general plight of ailing monuments. UNESCO suggested the need for a private sector organization for worldwide conservation of art and architecture. Returning to the United States, Col. Gray opened a fledgling not-for-profit in a small office in New York.

The World Monuments Fund's international scope was evident from its first projects—the medieval rock-hewn Coptic churches of Lalibela in Ethiopia and the mysterious monumental statues of Easter Island. Acknowledging his lack of formal training in the arts, Col. Gray focused on the technical and managerial challenges of preservation. Hiring

Figure 1. Interior view of the Pietà, Venice, Italy. The church of the Pietà (Santa Maria della Visitazione) was the first project to be restored with funding from the Kress Foundation to the World Monuments Fund, 1971-78.

appropriate international experts, he concentrated on project organization and administration, guaranteeing the quality of the work and fiscal accountability, essential precedents for the organization's future.

Following the disastrous floods of November 1966, Col. Gray returned to Italy to lead the American response in the UNESCO campaign for Venice. Among the early sponsors was the Kress Foundation, which "adopted" the complete restoration of the church of the Pietà with its soaring Tiepolo fresco cycle (figure 1). Other donors to WMF likewise assumed full financial responsibility for conserving their chosen Venetian sites, almost 30 projects in all.

The partnership between the Kress Foundation and WMF produced a chain of successful restorations in Italy, Spain, and Ireland during the 1970s and early 1980s. As a lasting contribution to preservation science, a research laboratory for stone conservation was established in Venice. Other contributors during this period supported new WMF activities in Nepal and Haiti.

For 20 years all of the World Monuments Fund's field projects were personally supervised by Col. Gray. When he retired in 1984, his legacy was a small but dedicated organization and a long list of meticulously restored sites.

Yet, considering the magnitude of the need, could WMF do more? Under the leadership of Bonnie Burnham, an expert on cultural property law and the former director of the International Foundation for Art Research, the World Monuments Fund accepted the challenge of creating a professional international preservation organization from the private sector. Between 1985 and 1990 the first steps were taken. With new donors, a growing membership, and new professional staff, WMF responded to the effects of the Mexican earthquake, commissioned a book about the destruction of Romania's architectural heritage, created a Jewish Heritage Program, initiated a project at Angkor in Cambodia (figures 2, 3), expanded its European field work to France, and established affiliates in western Europe. Simultaneously, the organization began to convene conferences, to publish technical reports, to oversee on-site training, and to take on an advocacy role. Emphasizing the importance of the cause, an annual benefit luncheon in New York honored international leaders in the realm of cultural heritage with the Hadrian Award (named in tribute to the ancient Roman Emperor).

Figures 2, 3. Before and after views at Preah Khan, Angkor, Cambodia. The temple complex of Preah Khan in the Historic City of Angkor is being restored as a partial ruin by the World Monuments Fund. On-site training of Cambodians is a major component of the project, which began in 1991.

Mutual Benefits of Cooperation

In 1987 the Kress Foundation sponsored a new European Preservation Program with WMF that heralded a fundamental shift in both organizations' approach to field preservation. A series of on-site visits by the Kress

Figure 4. The Pitareti Monastic Complex in the Tetritskaro District of Georgia was listed on the World Monuments Watch in 1996 and received a grant for emergency stabilization from the Kress Foundation, the country's first international funding for cultural heritage. The Watch listing also generated substantial local publicity and a Georgian television documentary about the complex.

Trustees confirmed the widespread need for help throughout Europe and the chronic funding problems that discouraged local action. What was needed was a means to generate attention and new support. The Kress Board approved an American-style challenge program for European cultural heritage with an initial commitment of $1 million over five years.

The new program invited applications for a range of competitive grants for initial planning, documentation, emergency repairs, clearly identified phases of work, and on-site training. Some support was also available for conferences, publications, and advocacy. Larger awards required matching funds from other sources. By inviting applications from the field, the program encouraged local sponsors to take the measure of their needs and to present the case for their sites. An award signaled international attention, provoked public pride, and generally elicited new support from the local community or the national government. In most cases it guaranteed that the project would continue.

Over the past decade the Kress Foundation has granted more than $4 million to the World Monuments Fund for European preservation activities and supported more than 100 preservation projects in 31 countries. Virtually every category and type of traditional structure has been aided: archaeological sites and catacombs, Armenian and Byzantine ruins, medieval and later churches, fortifications, palaces, synagogues, a mosque, gardens, chateaux, landscape follies, theatres, civic buildings, houses, even a tea room in Glasgow. Each award is a spotlight on a project in need, and sites from Portugal to Sweden, from Albania to Georgia, have benefited (figure 4). Significant new resources for preservation activities have been "leveraged" by Kress funds, at an average of at least three dollars to one (and often much more).

For the Kress Foundation the program provides a means of responding at many levels to the myriad problems afflicting the artistic heritage of Europe, both through financial aid and, as needed, WMF's professional expertise. For the recipients—institutions, local organizations, private sector groups, and public agencies—grants from the Kress/WMF program have offered fresh funds, new partners, and international distinction for deserving preservation projects. Recently, the program was increased to $500,000 per year for the next five years and includes a new category of institutional cooperation.

World Monuments Watch

For WMF the breadth of response to the Kress program opened a vista to the possibility of addressing the most compelling and difficult issues of international preservation—defining cultural heritage, recognizing how it is endangered, and resolving what must be done to preserve it. These are the primary questions that underlie the World Monuments Watch, a biennial *List of 100 Most Endangered Sites*, which was launched in 1996 with major funding from American Express (a commitment of $10 million over 10 years).

The Watch is the only international register of cultural heritage in immediate peril (figure 5). Nominations are solicited from governments, preservation organizations, and others concerned with site conservation throughout the world. Nominators propose cultural sites for Watch listing according to three primary criteria: *significance* (or meaning) within its context, *urgency* of immediate action to reverse serious threats, and the *viability* of appropriate solutions. An international jury separate from WMF convenes to debate the merits of each nomination. An engrossing selection of 100 sites is compiled; an illustrated catalogue is published; and the new list is presented at a press conference. American Express, the Kress Foundation, and other donors select sites that will receive their financial help.

Collectively, the World Monuments Watch *List of 100 Most Endangered Sites* enumerates the enormous range of the crises confronting our heritage on every continent and in every country. It is at once a stunning display of human creativity and ingenuity; of the meaning of our shared legacy from the past; and of our irresponsibility, negligence, and indifference, or worse. At the level of individual entries the list indicates how each site can still be saved and thus is also an instrument of hope.

Now in its third round the World Monuments Watch has generated significant new funding—well over $30 million—for endangered heritage from prehistory to the modern age. Even more importantly, it has created new sensitivities about the meaning and value of cultural sites and new partnerships to work on their behalf. American Express remains the largest

Figure 5. House of the Silver Wedding Anniversary, Pompeii, Italy. The grave conservation problems at Pompeii were highlighted by the World Monuments Watch. Major funding from the Kress Foundation has sponsored an in-depth analysis of the House of the Silver Wedding Anniversary and its surrounding insula by a team of international experts that will lead to a conservation manual for the entire site.

corporate sponsor, but WMF has been joined by the Aga Khan Trust for Culture on several Islamic projects; by banks in the Czech Republic and Mexico; by several local preservation groups; by national governments; and by the World Bank on projects in Bosnia, Ethiopia, and Romania. Many of these donors also have generated matching funds from the Wilson Challenge for Conserving Our Heritage, a program created by WMF Trustee Robert W. Wilson to encourage international partnerships.

As a worldwide synthesis of cultural heritage in peril, the World Monuments Watch has become a vital tool in the struggle to protect our cultural legacy. For threatened sites it serves to pinpoint need, attract attention, and provide a means to move forward. For communities and governments it serves as a lens by which to re-value their treasures. For citizens of the world it offers insight into the astonishing multiplicity—and fragility—of our heritage. For the World Monuments Fund it is an essential element in the larger challenge, for which other means must still be found, to protect, maintain, and enjoy—that is, to celebrate the meaning of—the great human achievements of our world. ■

Illustration Credits

The Illustration Credits are listed in Part and chapter order by chapter author's last name.

Acknowledgments

Achva Benzinberg Stein.

Introduction

Cristiano Mascaro.

Part I

Part I opener: Center for Jewish Art. Nasr: fig. 1: Hasan Uddin-Khan. Narkiss: courtesy Center for Jewish Art at the Hebrew University of Jerusalem. Tokoro: courtesy Future Generations Alliance Foundation, Kyoto. Bianca: courtesy Aga Khan Trust for Culture. Koonce: Robert C. Lautman.

Part II

Weffort: figs. 1, 2 by Cristiano Mascaro; fig. 3 by Ephim Shluger; fig. 4: C. Mascaro. Neto: fig.1: E. Shluger; figs. 2-4, 6: C. Mascaro; fig. 5: Marisa Vianna. Elbers: author. Myrvoll: Figs. 1-4: courtesy author; figs. 5,6: courtesy Heritage Management Office, Bergen. Sorkin: author. Cernea: figs. 1-3: courtesy Aga Khan Trust for Culture; figs. 4, 5: Curt Carnemark; fig. 6: Ekaterina Massey.

Part III

Croci: figs. 1-9, 11, 12: author; fig. 10 from Ismail Serageldin, "Very Special Places: The Architecture and Economics of Intervening in Historic Cities" Culture in Sustainable Development series, World Bank,

Washington, D. C., 1999, 4. Sabini: 1, 3-5: author; fig. 2: E. Shluger. Read and Ebbe: C. Carnemark. Govela: Lourdes Grobet. Vieira: courtesy Banco Safra.

Part IV

Bonnette: E. Shluger. Ruble: fig. 1: from *Historic Architecture of St. Petersburg*(Leningrad: Aurora Editions, 1982), 29; figs.2-3, E. Shluger; figs. 4A, 4B: author. Polishchuk: E. Shluger. Limonov: fig. 1: Leontief Centre (International Centre for Social and Economic Research), "The Strategic Plan for St. Petersburg. Approved by the General Council December 1st 1997," St. Petersburg, Russia, 1998, pp 54-55; fig. 2: E. Shluger. Mehrotra: author. Armaly and others: opener: Fritz Wentzel, Volkmar Wentzel Collection; figs. 1-3: from J. Marasovic in "Rehabilitation of the Historic Core of Split 2," ed. D. Marasovic, 2d rev. ed., City of Split-Agency for the Historic Core, Split, Croatia, 1998, pp 50, 60, 63, and 67 respectively; figs. 4, 5: M. Armaly. Shuaibi: author. S. Ibrahim: courtesy Aga Khan Trust for Culture.

Part V

Part V opener: H. Uddin-Khan. Darling: figs. 1, 2: C. Mascaro; fig. 3: E. Shluger; fig. 4: Eduardo Rojas. Smith: courtesy U. S. National Trust for Historic Preservation. Varma: courtesy Municipal Corporation, City of Ahmedabad, India. Birnbaum: figs. 1, 2, 6, 8, 12-14: author; figs. 3, 4: Jack Boucher for HABS; figs. 5, 7, 11: courtesy U. S. National Park Service; figs. 9, 10: courtesy Carol R. Johnson & Associates; fig. 15: courtesy Central Park Conservancy; fig. 16: courtesy Waterford Foundation. Desthuis-Francis: courtesy Aga Khan Trust for Culture. M. Serageldin: courtesy Aga Khan Trust for Culture.

Part VI

Part VI opener: Digital Stock, Inc. "Indigenous Peoples." Cherry: figs. 1–3: author; fig. 4: courtesy English Heritage. Nakagawa: fig. 1: Shin-ichi Nishimoto; fig. 2: author; figs. 3–5: "Report on the Restoration Work at the Tenneiji Temple: An Important Historic Spot of Tokyo-to" (1983). Stein: figs. 1, 2, 4–6: author. fig. 3: David Stein. Pereira: fig. 1: Ministerio da Cultura Divulgacao. Cohen-Mushlin: courtesy Center for Jewish Art of the Hebrew University of Jerusalem. Grellert: author and students, Darmstadt University of Technology, Darmstadt, Germany. The Center for Jewish Art of the Hebrew University of Jerusalem: Sokolova (figs. 1–4C): courtesy Center for Jewish Art; Castiel (figs. 5–7): author; Bergman (figs.8–18): Jewish Historical Institute, Warsaw; Kravtsov (figs. 19–26): courtesy Center for Jewish Art; Messinas: fig. 27: X. Zarkada, K. Trakasopoulo; figs. 28, 29, and 31B: author; fig. 30: DEIEB Ifaistos, Veroia; fig. 31A: Jewish Museum of Greece; Ceresnjes (figs. 32–39): courtesy Center for Jewish Art. Narkiss-Index: 1–4, 6–15: courtesy Center for Jewish Art; fig. 5: British Library, London, ms. Or. 2884, fol. 17. Thies: figs. 1, 2, 5, 8–11 courtesy author; figs. 3, 4: Berlin, Kunstbibliothek; figs. 6, 7: author.

Part VII

Part VII opener: H. Uddin-Khan. Parker: fig. 1: Navajo Nation Historic Preservation Department; figs. 2, 4: author; fig. 3: Don Doll, S. J; fig. 5: Chris Arend; fig. 6: courtesy U. S. National Park Service. Terena: author. Sekler: figs. 1–4, 6, 8: author; figs. 5, 7: Mary Patricia Sekler; figs. 9–11: courtesy UNESCO. King: author, ICCROM. Mann: fig. 1: The Metropolitan Museum of Art, Rogers Fund, New York, 1918, 18.31; fig. 2: Archive of the Jewish Museum, New York; fig. 3: Museum of Turkish and Islamic Arts, Istanbul, no. 1632; fig. 4: Staatliche Museen zu Berlin, Islamisches Museum, Berlin, I.27; fig. 5: Photo Archive of the Jewish Museum, New York; fig. 6: The Metropolitan Museum of Art, Fletcher Fund, New York, 1946, 46.156.16; fig. 7: Minneapolis Institute of Arts, 93.25.2; fig. 8: after *Al-Andalus*; fig. 9: Add. 14761, fol. 65v, courtesy Print Collection, The Jewish Theological Seminary; fig. 10: Museum of Turkish and Islamic Arts, Istanbul, no. 3. Lévi-Strauss: opener: E. Shluger; fig. 1: Diane Rothschild; fig. 2: E. Massey.

Part VIII

Part VIII opener: J. King, ICCROM. Hannah: fig. 1: F. Wentzel, Collection of Volkmar Wentzel; figs. 2, 3: World Monuments Fund. Rojas: figs. 1, 2, 5: author; fig. 3: Sivio Mendes; fig. 4: C. Mascaro. Williams: E. Shluger. Monreal: David Herald. Perry: fig. 1: Mark Smith; figs. 2, 3: World Monuments Fund/J. Stubbs; fig. 4: Merab Bochoidze; fig. 5: J. Stubbs/World Monuments Fund.

Cover

For many generations the Old Bridge in Mostar, Bosnia, built from 1557-66, connected a community formed by Muslims, Orthodox Christians, Catholics, and Jews. They shared a common space and history. During the 1992-95 civil war in Bosnia the bridge and parts of Old Mostar were destroyed. The built heritage of Mostar, which is listed as a World Heritage Site, is now part of a post-conflict reconciliation and reconstruction project supported by a partnership of international agencies and other donors. Rebuilding the social and cultural cohesion among the peoples of post-war Bosnia is a clear prerequisite to rebuilding the economy. Rebuilding the Old Mostar Bridge is both a physical and symbolic means to the road toward peace and economic renewal.